# Fundamentals of Finance

**FIFTH EDITION**

Financial and property markets, institutions, personal finance and financial management

# Fundamentals of Finance

Original edition by Andrea Bennett, Jenny Parry et al.

MASSEY UNIVERSITY PRESS

# Contents

| | |
|---|---|
| Preface | xi |
| Features of this book | xii |
| Key learning tools | xiii |

## PART 1: FINANCIAL SYSTEMS

### Chapter 1: An overview of finance

| | |
|---|---|
| Introduction | 3 |
| Definition of finance | 4 |
|     The financial system | |
| Finance as a discipline for study | 5 |
|     The interdisciplinary nature of finance | |
| Finance and business | 7 |
|     The business environment and stakeholder protection • The four levels of financial decision-making • Personal level • Sole proprietorship level • Partnership level • Corporation level | |
| The ethics dilemma | 13 |
|     Agency problems • Conflict of interest | |
| Financial markets | 13 |
|     The existence of private wealth • Freedom of choice • Incentives • Efficient markets • The role of government | |
| Conclusion | 17 |
| Self-test question and answer | 18 |
| Questions and problems | 18 |

### Chapter 2: Financial and property markets

| | |
|---|---|
| Introduction | 19 |
| Financial assets | 19 |
|     Debt versus equity claims • Prices of financial assets • The roles of financial assets | |
| Financial markets | 21 |
|     The roles of financial markets • Market participants • Types of financial market | |
| Money markets | 24 |
|     Market operation and participants • Types of instruments traded | |
| Capital markets | 25 |
|     The debt markets • The equities market | |

| | |
|---|---|
| Foreign exchange (FX) market | 28 |
|    *Market operations and participants • Types of instruments traded* | |
| Derivative markets | 29 |
|    *Types of derivative instruments • The operation of the market •* | |
|    *Participants in the futures market • Forward contracts •* | |
|    *Options contracts • Participants in the options market* | |
| Cryptocurrency markets | 35 |
| Property markets | 36 |
|    *Characteristics of property • Indirect vs direct investment •* | |
|    *Valuation and pricing • The role of the housing market in the economic cycle* | |
| Conclusion | 41 |
| Self-test questions and answers | 42 |
| Questions and problems | 42 |

## Chapter 3: Financial institutions

| | |
|---|---|
| Introduction | 43 |
| The development of the modern financial system | 43 |
|    *The modern role of government in the financial intermediation process •* | |
|    *Regulations to control the soundness of the financial system* | |
| Credit creation | 48 |
|    *Credit multiplier* | |
| Monetary policy – three control mechanisms | 49 |
|    *The official cash rate • The inflation problem* | |
| Modern financial intermediaries | 52 |
|    *Depository institutions • Non-depository institutions • The benefits* | |
|    *of financial intermediation* | |
| Ethics and financial institutions | 56 |
| Classifying types of financial transfers | 56 |
| Conclusion | 57 |
| Self-test questions and answers | 58 |
| Questions and problems | 58 |

## PART 2: FINANCE TOOLS

### Chapter 4: Time value of money – Single payments

| | |
|---|---|
| Introduction | 60 |
| Simple interest and future value | 61 |
| Simple interest and calculating the present value | 63 |
| Compound interest and future value | 63 |
|    *Other methods of calculation* | |
| The present value of a single payment | 67 |
| Compounding frequency | 70 |
| Continuous compounding/discounting | 74 |
| Nominal and effective interest rates | 75 |
| Solving for an unknown interest rate | 77 |
| Solving for an unknown time period | 78 |
| Conclusion | 80 |

Self-test questions and answers 80
Questions and problems 82

## Chapter 5: Time value of money – Multiple payments

Introduction 84
Multiple cash flows 84
    *Future value of multiple cash flows • Present value of multiple cash flows*
Level cash flows: Annuities and perpetuities 87
    *Future value of an annuity • Present value and annuities*
Finding the amount of a regular payment 93
Annuity due 95
Perpetuities 97
Asset valuation: Capitalisation method of property valuation 98
Asset valuation: Calculating the price of a bond 100
Loan types 104
Multiple payments per annum and compounding frequency 106
Conclusion 107
Self-test questions and answers 108
Questions and problems 108

## PART 3: PERSONAL FINANCE

### Chapter 6: Risk and return

Introduction 112
Risk-free assets 113
    *The two components of a return • Nominal interest rate*
Term structure of interest rates 115
    *Shape of yield curves*
Risky assets 117
Risk and return – the trade-off 119
Measuring historical risk and return 121
    *Returns from investment • Holding period yields or return •*
    *Standard deviation as a measure of risk*
Measuring future risk and return 127
The benefit of diversification 129
The capital asset pricing model and the security market line relationship 133
Conclusion 135
Self-test questions and answers 136
Questions and problems 141

### Chapter 7: Personal financial management

Introduction 142
The personal financial planning activity 142
Money management 144
    *Gathering financial information • Preparing an income statement •*
    *Budget preparation • Developing a personal balance sheet*
Financial planning for life 147

| | |
|---|---|
| Financial goal attainment | 149 |
| Funding a retirement plan | 150 |
|     Retirement income gap • KiwiSaver • Choosing a KiwiSaver fund | |
| Residential property and mortgages | 155 |
| Property investment: Rights and ownership | 156 |
|     Property concepts • Definition of land and land ownership • Forms of ownership | |
| Land registration and record of title | 160 |
|     Resource Management Act 1991 | |
| Financing the purchase of residential property | 164 |
| Starting or buying a business | 166 |
|     Personality traits • Preliminary evaluation • Business plan | |
| Conclusion | 171 |
| Self-test question and answer | 172 |
| Questions and problems | 175 |

## PART 4: FINANCIAL MANAGEMENT

### Chapter 8: Financial management

| | |
|---|---|
| Introduction | 177 |
| Role of financial management | 178 |
|     Financial management • Organisational context | |
| Objective of financial management | 180 |
|     What about profit maximisation? • Time value of money • Cash flows • Risk • Managers as agents • Economic implications of wealth maximisation | |
| Corporate governance and business ethics | 187 |
|     Reconceiving products and markets • Redefining productivity in the value chain • Enabling local cluster development • Ethical considerations in property | |
| The external environment | 189 |
|     Financial markets • Regulatory environment | |
| Risk and return | 190 |
| Conclusion | 193 |
| Self-test questions and answers | 194 |
| Questions and problems | 195 |

### Chapter 9: Investment in net working capital

| | |
|---|---|
| Introduction | 199 |
| Net working capital | 199 |
| Risk–profitability trade-off | 200 |
| Management of net working capital | 200 |
| Managing cash | 201 |
|     Cash and near-cash • Motives for holding cash • Forecast cash flow statement | |
| Management of accounts receivable | 204 |
|     Setting credit policy | |

| | |
|---|---|
| Management of inventory | 205 |
|    *Economic order quantity model • Computerised inventory control system • Just-in-time system* | |
| Management of current liabilities | 206 |
| Cash conversion cycle | 211 |
| Conclusion | 213 |
| Self-test questions and answers | 214 |
| Questions and problems | 216 |

## Chapter 10: Financing the firm

| | |
|---|---|
| Introduction | 222 |
| Features of debt and equity | 222 |
| Funding a firm's life cycle | 223 |
|    *Start-up stage • Growth stage • Maturity stage* | |
| Choosing the financing mix | 237 |
|    *Short-term or long-term sources? • Internal or external funding? • Debt or equity finance?* | |
| Cost of capital | 240 |
|    *Cost of debt capital • Cost of equity capital • Weighted average cost of capital* | |
| Conclusion | 245 |
| Self-test questions and answers | 246 |
| Questions and problems | 248 |

## Chapter 11: Investment in long-term assets – Concepts

| | |
|---|---|
| Introduction | 255 |
| Capital budgeting process | 255 |
| Measuring the costs and benefits | 256 |
|    *Investment outlay • Operating cash flows • Terminal value* | |
| Conclusion | 266 |
| Self-test question and answer | 267 |
| Questions and problems | 269 |

## Chapter 12: Investment in long-term assets – Evaluation techniques

| | |
|---|---|
| Introduction | 271 |
| Techniques of investment evaluation | 271 |
|    *Accounting return on investment • Payback period • Net present value • Assumptions of the weighted average cost of capital • NPV(ER) • Internal rate of return • Comparing NPV and IRR* | |
| Other capital budgeting considerations | 284 |
|    *Capital budgeting and inflation • Capital budgeting and risk* | |
| Conclusion | 287 |
| Self-test question and answer | 287 |
| Questions and problems | 288 |

## Chapter 13: Investment in long-term assets – Property

| | |
|---|---:|
| Introduction | 295 |
| Why invest in property? | 296 |
| Analysis of a property investment | 298 |
| *Investment purpose • Property investment risk • Property investment return • Single-period methods • Investor-specific considerations • Multi-period methods • Feasibility analysis • Capitalisation of property income • Financing property investments* | |
| Conclusion | 311 |
| Self-test question and answer | 312 |
| Questions and problems | 316 |
| **Glossary** | 318 |
| **Appendix 1 – Some useful formulae** | 329 |
| **Appendix 2 – Suggested solutions for selected end-of-chapter questions and problems** | 333 |
| **Acknowledgements** | 335 |
| **About the original authors** | 335 |
| **Index** | 336 |

# Preface

*Fundamentals of Finance* is an introductory finance textbook. It is purposely written to ensure students gain a broad understanding of finance, incorporating the key assets and markets, the financial system and how it operates, personal financial management, risk management, investments and business finance.

Students need to understand the workings of the financial system in order to gain a perspective of the context in which financial decisions are made; they also need to learn how to make financial decisions, both in their personal lives and in their workplaces. Furthermore, students in New Zealand require material that facilitates an understanding of finance in both the Australasian and the global settings. This book is also of value and interest to the general reader.

To keep current with changes in financial institutions and markets, personal finance and financial management, all chapters in this fifth edition have been updated. The major change in this edition is the inclusion of property, which is a key asset class, throughout the textbook. A new Chapter 13 evaluating property investment represents a capstone topic, drawing on concepts, tools and techniques from throughout the textbook to evaluate property investment decisions.

## Features of this book

*Fundamentals of Finance* provides a unique overview of contemporary finance from an Australasian perspective. We introduce the fundamental tools, techniques and concepts used in finance, then apply them to three major sectors of finance:

- financial institutions and markets
- personal finance
- business finance.

The broad coverage reflects the impact which finance has upon the economy, businesses and individuals, and allows for a more complete perspective of finance than traditional introductory finance textbooks have offered.

*Fundamentals of Finance* has a strong practical orientation and provides both a suitable foundation for further finance study and an overview for those students who simply want an introduction to finance.

The book is divided into four parts.

- Part 1 assists the reader to understand financial markets and the institutions that operate within them. This provides readers with a foundation upon which to build a more complete understanding of how financial markets assist the flow of funds between individuals and business organisations.
- Part 2 covers the tools, techniques and concepts used in finance. These chapters provide the methodology for applications introduced throughout the book.
- Part 3 explains the concepts of risk and return, and introduces personal financial management techniques that can assist readers to achieve their own financial goals.
- Part 4 describes a business organisation, how it is managed and financed, and its short-term and long-term operating strategies. The analysis of potential investments is an important process that is critical in ensuring that anticipated returns will be sufficient to meet financing costs. Upon reaching the final chapters, the reader will realise that many of the techniques used to achieve personal financial goals are also used by business organisations.

## Key learning tools

*Fundamentals of Finance* features several key tools to encourage the learning process.
- Learning objectives are presented at the beginning of each chapter to help students focus on the most important material.
- Definitions of new terminology are highlighted in bold when they are first introduced, then defined inside a box in the margin of the same page as well as in a glossary at the end of the book.
- Where equations are presented, they have been worked in detail so that students can see how each one works. A summary of key equations used in the book is presented in Appendix 1.
- At the end of each chapter, questions and problems are provided for students to test their comprehension of concepts and techniques covered in the chapter. Solutions to selected end-of-chapter questions and problems are included in Appendix 2.

# PART 1

# Financial systems

In this section, a number of regularly used financial terms and phrases are introduced and explained, so that when they are used in other parts of the text readers should recognise them and understand their meaning. In order to make this learning process easier, new finance terminology will be highlighted in bold print, and defined both alongside the text and in a glossary at the end of the book.

This part of the book introduces the financial system that operates in New Zealand, which is similar to those systems operating in most free-market economies. The financial system deals with the environment in which financial assets are created, held and traded in the economy. Essentially, it facilitates payments, lending and risk transference. Financial assets are held in many forms, from cash to the electronic record for a share. An understanding of the system is important for all types of financial decision-making.

Chapter 1 introduces a number of the concepts covered in later chapters. Finance is defined, and the reasons why it should be studied are explained. Important financial decisions must be made by individuals and organisations, and these decisions are influenced by the financial environment in which we live and operate.

In Chapter 2 the financial assets created by government, financial intermediaries, corporations and individuals are described. Before financial assets can be bought or exchanged, a price has to be set or agreed upon. When a financial asset is being sold for the first time it is called 'a primary issue' and is sold in a primary market; the price could be set by the seller, or the market could determine the price with the new financial assets sold to the highest bidder. Secondary markets exist for the trading of existing financial assets. In these marketplaces, the price set will be the lowest price a seller is prepared to accept and the highest price a buyer is prepared to pay. As new information becomes available in the marketplace, it will be incorporated into financial asset prices.

Chapter 3 looks first at why, when compared with most industries, the financial system is highly regulated. Recurring bank failures with large losses to depositors led to government intervention, as governments are concerned with the stability of the financial system and the role of the central bank – in the case of New Zealand, the Reserve Bank – in promoting it. It then looks at financial intermediaries that facilitate cash flow in the financial system, why they take the form they do, and why this form is constantly changing. Markets have developed over centuries in response to the changing financial needs of participants as well as the changing regulatory controls, and will continue to evolve.

# An overview of finance

**CHAPTER 1**

## Learning objectives

By the end of this chapter, you should:
- understand the interdisciplinary nature of finance
- be familiar with the concept of finance and the levels of financial decision-making
- recognise the role that financial markets play in the allocation of scarce resources
- understand the foundations of the market system and the regulatory environment that affect both individuals and organisations.

## Introduction

This chapter sets the foundation for the remainder of the book by giving an overview of the topics that are to be covered. At the same time, some of the basic concepts referred to throughout the text will be introduced. A definition of finance is given, as well as the applications, strategies and goals that should be established to ensure that individuals and corporations achieve their objectives within the existing business or regulatory environment.

It should become apparent by the end of the chapter that the **financial planning activities** relating to money management, performed by individuals and households, are very similar to those undertaken by small, medium and large companies. In addition, very few financial decisions can be made without an understanding of the role played by **financial markets** in the allocation of scarce resources.

In fact, the role financial markets play in distributing funds between borrowers and lenders and between individuals and companies is central to the material covered in this book. If financial markets and financial intermediaries did not exist, then individuals would not be able to save or borrow money readily, and companies would find it difficult to raise funds in order to expand their operations. Both individuals and companies use financial intermediaries to obtain funds in order to acquire **real** and **financial assets**, as shown in Figure 1.1. Corporations use financial intermediaries to issue financial assets on their behalf for purchase by other companies and individuals.

The tools used to determine the outcome of any financial planning activities are **time value of money** concepts, and these are covered in Chapters 4 and 5. These tools permit borrowers and lenders to calculate the value of any financial decision in today's dollars so that the best alternative can be selected. Given the uncertainty of outcomes that are to occur in the future, an element of **risk** is associated with these decisions. Risk and the effect it may have on the outcomes (or returns) to be received from financial planning activities conclude this section of the text.

> **Financial planning activities**
> Those activities relating to managing money.
>
> **Financial markets**
> Markets used to transfer financial assets between borrowers and investors.
>
> **Real assets**
> Assets that are tangible, such as land, buildings and machinery.
>
> **Financial assets**
> Securities issued by a corporation or economic unit for purchase by another individual or corporate investor.
>
> **Time value of money**
> The concept that a dollar owned today is worth more than the same dollar would be worth in the future.
>
> **Risk**
> The variability of returns resulting from an investment.

# Definition of finance

The definition of finance has changed over time as its role has been developed and refined. In the early part of the twentieth century, finance was concerned with the receipt and administration of funds on behalf of individuals and companies. Emphasis was placed on the **securities** (or **financial instruments**) used to transfer wealth, the institutions that acted as intermediaries between **lenders** (investors) and **borrowers**, and the financial markets in which they operated. Over time, the definition was broadened to encompass the financing requirements of a firm and, as a result, the emphasis has changed from an external (or outside the firm) approach to one that considers the internal financing requirements of a firm.

> **Securities**
> Financial instruments used to finance an organisation's operations.
>
> **Financial instruments**
> Instruments, such as convertible debt or preference shares, that allow funds to be transferred between investors (or lenders) and borrowers.
>
> **Lender**
> Person who grants the use of money or any other asset to another for a set period of time and receives income in return.
>
> **Borrower**
> An individual, or organisation, who obtains or receives something, such as money, temporarily from another individual or organisation, with the intention of repaying it.

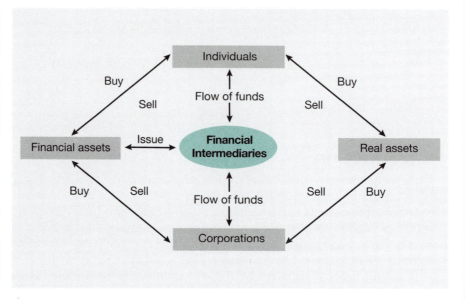

Figure 1.1 The parties involved in the acquisition of real and financial assets

Therefore, it can be said that **finance** is concerned with the allocation of scarce resources over time. These resources may be financial (money, **shares**, **bonds**) or real (property, minerals, goods) and, hence, require different types of decisions to be made. Financial decisions involve obtaining funds and then allocating them for a particular purpose. It is important to determine the costs and benefits associated with financing and investment activities because:

- they are spread out over a period of time
- they are not known with certainty.

In other words, because the costs and benefits arise in future periods, there is an element of uncertainty as to whether or not these forecast costs and benefits will actually occur.

> **Finance**
> The allocation of scarce resources, such as money, over time.
>
> **Shares**
> Entitlement to a proportion of the ownership of a company or firm.
>
> **Bonds**
> Fixed-interest investments whereby the individual receives a number of payments at fixed intervals until the bond is repaid. They represent the long-term debt obligations of a company or government.

## The financial system

When a decision is made to **invest** today, the current consumption of funds is foregone in order to receive a **return**, or profit, in the future; that is, the use of those funds is transferred from one period to another. Figure 1.1 shows that this activity may be concerned with acquiring either a real asset (such as land or a car) or a financial asset (such as shares or bonds) for your own personal use or

> **Invest**
> To apply or put money to some use in order to defer consumption and receive a return in the future.

for use within a company. Once a **company** has decided to invest in a major **asset**, the financial manager will make a financing decision as to the choice of funds to be used to finance the required asset. One of the major objectives of finance is to acquire funds at the lowest possible cost and then use these funds efficiently in order to obtain the desired benefits from the investment.

When implementing the decision to invest, or the decision concerning how to finance a large asset, people look to the financial system to meet their requirements. The **financial system** assists the financial decision-making process by bringing together investors and borrowers. The system operates via a set of **markets**, such as markets for shares, bonds, **foreign exchange** and other financial instruments. **Financial intermediaries**, such as banks, insurance companies and finance companies, act as 'go-betweens', and are used to assist the flow of funds between investors and borrowers. Investors are those who have surplus funds, whereas borrowers are those who require additional funds to meet their financial commitments.

Other parties to the financial system include financial service organisations and regulatory bodies. Financial service organisations provide financial advice to individuals and corporations on either a fee or a commission basis, while regulatory bodies exist to oversee and govern the activities of those who participate in the financial system. The roles of financial markets and the effect of regulation will be discussed later in the chapter.

## Finance as a discipline for study

Why study finance? The study of finance involves money management, and being able to manage funds successfully in a personal or corporate context is essential for the financial well-being of any person or company. There are three main areas of finance:

- financial institutions and markets
- investments
- corporate finance.

Financial institutions and markets are essential for permitting the flow of funds between individuals, corporations and governments. Financial institutions take in funds from savers and lend them to businesses or people who need funds. Financial markets offer another way to bring together those with funds to invest and those who need funds. Securities are issued and sold in financial markets, and there is overlap between the areas of finance because financial institutions operate in financial markets. These markets are important for determining interest rates, pricing securities and trading. The management of funds moving between countries is important for financial managers because of the effect that changes in currency values can have on the cost of imported and exported goods.

A knowledge of investment concepts allows investors and corporate managers to understand how real and financial securities are priced, as well as the risks associated with them. A knowledge of the complexities of the operations of the markets for these assets and the rules and regulations that govern them ensure that informed financial decisions are made.

Corporate finance provides the basis for financial decision-making in companies, where the financial manager's ability to make sound financial decisions is essential to maximising the value of the organisation. Successful decisions benefit both the company and its owners, and good cash (or fund) management is critical to a

---

**Return**
Gains or losses received from the investment of funds for a given period of time.

**Company**
A legal entity that operates and functions independently from its owners and, as such, is responsible for all debts incurred in the course of business.

**Asset**
A commodity or quality that is useful or valuable.

**Financial system**
A network which operates via a set of financial markets, bringing together investors and borrowers who buy and sell both real and financial assets; includes financial intermediaries, individuals, corporations, regulatory bodies and financial service organisations.

**Market**
A network whereby buyers and sellers are able to come together, either physically or through communication channels, to trade goods and/or services.

**Foreign exchange**
The process of converting New Zealand dollars into the currency of another country.

**Financial intermediaries**
Banks, insurance companies and other organisations that facilitate the flow of funds between investors and borrowers.

company's survival. For example, astute credit policies ensure that funds owing to the company are collected on time, while appropriate financing decisions ensure that the company can borrow funds when needed to finance projects and expansion.

However, perhaps the most important reason to study finance is to attempt to understand how to cope with uncertainty. Financial management deals with the risks and uncertainties of activities that may arise in the future. Financial management is forward-looking, and therefore sets objectives in order to achieve a desired result that can be measured in financial terms. Business people require an appreciation of the risks associated with decisions made in an uncertain world so that better-informed financial decisions can be made. This requires an understanding of how the financial system works and how individuals and organisations operate within it.

## The interdisciplinary nature of finance

Finance, by its very nature, draws from, or builds on, a number of other disciplines, including accounting, the decision sciences, economics and the behavioural sciences, as shown in Figure 1.2.

Finance draws from accounting by using the information gathered and presented by accountants in order to obtain an understanding of the past or present position of an organisation's activities. This information provides financial managers with the data required so that decisions about future projects or funding requirements can be made. In other words, finance concentrates on future company operations and draws from activities occurring in the economy and financial markets in order to be able to make informed financial decisions that will add value to the company. Individual **investors** also use the financial reports generated by accountants in order to assist their personal **investment** activities.

There are two key differences between the disciplines of accounting and finance. Firstly, accountants use an **accrual** method of recording data for compiling financial statements and, in the process, follow established accounting procedures. They report the **profits** (or losses) that have been made from the company's operations. Financial managers, on the other hand, emphasise the inflow and outflow of the company's **cash flows,** and manage these funds to maximise the firm's value. By doing this they make sure that there are sufficient funds available to meet the organisation's financial obligations and schedule of investment in new projects. Secondly, accountants record and report financial information, whereas financial managers evaluate this information and use it as the foundation for collecting additional information. This information is then used to make decisions concerning the expected future returns and risks of the firm's operations.

The analytical tools and techniques that are used in finance to assist financial decision-making are drawn from the decision sciences. These techniques attempt to model reality by describing, for example, the relationship between cash inflows and outflows and, hence, permit comparisons between various projects. Spreadsheet packages, such as Excel, greatly assist the quantitative analysis of projects and their associated risks. For example, the effect of changes in certain expenses on cash flows can be analysed using Excel's 'what-if' and 'scenario analysis' tools.

Economic theories underpin many of the concepts and techniques used in finance. For instance, all individuals and businesses operate within the New Zealand and global economy and, hence, it is necessary to understand the effects of this economic framework on financial decisions. For example, the **monetary policies** of New Zealand's trading partners will affect the value of

---

**Investors**
Individuals who acquire the financial assets of corporations or other organisations in order to receive compensation for the loan of their funds.

**Investment**
The activity of investing in real and/or financial resources.

**Accrual**
Accrual accounting records cash and credit transactions as they are incurred and not when the cash flows arise.

**Profit**
Excess of income over expenses. Alternatively referred to as *net profit*, *net income* or *net earnings*.

**Cash flows**
The inflow (receipts) and outflow (disbursements) of funds.

**Monetary policies**
The management of a nation's money supply, and how this relates to interest rates, prices and other economic variables.

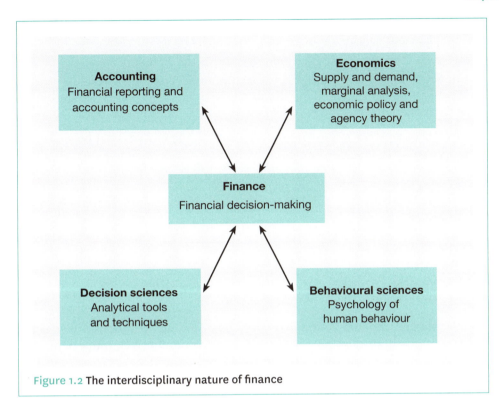

Figure 1.2 **The interdisciplinary nature of finance**

their **currencies**, and this in turn will cause adjustments to the New Zealand dollar. Movements in currencies cause interest rates to fluctuate so that the costs associated with borrowing or lending money may increase or decrease. The supply and demand for securities or goods is another factor that affects their prices. These concepts are found from studying economics. In addition, when considering financial decision-making, the economic concept of **marginal analysis** is often drawn on. By using this technique, the decision to accept or reject a new project will be made only if the marginal costs associated with the project are less than the marginal benefits to be derived from it.

The behavioural sciences help us to understand human behaviour. In the context of finance, an understanding of human behaviour allows us insights into the reasons for the investment and financing decisions made by personal investors and business managers. Everyone has their own perceptions of risk and the rewards they are prepared to accept for taking risks. Therefore a knowledge of the varying personality traits individuals possess will assist those providing investment or financial advice.

**Currency**
An exchange medium within a country; that is, money.

**Marginal analysis**
Technique used in managerial finance whereby a proposal is accepted only when the added benefits exceed the added costs.

## Finance and business

### The business environment and stakeholder protection

Financial decisions made by managers not only affect the firm's **shareholders** but often also impact upon other **stakeholders**, such as the firm's creditors, suppliers, employees and customers. Stakeholders are defined as those who have a claim on a company's cash flows. For example, cash flows generated by the company will:

- pay employees' salaries and wages
- pay suppliers for the goods and services they provide

**Shareholder**
Any individual or entity owning shares in a company.

**Stakeholders**
Groups such as investors, suppliers, regulators, employees, customers and the public with interests in a firm.

- pay creditors interest on the funds they have loaned to the company as well as the principal required to be repaid at maturity
- pay taxes to the government from any surplus the company makes.

As shown in Table 1.1 any surplus (or uncommitted) cash flows will be paid to the owners (i.e. the shareholders) of the company in the form of dividends and/or be reinvested in the company to enable it to expand its operations.

Table 1.1 **Allocation of company cash flows**

| Company cash flows ||
|---|---|
| **Committed** | **Uncommitted** |
| Employees' salaries and wages | Reinvested in company |
| Payments to suppliers | Dividends paid to owners |
| Payments to creditors | Debt repayments beyond |
| Government tax payments | minimum requirements |

**Finance company**
Finance companies lend the funds they have raised in the markets to people and businesses who need money to finance the purchase of durables, such as equipment, cars and home improvements. They normally charge higher interest rates to compensate for the riskier lending.

**Financial crises**
Major disturbances in financial markets typified by steep declines in asset prices and widespread company failures.

**Global financial crisis**
A worldwide financial crisis that occurs when financial-market participants recognise the risk and overinflated values of financial contracts, leading to a severe contraction in the flow of funds and rapidly declining asset values.

**Act**
A codified decision provided by a legislative body.

The decision of a **finance company** to curtail its lending operations due to some customers defaulting on their loans will affect a number of groups. Property developers who have borrowed money from the finance company for housing projects and require additional funds will be unable to complete projects that are already underway. Investors in finance company securities may lose some, or all, of their money. Apart from these two groups, the suppliers of goods to the developer might be affected if they are not paid, and a number of employees might lose their jobs because the money to pay their salaries has dried up. There have been many **financial crises** over the centuries: the Dutch tulip-bulb price boom and crash in 1637, the bank panics and collapses in the eighteenth and nineteenth centuries, the Wall Street stockmarket crash and Great Depression of 1929 to 1939, and the **global financial crisis** (GFC) of 2007 to 2008.

Financial crises can start in several ways: asset price booms and busts; overall uncertainty caused by failures of major financial institutions; mismanagement of financial reforms; or the introduction of new financial products. The GFC, which began in the United States, had its origins in a complex interplay of events, including readily available funds for borrowing, low interest rates, rapid growth in housing markets, and financial mismanagement. When US house prices fell, banks and other financial institutions became unwilling to lend to each other for fear that the other parties might have large exposures to the large number of home loans in default.

Security products tied to these home loans also declined hugely in value and, due to the financial links between countries, a large number of overseas financial institutions were also affected. Many, particularly in the United Kingdom and Europe, required government funding assistance to prevent their collapse. Government regulatory systems and corporate governance were deemed inadequate, so governments worldwide have been working on improving both in order to promote an efficient and transparent financial environment. These problems will be discussed further in Chapters 2 and 3.

Given the potentially wide-reaching adverse impacts that can result from business decisions, regulatory bodies play an important role in imposing constraints on such activities in order to protect stakeholders.

Consumer protection laws are embodied in a number of **Acts** that govern the sale of goods and services. The earliest of these is the Sale of Goods Act 1908, which was amended in July 2003 to encompass computer software. This Act ensures that the buyer of a product or service receives the product or service of the quality expected within a specified time and at the agreed price. However, the Act's powers have been reduced by the introduction of the Consumer Guarantees Act 1993, so that its current application is to wholesalers who supply retailers with goods. The Consumer Guarantees Act 1993 is concerned with non-private consumer transactions (i.e. those transactions undertaken with retail organisations) and contains various implied warranties for goods and services supplied or sold to consumers. The Act includes protection for consumers by ensuring that the goods or services they acquire are of the quality and type advertised. Further, it sets out the type of compensation that consumers can expect to receive from the suppliers and manufacturers if any of the goods or services are found to be inferior. The Fair Trading Act 1986 also serves to protect consumers from misleading or deceptive conduct in trade, as well as from the supply of unsatisfactory or unsafe goods and services. These Acts encourage ethical behaviour in the marketplace and put the onus on businesses to provide consumers with products that comply with established safety guidelines and that live up to the promotional promises made.

Another important Act is the Companies Act 1993, which contains provisions for the formation, administration, acquisition and winding up of companies, as well as for the protection of those stakeholders who have contractual obligations with a company. It defines the relationship between the company and its stakeholders by considering the duties of company directors, and sets out the potential liabilities that may be imposed if the directors breach their duties. For example, while it gives directors a great deal of discretion in their business dealings, it seeks to protect the owners (i.e. shareholders) and creditors against any abuse by those in charge of the company's operations. In 2014, the Companies Amendment Act No. 4 was introduced in order to prevent directors acting in bad faith or incurring additional debt if a company was insolvent.

The task of ensuring that the Companies Act is enforced has been delegated to a regulatory body, the Financial Markets Authority (FMA). The FMA is the country's primary investment regulator, and its objective is to promote investor confidence as well as encourage capital investment in New Zealand. The FMA was established in 2011 following criticism that the previous regulatory regime (the Securities Commission of New Zealand) had failed to prevent numerous finance company collapses during 2007 to 2008. The FMA undertook investigations in order to determine whether or not investors were misled by the information provided in **prospectuses** produced by these finance companies prior to receivership.

**Prospectus**
A document required by law to inform prospective investors in a firm of the details of the security and the firm's financial position.

The FMA also regulates the Financial Markets Conduct Act 2013. This Act seeks to ensure that investors have confidence in the financial markets, as significant abuses in securities trading had occurred in the past. Poor information disclosure and ineffective trading procedures also made the financial market's operations inefficient. An efficiently operating stock exchange is essential in any financial market in order for market participants to feel confident that they are operating in a transparent, fair and competitive market. In order to ensure that the performance of the New Zealand's securities market, known formally as the New Zealand Exchange Ltd and referred to as the NZX, is satisfactory, the FMA reviews its operations annually. During the 2007 annual review, the Securities Commission (the regulator before the FMA) recommended that any attachments to company announcements should immediately be placed on the NZX's website so that all interested parties receive the information as soon as it is made public. Future reviews are expected to focus on specific issues with regard to how the NZX carries out its own market supervision, since it has a statutory responsibility to do so as well.

In some cases the government is a stakeholder acting on behalf of the public. For example, income taxes collected by the government can be used for the benefit of the nation, including providing for the health and education of its citizens. The level and type of tax that should be collected from companies and individuals is covered by the Income Tax Act 2007. All stakeholders should consider the effect of income taxes when analysing investment alternatives, selecting suitable financing arrangements and paying out returns to owners. In the late 1980s, the New Zealand government introduced a dividend imputation system that significantly changed the taxation of income for companies and their shareholders. This system, in effect, eliminated the incidence of the double taxation of profits that had existed previously. Under the old (classical) system, companies were taxed on their earnings and then, when the earnings were distributed as **dividends**, they were taxed again as income in the hands of the shareholders. The new imputation system has affected the relative desirability of different forms of business organisation, and has influenced many of the major financial decisions made by companies and investors.

Finally, there are two Acts that have been designed to protect the environment for the current and future benefit of stakeholders. The first, the Resource Management Act 1991, was passed with the objective of ensuring that the use, development and management of New Zealand's resources were undertaken in order to provide for the well-being of its citizens. The aim of this Act is to protect the physical and natural resources of the country as well as the air, water, soil and ecosystems that are necessary to sustain a good quality of life.

In 2002, as part of concern over the increasing level of greenhouse gases in the atmosphere and their impact upon the environment, New Zealand signed the Kyoto Protocol. In the spirit of this accord, the Climate Change Response Act 2002 was passed. This Act was amended in 2012 and seeks to stabilise the level of greenhouse gas emissions in order to minimise the potentially harmful effects of global warming. International concern about the impact of global warming on natural ecosystems and food production came into focus in late 2015 at the Paris climate change conference (COP21). New Zealand signed the subsequent Paris Agreement, which will commit the country to carbon reduction initiatives.

## The four levels of financial decision-making

There are two segments into which the four main levels of financial decision-making fall, as shown in Figure 1.3. The personal segment comprises the personal level and is present throughout your lifetime, whereas the organisational segment may only affect some members of the population. This latter segment can be further subdivided into three levels whereby a sole proprietor may progress to a partnership and, in time, their organisation could become a corporation. The two middle levels can be interchangeable and, in some instances, one may be omitted. All four levels are described below.

> **Dividends**
> The portion of a company's net profit paid to its shareholders (owners).

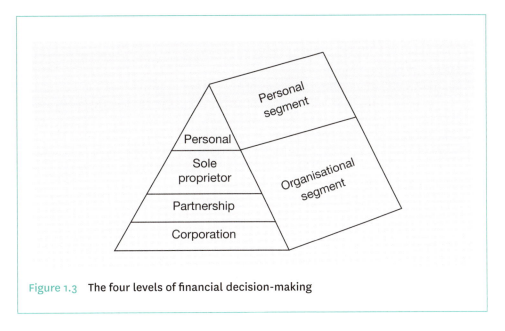

Figure 1.3 The four levels of financial decision-making

## Personal level

At the personal level, decisions may be made for a household comprising either a single person, a number of people sharing a house, or a family. At this level there are three financial decisions which are usually considered. These are the decisions to:

- consume or save current wealth – that is, to decide whether all income should be spent as it is earned or whether some of the funds could be deferred in order to be used at some time in the future
- borrow additional funds from others in order to help household members achieve their preferred consumption and investment plans
- manage the risks associated with any financial decision in order to determine whether the risks should be reduced or increased.

## Sole proprietorship level

These businesses or firms offer goods and/or services, but are owned and operated by one person in order to make a profit. Examples are the corner dairy, the shoe repairer, dry cleaners, etc. The owner of the business may hire a few employees but they make all the decisions concerning the operation of the firm. Funds to operate the business are obtained from personal resources or by borrowing from family members, friends or the bank. The owner assumes **unlimited liability** for the funds invested in the firm. This means that if insufficient revenue is earned to pay interest charges on any loans, the owner's personal wealth may be used to satisfy the financial obligations of creditors.

> **Unlimited liability**
> The state of being personally liable for all debts and monies owed by a business or organisation.

## Partnership level

Partnerships are firms made up of two or more owners working together to make a profit. These firms pool funds and expertise to finance their operations. A partnership agreement sets out the proportion of total funds to be paid into the firm by each partner, the proportion of profits to be allocated to each partner, and the management decision-making process. A partnership has a finite life, because when one of the partners dies or leaves the firm the existing partnership is dissolved and a new partnership agreement must be drawn up by the remaining partners as well as any new members.

Most partners have unlimited liability so that, in a similar fashion to the sole proprietor, they are jointly and severally responsible for all debts relating to the partnership. Examples of this type of business are professional organisations such as accountancy, legal, architectural and engineering firms.

However, in some cases a limited partnership may exist in New Zealand, whereby one or more partners may hold a **limited liability** in the firm, as long as there is at least one unlimited partner in the organisation. Limited partners do not usually participate in the firm's management.

> **Limited liability**
> The state of being liable for all debts and monies owed up to a pre-defined amount.

## Corporation level

These organisations are entities that have been created by law. They are distinct from their owners and, as such, are responsible for all debts incurred during the course of their business operations. A corporation, or company, can sue and be sued, acquire property and enter into contracts. The company pays its own taxes and is governed by its constitution. The constitution lists the purpose of the business, the number of shares to be issued by the company, the number of directors to be appointed to the board, as well as any other rules that will govern its operations.

Companies raise two forms of finance to support their operations. These are debt and equity. **Debt** is raised from individuals, and institutions, who have surplus funds and who invest their money in the company. The company pays interest to investors who have lent them money, and considers the debt to be a liability because at a designated future date they will have to repay the money they have borrowed.

> **Debt**
> An obligation of one party (the borrower) to repay a specified amount of money to another party (the lender).
>
> **Equity**
> Money, in the form of shares, supplied to a company or organisation by its owners.

**Equity** is the other form of finance used by companies; in this case, the company issues shares to individuals and institutions who become owners of the company. The proportion of ownership they hold depends on the number of shares purchased. The shares can be held indefinitely, or sold at the investor's (owner's) discretion. The investors usually receive a dividend for each share they hold.

Although there are a number of private corporations in existence, in this book we will focus mainly on publicly traded companies. These companies issue shares to the public, who then become the owners (shareholders) of the company. However, although the shareholders own the company, they do not manage its day-to-day operations. In order to do this, they appoint a board of directors who, in turn, appoint managers to conduct the company's affairs. Hence, the board acts as the representative of the shareholders, and it attempts to appoint managers who will act in the owners' best interests.

The separation of ownership and management is a distinct feature of corporations, as it ensures that the company is set up as a permanent entity; that is, it does not have a finite life. In addition, the structure permits shareholders to transfer the ownership of their shares to others, and allows managers to leave the organisation without causing major disruption to its operations. In other words, the separation of these two activities creates flexibility and continuity.

> **Liquidation**
> The process of winding up the assets of an organisation and distributing the funds to creditors and owners.

Corporations have limited liability, which means that the owners' personal wealth is protected, although if the corporation cannot service its debt then it can be **liquidated**. In this case, all creditors will be paid from the sale of company assets, and shareholders will receive only those funds that remain; that is, shareholders receive the residual funds on the winding-up of the company's affairs.

# The ethics dilemma

**Ethics** in general deal with morality, or the ability to know the difference between right and wrong. In the case of business, ethics relate to the moral principles by which a company operates. Many organisations possess a code of ethics that sets out the standards of professional conduct for employees to follow in dealings with other employees, stakeholders and customers.

There are two main areas where ethical issues associated with companies most commonly arise: agency problems, and conflicts of interest.

> **Ethics**
> The ability to know the difference between right and wrong.

## Agency problems

**Agency problems** may arise when managers, who are hired as agents of a company's owners (or shareholders) and are thus expected to work in the owners' best interests, have different goals from the owners. To some extent this problem may be overcome by structuring the remuneration packages paid to senior management so as to be directly based on performance. In most cases the package would consist of a salary plus incentives and/or bonuses; the incentive might include share acquisition, so that a manager has a direct interest in the performance of the company. As an owner of the company, a manager will want it to succeed so that its value will increase, as they will in turn receive compensation from an increasing share price and an increasing dividend stream.

An example of agency conflict would be when a managing director uses the company's resources to fund their own personal interests in related companies. The funds for these expenditures may not be disclosed in financial statements, so that the owners and stakeholders are unaware of the additional liability carried by the company. In this situation the company employing the managing director is unknowingly acting as a source of funds for the managing director's other ventures.

> **Agency problems**
> Issues that arise when managers, who are hired as agents of a company, work in their own interests rather than in those of the shareholders.

## Conflicts of interest

**Conflicts of interest** arise when a manager or director uses information pertaining to the company to benefit themselves or another organisation. For example, a director and/or shareholder might try to persuade the company's owners that a segment of the organisation is not performing well and is unlikely to do so in the future; they could then suggest that it is in the company's best interests for this segment to be sold to a consortium in which the manager or director has an interest for a nominal sum.

There are a number of organisations that ensure that ethical behaviour is observed in the New Zealand marketplace. The FMA oversees the conduct of the financial markets to ensure that operations are transparent and efficient, while NZX oversees publicly listed companies to ensure that they operate in an ethical manner. The companies themselves have trustees and auditors whose job it is to make sure that a true and fair picture of the company's operations are portrayed in its literature. If trustees or auditors find inaccuracies that might affect the performance of the company, it is their duty to detail these problems so that suppliers, creditors and investors can make informed decisions.

> **Conflicts of interest**
> Issues that arise when a manager, or director, uses company information to benefit themselves or another organisation.

# Financial markets

Individuals, sole proprietorships, partnerships and corporations all receive and disburse funds. Surplus funds are put away for use at a later time. In today's environment, people and businesses are using electronic means of transferring cash from one source to another. In each instance, banks facilitate these transactions. Banks do not operate in isolation, but are part of a market system which facilitates the flow of funds between entities within New Zealand and throughout the world. Being part of a market means the banks and, in particular, the corporations compete, create and transfer wealth and, in the process, face the risks associated with doing this.

The modern financial system has developed as a consequence of the features of capitalism and the rights that it endows. These include:

- the existence of private wealth
- freedom of choice
- incentives
- efficient markets
- the role of government.

Each of these concepts will be discussed further below.

### The existence of private wealth

Physical assets such as money, houses, cars, plant and machinery, and human capital in the form of education and intellectual property, are all forms of wealth. Historically, the proportion of ownership and wealth has oscillated between the state and individuals. However, if a **pure market system** existed, then all wealth would be owned by private individuals.

Private wealth endows owners with legally enforceable rights. If wealth is owned by an individual, or organisation, then the owner has the right to decide how the wealth will be used. For example, if you own a house, then you have the authority to decide who will live in it. However, if you are renting the house then the owner has the right to ask you to move out. The same exists with any asset: the owner has the power to determine how and when that asset can be used.

Furthermore, the ownership of private wealth means that individuals will utilise their own resources efficiently; that is, they will seek more wealth, not less. In this way, they will try to maximise their wealth by optimising its use and allocating their scarce resources in a manner that will provide more opportunities for everyone. In other words, by owning wealth, such as a car, you will look after it better than a tourist would look after a rental car.

> **Pure market system**
> A system in which all scarce resources are freely allocated so that the maximum benefit is received by everyone as a result of the allocation.

### Freedom of choice

A market system permits different options to be tried and different participants to freely enter and exit the market. In such a system, organisations and entrepreneurs will compete for scarce resources, and if their choice of investment alternative is successful, they will continue to invest in other projects. However, if bad choices are made, then the organisation will become unproductive and fail. In the market system, some people will succeed whereas others will fail. It is competition and successful decisions that determine the winners and losers. In this system, losers exit the market because there is no safety net to catch them if they fail and, therefore, they are prevented from continuing to inefficiently allocate scarce resources.

### Incentives

Incentives are motivators – they motivate people to take risks. Without incentives, many people would undertake only the projects that they were convinced would succeed and, in the process, might implement only those projects generating a low level of profit. The workers would avoid the risky and more lucrative projects. Under the market system, incentives encourage workers to undertake riskier projects that would generate significantly higher profits. It is the motivation of increased profits which permits an allocation of scarce resources in such a way that the goods and services offered match those the consumer demands. Therefore, it is apparent to all that the allocation of resources has been careful, efficient and self-sustaining.

## Efficient markets

In order for markets to work, all participants need to be informed, therefore an **efficient market** is said to be one where the price of any good (i.e. asset) fully reflects all information associated with it. However, the market consists of individuals whose interpretation of this information will differ, so that whenever goods are traded, it is the forces of supply and demand which will determine the price that will clear the market of all goods offered for sale. If prices do not reflect all information, based on the information individuals have received and incorporated into the price they expect to pay for an item, the market for the product may not be satisfied. In other words, the price may be too high for purchasers to pay or too low for sellers to accept.

> **Efficient market**
> This market exists when the price of any good (asset) fully reflects all information associated with it.

Government planners seek to have a market that is efficient by encouraging competition and the provision of good-quality information in order for traders to be confident they are in possession of all relevant facts. Some of the conditions this market should possess are that:

- supply and demand determines the price of **homogeneous** goods
- prices reflect all available information
- many individuals and firms are able to trade
- there are no transaction costs (or costs are minimal)
- participants are free to enter and exit the market at any time.

> **Homogeneous**
> Something that is of a similar kind or nature.

The presence of an efficient market implies that a person who has access to all available information is able to make a fully informed decision. However, there is no guarantee that the individuals themselves will make the right decision. Furthermore, in an efficient market, competition between traders provides the incentive signals to ensure resources are allocated efficiently so that the maximum benefit will be received. No resources will be wasted, because supply and demand will be equalised through the mechanism of price changes. For example, if the price of a particular line of goods being offered for sale is set properly, all the goods will be purchased; that is, the supply of the goods will meet the demand for them.

## The role of government

The market system that has been described above is, in the main, self-regulating. However, there is still a role for a government to play to make sure that the market system operates properly. The tasks required from a government are to:

- act as an umpire whenever disputes among traders in the market occur
- maintain a legal system that enforces contracts and keeps the playing field level and fair
- provide quality information disclosure so that market participants can make better decisions

- maintain a defence system to protect the nation's borders, as well as a police service to protect the public's interests
- create a climate that will encourage individuals to engage in business by giving them the right to own property and operate in an efficient market, receive the full enjoyment of the incentives resulting from their labours, and have minimal disincentives such as compliance costs and taxes.

The government should also grant solutions to economic problems that the market cannot or will not provide. Examples of these are **public goods** and **externalities**. Public goods are those products or services, such as education, health, bridges and roads, which may not generate a profit for the resources allocated to them. These goods are public because everyone usually has the right to use them and no firm or individual should be denied access. As a result, it is not possible to charge for the use of these goods, and therefore it must fall to the government to provide and maintain them.

Externalities are those outcomes from the production and exchange of goods that are deemed to be undesirable, such as pollution or exploitation. They do not necessarily arise from the use of the market system as such. Pollution may occur because no single individual or firm owns the air or water. As a result, there is no incentive provided by the market system to keep the environment clean. This situation means that the polluter is able to charge less for the goods produced because they do not have to have systems in place to control the emissions. One way to overcome the problem is to regulate the polluters and prevent the production of any goods that pollute the environment. However, the ideal would be a market-determined price that would permit the goods to be produced at a price that would allow the firm to instal systems to minimise pollution while at the same time making a profit on its operations.

In conclusion, a market system will affect the decisions of individuals and firms on the one hand, but on the other hand the main outcome of a competitive system is a more efficient utilisation of resources that provides greater community wealth. This system permits an optimal economic solution to resource allocation, and is also an ethical solution because it encourages responsible behaviour by individuals in order to succeed. For example, if traders do not have a good reputation, then the market will punish them by not allowing them to trade and make a living. In addition, an efficient market only discriminates on the price an individual is prepared to pay for goods, thus making it a fair system that requires only an individual's ability and willingness to work hard for them to be successful.

> **Public goods**
> Goods or services, such as education, provided by the government for use by members of its society.
>
> **Externalities**
> Influences on the activities of an individual or business that are not controlled by the individual or business.

# Conclusion

The purpose of this chapter was to lay the foundations of the areas to be covered in this book. Finance is described as involving the allocation of financial and real assets over time. One objective of finance is to acquire funds at the lowest possible cost and to use these funds efficiently to obtain the desired benefits from the investment. By its very nature, finance is interdisciplinary and draws primarily on accounting and economic principles in order to obtain the information from which informed decisions concerning the financing and investment of assets can be made. None of these decisions can be made in isolation, and the financial markets play a pivotal role in determining the allocation of scarce resources. Both individuals and organisations (at all levels of the organisational segment) make similar financial decisions and, as a result, both segments benefit from some knowledge of the regulations governing the business environment.

The next two chapters of Part 1 provide an overview of financial markets and the financial intermediaries that assist with the receipt and disbursement of funds between borrowers (issuers) and lenders (investors). No individual or organisation operates in isolation, and it is important that the financial environment in which they operate is understood.

Part 2 covers the tools required to value financial decisions. These chapters help you to understand time value of money and how it affects financing and investment decisions. For example, time value of money techniques help us to understand how interest is charged on things like a student loan or a home mortgage, how a savings goal can be achieved, and so on.

Personal finance is introduced in Part 3 to help you to plan for your own financial well-being. Financial decisions involve differing levels of risk, and Chapter 6 describes the relationship between the risk of an investment and the returns required by investors. Chapter 7 describes the short-term and long-term financing requirements of individuals, such as financing the purchase of a house or planning for retirement, then concludes by covering financing requirements and the development of a business plan for purchasing a small business.

Finally, in order to complete the progression from individual financial decision-making to business, the investment and financing aspects of larger companies will be described. Part 4 commences with an overview of the goal of the firm and the role of the financial manager, before describing the management of the firm's short-term resources and the financing of the firm. The final three chapters evaluate investments in long-term assets, such as plant and equipment, and property. The analysis of potential investments is an important process that is critical in ensuring that the anticipated returns will be sufficient to meet the financing costs.

> **SELF-TEST QUESTION**
>
> A bank is a financial intermediary that can be used by individuals, sole proprietors, partnerships and corporations to assist their financial management objectives. Describe the role banks play to enable these objectives to be achieved.
>
> **ANSWER TO SELF-TEST QUESTION**
>
> **Personal**
> - Permit individuals to deposit surplus funds that will earn interest.
> - Provide loans, to acquire real assets, in the form of mortgages and personal borrowings.
> - Provide access to foreign currency when required for overseas travel or the purchase of goods and services.
>
> **Sole proprietor/partnership**
> - Act as a depository for surplus funds from business operations.
> - Provide loans to fund the organisation's growth or acquisition of real assets.
> - Provide the foreign exchange required for the importing and exporting of goods and services.
>
> **Corporations**
> - As in sole proprietorship/partnership.
> - Act as the intermediary for the issue of the company's financial assets (i.e. debt or equity) to external parties such as individuals or institutions.

**QUESTIONS AND PROBLEMS**

1. Define the term *finance*.
2. How does financial decision-making differ from decision-making concerned with real resources?
3. List and describe the four levels of financial decision-making.
4. What are the basic foundations of a market system? List and describe them.
5. Explain how the financial markets and financial intermediaries assist individuals and companies.
6. What do the words *decision to invest* mean?
7. How does studying finance assist an individual in managing their financial affairs?
8. Compare and contrast the disciplines of finance and accounting.
9. Describe the dividend imputation system that exists in Australia and New Zealand.
10. Define the word *stakeholder*.
11. Describe ethics and the role of ethics in a business environment.
12. Builderup Ltd, a property development company, is constructing an apartment building and has been forced into liquidation. Who are the stakeholders likely to be affected, and how will they be affected?

# Financial and property markets

**CHAPTER 2**

◼ **Learning objectives**

By the end of this chapter, you should be able to:
- describe the broad asset classes for investment
- explain the functions served by financial markets
- describe the various types of financial markets, their operations and the instruments traded in them
- identify the market participants for each type of market
- describe how an individual or company may participate in the various markets
- describe property markets and their various characteristics.

## Introduction

Over time, societies have developed markets to make the efficient exchange of goods and services between buyers and sellers possible. The prices of such goods and services are determined by the forces of supply and demand.

The types of market in a modern economy can be classified as:
- product markets for manufactured goods and services
- factor markets for the factors of production of labour and capital.

For a market economy, prices act as a signal to direct resources to their best use.

We will consider one part of the factor markets, called the financial markets, that deals with financial assets. In this chapter we discuss the role of financial markets and the financial assets that are bought and sold in them. Markets are important as, with the aid of **intermediaries**, they enable the transfer of funds between those needing them and those with a surplus. This transfer of funds involves many types of financial assets. The chapter concludes by exploring property markets.

> **Intermediary**
> A financial institution that facilitates the transfer of funds between borrowers and lenders.

## Financial assets

We have discussed financial assets previously, in Chapter 1. An asset is defined as anything of value, and can be either of a tangible or an intangible type. Tangible or real assets are resources such as buildings, land and commodities. Financial assets are intangible 'paper' claims to a portion of the ownership of an underlying real asset. So real and financial assets are linked together; for example, when a company issues a debt or equity security to acquire the funds to invest in real assets such as a new machine. Figure 2.1, reproduced from Chapter 1, shows the linkages between real and financial assets and the participants in the financial system.

Financial assets, often referred to as financial instruments or securities, enable the transfer of funds from units with surplus funds (lenders) to units that are deficient in funds (borrowers). The borrower is the entity who agrees to make future cash payments to the lender and issues the security to the lender. The lender can

retain the security and also be the investor. Or the lender can resell the security so that another person becomes the investor or holder of the financial asset. It is important for the modern financial system to have a wide range of financial assets with different return, risk and time characteristics to meet the needs of the lenders or investors and the borrowers. Here are some examples of financial assets:
- a share issued by listed New Zealand telecommunications company Spark
- a loan by the ANZ bank to a student to buy a car
- a bond issued by the New Zealand government.

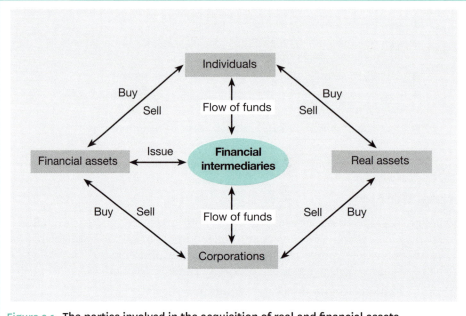

Figure 2.1 **The parties involved in the acquisition of real and financial assets**

## Debt versus equity claims

The claims of financial asset holders fall into two basic types: debt and equity. A debt instrument is one where the holder has a contractual entitlement to future cash flows from the borrowing issuer. New Zealand government bonds, Treasury bills, and a car loan are all examples of debt instruments. The holder of a bond is paid fixed payments, usually every six months. At end of the term, or at maturity, the borrower repays the individual, company or government their principal (based on its face value or par value).

A short-term debt instrument called a **bill** has a life or maturity of up to a year, is issued at a **discount** to face value, and is often called a **discount instrument**. This means no interest is paid during its lifetime, but at maturity the repayment includes both principal and interest. As an example, a 90-day bill may be sold (issued) by a company for $95 000 to an investor to raise debt funds for the company. At maturity after 90 days, the investor receives $100 000 (principal plus interest) from the company or an agent acting on the company's behalf.

An equity claim requires the issuer to pay the holder an amount based on earnings after the debt holders have been satisfied. The issuer is not obligated to pay an equity claim, and hence it may be referred to as a residual claim. An ordinary share, sometimes referred to as common stock, is an example of an equity claim; it represents part-ownership of a company and appears on the company's

**Bill**
A short-term debt instrument that is issued at a discount to its face value.

**Discount**
The difference between the face value and the price of a financial asset, such as a bond or bill, where the face value exceeds the price.

**Discount instrument**
Financial asset that, when first issued, is below its face or par value, and when repaid at maturity includes principal and interest.

**balance sheet** as a financial asset. Note that government bonds and bills are often misleadingly referred to as government stock, but they are, in fact, debt instruments and appear on the government's balance sheet as liabilities. The advantage of holding shares for an investor, on the one hand, is that shareholders may benefit from any increases in the companies' asset values or profitability and they may receive periodic payments (dividends). On the other hand, the debt holders are paid their fixed dollar amount before equity holders, but do not share in any gains.

> **Balance sheet**
> Statement of an individual's or organisation's assets, liabilities and equity at a given date.

## Prices of financial assets

The prices of financial assets are a reflection of future cash flows and their degree of certainty. The pricing includes estimates of risk associated with the cash flows. A common approach to finding a current value or the current worth of a financial asset is to use the time value concepts discussed in Chapters 4 and 5, and discount future expected flows so that the sum of the present values of the expected future cash flows is the price. The type of financial asset and the characteristics of the issuer will determine how certain future cash flows will be. We regard debt instruments issued by governments as free of default risk, or risk-free, as the cash flows to the holder are certain.

However, such financial assets are not free from other types of risk, as changes in interest rates can affect the prices of financial assets. It will be seen from the formula for finding the price of a bond in Chapter 5 that if the interest rate changes, it has a direct effect on the bond's price. Generally, if interest rates go up, bond prices go down and vice versa. So, we say there is an inverse relationship between bond prices and interest rates. Assume that a long-term government bond such as a three-year bond with a coupon rate of 5% is sold in the market before its maturity, and the market interest rates have moved upwards to 8% since its issue. The price of the bond will decrease consequently and the seller will be facing a capital loss.

In addition, if an investor bought a bond issued in a foreign currency (such as the US dollar) then the investor faces another risk – called foreign exchange risk – that exchange rate changes will adversely affect its cash flows.

## The roles of financial assets

An important role of financial assets is to aid the transfer of funds from those with excess funds to those deficient in funds; for example, to those who need funds to invest in capital projects. In addition, they aid in the transfer of risk for market participants (to be discussed later in the chapter).

# Financial markets

A financial market is a market that trades in financial assets. It is not essential for a financial market to exist in order for financial assets to be created and exchanged, but in most economies financial assets are created and then traded in some type of financial market. Financial markets play an important role in helping businesses and governments to raise new funds, as well as allowing investors to trade among themselves. The development of financial markets has also made the exchange of value of goods and services much easier. The existence of financial markets improves the attractiveness of financial assets, both for prospective buyers and for sellers. The market that deals with the immediate delivery of financial instruments is called the spot (cash) market; for example, the stock market. The markets that deal with financial instruments for delivery at some future date are called the derivative markets and will be discussed later in the chapter.

## The roles of financial markets

### Reduction of costs

One of the key roles of a market is the reduction of **transaction costs** for the participants. The existence of a market reduces both the search and information costs for the buyers and sellers. The lenders, or buyers, of financial assets do not have to spend large resources to determine the creditworthiness of the borrowers or sellers of the financial assets. Nor do they have large costs in locating the borrowers. An organised exchange can do this task for them and lower the cost through **economies of scale**. In addition, exchange rules that protect the financial safety of market participants help lower costs.

### Establishing prices

Markets help to establish prices for financial assets. This is another key role known as **price discovery**. By having a market where many similar securities trade at the same time, buyers and sellers can establish a fair market price at any one time. In other words, by having securities with similar formats for the contracts they represent, traders can compare prices and a fair price can be established. For example, this can be for listed company shares or the price of money (interest rates). We talk about **deep markets** if there are many securities bought and sold at one time, and **thin markets** when low volumes of financial assets are being traded.

The existence of numerous traders who are actively trading is another aspect of markets that helps establish prices. If traders see a security for sale that they believe is temporarily undervalued, they will buy the security. This demand for the security will cause its price to rise. And traders will keep buying the security until its price rises to what they believe is a fair market price. Likewise, if traders believe a security is overpriced, they will sell it, causing its price to drop. Again, they will keep selling it until its price has dropped to what they believe is a fair value.

With the expanded markets, such as the international markets for financial assets, provided such markets are free from trade restrictions, then the principle of **arbitrage** should ensure that equivalent financial assets being bought or sold in different markets have similar prices. The term *arbitrage* refers to the process of simultaneously selling overpriced assets and buying the same or similar assets that are underpriced elsewhere. For example, the New Zealand Spark ordinary shares are listed on the New York Stock Exchange in the United States, and the process of arbitrage ensures that the price of Spark in New Zealand and in the United States is similar, barring transaction costs and exchange rates.

### Maintaining liquidity

The liquidity function is an important component of any market. **Liquidity** refers to the ease of selling a financial asset for cash, so that a *liquid* asset is one that is easily converted into cash. An *illiquid* asset is one that is not readily converted into cash, and the seller might have to accept a large drop in price and/or wait for some time before a buyer can be found. If a financial market is liquid, this means financial assets can be traded readily without overly affecting prices. During the global financial crisis, financial institutions tried to sell financial securities for

---

**Transaction costs**
The costs involved in making financial deals, such as the costs of issuing new securities.

**Economies of scale**
Economies of scale occur when the average cost of producing a product or service decreases as the amount produced increases.

**Price discovery**
The revealing of information about future cash market prices.

**Deep markets**
Markets where there are numerous buyers and sellers.

**Thin markets**
Markets in which there are not many buyers or sellers.

**Arbitrage**
The simultaneous buying and selling of a product to take advantage of price differences. In this process, the price differences are reduced.

**Liquidity**
The quickness and ease of converting assets into cash. Sometimes called 'marketability'.

funds, but the liquidity of the securities had 'dried up' so the institutions sold them far below their previously recorded market price. The drying up of market liquidity was one of the reasons the credit crisis spread from the United States to other parts of the world. Many real assets such as residential property are regarded as mainly illiquid, as well as some financial assets such as shares that are closely held by one entity.

So, the more liquid the security and the lower the cost of trading, the more efficient a market can be in pricing securities. As a result, markets can increase investment opportunities by providing a large range of financial assets with different characteristics of return and risk to interest both borrowers and lenders. By having a wide range of financial assets the markets fulfill an **intertemporal** function; in other words, they allow consumption for savers to be smoothed over time. For example, individuals, instead of consuming all of their income today, could invest the surplus in shares and over the next few years they could gain extra income by selling off parcels of shares.

**Intertemporal**
An adjective meaning *across time*.

### Transfer of risk

The financial markets also allow for the transfer of risk from those wishing to reduce risk by **hedging** to those who are willing to take risks. One important example of this is the development of products and markets that deal with risks associated with increased volatility in interest rates. Products such as forward contracts are available which fix the price of foreign currency today but are not completed until some future date. Using **forward contracts**, importers can lock in a foreign currency price today and remove the risk of the domestic currency dropping in value when they have to pay for their imports.

**Hedging**
The practice of managing risk exposure, often by using contracts (such as derivatives) that have an offsetting exposure.

**Forward contract**
An agreement by two parties to carry out a financial transaction at a future (forward) point in time.

### Market participants

Households, companies and partnerships, governments and supranational bodies such as the World Bank can either borrow or lend through the financial markets. They can deal directly with the markets or through an intermediary. If they are individuals with small amounts, then they deal in the markets that cater for relatively small amounts, called retail markets. For institutions dealing in large amounts, for example $100 000 or more, the wholesale markets are available, where the larger denominations can lead to lower transaction costs. Institutions can also buy large amounts and break them into smaller parcels for individuals.

### Types of financial market

Financial markets can be distinguished in a number of ways.

- *Time frame*
  For example, the market for short-term debt is called the **money market** and deals with debt securities of less than a year in maturity. The market for longer-term instruments is called the **capital market**.
- *Type of financial claim*
  For instance, debt markets and equity markets are so called because of the instruments traded in them.
- *Newly issued or existing claims*
  For example, there is a **primary market** for newly issued securities. It is usual for a financial institution to be involved in the issue (i.e. sale) of new securities or

**Money market**
A market in which short-term debt instruments with maturities up to a year are traded.

**Capital markets**
The financial markets where the longer-term, relatively riskier debt and equity securities trade.

**Primary market**
Financial market in which new securities are sold and most of the funds raised go to the issuer.

> **Secondary market**
> Financial market in which existing securities are bought and sold between investors.
>
> **Auction**
> A market where the orders of traders are matched directly by the brokers.
>
> **Dealer**
> In the case of financial markets, an agent that takes ownership of the financial assets, and then makes a market by buying and selling those assets to investors.
>
> **Intermediated**
> Parties are brought together by the help of a mediator.
>
> **Bank bills**
> Unsecured short-term marketable securities issued by companies with payment arranged through a bank.
>
> **Broker**
> An agent who, for a fee or commission, carries out transactions such as the buying and selling of shares for a client.
>
> **Over-the-counter (OTC) market**
> A market that is not organised by an exchange organisation.
>
> **Repos**
> Repurchase agreements where financial institutions sell some of their government securities in exchange for cash, simultaneously agreeing to buy them back at a fixed later date.

the raising of funds for a company or government department. The **secondary market** for existing securities allows the lenders or investors to change their holdings of securities over time as well as performing a price discovery role.

- *Cash or derivative markets*
  For example, banks quote spot FX (foreign exchange) rates, and they also quote derivative FX contracts for rates in a month's time.
- *Organisational structure*
  For instance, a market can be an **auction**, **dealer**, or **intermediated** market. Dealers may help market liquidity by being willing to buy or sell securities.

## Money markets

Money markets deal with the trade of short-term debt instruments that are usually highly liquid with maturities less than a year. So the term 'money' is a misnomer. This market is an important source of short-term funding for companies as well as for governments. Cash flows and outflows rarely occur at the same time, so the money markets help to solve this problem. Creditworthy companies looking for short-term finance can borrow money in this market by issuing debt securities of large denomination called **bank bills** in its primary market. Wealthy individuals and financial institutions lend the companies money on a short-term basis by buying these securities. In addition, companies with temporary surpluses of funds can invest in these short-term instruments: if their circumstances change and they need the funds back, then the money market instruments can be sold quickly in the secondary market with little loss of value as they have little liquidity risk. Because of this and other factors, such as the large volume of securities being traded (deep markets), money market participants accept lower returns because of perceived lower risk compared with long-term markets. This means the rates on money market securities are generally only a small percentage higher than the rates on comparable short-term government securities.

### Market operation and participants

The money market operates through a network of phones and electronic screens. Market players buy and sell on their own behalf as dealers, as well as being **brokers** for their clients. This type of market, having no formal structure and no physical location, is known as an **OTC market** (over-the-counter). One of the features of an OTC market is that there is no formal structure to guarantee payment of bought and sold financial assets. The market depends on the trustworthiness of the participants to meet the payments. So the main market participants are the financial institutions, the government and large companies.

### Types of instruments traded

In the New Zealand money market, types of instruments traded can be grouped into:
- cash and **repos**
- the New Zealand government (Crown) instruments of **Treasury bills**
- corporate bill instruments (mainly bank bills)
- **certificates of deposit** (CDs)
- **promissory notes** (**commercial paper**).

These short-term debt instruments are discount instruments, priced using the techniques discussed in Chapter 4.

Table 2.1 **Money market instruments in New Zealand**

| Instrument | Uses |
| --- | --- |
| Treasury bill | Funding government expenditure |
| Bank bill | Short-term borrowing and investing |
| Certificate of deposit | A source of short-term funding for banks |
| Promissory note | A source of funding for companies with a good credit rating |

# Capital markets

The capital markets are made up of the equities market (otherwise called the share market or stock market), the bond markets (debt markets), and other markets involving financial instruments with maturity greater than one year. These markets deal with the savings for longer-term investment plans for investors and longer-term financing of large amounts for companies, generally longer than one year in maturity.

## The debt markets

Many long-term debt instruments in New Zealand are traded in an OTC market. As in the case of the money market, this trade takes place via electronic screens and by telephone. In addition, the New Zealand Exchange company NZX that operates the stock market (NZSX) also operates the debt market (NZDX) and has an increasing number of listed debt instruments. How bond traders price these instruments is discussed in Chapter 5. These can be bought through an NZX adviser. The main participants in the bond market are the Reserve Bank of New Zealand, the government, financial institutions and overseas investors.

### Types of instruments traded in the debt markets

Again, the instruments traded can be classified as Crown or non-Crown instruments. The Crown instruments are government bonds, usually three- and ten-year maturity, inflation-indexed bonds and retail Kiwi bonds. The minimum bid amount of $1 million for government bonds can be broken down into smaller parcels by financial institutions for the small investors in the secondary markets. The corporate, local government and state-owned enterprise (SOE) bonds are issued as a way of meeting these bodies' long-term funding needs. The majority of the securities traded are government bonds where a good proportion is held by non-residents. The market for government bonds has become reasonably liquid since deregulation in 1985.

Investors holding the retail instruments inflation-indexed bonds reissued in 1998, and the retail Kiwi bonds first issued in 1985 by the government, tend to retain them to maturity. For the larger corporations and SOEs, the bond market is relatively illiquid with little trading. If bonds are traded, then there is a margin over the **yield** on government bonds due to the illiquidity and higher default risk. In other words, if the government bonds are yielding 4.5% per annum (the risk-free

**Treasury bill**
Short-term debt instruments issued by the government for short-term financing.

**Certificates of deposit (CDs)**
Short-term debt instruments mainly issued by banks requiring short-term funding. Investors providing the funds do have the flexibility to sell them in the liquid secondary market before the deposit held by the bank matures.

**Promissory note**
A written promise by the borrower to pay the lender a specified amount of money at some future specified date. Usually a short-term instrument issued by a corporate of good credit standing.

**Commercial paper**
A short-term debt instrument issued directly into the market by companies with good credit ratings, with the aid of a financial institution, and known in New Zealand as *promissory notes*.

**Yield**
The return on an investment, normally expressed as a percentage of its current value. By convention, it is quoted as an annual rate.

> **Capital notes**
> Bond issues that are not supported by any underlying security and pay higher interest than corporate bonds supported by underlying assets.

rate), and corporate bonds are yielding 7%, a risk premium of 2.5% is required over and above the government bond yield.

**Capital notes** are another type of debt instrument, which pay a fixed rate of interest just like bonds but rank below all other debt offerings of the company, and only just above the equity holders in the event of the company becoming insolvent. So the interest rate on capital notes generally contains a premium over the risk-free rate to reflect this risk. In addition, at their maturity date, the holder may have the option of holding the notes for another period but at a new interest rate, or may be able to convert them into shares, generally at a discount to the share price at maturity.

## The equities market

As with the other financial markets, the equities market involves the trading of financial assets known as shares or common stock or equities. Often the equities market is known as the share market or stock market, but these days it often trades other instruments such as debt as well as shares. Equity financing by a company is another way of raising funds for the company, generally at higher cost compared with debts due to factors such as dividends being paid out of after-tax income, unlike debt interest payments that are deducted from income before tax is calculated, and the issue costs. Note, however, that the subsequent trading of the shares on an exchange does not provide any more funds for the company.

### Types of equity traded

Equity instruments traded are ordinary shares, options, rights, **preference shares** and **convertible notes**. The last two are called hybrid securities as they possess features of debt and equity. For the investor supplying funds to the company, ordinary shares represent a claim on the residual cash flows after all of the other expenses – such as debt, costs of goods and services, and taxes – have been met. In addition, a share represents an ownership stake in the company and, indirectly, the right to a voice in the overall management of the company.

Preference shares, which are no longer common in New Zealand, receive a fixed dividend only after payments to debt holders have been made, but before any payment to shareholders. Preference shares are similar to debt but have some features of equity – there may be no maturity date and payments of dividends are not legally binding as with debt.

A convertible bond or note is a debt instrument that allows the investor to convert debt into equity at maturity at a predetermined ratio. For this reason, they are often included as equity in the balance sheet of the company.

When a company wants to raise funds by equity instead of by debt, it can issue new share capital in the primary market. Examples of this are the flotation of new shares to the investing public, and **rights issues** where shareholders are offered additional shares as a percentage of their current holdings. Occasionally, companies sell shares directly with the help of an institution that 'places' them with a small number of banks and other investment institutions. This may reduce costs and the time taken to raise the funds. In a primary issue, the company receives the proceeds from the sale of equity minus the issue costs. Existing listed shares are traded between investors in the secondary market of the stock market but the company receives no direct benefit. However, without the existence of a secondary market, investment in shares could be far less, because investors would not be able to liquidate or change their shareholdings easily. So, shares listed on an organised

> **Preference shares**
> Shares that give their holders priority over ordinary shareholders and have some characteristics common to debt instruments.
>
> **Convertible notes**
> Debt instruments that can be converted into shares.
>
> **Rights issue**
> If a company is seeking extra funds, it may offer the existing shareholders the right to subscribe for the extra shares. The right is renounceable if it can be sold to another party. The right is non-renounceable if it can be exercised only by the shareholder and not be sold.

exchange such as the NZSX are more liquid, an important attribute when listed shares are compared with unlisted shares.

## Market operations and participants

Participants in the equities market are individuals, companies, and institutional investors such as the large New Zealand insurance company AMP. The importance of institutions has increased in the stock market as the pattern of investing is changing from individuals holding shares directly to individuals holding shares in such assets as unit trusts and superannuation funds. Currently, there are several ways in which an individual can invest directly in the stock market. These vary according to the cost and the share advisory service. They are:

- a full advisory service where an individual uses a client adviser with a share broker to help with share purchase/sales and management
- a telephone trading account where an individual places orders with or without advice
- an online trading account where an individual can make trades via the internet.

Often share brokers' web pages include research analysts' reports, giving analysis of companies with recommendations to assist investors in making their decisions.

If, for example, you want to trade shares directly over the telephone, you will tell the broker which shares (and how many of them) you wish to buy or sell, and you will inform the broker at what price, or within what price range, you will buy (or sell) them. For selling shares in New Zealand, share brokers require your personal financial identification number (FIN), which has been given to you by the share registry, as well as your common shareholder number (CSN) for the company whose shares you intend to buy (or sell). This is because an electronic record of share ownership is now in place in New Zealand.

After you have made a share transaction over the telephone, the share broker will notify you of the details, via post or email. Later, you will receive an official legal contract for the transaction. Share traders will receive a share statement, similar to a bank statement, from the share registry, usually within a week of any new transaction. Generally you need to set up an account before trading and a broker will charge a percentage commission, usually based on the value of shares bought or sold.

Online brokerage rates are generally a smaller percentage than those charged for telephone trading – for example, 0.3% rather than 0.7% – and there is a smaller minimum dollar fee for each transaction if you choose to trade via an online share account. Currently you will need to give details on the internet broking form as to whether you are placing a 'buy' or a 'sell' order, how many shares you wish to trade and on which stock exchange (New Zealand's or Australia's), the share code and whether you want to buy or sell at the current market price or prefer to place a limit on the price you buy or sell at. Information on how many buy orders and sell orders there are and on the depth of trading for each share is generally available for regular internet share traders to use. There are advanced trading options available; for example, a Stop Loss order that permits a share trader to place a sell order into the system at a specified price for a share, which will only be carried out if the selected share trades at or below the specified trigger price.

NZSX operates a continuous auction market with the use of electronic screen trading from exchange members' offices throughout New Zealand, currently

> **Market index**
> A measure of price levels in a market.

between the hours of 10 am and 5 pm. Electronic trading matches orders of buyers and sellers on an established price and time priority framework. Market clearing, settlement and registration are handled electronically. Both the FMA and the NZX oversee and regulate the New Zealand stock exchange. Share price quotations and **market indices**, such as the one for the top 10 companies in New Zealand called the S&P/NZSX10, can be found in major daily newspapers.

## Foreign exchange (FX) market

This market is the most active of the financial markets. Foreign currency is bought and sold in large volumes virtually every minute of the day through a vast system of telephones and computers that form the OTC FX market. Because of the large volume of transactions (in 2013 over $5.3 trillion per day worldwide) and the rapid flow of information between traders, this market is very efficient and acts like a centralised market. Originally this market dealt with the exchange of currency as a result of commercial or financial transactions; in other words, trade transactions. Now it is dominated by cash flows between institutions, of which trade flows are a small part. As it is an over-the-counter market, it is not formally regulated.

### Market operations and participants

> **Spread**
> The difference between buying and selling quotations.
>
> **Exchange rate**
> The price at which one foreign currency can be exchanged for another.

The major players in the FX market are individuals and firms involved in international transactions, banks and non-bank dealers, and the government. The dealers in the banks and non-bank financial institutions act as principals in the FX market by quoting two-way prices (the prices at which they are prepared to buy and sell currency), with the major banks handling the greatest volume. The difference between the two prices is called the **spread**. For the retail investor, foreign exchange quotes are displayed in the major banks, and the spread between the buy and sell quotes represents the bank's fee. For larger wholesale FX transactions the spread is usually smaller.

The **exchange rate** is the price at which a foreign currency can be exchanged for another. It can be quoted in two different ways: a direct quote is when the foreign currency is written in terms of the local currency. For example, for a US manufacturer in the United States wanting NZ dollars, 1 NZ dollar = 0.60 US dollars is a direct quote for the NZ dollar. An indirect quote is when the local currency is written in terms of the foreign currency. For the US manufacturer, the quotation 1 US dollar = 1.66 NZ dollars is an indirect quote for the NZ dollar. Notice that quotes in New Zealand are written as indirect; for example, a New Zealand manufacturer who wants to buy US dollars is quoted 1 NZ dollar = 0.60 US dollars. Most currencies in the world are expressed in relation to one US dollar per unit of local currency, i.e. as direct quotes, except some former British Empire countries. This is because the US dollar is accepted in most countries. For two non-US currencies, say New Zealand and Malaysia, NZ dollars are first converted into US dollars and then into Malaysian currency.

In small open economies such as New Zealand's, exporters and importers are particularly affected by changes in foreign exchange rates. For example, New Zealand dairy exporter Fonterra experiences increased export earnings when the New Zealand dollar falls in value relative to the currency of its main customer, the United States. Conversely, the value of Fonterra's overseas sales falls when the value of the New Zealand dollar rises. Similarly, importers experience changes in the value of their overseas purchases whenever the New Zealand dollar foreign exchange rate changes. To protect their cash flows from fluctuations in the exchange rate, many exporters and importers use risk-management instruments.

## Types of instruments traded

Instruments traded can be traded on the **spot market** for immediate delivery, or on the **forward market** for future delivery. For instance, the spot exchange rate is the exchange rate for the spot FX transaction, and the observed interest rates are called the spot interest rates. In reality, the convention for payment for a spot transaction such as FX is settlement within two working days. Forward markets deal with forward contracts: agreements by two parties to carry out a financial transaction at a future (forward) point in time. Contracts traded, such as forward FX, are examples of derivative instruments, which are discussed in the next section. Such contracts have been developed to manage the increased risk of losses for individuals and institutions arising from large fluctuations in economic variables such as interest rates and foreign exchange rates.

Foreign exchange rates have been very volatile in recent years as there is a large number of factors that affect the exchange rate, including the relative inflation rates, the relative interest rates between countries, a country's monetary policy (discussed in the next chapter), and the forces of supply and demand. A method of handling the risk associated with adverse changes in foreign exchange is discussed in the next section.

> **Spot market**
> A market that involves transactions that are settled without delay.
>
> **Forward market**
> A market for forward contracts that involve delayed settlement.

## Derivative markets

So far, we have considered the spot or physical markets for financial instruments. With the development of economies and international trade, and the need to manage risk associated with adverse price changes, contracts have been introduced that give the holder the obligation or the choice to buy or sell a financial instrument at some future date. The price of such contracts is derived from the underlying financial assets, interest rates or financial index. These contracts are called **derivative instruments** and can be traded in their own derivative markets. Futures and options are common types of derivative. Borrowers and lenders can use these products to manage risk associated with their capital market transactions, as well as risks arising from changes in interest and exchange rates. Such contracts can be thought of as insurance-type products.

## Types of derivative instruments

A **futures contract** is a legal agreement to buy or sell a specified amount of a product at a specified price at some predetermined date in the future. So, the price of the product is fixed today, but the transaction will occur at a predetermined date in the future called the **settlement date** or **expiry date**. An early example of a futures contract occurred in Japan in the 1600s when the Japanese rice farmers locked in the price of rice before harvest by an agreement with the buyers. The first futures contracts were based on agricultural commodities such as sugar, but at the present time the majority is based on financial instruments or indices.

To illustrate, Company X wants to buy an asset ABC and there is a futures contract traded on the futures exchange where the underlying product to be bought or sold is asset ABC. The contract's settlement date is three months from now. So Company X buys the futures contract and another company, Y, agrees to

> **Derivative instrument**
> Any instrument whose value is derived from the underlying asset on which it is based.
>
> **Futures contract**
> An exchange-traded, legal contract between a buyer, who agrees to take delivery of a specified asset at a predetermined time, and a seller who agrees to deliver the asset.
>
> **Settlement date**
> Also known as *expiry date*. It refers to the date when a contract expires.
>
> **Expiry date**
> The date when an option terminates, also known as the *expiration date*.

sell Company X the futures contract by way of the futures exchange market and to deliver the asset in the future for the price of $1 000. So $1 000 is the futures price, and at the settlement date Company Y will deliver asset ABC to Company X.

If the future price of asset ABC in the physical market increases before the settlement date, then the company that has bought the futures contract will make a profit. In this instance, the seller of the futures contract for asset ABC will realise a loss as they have agreed to sell at $1 000 whereas the futures price may now be $1 500. If, on the other hand, the price of asset ABC decreases to $800, then Company Y will make the profit as it has agreed to sell at $1 000 and Company X has to buy at $1 000.

In the jargon of the futures markets, we say that when an investor buys a futures contract – that is, agrees to buy at the future date – they are in a **long position** or long futures position. If, instead, the investor's opening position is an agreement to sell something – that is, the sale of a futures contract – they are said to be in a **short position** or short futures position.

> **Long position**
> To agree to buy at a future date.
>
> **Short position**
> A selling position – the sale of a financial asset.

In general, if the futures price increases before the settlement date, then the buyer of a futures contract will make a profit. Likewise, if the futures price decreases, the seller of a futures contract will realise a profit. However, if they held positions in the underlying physical markets then any loss they made in one market would be offset by a profit made in the other market. This is the basis of hedging, to be discussed further on in the chapter.

### The operation of the market

Futures are sold through organised exchanges. The NZX has an NZX derivatives market, where it offers a range of futures and options on dairy products as well as some derivatives on New Zealand equity indices and companies. The Australian futures market that is part of the Australian Stock Exchange (ASX) also offers New Zealand derivatives on short-term interest rates, bonds and electricity contracts. One of the largest futures exchanges, based in Chicago and owned by CME Group, has a huge range of futures contracts from oil futures to futures providing protection from hurricanes. Another derivative market that is OTC involves the major banks, which offer forward contracts and **swaps**. Forwards are discussed later in this chapter.

> **Swaps**
> Financial instruments that involve the exchange of cash flows between two parties.

A futures exchange is an organisation composed of members holding seats on the exchange. Seats are traded on an open market, and individuals who want to become members and who satisfy the exchange rules for financial integrity may buy seats. Each exchange works out what kind of goods it will trade and the contract plans for each of those goods. The products offered by the exchanges are therefore standardised ones, with the quantity, quality, time, and place of delivery of the goods for the contract being specified at the outset.

Examples of contracts offered by the ASX are shown in Table 2.2 on the next page.

Table 2.2 **Sample of contracts offered by the ASX**

| Futures contracts | Options on futures contracts |
|---|---|
| NZ 90-day bank bill futures | NZ 90-day bank bill futures |
| ASX200 Index Options | New Zealand electricity options |
| 10 Year Australian Bond | Qantas Airways Limited options |
| **Commodities** | |
| Eastern Australian Feed Barley | |

Source: www.asx.com.au/prices/asx-futures.htm

## Margin requirements

To enter into a futures contract, the buyer or seller does not have to put all the money up front, but is required to provide the member of the exchange, the broker, with a deposit called an **initial margin**. In addition, if the underlying instrument has changed in price, the client is required to top up this initial deposit with the broker on a daily basis. This process is called **marking to market**. If the client's credit has declined, then they will have a **margin call** and will need to supply extra funds. This process protects the **clearing house**. As a consequence of this margin process, where the deposit might have a value equal to 5–10% of the goods represented by the contract, small changes in the underlying asset may be magnified. This is one of the reasons why derivatives are perceived as being risky, although their basic functions are risk reduction and transference: holders of futures contracts may be called upon to provide funds on a daily basis.

## The role of the clearing house

The trade from a client must be executed through a broker who is usually a member of the exchange. So the two parties to the transaction may be in different physical places and not know each other. This raises the problem of creditworthiness and whether the traders will perform as they have contracted to do. To solve this problem, every futures exchange has a clearing house. The clearing house is a separate financial institution that guarantees the contract performance of both parties. Figure 2.2 shows the linkages between the parties involved in a futures contract.

## Fulfilment or closing out a contract

A futures position, once entered into, can remain open until maturity when the contract must be carried out; that is, the underlying instrument must be either bought or sold according to the contract's specifications. However, most futures contracts are settled (closed out) by a reversing trade. This means the buying or selling of a similar contract that has delivery in the same month but is the opposite of the original trade. Recall Company X that bought a futures contract for asset ABC. It would sell a futures contract for ABC that it would obtain through the futures market before, or at, the expiry date. Rarely is there physical delivery of the underlying asset.

**Initial margin**
The preliminary amount that needs to be deposited with a broker by the market player so that a futures contract may be bought or sold.

**Marking to market**
The process of adjusting an initial deposit of a good to its current market value. Usually occurs daily in the futures market.

**Margin call**
The call for extra funds when adverse movements in the price of a contract erode the initial deposit to below a specified level.

**Clearing house**
A financial institution that guarantees the contract exchange between buyers and sellers of financial contracts; for example, futures contracts.

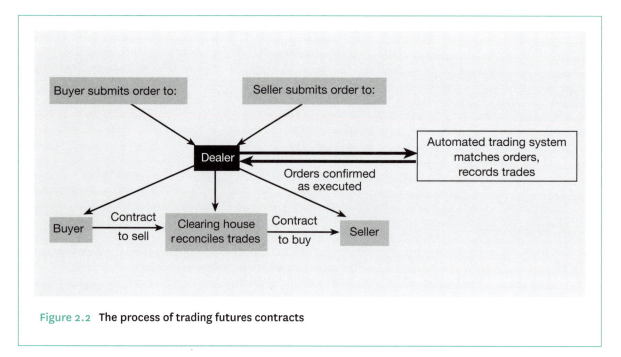

Figure 2.2  The process of trading futures contracts

## Participants in the futures market

Who uses derivatives? *Hedgers, speculators* and *arbitrageurs* are the terms for the important market players. A **hedger** is a market player who wants to protect an existing position from future unfavourable price movements. This could be a commodity producer, such as the New Zealand company Fonterra (dairy products), or a commodity consumer, such as the New Zealand manufacturer Fletcher Building Ltd (steel). So they may use futures contracts to hedge in order to protect their position in the physical or cash markets. To perform a hedge, a market player needs to take an equal and opposite position in the futures market to the one held in the physical market.

There are two types of hedge – long and short. In a **long hedge**, the market player takes a *long (buy) futures* position to offset an existing short position in the physical market. For example, a steel manufacturer could buy iron ore futures contracts today to lock in the buying price for iron ore they wish to buy in one month. In a **short hedge**, the market player takes a *short (selling) futures* position to offset an existing long position in the physical market. For example, Fonterra could enter into a futures contract to sell butter (in market jargon, to short butter) to offset an existing long position in the physical market with the actual stocks of butter it holds and protect itself from any decline in the price of butter. Alternatively, a fund manager holding a portfolio of stocks and intending to sell them in two months, could hedge against stock prices falling by selling stock index futures contracts.

It is important to realise that a hedge involves offsetting transactions – any loss you make in one market is offset by your gain in the other market. In the example of the steel manufacturer, prices of iron ore could move up in the physical market over the month so that they would have to pay more for the ore. However, as they hold a futures contract that enables them to buy the ore at a price established

**Hedger**
A market player who wishes to protect their existing position by reducing risk.

**Long hedge**
This is when a market player buys a futures contract to protect an underlying physical position.

**Short hedge**
This is when a market player sells a futures contract.

before prices moved up, the steel manufacturer can make a profit that cancels out the increased price in the physical market. Consequently, the risk associated with future adverse price movements is reduced.

A **speculator** is a market player who accepts the risk that hedgers want to transfer. The speculator wants to make a profit and so takes a position based on their **expectations** of future price movements. So if speculators expect:

- futures prices to rise, they buy futures contracts (go long)
- futures prices to fall, they sell futures contracts (go short).

Without speculators in the market to provide liquidity, the protection desired by hedgers would be extremely expensive.

**Arbitrageurs** are the third main group. These are market makers and traders who buy and sell futures contracts, trying to profit from price differences between markets. Futures price quotations are available daily in the major newspapers or on the internet.

> **Speculator**
> A market player who takes on risk in order to make a potential profit.
>
> **Expectations**
> Beliefs or views about possible outcomes, such as the future direction of interest rates.
>
> **Arbitrageur**
> A market player who carries out arbitrage.

## Forward contracts

A forward contract is similar to a futures contract in that it is a contract to deliver an underlying asset at a predetermined price at the end of a specified period. There are forward contracts for commodities such as crude oil, and for underlying assets including interest rates and foreign exchange. A forward FX transaction occurs when a contract is entered into today, at an exchange rate fixed today, but with settlement at some specified point in the future. A forward FX transaction may arise, for example, when a New Zealand company knows it is going to pay in US dollars for some goods imported from the US in three months' time. If the importer is concerned that the US dollars may increase in price (appreciate), then the company may enter into a forward FX contract. This means the price of the US dollars is determined today but the **delivery date** is at some specified date in the future when the US dollars are paid for. So, forward exchange contracts offered by the major banks lock in an exchange rate for the exchange of two currencies at a specified future date, and can be obtained for almost any future date the client desires.

> **Delivery date**
> Date at which the contract expires and the specified transaction is carried out.

However, a forward contract is usually non-standardised, as the terms of the contract are negotiated between the buyer and the seller on an individual basis. Forward contracts are OTC products offered by banks and other agents, and there is usually no secondary market or clearing house. Unlike futures, there is no daily margin to meet, which is an important difference. The forward market for foreign exchange offered by banks is extremely large, whereby rates for future foreign exchange dealings can be fixed at rates determined today. Banks also offer a product for protection against fluctuating interest rates. This product, which is a forward rate agreement for interest rates, is known as an FRA. A company looking at borrowing funds in three months' time can buy an FRA and lock in current interest rates to reduce uncertainty.

## Options contracts

So far, the derivatives discussed have committed the parties involved to settle the transaction at the predetermined conditions. If a party did not want to commit itself, but wanted to wait and see what happened in the markets, it could buy an option.

An option on a financial asset gives the owner the right, but not the obligation, to buy or sell a specified asset at a specified price, called the **exercise price** or **strike price**, on or before the expiry date or expiration date. For example, if the shares of the New Zealand company Spark are selling at $6, an option on Spark shares that gives the investor the right to buy shares at $5 will have a value at least equal to the difference between $5 and $6.

### Types of options

There are two types of options: call options and put options. The holder of a **call option** has the right to buy a specified good at a certain price, with the right lasting until a certain date. Ownership of a **put option** gives the holder the right to sell a specified good at a certain price before a specified date.

Note that for every option there is a buyer and a seller. For a call option, the buyer pays a sum called the **premium** to the seller of the option, who is said to write the option for the buyer by agreeing to deliver (sell) the goods to the buyer of the call at a certain price up to the expiry date. Likewise, the seller (**writer**) of a put option receives payment (the premium) from the buyer of the put. The buyer of a put then has the right to sell a specified good to the seller of the put contract at a specified price up to expiry date.

It is important to remember that ownership of an option gives the right, but not the obligation, to the holder (buyer) to transact. For example, the holder of a call option may exercise the option to buy the good at the specified price during the option's lifetime, but is not obliged to. Similarly, a holder of a put option may exercise the option to sell the specified good before expiration.

However, the seller of an option is committed to delivering if the holder decides to exercise their right before expiry. They have received payment from the buyer and must deliver. If the buyer of a call option decides to exercise the option to buy the goods, then the seller of the call option must sell them the goods for the agreed price. Likewise, if the buyer of a put option decides to **exercise** their option to sell, then the seller of the put option must buy from them the goods at the specified price.

### Option exchanges

Options exchanges are similarly organised to futures exchanges, and in some places, such as Sydney, the two are combined. Buyers and sellers of exchange options can close out their positions before the expiry date in a similar fashion to futures contracts, provided that the contracts exist. The Sydney market is a small one and only liquid in a few contracts, whereas the US markets are deep and liquid.

### Participants in the options market

Who uses options? There are many players in the options markets. Hedgers can use options as a form of insurance to reduce or remove potential harmful price movements. They buy the required protection, but are not locked into the contract and so can take advantage of any favourable price movements. For example, a

---

**Exercise price**
The price at which an option is to be settled, also known as the *strike price*.

**Strike price**
The price at which an option is to be settled or exercised.

**Call option**
An option where the buyer has the right, but not the obligation, to buy the underlying asset at a predetermined price before a specified date.

**Put option**
An option where the buyer has the right, but not the obligation, to sell an underlying asset at a predetermined price before a specified date.

**Premium**
The payment from the buyer to the seller of an option.

**Writer of an option**
The seller of an option.

**Exercise an option**
When the holder of an option uses or takes up the option on or before the expiration date.

manager of a share portfolio (similar to that of one of New Zealand's top ten companies) may want to sell the portfolio in three months' time and so might purchase a put option on the S&P/NZSX10. This would enable them to sell their portfolio at the specified price even if the market falls during the three months.

There are many types of option writer. For example, producers of commodities could sell a call. As the producer holds the commodities, they are giving another party the option to buy the commodities at a set price. By writing a call, they receive income in the form of a premium if the option is not exercised. However, if the price rises, they face a loss as they would have to sell at a lower price. A portfolio manager could write a call for each share of stock held. Again they receive a premium for this. The strategy is not risk-free. If the call is exercised in a bull market, the manager simply delivers the stock. Other writers are speculators and arbitrageurs who are trying to profit by price movements or price differences.

## Cryptocurrency markets

**Cryptocurrency** markets emerged with the mining of the first Bitcoin, in January 2009. Unlike traditional currencies, digital forms of money, such as Bitcoin, operate using a decentralised technology known as **blockchain** and use cryptographic techniques to secure transactions. The decentralised peer-to-peer network involved means they can operate without the need for intermediaries, such as banks.

Cryptocurrency markets operate through a network of exchanges, digital wallets, and the process of mining coins. Exchanges, such as Coinbase and Binance, are digital marketplaces where users can buy, sell and exchange various cryptocurrencies such as Bitcoin, Ethereum and Ripple, among thousands of other cryptocurrencies (although only 20 cryptocurrencies make up around 90% of the total market). These platforms play a pivotal role in price discovery and liquidity provision. **Digital wallets** facilitate the secure storage and transfer of cryptocurrencies. **Mining** is an integral process of cryptocurrencies like Bitcoin and involves solving complex mathematical problems to validate transactions. The mining process not only creates new units of the cryptocurrency, but also plays a crucial role in maintaining the integrity and security of the blockchain.

Cryptocurrency markets attract a diverse array of participants who trade for investment, speculation and trade purposes, as well as for decentralisation ideals. In contrast to many financial markets, individual investors form the backbone of crypto markets. However, institutional investors, including hedge funds, asset managers and corporations, have increasingly entered the cryptocurrency arena. Despite their innovative potential, cryptocurrency markets are not without risks. Cryptocurrencies are known for large fluctuations in price, influenced by factors such as market sentiment and macroeconomic trends, as well as market failures and fraud, such as the collapse of FTX in November 2022. The regulatory environment poses another significant risk. With any new market or financial product, regulations change and evolve, often due to some market failure; these affect market accessibility and investor confidence. Investors are also concerned about security risks, including hacking, fraud, and vulnerabilities in both exchanges and digital wallets. Addressing these risk factors will be critical to moving cryptocurrencies into a mainstream market.

Beyond the currencies themselves, the blockchain technology is likely to play an increasing role in the future. The decentralised nature, security, transparency and efficiency of blockchain means it has the potential to reshape business transactions and enhance the way we record, store and transfer value and information.

---

**Cryptocurrency**
Digital or virtual currency commonly built on blockchain technology.

**Blockchain**
Decentralised, immutable (i.e. permanent, irreversible) ledger technology ensuring secure and transparent record-keeping for cryptocurrency transactions.

**Digital wallets**
Tools for storing and managing cryptocurrencies, providing secure access to private keys for transactions and balances.

**Mining**
Process of validating transactions and securing a cryptocurrency network by the solving of complex mathematical problems which is rewarded with new coins.

## Property markets

Property is a major asset class and in most economies is considered an integral part of the wider financial system. While property has a number of similarities with other forms of investment, such as the concepts of debt financing, cash flow analysis and risk considerations, there are important characteristics that differentiate property.

Investment in property usually refers to the ownership of property for financial investment returns such as rental or capital growth. However, in the wider sense, many firms and individuals also invest in property to use as a key business input or for residential occupation. Almost all businesses use property in some manner, whether it be office space, a factory or a shopfront. Even online and software-type businesses will likely require the use of warehousing/logistics or office space somewhere. On an individual level, everyone requires residential accommodation as either a renter or an owner/occupier. In this regard, many investment properties are a 'derived demand' product from an economic perspective and their success as investments are inextricably linked to the industries which use them as an input to production.

From an investment perspective, common categories of the property market include residential, commercial, retail and industrial. There are less common specialist investment sectors such as agriculture, horticulture and forestry. Also, within these categories there are combinations and subcategories, such as townhouses and apartments in the residential market, or light and heavy industrial properties. In addition to these investment sectors, there are also non-investment sectors such as Crown land[1] (e.g. parks and roads) and indigenous land holdings.

Property differs from other forms of investment in that it has distinct markets for 'consumption' and for 'investment', each with distinct but related supply and demand conditions. By way of illustration, there are separate markets (and supply/demand conditions) for retail shops for lease (consumption) and for retail properties for ownership (investment). It is quite conceivable that the investment market could be experiencing an oversupply of properties available for sale at the same time as the consumption market is undersupplied (i.e. few shops available for lease). Similarly, there may be a dual market for investment and consumption at the ownership level, most commonly encountered in the residential sector. Much of the housing stock is readily transferred between the owner-occupied and investment (purchased to lease or rent out) sectors. In this regard, investors can be seen as in competition with owner-occupiers within this market.

Property is an essential part of business and personal life, and an understanding of property is useful across many careers as well as personally. The key difference between property and many other asset classes already discussed in this chapter is that it is a physical asset rather than a financial/legal instrument and is therefore subject to physical deterioration and the constraints of space, meaning that each parcel of land is unique. For this reason, an understanding of the legal, physical and economic basis behind the financial and risk aspects of property is important.

### Characteristics of property

Property has three unique and distinct characteristics that need to be considered first separately and then as a whole to determine the potential for investment use of any

---

1 Crown land is land vested in His Majesty that is not set aside for any public purpose or held by any person in fee simple. Crown land in New Zealand is administered under the provisions of the Land Act 1948.

particular property. These are the physical, legal and economic characteristics of the property. A property could be physically able to support a particular investment, but this use may not be legally permissible (say a noisy industrial plant in a residential area). Similarly, a site may be legally and physically capable of sustaining, say, a significant retail complex on a site in a small town, but it may be uneconomic.

## Physical characteristics

Land can be used for many purposes, including agriculture, commerce, industry, residential accommodation and recreation. The use and value of an individual property will depend on its unique physical characteristics. One of the most important **physical characteristics of property** is location.

> **Physical characteristics of property**
> The tangible attributes such as size, location and structure that affect a property's value and use.

What might be the locational attributes of the Wellington apartment building in this picture that affect its value?

This apartment building is located on the Wellington Harbour close to downtown shopping. The waterfront location will contribute significantly to the value of the apartments. Residents are prepared to pay a higher price to have a harbour view and the benefits of living in a central city locality.

When assessing the use and value of a property investment, there are many physical attributes of land to consider. The physical features most easily recognised include shape, size, topography and aspect. For agricultural land, there will be a number of other factors such as soil type, climate and access to water.

The following cadastral plan has a number of sections. It demonstrates the importance of a range of physical characteristics.

Lot 1 in this plan is a much larger section than the other residential sections surrounding it. If it was a vacant site, it could possibly be subdivided into several smaller residential sections. It is currently occupied by a service station. This site is well suited to service-station use because of the size of the site, its square shape and flat contour, and its location on the corner of two busy roads.

Man-made improvements include improvements to the land as well as structures built on the land.

### Legal characteristics

The legal characteristics of land also affect its use and value. In free-market economies, land use is regulated within a framework of laws that recognise the possible conflict between private ownership and public use. Ownership of land is often compared to a **bundle of rights**, some of which are limited. Landowners have the right to construct buildings and carry out other improvements on their property; however, the use of the property and the construction techniques must meet the requirements of the local territorial authority.

Landowners may decide to lease out their property to another party. This will reduce the rights that the property owner has over their own property, as the tenant will be paying rent in order to have the right to occupy. Landowners may also encumber the property (e.g. raise a loan using a mortgage security against the title of their property). This will give some of the property rights to the mortgagee (the financial institution that has provided the finance).

It is also important to recognise the rights of the Crown over privately owned land. Except for Māori land, all other titles are granted on the basis that the Crown retains the right to resume its underlying right to the land (i.e. to resumption of ownership). The Crown has rights over mineral deposits, rights to charge taxes on land and rights to acquire or resume privately owned interests in land, for example for public works such as roads. These legal restrictions on land use will be covered in greater detail in Chapter 7.

> **Bundle of rights**
> Ownership rights encompassing possession, use, exclusion, and transfer of property.

### Economic characteristics

From an economic perspective, property is generally a derived-demand product, though less so in the residential consumption market. That is, its value is determined by the value of its use as an input to another economic activity. Land that can be used for a high-value activity (such as high-rise apartments or office buildings) has a high value. Land which can only be used for low-value activities (such as pasture) will have a lower value. In assessing the value of investment property, it is of primary importance to understand what the land could be used for.

Land has different economic characteristics to other goods because it is immobile. The **immobility of land** means that the market for the services a property has to offer is generally derived from a narrow geographical area, and advances in technology have not significantly changed this yet.

The immobility of land also means that land is heterogeneous, meaning no two parcels of land are the same. Ratcliff explains this characteristic.[2]

> **Immobility of land**
> The inability of land to move to another location, which affects its value.

> Each parcel of land occupies a unique physical relationship with every other parcel of land. Because in every community there exists a variety of land uses, each parcel is the focus of a complex but singular set of space relationships with the social and economic activities that are centred on all other parcels. To each combination of space relationships the market attaches a special evaluation, which largely determines the amount of the bid for that site which is the focus of the combination.

Another economic characteristic of land is that land ownership involves the outlay of relatively large sums of money compared to other forms of investment, which limits the number of buyers in the market.

---

2 Richard Ratcliff, *Urban Land Economics* (New York: McGraw-Hill, 1949), 283–84.

Land has the quality of permanence, which is one of the reasons it is such an important investment option. There are situations where land subsides or erodes and is lost. However, improvements on the land do deteriorate over time. Land is a scarce resource, the supply of land is limited, and only very small additions can be made by reclamation. Land is therefore a scarce resource and competition for its use affects its value.

## Indirect vs direct investment

**Direct property investment** means an investor owns a specific property; an **indirect property investment** could be investing in an investment entity such as a property company listed on a share market. An example of the latter is the purchase of shares in a listed property investment entity such as Precinct Properties or Argosy or Kiwi Property. Some of these investment entities offer a diversified portfolio, while others specialise in certain sectors. When a property is owned through an investment entity, some of the characteristics of the property investment – in particular the risk and liquidity aspects – change. There are two main reasons for this. Firstly, there is a significant change in liquidity because the holding of shares or units can be readily traded, in part or in whole. Secondly, there is an implicit reduction in direct control over the asset and the property knowledge required to invest in and manage the assets directly. However, as there are additional management costs associated with indirect property investment, returns on the property will be lower.

Indirect investment can also present opportunities with respect to diversification and access to certain sectors. For example, if you have $1 000 000 to invest, this could represent only one or two direct properties (lower-value properties, even with debt financing). Alternately, this could represent ten separate $100 000 investments in listed entities that invest in a substantial number of commercial, industrial or retail properties.

Implicit in this is that indirect investment is combined with an element of aggregation of investors. The comments above would not apply, for example, to an investor owning 100% of a private property investment company.

> **Direct property investment**
> Ownership of physical real estate for income or capital appreciation.
>
> **Indirect property investment**
> Investing in real estate through securities like listed property companies or real estate funds.

## Valuation and pricing

Perhaps one of the most unique financial distinctions of property is that there is no 'spot' price like we see for the traded financial assets we discussed earlier in the chapter. This stems from the fact that property is a heterogeneous product – no two properties are identical.

The value of each property can only be determined by a transaction at any particular time. An **'objective' valuation** is only really established via the price a property sells for in an **'arm's length transaction'**. It could be sold again the next week and the price could be different. Every financial analysis to determine the valuation of a property is subjective in some way. There is no 'spot' price for any particular property, only value estimates which become an 'objective' price at the time a transaction is completed. It is for this reason that there are significant careers in property analysis and valuation and that there is the potential to make returns significantly above (or below) industry averages.

> **Objective valuation**
> Unbiased assessment of a property's value based on market conditions and comparable sales.
>
> **Arm's length transaction**
> Fair, uncoerced property exchange between unrelated parties at market value.

## The role of the housing market in the economic cycle

The demand for housing is generally driven by population and demographics, income levels, employment rates and the availability and cost of credit. The supply of new housing will depend on house construction and can be restricted by environmental constraints on building.

The housing market is cyclical and is unique in its operation. Each property has unique physical and location attributes, making prices and price movements hard to measure. Prices tend to be slow to respond to an imbalance in supply and demand in a depressed market. Most vendors will choose to delay selling rather than take a reduced price. Instead, the inventory of unsold homes will gradually reduce over time as new building slows and new households are formed. Then prices will rise again when demand increases.

These fundamentals will lead to increases in the market over time, but when a housing bubble occurs – with rapid price increases that are not supported by fundamentals – there is a likelihood that prices will fall as a result of diminished demand. Case and Schiller[3] explain what happens during a housing bubble:

> During a housing bubble, homebuyers think that a home that they would normally consider too expensive for them is now an acceptable purchase because they will be compensated by significant further price increases. They will not need to save as much as they otherwise might, because they expect the increased value of their home to do the saving for them. First homebuyers may also worry that if they do not buy now, they will not be able to afford a home later.

Housing is very responsive to interest-rate changes. In many countries, including New Zealand, residential property prices initially fell during the 2020 Covid-19 lockdowns. However, as central banks responded to the expected economic downturn by lowering interest rates to historical lows, and governments increased spending and transfer payments to both individuals and businesses, property markets experienced a prolonged period of very rapid growth. Purchasers took advantage of the cheap and readily available loans, which resulted in prices being bid up on the limited supply of homes. As inflationary pressures built, the Reserve Bank of New Zealand (RBNZ) started increasing the official cash rate, in November 2021, and continued to do so through 2023. A house price correction occurred during the later part of 2022 and into 2023, which saw house prices drop by around 15% on average across New Zealand. This inevitably left some more-recent purchasers with homes that were worth less than the loans secured against them. In the scenario of lower property values and substantially higher interest rates when refinancing loans, some home purchasers will inevitably have to sell.

A similar but more severe situation occurred in the United States when collapsing house values led to the GFC from 2007 to 2008. The loss of collateral value from home mortgages in the United States was a key factor in the GFC. That crisis decreased consumer wealth in many countries and severely eroded the financial strength of banking institutions. As a result, many financial institutions around the world became insolvent and either went bankrupt or were bailed out by governments.

---

3   Karl Case & Robert Shiller, 'Is there a bubble in the housing market?', *Brookings Papers on Economic Activity* 2, vol. 34 (2003): 299–342.

The impact of the residential property market on the economy and health of the financial system leads policy makers, such as the RBNZ, to intervene in property markets. For example, the RBNZ might initiate or change policies in respect to loan-to-value or loan-to-income ratios to influence demand and dampen price increases, in order to reduce the probability of housing price bubbles forming, which could jeopardise the health of the financial system. As noted above, much of the housing stock is fungible between the owner-occupier and investment sectors, and this can result in competition between these sectors. It was for this reason that the RBNZ intervened to restrict the supply of loans to the investment sector during this period of unusually high growth in house prices, thereby reducing the aggregate demand.

## Conclusion

This chapter has provided the foundation for an understanding of the types of financial market and the individuals and institutions involved in these markets. The financial assets, operation and participants in the various markets have also been discussed. Financial markets are important as they help establish the fair value of securities and provide liquidity for investors. Financial markets are important as a source of funds for larger companies, financial institutions and for investors, and they provide a wide range of financial assets to meet their varying financial needs. We saw in the 2008 global financial crisis how important markets are: when they stop working properly, the result can be that the world ends up in a global recession. The secondary markets have undergone significant changes, one of which being that the major participants are now institutions rather than small investors. In addition, advances in computer technology have significantly changed markets and their operations.

### SELF-TEST QUESTIONS

1. If you are acting as an adviser to a country that has already a system of financial intermediaries but not well-developed financial markets, would you recommend establishing strong financial markets as well?
2. Briefly distinguish between the instruments of the main physical and derivative markets.

### ANSWERS TO SELF-TEST QUESTIONS

1. Financial markets facilitate transfers of funds between savers and investors. Primary markets raise funds for larger businesses, and governments and secondary markets allow lenders/investors to change their collection of securities as required. If they exist, the flow of funds for final investment purposes is higher and the cost of funds for borrowers is lower. So yes, you would recommend development of strong financial markets.
2. The instruments used in the physical markets allow funds to be raised/lent; that is, bank bills in the short-term money market, bonds in long-term debt in the capital markets, or shares in the equities market. The instruments used in the derivative markets (that is, futures market, options market, swaps market, forward rate agreements [FRAs]) allow users of physical instruments to manage the market risks they undergo.

### QUESTIONS AND PROBLEMS

1. Define a *financial market*, and identify its functions.
2. List the types of financial instruments created and traded in financial markets, briefly indicating the main differences between the various categories of instruments, and giving examples of each type.
3. Distinguish between primary and secondary markets, explaining the roles served by each, and giving examples of transactions in each category.
4. Distinguish between money markets and capital markets.
5. Explain the difference between an over-the counter (OTC) market and an organised exchange. Give an example of each.
6. What is a discount instrument such as a Treasury bill?
7. Identify and explain the motivations of the participants in futures markets transactions; namely, hedgers, speculators, traders and arbitrageurs.
8. Explain why options and futures are labelled 'derivative securities'.
9. What are the main cash flow differences between futures and forward contracts?
10. What are the two ways of discharging a futures contract?
11. How is property differentiated from other forms of investment?
12. What is 'objective' vs 'subjective' valuation in a property context?

# Financial institutions

**CHAPTER 3**

### Learning objectives

By the end of this chapter, you should be able to:
- explain why the transition from gold to paper money had extensive repercussions, including impacts on economic development, financial instability and regulation
- discuss the four safety and soundness regulations used by the central bank to control the financial system
- explain how banks create credit
- identify the three monetary policy control mechanisms
- describe the two primary functions of financial intermediaries – brokering and transformation
- describe the three ways, or channels, in which funds can be transferred from saver to borrower, and be aware of the related trends.

## Introduction

In this chapter, we will consider the part that financial intermediaries play in the financial system. Financial intermediaries have evolved from the gold lenders of the Middle Ages to the more sophisticated entities that provide a range of services today.

Financial intermediaries are an essential part of the modern financial system. In reality, in many countries they are the major source of financing for businesses. A financial intermediary is an institution that helps to transfer scarce loanable funds from those who save and lend (surplus budget units) to those who wish to borrow and invest (deficit budget units). Financial intermediaries aid in the creation of financial securities and in their transfer from issuers (borrowers) to investors (lenders). Financial assets or securities are liabilities issued by those units (households, business firms, governments) that borrow in order to spend more than their current income in consumption and investment.

## The development of the modern financial system

The modern financial system has evolved from simple to complex means of carrying out financial transactions. Money is a key financial security or asset that has evolved, as a means of payment or medium of exchange for goods and services, from being based on metals such as gold or silver (**commodity money**) to paper notes based on public confidence. The process of evolution from commodity money, or money based on metals and the like, really began with the activities of London goldsmiths who were early examples of bankers or financial intermediaries.

Consider the following stylised anecdote of the evolution of the modern financial intermediary. Gold was long used as money by individuals and merchants. However, it was not the most suitable means of exchange as it was heavy to carry

**Commodity money**
Money that has value in itself or is redeemable as something of value; for example, gold coins.

around. So the London goldsmiths stored the surplus gold and issued goldsmith notes (or receipts) in exchange. The receipts allowed individuals to obtain the gold at any time, and the goldsmith charged a fee for storing the gold. With the goldsmith acting as a secure keeper for the gold, there was the same number of receipts as gold on hand. So, if every depositor turned up at the same time there would be enough gold for everyone.

Instead of transacting in gold, the public began to accept goldsmith notes for payment – the first paper money. As long as the goldsmiths had unblemished reputations, individuals were willing to accept receipts for gold. Dealing with paper receipts lowered transaction costs for customers as receipts did not need to be exchanged for gold. The number of withdrawals from the goldsmiths' gold holdings decreased as the public used the paper money, and holdings stabilised.

Over time, the goldsmiths were able to estimate how much gold was likely to be withdrawn or deposited on any given day. Then goldsmiths realised that it was not really necessary to hold a 1:1 ratio of receipts to gold. They could supply loans to the community and earn extra income in addition to the storage fees. They knew the pattern of gold withdrawals and that there was little chance of all of the gold being demanded back by the rightful owners simultaneously. The goldsmiths issued loans to the public in the form of gold receipts (a typical example was a £5 note for 100 days at 10% per annum). In doing so, they exposed themselves to a **maturity risk** or mismatch, because short-term **callable deposits** were now backed by long-term loans rather than by gold holdings. That is, if the public did decide to redeem their deposits simultaneously, there would be a shortfall or liquidity problem. In addition, there was now an element of default risk, as the goldsmiths could no longer ensure that the depositors of gold would get their money back under every possible circumstance. So the interest charged on the loans had to cover these risks.

The extra receipts were readily accepted by the public as good money. (This acceptance of paper receipts as a means of exchange is a fundamental ingredient in the modern financial system.) However, there now developed a situation where there was an incentive (profit) for the goldsmiths to grant loans by printing notes, tempered by the fear of loss – that is, a system open to abuse in the pursuit of individual gain. When the receipts on issue exceeded gold holdings, it meant there was no longer enough gold to satisfy all of the outstanding claims. Because of the goldsmiths issuing loans, there had been a money-creating impact on the economy. To illustrate, suppose that a goldsmith after many years of experience knew the maximum amount of gold required to be held in reserve was 20% of deposits. Then the goldsmith could issue receipts until stored gold was 20% of the outstanding receipts. With a gold stock of $100, the maximum amount of receipts that could be issued could be found as follows:

$$\$100 = 0.20 \times \text{receipts}$$
$$\text{Receipts} = \frac{\$100}{0.20}$$
$$\text{Receipts} = \$500$$

If, for some reason, the number of short-term withdrawals exceeded the gold holding, the goldsmiths would be unable to satisfy all of the depositors' claims if they turned up at the same time. (In the long term, everybody would get paid as the loans were paid off, barring default on loans.) With different circumstances where the ability to convert paper money to gold failed (i.e. depressions), the

---

**Maturity risk**
The risk that changes in interest rates will adversely affect the prices or yields of long-term assets compared with short-term assets.

**Callable deposits**
Deposits that are available on demand from a bank without penalty for early payment.

goldsmiths would become insolvent. This happened in 1672 when King Charles II confiscated £1 million of goldsmiths' deposits held in his Treasury at 8%, which led to major defaults by goldsmiths (an effect known as **contagion**, where one goldsmith's bankruptcy affected another and led to their bankruptcy).

In order to safeguard depositors against losing their funds, the solution was to develop a bank that could lend to goldsmiths during a liquidity crisis – a central bank where resources were pooled. Simultaneously, the volume of banking grew so rapidly during the eighteenth century that it was advantageous for banks to pool their resources with a larger bank. One of the roles of a modern central bank – for example, the Bank of England – is to perform this role of acting as a *bank for the bankers*.

Unfortunately, the central bank requires almost unlimited resources in some circumstances. During the 2008 global financial crisis, we saw central banks providing funds to and bailing out a large number of institutions and businesses in complex arrangements. For example, in the United States, the government bought shares in some companies while providing others with massive financing at favourably low interest rates.

A central bank also has other important roles, such as that of controlling how much money is in the economy, supervising financial institutions, and often acting as the bank for a government.

> **Contagion**
> An effect in which the uncertainty about one bank's finances can spill over to other banks and lead to heavy withdrawals by depositors.

## The modern role of government in the financial intermediation process

As the financial system evolved, one of the roles of the central bank became one of **'lender of last resort (LLR)'**. This is usually taken to mean that it provides liquid funds to those financial institutions in need, especially when alternative sources of funds have dried up. So, gradually the modern banking system emerged.

However, with a central bank as an LLR, a new problem emerged. Goldsmiths/bankers loosened their lending restraints and there was the temptation to run down reserves of money or take greater risks with their deposits. This led to the introduction of the first regulation in modern banking – that of the requirement to hold certain reserve levels of financial assets.

Today financial institutions are one of the most heavily regulated of all businesses. The rationale for this arises from the desire to protect the public's savings, and to maintain public confidence in the financial system so that the public will continue to make funds available for productive investment to construct new buildings, purchase new equipment, set up new businesses and create new jobs.

> **Lender of last resort (LLR)**
> Banks which provide liquid funds to financial institutions in need.

## Regulations to control the soundness of the financial system

The liabilities (deposits) of financial institutions are a major source of the money supply that impacts on **macroeconomic** performance, so regulators seek to influence the operation of financial intermediaries. There are four goals in regulation:

- safety and soundness of the financial system
- consumer and investor protection
- fairness
- information disclosure.

Regulations to achieve these goals take various forms.

> **Macroeconomic**
> Describes the relationships and forces that affect variables such as national income, prices and employment.

### Safety and soundness

The main aims of safety and soundness are to avoid disruptions in the payments systems and prevent collapses of financial institutions. This is achieved by a variety of means, such as a framework for maintaining a stable payments system, using monetary policy to influence the level of prices, and supervising financial institutions. New Zealand's central bank, the Reserve Bank of New Zealand (RBNZ), supervises the payments system, the operations of the major banks, and the overall financial system. The central bank in Australia, the Reserve Bank of Australia, is responsible for the payments system and the overall financial system, but another authority, the Australian Prudential Regulatory Authority, supervises all the deposit-taking institutions.

Various methods are used around the world to supervise financial intermediaries. In many countries, reserve requirement regulations require a bank to hold a percentage of assets, such as 10%, usually with the central bank, to prevent banks from running their liquidity too low. However, New Zealand is a country where there is no such requirement by law.

In many countries, banks needing funds can borrow from the central bank in its LLR function. Such borrowing can also be used as a monetary policy tool, as higher central bank interest rates reduce banks' incentive to borrow from the central bank when short of funds. This is one tool that the central bank of the United States, called the Federal Reserve (the Fed), uses when it adjusts its lending rate to banks through the lending facility called the discount window.

A number of countries have deposit insurance. For example, all national banks in the United States must be insured by the Federal Deposit Insurance Corporation (FDIC). However, the excessive protection of depositors' funds leads to the set of problems called **moral hazard**. Depositors have little incentive to monitor their funds since the government takes this role; consequently, depository institutions may take higher risks with these funds. After the United States savings and loans institutions' huge losses in the 1980s, deposit insurance in the United States was changed to a risk-based deposit insurance premium system.

Equity requirements are imposed on banks, as the equity forms a cushion against the debt. Equity capital consists mainly of shares issued to investors by the bank, and retained earnings. However, the ratio of equity to total assets is quite low. Banks in New Zealand require fully paid-up capital of not less than $15 million of share capital. There is also the requirement for New Zealand banks to meet the internationally agreed capital requirements of the Basel Accords made between major countries' bank supervisors. The accords were later updated to take into account the different risks banks are exposed to, and became known as the Basel II capital accords. Now it has been superseded by Basel III, to be introduced before 31 March 2019.

During the 2008 global financial crisis, governments and central banks undertook unheard-of interventions in financial and economic systems. The crisis began in one part of the mortgage market in the United States, in particular: subprime mortgages issued to low-income individuals who had a high chance of defaulting on their loans.

House prices in the US had been rising steadily from 2000 onwards, and those on low incomes had been encouraged to borrow. Then, in 2006, house prices started to fall, and home owners began to default on their payments. Many banks had constructed new securities based on their mortgage portfolios, and had either kept some mortgage securities or sold them on to other institutions or even to overseas banks. As mortgage defaults increased, the value of mortgage-related securities

> **Moral hazard**
> A theory that the existence of insurance may induce undesirable behaviour. In relation to banks, it is the idea that banks may take excessive risks with depositors' funds.

plummeted, and banks became unwilling to lend to or borrow from each other in case the other bank owned some of these 'toxic' securities. Unable to source funds through the usual channels, many financial institutions were forced to either seek new equity funding or obtain emergency funding from the central bank, while yet others were bailed out by their government or filed for bankruptcy.

As a result, the financial crisis flowed into the main US economy: companies were unable to refinance their maturing debt, so jobs were lost, especially in the construction industry, and economic growth slowed considerably, with the US falling into recession in 2009. Meanwhile, many European countries had seen large increases in house prices, which were fuelled by excessive bank lending, and the US crisis was repeated, with many European banks needing to be supported by their governments.

Regulators and politicians have argued about the causes and spent time looking for ways to avoid repeating the crisis. One result is the updated capital accord Basel III, which includes improved rules that increase the levels of capital a bank should hold. These rules were gradually implemented globally.

## Consumer and investor protection

There are many regulations designed to protect consumers and investors, such as the Companies Act 1993, which we discussed in Chapter 1, and the Financial Markets Conduct Act 2013, which, according to the New Zealand Legislation website (legislation.govt.nz), 'governs how financial products are created, promoted and sold and the ongoing responsibilities of those who offer, deal and trade them'.

## Fairness and information disclosure

It can be argued that fairness should result from a market-based system that allocates goods and services on the basis of price. However, this allocation may not be efficient if markets do not have all the information. So regulation is essential to ensure disclosure of adequate information so that investors can make informed choices in their lending and borrowing decisions. For example, the NZX's listing rules include a continuous disclosure provision by the terms of which a listed company must keep the market constantly informed on issues that may affect the price of its security. As well, the FMA oversees all New Zealand's financial markets. In addition, a market system may not meet all of society's objectives, so regulators may intervene to obtain a more desirable allocation of resources.

## Banking regulation

Banking regulation arises as a natural outcome from the forces that give rise to banks. Once regulation aimed at instilling confidence in the system is passed, it creates its own moral hazards that necessitate further regulation, and so it goes on. In New Zealand the banking regulations have more of a market focus. Nevertheless, the RBNZ maintains a supervisory role over the banks, monitoring the public disclosure statements that banks in New Zealand are required to publish periodically concerning their balance sheets. But there is no longer a hands-on approach to banking supervision, as exists in the United States.

The reserves of assets that a bank holds play an important role in New Zealand's, and indeed in the world's, banking and monetary systems. Generally, the higher the growth rate in reserves, the higher the rate of change in the money supply.

Too high a change has been linked to inflation and its harmful effects. The United States has a fractional reserve banking system which means a bank must hold or 'reserve' some portion of funds that savers deposit, in a form approved by the US Federal Reserve. In New Zealand, no such requirement is laid down by law, but banks still hold a certain percentage as reserves for liquidity reasons.

Next we consider more fully why reserve requirements for banks are necessary.

## Credit creation

> **Credit creation**
> The process by which banks create money from their lending of investors' deposits.

The amount of money in an economy is far more than what has been issued by a central bank. **Credit creation** refers to the process by which banks can create money from their lending of investors' deposits. It is important to realise that the deposits of a bank are its liabilities, but when it lends out these deposits as loans, mortgages and the like, the bank forms new financial assets. So, there is an incentive for banks to lend out as much as they can in order to increase their profits. For this reason, many countries have regulations to stipulate the amount of reserves kept by banks.

However, suppose banks in New Zealand want to hold 20% of deposits in reserve. This means that they can lend out the remaining 80% of deposits. Assume, for this example, that money is first created by $1 000 being injected into the public's hands through the central bank buying back bonds from a financial institution. By issuing cash or writing cheques on itself, the central bank pays $1 000 to the financial institution (say Bank A) which now is able to loan funds to the public. This can be illustrated using the example balance sheet following:

| Bank A's Balance Sheet | |
|---|---|
| **Assets** | **Liabilities** |
| Reserves = $200 | Deposits = $1 000 |
| Loans    = $800 | |

Keeping $200 as reserves, Bank A lends $800 to Customer A, who deposits the entire amount in Bank B. However, Bank B only has to hold 20% for reserves and so Bank B lends $640 (800 × 80%) to one of its customers, Customer B. Customer B then deposits $640 in Bank C. Bank C lends $512 to another customer, who deposits it in Bank D, and so on. This process can be recorded as follows:

| Bank A's Balance Sheet | | | Bank B's Balance Sheet | | | Bank C's Balance Sheet | |
|---|---|---|---|---|---|---|---|
| **Assets** | **Liabilities** | | **Assets** | **Liabilities** | | **Assets** | **Liabilities** |
| $200 | Deposits = $1 000 | | $160 | Deposits = $800 | | $128 | Deposits = $640 |
| $800 | | | $640 | | | $512 | |

Notice that each time a bank lends, the amount that can be lent to each subsequent borrower decreases, but the total amount of deposits increases.

The central bank's position has increased by $1 000 from the bond buyback and the banking system would have loans of $4 000. The change in money supply totals $5 000 as a result of the process summing $1 000 + $800 + $640 + $512 …

To work out the total deposits created in the credit creation process, a formula involving the credit multiplier is used.

## Credit multiplier

This is a ratio that gives the maximum amount of loans that result from an initial deposit.

> **Example 1: Finding the maximum amount of money creation**
>
> Using the $1 000 deposit above, and a reserve ratio of 20%, find the maximum amount of money that can ideally be created.
>
> **Solution**
> $$\text{Credit multiplier} = D/\text{reserve ratio}$$
> $$= \$1\,000/0.2$$
> $$= \$5\,000 \text{ (or 5 times)}$$
>
> where reserve ratio = 20%
> D = initial deposit

Thus, from an initial amount of $1 000, a total of $5 000 was created. The value of the reserve ratio affects the limit of credit expansion. Consider the following: if the reserve ratio = 0.10, what would the credit expansion be? The answer is $10 000 ($1 000/0.10). It is worth noting that this is under ideal conditions. In reality, some money 'leaks' from the system, say as a company pays its taxes due.

Changes in the amount of money affect the level of interest rates, the availability of credit from financial institutions, and thereby the economic well-being of the economy. Because changes in the amount of money are more important for the economy than changes in the amount of other commodities, governments wish to control the money supply – a policy known as monetary policy. This policy is usually carried out by the central bank.

## Monetary policy – three control mechanisms

Monetary policy involves adjusting the level of money supply in a way that slows down or speeds up an economy. When a central bank increases the amount of money in an economy, interest rates will generally fall. Recall that the interest rate is the price of money; therefore, if the supply of money increases relative to demand, interest rates will fall.

Decreasing interest rates tends to stimulate an economy, as lower interest rates make it cheaper for firms to borrow. Through higher investment in new equipment, plant and other production factors by firms, more jobs may be created, so there may be higher employment and ultimately increased economic activity. Likewise, if a central bank believes that an economy is growing too fast and that a rise in inflation is likely, then it can slow down the economy by decreasing the money supply. This acts to increase interest rates by making borrowing dearer, thus slowing firms' investment.

Central banks implement monetary policy through a number of mechanisms, which are described below.

- Reserve requirements, discussed earlier, limit banks' ability to expand their lending and credit creation. However, in New Zealand's case there is no reserve requirement. Instead, New Zealand has a system based on an 'official cash rate' – the interest rate the Reserve Bank will borrow and lend at, as discussed below.

- Open market operations (OMOs) occur in many countries on a daily basis when the central banks buy and sell short-term government securities to influence the level of short-term interest rates and so try to control the amount of money in the financial system. For example, to tighten monetary policy in the United States and try to drive interest rates up, the Fed could sell government bonds to the financial institutions. This reduces the financial institutions' funds as they need to pay the Fed, and therefore reduces the funds they have available to lend. This will result in a reduction of the amount of cash in the system, and will force the financial institutions to compete for funds in order to balance on a daily basis, thus driving up interest rates. The higher interest rates should have a dampening effect on the economy, reducing economic activity and people's desire to borrow. Likewise, to simulate economic growth, the central bank can buy government securities from the major banks, which receive payment for them; the banks will then have more funds to lend out and create more credit.
- An adjustment in the interest rate the central bank charges on loans. An increase in the interest rate for borrowing from a central bank (often called the discount rate) reduces the incentive for banks to use it as a LLR when they are short of funds.

### The official cash rate

In 1999, the RBNZ introduced a base interest rate called the official cash rate (OCR), which is the rate at which the bank will borrow and 'lend'. The OCR is now the key economic indicator of monetary policy in New Zealand. This change has been implemented in order to reduce the volatility in interest rates.

The major banks must settle all of the financial transactions between themselves and the RBNZ at the end of every day and be in credit. However, the major banks hold cash in settlement accounts with the RBNZ in order to settle the flow of funds between themselves, the government and the public. If a major bank has insufficient money in its settlement account to settle with other banks, it can borrow funds either from the RBNZ or from other banks. If it borrows from the RBNZ, it will pay interest at a rate that is just above the OCR. However, if the bank (let's call it Bank A) needs funds and borrows from another bank (Bank B), it will be charged an interest rate close to the interest rate that the RBNZ charges. This is because other banks could undercut Bank B, which is offering the funds, by using cheaper funds from the RBNZ.

Instead of borrowing from the RBNZ or each other and the settlement banks in order to settle every day, the banks can enter into repurchase agreements (repos). This is where the RBNZ buys securities from the major banks, thus giving them cash if they need it to balance. Then the banks will buy the securities back either later on that day or overnight, so effectively the RBNZ is making a short-term loan to them – but only overnight. In 1998 the RBNZ introduced real-time gross settlement for wholesale transactions, so that large sums such as $1 million are now settled immediately instead of waiting until the end of the day, so reducing risk of default.

Therefore, by acting as banker to the major banks, the RBNZ sets the benchmark price of money for the banking system and the economy.

In the past, the monetary policy actions of the RBNZ, in common with other central banks, have been the use of open-market operations, as discussed previously.

Now the OCR system of the RBNZ focuses on the short-term interest rate (price), and to a much lesser extent on settlement cash that banks use in settling their transactions with one another and the RBNZ, thus influencing the level of other short-term rates and ultimately monetary conditions. Open-market operations for the purpose of smoothing short-term imbalances are still carried out to complement the OCR system.

## The inflation problem

Inflation can result when the money supply expands beyond what a fully employed population in an economy requires. An important goal of monetary policy is to control inflation and keep it within a certain range. For example, in New Zealand the range is currently 1–3%. Changes in the money supply can influence people's spending. An increase could lead to more spending on real assets, such as cars, or financial assets, such as shares. Then the increased demand for goods and services could increase their production as well as their prices.

Inflation can also result from a rise in the prices of imported goods, such as oil, but this kind of inflation is usually more 'transient' than the inflation caused by too much money chasing too few goods or services.

Why is inflation a bad thing? A major problem with inflation is that it results in wealth transfers between parties, if the parties are unable to adjust to the anticipated inflation and large price increases. Those people with fixed-interest income usually are unable to adjust their investments, and consequently experience difficulty through the loss of purchasing power, as the following example illustrates.

| Example of out-of-control inflation | | Germany 1919–23 | | |
|---|---|---|---|---|
| Year | Month | Paper currency millions | Inflation index 1913 = 1 | FX rate 1USD = RM[1] 1913 = 1 |
| 1919 | December | 50 065 | 8.03 | 11.14 |
| 1920 | December | 81 387 | 14.40 | 17.48 |
| 1921 | December | 122 497 | 34.87 | 43.83 |
| 1922 | December | 1 295 228 | 1 475 | 1 750.83 |
| 1923 | December | 496 585 345 900 000 | 1 200 400 000 000 | 1 000 000 000 000 |

[1] RM refers to a German mark.

A 50 000 RM note changed in value as follows:
- in June 1922 it bought 625 lb (about 284 kg) of potatoes
- in June 1923 it bought 25 lb (about 11 kg) of potatoes.

By November 1923, a German citizen needed 1 050 000 RM notes to buy 1 lb (about 450 g) of potatoes. The example illustrates one of the fastest rates of inflation periods in modern times, and how inflation inflicted huge costs on German society. More recent examples include Zimbabwe and Argentina, which have both experienced out-of-control inflation, imposing huge costs on their economies and citizens.

In addition to targeting short-term interest rates to control inflation, monetary policy is also used to try to smooth out fluctuations in the economy between periods of faster and slower economic growth in order to avoid destructive boom-and-bust cycles. Monetary policy can also help to prevent large swings in employment; for instance, one of the stated goals of the US Fed is to promote high employment. Therefore each country around the world has its own central bank that conducts monetary policy to achieve its economic goals, which may include elements such as low inflation, price stability or low unemployment.

## Modern financial intermediaries

Financial intermediaries are institutions that intermediate between the providers and the users of financial capital. They collect the funds of savers and lend them or invest them in businesses or people who need the funds. There has been a steady growth in the size of such intermediaries over the past few decades. They can be grouped into two categories: depository and non-depository institutions.

### Depository institutions

Banks, savings institutions and credit unions are depository (deposit-taking) institutions. Banks are the most familiar, as most people deal with them on a daily basis. Banks deal with a variety of savings and term deposits, and use the funds to make individual, business and mortgage loans. They seek to have a positive difference (spread) between the rate earned on loans (their assets) and the cost of funds (their deposits). For example, a bank may pay 4% on bank deposits and charge 5.5% for borrowers wanting a mortgage. From this spread, banks must meet their operating expenses and earn a reasonable profit on their capital. In New Zealand, savings institutions consist of building and investment societies that provide housing mortgages and consumer lending in local regions. Credit unions are small, co-operative, consumer organisations whose investments are almost entirely short-term consumer loans made to the member-customers who have deposits with them. An example of such an organisation is Unity Credit Union (trading as Unity).

### Non-depository institutions

There are financial institutions that accept funds for investment but do not take deposits. Insurance companies do not raise funds by taking deposits, but take in funds by selling insurance policies that enable their buyers to protect themselves from various risks – for example, disability, ill health, and damage to property. Insurance companies have a relatively steady inflow of premium funds under long-term arrangements with policy holders, and the companies invest these funds in capital market securities such as bonds and equities, but also hold some short-term securities in order to provide cash quickly in order to meet customer claims.

Banks, insurance companies and other financial intermediaries may sell **superannuation** (super) schemes to individuals, who then pay on a regular basis into their super accounts. By putting savings into their super accounts over their working lives, individuals may build up assets to generate income in their retirement. These financial institutions pool and invest the funds in a variety of shares, bonds and other assets in the expectation that the value of the funds will increase. Note that superannuation schemes are often called 'pension plans' overseas.

The New Zealand superannuation industry is benefiting from an inflow of funds since the introduction of the **KiwiSaver** scheme in 2007. This is a 'voluntary'

---

**Superannuation**
A scheme that allows individuals to invest funds over their working life to create income for when they retire.

**KiwiSaver**
A voluntary, mainly workplace, incentive savings scheme open to all New Zealanders to save for their retirement via a variety of investment options, from conservative to growth, offered by various financial intermediaries.

savings scheme in which new employees are automatically enrolled. However, there is a brief period during which employees may opt out of the plan. Investors in KiwiSaver schemes benefit from mandatory employer contributions as well as government incentives.

Finance companies raise funds through loans from banks or related companies, and through the issuing of short- to medium-term debt securities to retail investors or via the capital markets. They provide loans and lease financing, mainly to individuals and small and medium-sized companies for business projects involving a degree of risk. Given this, interest rates for borrowers and investors have often been higher than bank rates. The collapse of many finance companies between 2006 and 2012 indicated that the rates did not offer enough return to compensate investors for the risks to which they were exposed. Finance companies have also been raising funds by **securitisation** of their assets. An example is MTF Finance, which offers car and other vehicle loans, as well as personal and business loans including finance leases. This involves the finance company issuing debt securities based on an underlying pool of loans. The interest and principal from the underlying loans are used to pay the security holders.

> **Securitisation**
> The process of repackaging and grouping loans so they have the characteristics of more liquid securities. For example, many of the mortgage loans in the United States have been repackaged into securities called collateralised mortgage obligations (CMOs).

Another type of non-depository institution is investment companies or managed funds (called mutual funds in the United States), which pool funds from investors and use them to buy real and financial assets such as shares or bonds. For example, a unit trust (a managed fund where an investor buys units) offers a small investor the advantages of: reduced investment risk from diversification; professional management of funds; and reduced transaction costs from economies of scale. One common unit trust is a cash management trust, which pools investors' funds so that they can access indirectly the wholesale money markets and earn higher returns on their short-term funds. However, there are a number of fees associated with managed funds, such as entry fees and ongoing management fees, which act to reduce the returns on managed funds.

**Investment banks** (otherwise known as merchant banks) are also a type of non-deposit-taking institution, and operate both as intermediaries and agents. Originally, they were involved with short-term deposits and lending, but their operations have expanded to include advice to companies on matters including mergers with and acquisitions of other companies, and fund-raising via securities such as new share issues. For example, in New Zealand, for the share float of the previously state-owned electricity company Meridian Energy, the investment banks Goldman Sachs Group Inc. (United States), Macquarie Group (Australia) and a partnership of Deutsche Bank AG (Germany) and Craigs Investment Partners (New Zealand) were involved.

> **Investment banks**
> Institutions or divisions of firms that originate and distribute securities to open-market investors.

## The benefits of financial intermediation

Financial intermediaries are needed because we live in a world of imperfect information and actions. Individuals and companies require help with their financial needs, such as borrowing and lending, buying and selling financial assets, and managing risk exposures. Costs are involved in moving funds between lenders and borrowers. Some of these are search and information costs, where lenders are found and matched with borrowers who must be checked for creditworthiness; drawing up of contracts costs; and monitoring of loans. Intermediaries have become skilled at performing low-cost transactions, which are discussed below. They carry out two main roles, a brokering role and a transformation role, by repackaging funds into marketable parcels.

### Brokerage

The use of a broker can cut the costs of searching for lenders. For this service, they charge a brokerage fee. Consider the case where 100 lenders are looking at 100 potential borrowers. To become fully informed about the borrowers, they could spend, say, $25 on monitoring each borrower. The combined cost of evaluation would be $250 000 (100 × 100 × $25). However, if a broker steps in, the costs are reduced. Assume the evaluation cost is the same for the broker, at $25 per head, so the aggregate cost is now $2 500 (100 × $25). If the information is distributed for an insignificant cost, the saving in total monitoring costs is $247 500 ($250 000 – $2 500). Even after allowing for brokerage fees the savings are substantial.

Note that the savings increase markedly with the size of the sample of people involved. This is because the information collected about borrowers can be reused. So the fixed costs are spread over a larger number of people, thus leading to greater possible savings through economies of scale. The broker function involves no risk – beyond the cost of collecting unwanted information. Brokers do not take funds onto their balance sheet positions; they simply connect those with funds to those in need of funds.

For example, the New Zealand sharebroker ASB Securities enables its clients to trade securities including shares and bonds for a fee. Sharetrading apps such as Robinhood (United States), Hatch and Sharesies (New Zealand) have been credited with democratising investing by making securities more accessible to the general public.

### Transformation

Because the investor often has different characteristics and needs to those of the borrower, as shown in Table 3.1 on the next page, the financial intermediary receives funds in one form suitable to investors, then lends these funds out in another form more suitable to the borrower. Some of the asset transformations made by financial intermediaries are:

- maturity transformation, whereby short-term deposits become 10-year mortgages in the case of a bank
- liquidity transformation, whereby fairly liquid term deposits are matched with illiquid term loans
- size or denomination, whereby relatively small deposits can be pooled to make a large loan
- risk transformation for credit or default risk, whereby a bank will monitor loans carefully.

Notice that every transformation involves a mismatch, and thus involves risk-taking by the financial intermediary. For instance, receiving deposits on-call and lending them out on a term basis involves interest-rate risk if interest rates rise sharply. The bank takes on the risk that the value of its assets will fall from a drop in price.

Investors typically have different investment requirements than those offered by borrowers.

Table 3.1  Borrowers' and investors' requirements

| Investors' needs | Borrowers' characteristics |
| --- | --- |
| Security and low default risk | |
| Liquidity, be able to withdraw funds quickly without loss | Want to borrow on a long-term basis |
| High return | Want funds cheaply |
| Small denomination investments | Want large sums of money |

The process of transformation of assets by a financial intermediary involves changes in the financial instrument(s) held by the ultimate investors. Financial intermediaries issue securities of their own, such as deposits, to ultimate lenders, and at the same time accept promises to pay (IOUs) from borrowers as loan contracts. The roles of financial intermediaries are summarised in Figure 3.1.

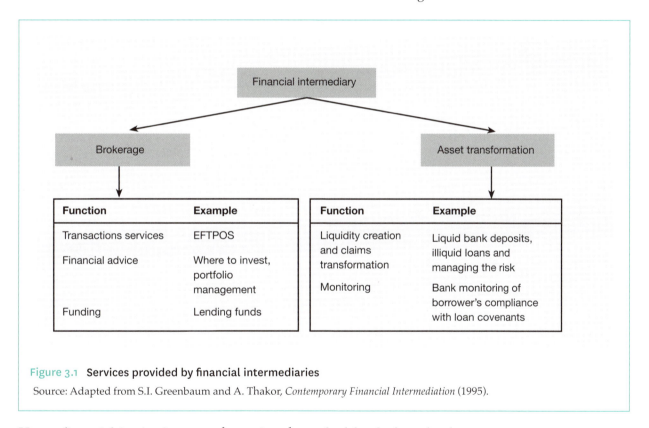

Figure 3.1  Services provided by financial intermediaries
Source: Adapted from S.I. Greenbaum and A. Thakor, *Contemporary Financial Intermediation* (1995).

Hence financial institutions are the major channel of funds from lenders to borrowers, especially for businesses. Without a financial intermediary, funds transfer may not take place. This is mainly due to how financial intermediaries can diversify their risks, and also to how they lower the information and monitoring costs of loans – the costs of seeking out information and of the transaction itself may be prohibitive for individual households.

Part of the transaction cost arises from the mismatch in information between the lender and the borrower, where the borrower generally has better knowledge of what the borrowed funds are going to be used for and how they intend to repay the funds. Financial intermediaries help to reduce this mismatch by collecting and using information about borrowers' financial capabilities for future loans. Given the importance of financial intermediaries, the New Zealand Reserve Bank, in addition to its supervision of depository institutions, has taken over supervising non-depository institutions, such as insurance companies and large finance companies.

## Ethics and financial institutions

As efficient as financial institutions and markets appear to be, market critics contend that there is still a great deal that is imperfect in our financial system. They argue that not all financial markets are fully competitive and that price fixing or defrauding unsuspecting members of the public does occur quite frequently. For example, some New Zealand finance companies borrowed investors' funds allegedly to buy property, but the property deals never came to pass. Some US fund managers have been charged with **unethical behaviour**, because they allowed a few favoured clients to trade after the close of the markets at favourable prices, and so these clients benefited at the expense of others. Unsound bank-lending practices in a relatively small part of the US mortgage market contributed to a credit crisis that spread globally, resulting in the bank failures of Northern Rock in the United Kingdom and Indy Mac in the United States, and governments in Europe having to bail out their banks. These problems raise questions about how improvement in marketplace behaviour can be achieved. Should it be achieved by means of more government regulation, higher industry-imposed standards or improved professional ethical codes? We are reminded that financial markets and intermediaries are fragile entities and rely on the support and the confidence of stakeholders such as the government and the public to operate efficiently and perform their essential functions.

> **Unethical behaviour**
> A breach of a written or unwritten moral code.

## Classifying types of financial transfers

This chapter concludes with a classification of the types of financial transfers that occur in the financial system. Funds can flow between lenders and borrowers in the following three ways.

- *Direct transfers*
  
  This is when investors place funds directly with businesses by buying their debt or equity securities. This is relatively uncommon because the matching of investor/borrower needs is unlikely. Companies generally need a high credit rating to borrow funds directly. Some examples are direct company issues of debentures and shares, especially to family.

- *Indirect transfer through investment banks*
  
  This transfer involves brokers who take a fee or commission in order to source funds for borrowers. This has become increasingly common in New Zealand, with many companies now being credit-rated. Companies with good credit ratings may seek the assistance of investment banks in order to operate their own commercial paper programmes in the money markets. An example has been New Zealand Spark with its issues of commercial paper. Borrowing directly from the capital markets with the aid of a broker can lower the cost of long-term borrowing. Many well-rated companies have issued capital notes that are then listed on the NZX; for example, Fletcher Building. Investment banks have also arranged first-time share issues; for example, for the New Zealand electricity company Meridian Energy. Note that most new share issues are organised through this type of go-between.

- *Indirect transfer through financial intermediaries*
    This involves the services provided by financial intermediaries of brokering and asset transformation. In this process, financial assets are transformed. It is the most common form of debt transfer between lenders and borrowers. Banks are the major financial intermediaries in the modern society.

## Conclusion

We have discussed how the financial intermediaries of deposit-taking financial institutions developed out of the activities of goldsmiths. The storage of gold and the issue of receipts made transactions easier, but led to the development of fractional reserve banking with the issue of extra receipts. This required institutions to make sure they had sufficient assets in reserve to manage liquidity. However, it introduced the problem of limiting the supply of receipts so as to maintain value. Thus, the use of paper receipts required the development of a central system that was initially a group of banks. Over time this system proved insufficient to withstand economic crises, such as recessions, and so the supervisory and LLR functions were taken over by central banks.

Financial intermediaries became adept at offering other financial services apart from payments, such as managing the risks involved in funds transfer. As the financial needs of individuals and companies change, the financial sector produces new products that meet these needs. A goal for individuals and financial managers of companies is to secure low-cost, low-risk funding. Risks, barriers, frictions and imperfections in the marketplace inhibit the transfer of funds from savers to firms. Intermediaries are required to 'broker' and 'transform assets' to bridge the gap. We have seen in this chapter how important the role of financial intermediaries is to the economic system. If corporations want to access funds directly they must market securities that are attractive to investors, and to do this they may have to reduce the risk to investors. Corporations can facilitate this process by providing investors with good-quality information and by reducing operating risk.

## SELF-TEST QUESTIONS

1. Explain the concept of financial intermediation and how it can increase the efficiency of the financial system.
2. Bank regulation is considered necessary in the public interest, as bank failures are considered to have a greater impact upon the economy than the failure of other types of business would have. Do you agree with this statement?

## ANSWERS TO SELF-TEST QUESTIONS

1. Financial intermediation describes the process by which financial intermediaries intercede between the borrower (the unit deficient in funds) and the lender (the unit with surplus funds). Financial intermediaries transform financial assets in such a way as to make them more appealing to both units. For example, short-term deposits are altered into the long-term mortgage. Intermediaries are able to do this because they reduce search costs, and they process and reuse the information they have obtained.
2. Bank failures occur infrequently but can have a large impact on the economy because of their payments role, the contagion effect where the failure of one bank can raise fears about the solvency of other banks, the reduction in the money supply, and the loss of depositors' wealth.

## QUESTIONS AND PROBLEMS

1. How did goldsmiths print money, and what repercussions did this have in terms of financial instability and regulation?
2. Why did the Bank of England become a lender of last resort (LLR) to the UK banking system?
3. Describe how open market operations (OMOs) can be used by the central bank to control the monetary system.
4. Explain what the two primary functions of financial intermediaries are, and indicate how they are important.
5. Explain the term *denomination intermediation*.
6. Why has the indirect transfer method of raising finance through investment banks become more common in today's financial markets?
7. Explain what 'spread' is in relation to financial intermediaries, and in what way it is important for them.
8. What is fractional reserve banking, and how does it affect money creation?
9. List some of the roles of a central bank.

# PART 2

# Finance tools

Part 2 of this book introduces the finance tools that are required to solve many of the financial problems faced by businesses and individual investors. Both companies and individuals invest money today in the hopes of receiving more money in the future. These investment decisions require them to be able to make comparisons of cash flows at different points in time.

A crucial question in finance is: What is the value today of cash flows to be received at a later time? For example, what would a lottery winner's decision be if they were offered a prize of $10 million today or $1 million paid every year for the next ten years? The winner would most likely take $10 million today, as a a higher value is placed on the funds in hand.

The value of assets depends on when the cash flows they generate will arrive. Investment decisions depend on whether the value of future cash flows is greater than the initial investment.

In Chapters 4 and 5, we introduce the financial mathematical tools required to analyse financial decisions. The 'time value of money' concept deals with the relationship between values of dollars today, and values of dollars at a later point in time.

Chapter 4 deals with how a single amount invested today at a specific interest rate will grow over time, and how to find a value today for future cash amounts. The trade-off between the value of money today and money in the future depends on, among other things, the rate that can be earned by investing.

Chapter 5 further explores the relationship between present and future amounts by valuing multiple cash flows. It describes some shortcuts for working out the value of multiple cash flows.

The topics covered in Chapters 4 and 5 are central to any investment or financing analyses performed by individuals or firms.

# CHAPTER 4
# Time value of money – Single payments

**Learning objectives**

By the end of this chapter, you should be able to:

- explain the concept of the time value of money, and understand the relationship of present value to future value
- describe the concept of simple interest and the process of compounding
- calculate future values using compounding, and calculate present values using discounting
- calculate effective rates of interest, and understand their relationship to nominal rates
- calculate unknown interest rates and time periods from the time value of money equation.

## Introduction

In the next two chapters we will look at the relationship between the value of dollars today and that of dollars in the future. This is a fundamental concept of finance. Under this concept, individuals prefer to receive a dollar today to receiving that same dollar promised in a year's time. This is because in the interval we could have earned interest on today's dollar and so end up with more than a dollar in a year's time.

As a result, it means we cannot add and subtract or otherwise accurately compare dollar amounts which occur at different points in time unless we first change them to the same value base. In other words, a $10 000 lump sum today cannot be compared with receiving $10 000 in a year's time unless changed to the same time frame.

In this chapter we study the time value of single payments, and in Chapter 5 we will analyse the time value of a series of cash flows. The principles of time value of money will be applied throughout this text. For example, one of the functions of financial markets is the determination of prices (or values) of financial assets traded in the markets, by finding the relationship between present and future values.

For an individual to be indifferent to an amount received today and an amount to be received later (the **future value**), the later amount must include some additional compensation in the form of interest for individuals or companies who forego their consumption. **Interest** is the cost of funds to a borrower (lacking in funds and wanting to receive funds) or part of the return for a lender or investor (the supplier of funds). As far as the suppliers of funds are concerned, the compensation they require is a reward – firstly for not consuming, and secondly for the risks they are accepting; for example, the risk that the borrowers may default on their payments. Therefore, the interest rate for lenders represents the minimum required return they expect. The borrowers pay interest for 'renting' the funds, and in addition they have a **liability** to repay the lender (who initially provided the funds) the principal

---

**Future value**
The value of a sum after receiving interest on it over one or more periods. Also called *compound value* when interest is compounded.

**Interest**
The rate paid for borrowing or lending money.

**Liability**
Debts of an individual or company that represent obligations for repayment.

amount at the end of the term of the loan.

There are many interest rates in the marketplace. For example, interest rates on three-year government bonds will be lower than the rate on a three-year **mortgage**, while the rate for a business **term loan** is likely to be higher than the mortgage rate. Factors that affect interest rates will be discussed in Chapter 6, but first we will examine how interest rates are measured.

There are two ways, discussed below, of measuring the rate of interest:

- using a simple interest basis
- using a compound interest basis.

> **Mortgage**
> A form of financial asset where the lender (mortgagee) has the right to recover their money by selling the property if the borrower (mortgagor) defaults on payment.
>
> **Term loan**
> A loan from a bank with a specific maturity.

## Simple interest and future value

Future value (FV) refers to the amount of money that an initial amount will grow to over some period of time at a given interest rate. In other words, future value is the cash value of some investment at some future date. When we calculate **simple interest** on a base amount or **principal**, it is calculated on the principal only.

Suppose we deposit $10 000 for a year into an account that will earn 5% per annum interest income on the principal only. What will this deposit (principal) be worth at the end of one year? That is, what is its FV? The interest earned during one year is $10 000 × 0.05 = $500. So the value of the account after one year is $10 500 (i.e. $10 000 + $500). Similarly, the interest earned for the second year is $500, taking the total amount after two years to $11 000 (i.e. $10 000 + $500 + $500).

Generally, the amount of simple interest (I) is equal to the principal amount (P) times the (simple) rate of interest per annum (r) times the number of periods in years (n):

$$I = P \times r \times n = Prn$$

*Equation 4.1*

> **Simple interest**
> Interest calculated on the original amount.
>
> **Principal**
> The outstanding balance owing on a loan.

If n is a fraction of a year, say 60 days, it must be substituted into Equation 4.1 as a fraction of a year, such as 60/365.

---

**Example 1: Calculating simple interest**

Find the simple interest on $1 239 at 7% per annum for:

a  two years
b  90 days.

**Solution**

a  I = Prn
   = $1 239 × 0.07 × 2
   = $173.46

b  I = $1 239 × 0.07 × 90/365
   = $21.39

---

**Mathematical hint**

To avoid rounding differences in calculations, keep all numbers in your calculator. For ease of writing, calculations are usually shown to five decimal places. But all the numbers are kept in the calculator and then are rounded to TWO decimal places at the end where necessary.

The total amount (FV) the depositor has at the end of n years equals the original deposit plus the interest earned. Therefore,

$$FV = P + I \qquad \text{Equation 4.2}$$

Substituting Equation 4.1 for I in Equation 4.2 gives:

$$\begin{aligned} FV &= P + P \times r \times n \\ &= P + (Prn) \\ &= P(1 + rn) \text{ by algebraic factorisation} \qquad \text{Equation 4.3} \end{aligned}$$

Notice that the annual interest rate is entered as a decimal and n is in years. So for our first example of $10 000, the future value after two years is:

$$\begin{aligned} FV &= \$10\,000(1 + 0.05 \times 2) \\ &= \$10\,000(1 + 0.10) \\ &= \$10\,000 \times 1.10 \\ &= \$11\,000 \end{aligned}$$

> **Mathematical hint**
>
>
>
> **Order of mathematical operations for ordinary calculators**
> To remember the order of operations, the acronym BEDMAS may be used, where BEDMAS stands for: do Brackets first, then Exponents or powers, then Division and Multiplication followed by Addition and Subtraction last.

### Example 2: Future value of a single amount

If $10 000 was borrowed for three years at a simple interest rate of 5% per annum, what would the total lump sum repaid after three years be?

**Solution**

$$\begin{aligned} FV &= P(1 + rn) \\ &= \$10\,000(1 + 0.05 \times 3) \\ &= \$10\,000(1.15) \\ &= \$11\,500 \end{aligned}$$

Simple interest is used for short-term financial assets in the **money markets** (also called the *short-term debt markets*), where companies can borrow or invest in the short term. When applied to these assets, however, the time period will be a fraction of a year, such as 90/365.

### Example 3: Application of simple interest

Suppose a large company invests their temporary surplus of $100 000 in the money markets for 180 days at 4% per annum.

What amount of money would be repaid at the end of 180 days?

**Solution**

$$\begin{aligned} FV &= P(1 + rn) \\ &= \$100\,000(1 + (0.04 \times 180/365)) \\ &= \$100\,000(1 + 0.019726) \\ &= \$101\,972.60 \end{aligned}$$

## Simple interest and calculating the present value

So far, we have discussed the future or accumulated values of original amounts invested or borrowed. Often we want to work out how much the money we expect to receive in the future (e.g. to be received in two years' time) is worth today. The amount today is known as the **present value** and can be thought of as the necessary sum invested or borrowed today, to yield a particular value in the future. As the future value equation (Equation 4.3) has four variables: FV, P, r and n, it can be rearranged to calculate any one of the four variables.

The present value (PV) of a future amount can be found by rearranging Equation 4.3:

$$PV = \frac{FV}{(1+rn)} \qquad \text{Equation 4.4}$$

This formula states that the present value (PV) of a future amount is calculated as the future amount (FV) divided by the simple interest factor of (1 + rn). This in effect **discounts** the future sum so that it refers to the value of this amount in today's dollars. In other words, we remove the interest component from the future sum in order to arrive at payments made today.

> **Present value**
> The value of a future amount discounted at the appropriate market interest rate; that is, the current dollar value of a future amount.

> **Discounts**
> This means to find the present values of future amounts. This is the inverse of compounding interest.

### Example 4: Present value of a single amount with simple interest

What is the present value of a money market instrument that will pay 10% per annum simple interest and will pay its holder $100 000 in 120 days?

**Solution**

$$PV = \frac{FV}{(1+rn)}$$

$$= \frac{\$100\ 000}{(1 + 0.10 \times 120/365)}$$

$$= \frac{\$100\ 000}{(1 + 0.03288)}$$

$$= \frac{\$100\ 000}{1.03288}$$

$$= \$96\ 816.98$$

Simple interest is easy to calculate, but is used mainly for money-market instruments and interest-only loans where interest is always paid on the initial loan deposit and not added to it.

## Compound interest and future value

For most loans and investments, we use **compound interest**. In calculating compound interest, interest is worked out on both the principal and the accumulated interest from previous periods. In the bank deposit example of $10 000, suppose interest for the second year is calculated on the principal and the first year's interest of $500. We know that the value of the account at the end of

> **Compound interest**
> Interest is calculated each period on the principal plus any interest. It is then added to the principal.

the first year is $10 500. This becomes the new principal for the second year that will earn 5% interest over that year. Thus the value after two years is:

$$= \text{value after 1 year} + \text{interest in year 2}$$
$$= \$10\,500 + 0.05 \times \$10\,500$$
$$= \$11\,025$$

Likewise, the value after three years is:

$$= \text{value after 2 years} + \text{interest in year 3}$$
$$= \$11\,025 + 0.05 \times \$11\,025$$
$$= \$11\,576.25$$

The process of **compounding** can be simplified by rewriting the steps and deriving a general formula as shown below.

The future value after one year can be written:

**Compounding**
The process of finding future amounts where interest is paid on interest already earned.

$$FV = \$10\,000 + 0.05 \times \$10\,000$$
$$= \$10\,000 \times (1 + 0.05)$$
$$= \$10\,500$$

Note the $10 000 has grown by a factor of $(1 + 0.05)$ or 1.05.

The future value after two years is:

$$FV = \$10\,500 + (\$10\,500 \times 0.05)$$
$$= \mathbf{\$10\,500} \times (1 + 0.05)$$
$$= \mathbf{\$10\,000 \times (1 + 0.05)} \times (1 + 0.05)$$
$$= \$10\,000 \times (1 + 0.05)^2$$
$$= \$11\,025$$

Finally, the value after three years is:

$$FV = \mathbf{\$11\,025} + (\$11\,025 \times 0.05)$$
$$= \mathbf{\$10\,000 \times (1 + 0.05) \times (1 + 0.05)} \times (1 + 0.05)$$
$$\text{or } = \$10\,000 \times (1 + 0.05)^3$$
$$= \$11\,576.25$$

Now we will develop an equation for future value.

Consider a deposit of PV dollars. If this deposit is repaid after n years and interest is compounded annually at r%, then the future value of the deposit is:

$$FV = PV(1 + r)^n \qquad \textit{Equation 4.5}$$

If we compare the two methods of calculating interest, using the $10 000 and 5% interest rate, the simple interest method will provide a future value after two years of $11 000. If the compound interest method is used, the value after two years is $11 025. The additional $25.00 is 5% interest earned in the second year on the year one interest; that is, $0.05 \times \$500$. The additional interest earned on year one's interest is due to compounding.

## Other methods of calculation

### Financial calculator solution

As well as using an equation to find future value with an ordinary calculator and its power (exponents) key, we may also use the financial functions on a financial calculator or a spreadsheet. Financial calculators do vary in their programming, so it is important if you have one to understand how it works.

Most financial calculators have a present value (PV) key, a future value (FV) key, a number of time periods (N or n) key, an interest rate (i%) key, a payments (PMT) key and a compute (COMP or CPT) key.

If you have a financial calculator, you can use it to check the answer for the previous three-year example. First, check that the calculator's memory is cleared. Then enter −10 000 and press the PV key. (Note some calculators need you to enter PV as a minus amount [i.e. −10 000] as it is an outflow or investment.) Make sure you use the +/− key on your calculator for the minus sign. Next, enter 5 and press the i% key (unlike the equations, most financial calculators work so that you enter whole numbers for the interest rate instead of decimals). Next, enter 3 for the number of time periods (in this case, years), then enter 0 for the payments (PMT) and finally press the COMP/CPT key followed by the FV key to calculate the future value of $11 576.25.

---

**Financial calculator solution**

Inputs:         −10 000          5          3          0
                  PV             i%         N         PMT

Press:           CPT            FV

Solution: $11 576.25

---

Note that on the financial calculator there is a key for payments (PMT) during the period. In this case PMT is zero, as there is a single cash flow. It is useful in time value money problems to realise there are basically four inputs and we are solving for the fifth input or variable. Spreadsheet programs exist for calculating future values. Next we have the same example solved using an Excel spreadsheet program.

### Spreadsheet solution

We first show how a spreadsheet such as Microsoft Excel can be used to solve the single-cash-flow example. We may set up a spreadsheet with the inputs of PV, i and n in the cells, with the FV equation formula in another cell, and solve for FV as if the spreadsheet was a calculator. However, it is far easier to use the built-in financial functions via the function $f_x$.

Open up the Excel spreadsheet and click on the function sign ($f_x$) in the function input line above the actual spreadsheet. An equals sign (=) will appear in the cell input window and you will be asked what function you want to use. Click on Search to find function FV, or you can search in the category 'Financial' for FV. Then you can select FV, and on the spreadsheet screen the description 'Returns the future value of an investment based on periodic, constant payments and a constant interest rate' shows. When you click OK for FV, a dialogue box in the screen FV (Rate, Nper, Pmt, Pv, Type) will appear and you enter the variables for the problem.

The Rate is 0.05; Nper is the number of periods (3 in this example); Pmt is 0 as no periodic payments occur; Pv is −10 000 and Type is 0, reflecting payments occuring at the end of the period. So we have FV(0.05,3,0,–10 000,0). Clicking on OK gives $11 576.25. It is important to note the interest rate is entered as a decimal, and the initial deposit Pv is entered as a negative number with no comma. If you omit the negative sign then FV will appear as –$11 576.25.

### Spreadsheet solution

Using the financial function *fx* and its pull-down window we solve for the future value as follows:

$$=FV(Rate, Nper, Pmt, Pv, Type)$$
$$=FV(0.05, 3, 0, -10000, 0)$$
$$= 11\ 576.25$$

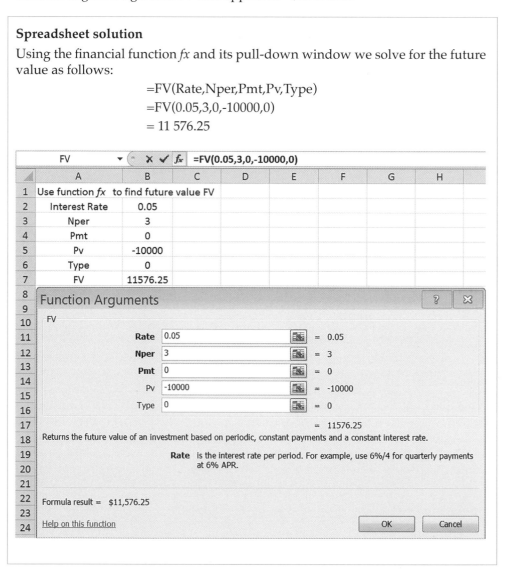

The example on the next page demonstrates the effect of compounding on future value.

> **Example 5: Compounding and future value**
>
> Suppose you deposit $1 254.50 into an account earning an annual interest rate of 3.5%. How much can you withdraw at the end of six years if interest is compounded annually?
>
> **Solution**
>
> $$\begin{aligned} FV &= PV\,(1+r)^n \\ &= \$1\,254.50 \times (1.035)^6 \\ &= \$1\,254.50 \times 1.22926 \\ &= \$1\,542.10 \end{aligned}$$
>
> This implies that, if somebody offers you $1 254.50 today or $1 542.10 at the end of six years, and your **opportunity cost** of funds is 3.5%, you would be indifferent as to the two alternatives.

**Opportunity cost**
The next best rate of return that would be achieved through an alternative course of action: the rate of return (market yields) in the financial markets is often used as a benchmark for opportunity costs.

> **Mathematical hint**
>
> **Using a calculator with exponents (powers)**
>
> In Example 5, the quantity $(1.035)^6$ can be worked out using the power key ($Y^x$, $X^y$ or $\wedge$) on any scientific or business calculator that has the key. Enter 1.035 in your calculator, press the power key, followed by the button for the number 6, and finally the equals key. This gives the number 1.22926, which can then be multiplied by the principal $1 254.50 to give the answer of $1 542.10.

The interest rate and the amount of time between the present and future amounts relate the present and future values mathematically. Note that unless specified, the word interest involves compound interest and the nominal interest rate means the nominal *annual* rate of interest. For example, a quoted rate of 6% means 6% compounded per annum. Interestingly, we can use a nominal interest rate to get a rough approximation of how long it will take an investment to double in value. Divide the interest rate into 72 to find the number of years it will take to double in value; in this case, the answer is 12, so it will take roughly 12 years for an investment returning 6% to double in value. In practice, this is referred to as the Rule of 72.

## The present value of a single payment

If a certain amount will be received in the future we may want to know what it is worth in today's dollars given a certain required rate of return or opportunity cost. Most financial management decisions require present values (PV) rather than future values (FV). For example, a financial manager who is considering buying an asset wants to know what the asset is worth today rather than what it will be worth in the future. On the other hand, savers (investors) may want to know how much deposited today will grow into a required future amount. The process of finding the present value of a future amount by decreasing a future value (FV) at a compound rate is known as **discounting**. The calculation is therefore referred to as a discounted cash flow (DCF) calculation, and the interest rate r is known as the discount rate. The present value (PV) in the case of compound interest can be found by rearranging Equation 4.5 to give:

**Discounting**
The process of finding current amounts by the process of present value.

$$PV = \frac{FV}{(1+r)^n}$$

*Equation 4.6*

Note: The equation can also be written as $PV = FV \times (1+r)^{-n}$ with the power of the denominator changing to negative and multiplying FV by $(1 + r)^{-n}$.

The relationship between the interest rate, the number of years and the present value of $1 is shown in Figure 4.1.

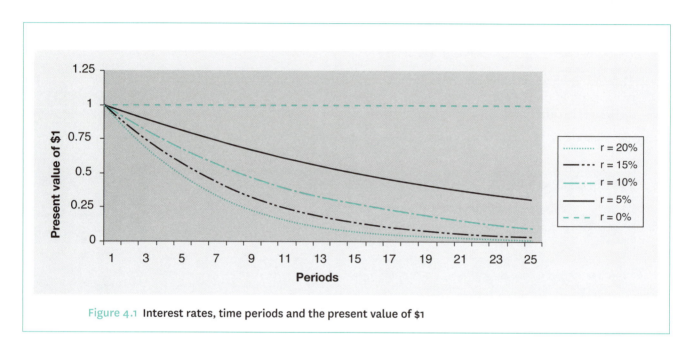

**Figure 4.1** Interest rates, time periods and the present value of $1

Figure 4.1 shows that the present value decreases with increases in the discount rate and time until the future funds are received. The longer you have to wait for your money, the less it is worth today. However, for an interest rate of 0%, the present value always equals the future value.

#### Example 6: Present value and compounding

You know you will need $2 000 at the end of three years. If your money can earn 5%, how much should you deposit into your account today?

Another way of asking this question is: 'What is the present value (PV) of $2 000 to be received at the end of three years?'

**Solution**

Use Equation 4.6 to solve the unknown PV.

$$\begin{aligned} PV &= FV(1+r)^{-n} \\ &= \$2\,000\,(1.05)^{-3} \\ &= \$2\,000\,(0.86384) \\ &= \$1\,727.68 \end{aligned}$$

> **Mathematical hint**
>
>  With many calculators, for PV = FV × (1 + r)$^{-n}$, you may put in (1 + r), press the power key (Y$^x$, X$^y$ or ^), press the power number followed by the +/- key for the negative, and finally the equals key. Or you may use the reciprocal key 1/x, as 1/x is x$^{-1}$ with the first form of Equation 4.6.

As noted, financial calculators have a present value (PV) key, a future value (FV) key, a number of time periods (N or n) key, an interest rate (i%) key, a payments (PMT) key and a compute (CPT or COMP) key. To check the answer for Example 6 using a financial calculator, first make sure the calculator's memory is cleared. Then enter –2 000 and press the FV key. (Note some calculators require you to enter FV as a minus amount, as it is an outflow or investment.) Next, enter 5 and press the i% key, followed by 3 for the number of time periods (in this case, years). Finally press the CPT key followed by the PV key to calculate the PV of $1 727.675, which rounds to $1 727.68.

---

**Financial calculator solution**

Inputs:      –2 000       5       3       0
              FV         i%      N      PMT

Press:       CPT         PV

Solution: $1 727.68

Note that on the calculator there is a key for payments (PMT) during the period, but in this case PMT is 0 as shown in the solution.

**Spreadsheet solution**

Spreadsheet programs exist for calculating present values. Following is the same example solved using an Excel spreadsheet.

Use the financial wizard function sign ($f_x$) in the function input line above the actual spreadsheet. Click in Search to find the function PV or click on Financial, then PV, and a dialogue box will open in the screen PV (Rate, Nper, Pmt, Fv, Type). Enter the variables for the problem. The Rate is 0.05; Nper is the number of periods (3 in this example); Pmt is zero, as no periodic payments occur; Fv is –2 000; and Type is 0, reflecting payments occuring at the end of the period. So we have PV(0.05,3,0,–2 000,0). Clicking on OK gives $1 727.68.

Note that the interest rate is entered as a decimal, and PV is entered as a negative number with no comma. If you omit the minus sign then PV appears as –$1 727.68.

As a three-step process, the present value of a single amount is:

=PV(rate,Nper,Pmt,Fv,Type)
=PV(0.05,3,0,-2000,0)
=1727.68

### Example 7: Investment decisions

An elderly aunt wishes to test your finance skills and offers you the opportunity to receive either $3 000 two years from now or $2 620 today. If you can earn 7% on your investment, which offer should you take?

**Solution**

$$\begin{align} PV &= FV(1+r)^{-n} \\ &= \$3\,000\,(1.07)^{-2} \\ &= \$3\,000\,(0.87344) \\ &= \$2\,620.31 \end{align}$$

In other words, it is of no consequence whether you receive $3 000 in two years' time or $2 620.31 today.

### Example 8: Current price of a future amount

Find the current price (PV) of a security that pays interest and principal of $1 000 at maturity in two years' time if the current market interest rates are:

a  8%
b  5%

**Solution**

a
$$Price = \frac{FV}{(1+r)^n}$$
$$Price = \frac{\$1\,000}{(1+0.08)^2}$$
$$= \frac{\$1\,000}{1.1664}$$
$$= \$857.34$$

b
$$Price = \frac{\$1\,000}{(1+0.05)^2}$$
$$Price = \frac{\$1\,000}{1.1025}$$
$$= \$907.03$$

Note: For Example 8, the change in today's value for the security shows the impact of a change in interest rate, as it moves from 8% to 5%. As the interest rate falls, prices of financial assets may rise. This inverse relationship between an asset's price and interest rates will be met again in later chapters.

## Compounding frequency

So far, we have focused on calculating the present value or future value of a single lump-sum payment with an annual interest rate. If we increase the number of compounding periods per year, then we end up with different annual yields. The frequency for compounding interest varies widely. For example, bank accounts can pay interest semi-annually (twice a year), quarterly, monthly or daily. If compounding or discounting takes place more frequently than once during a year, we need to modify the future and present value equations from the previous section to take this into account. Any increase in the frequency of compounding, all else being equal, will increase the future value of the funds to be received.

To show how this principle works, we calculate the future value of an initial investment of $1 000 compounded semi-annually at 10%. After the first six months, the amount is $1 050 = $1 000 × (1 + 0.10/2). At the end of the second six-month period the total is $1 102.50 = $1 050 × (1 + 0.10/2). An easier way to calculate the value is to recognise that $1 000 is being invested for two six-month periods at an interest rate of 5% per period. That is,

$$FV = \$1\,000 \times (1 + 0.05)^2$$
$$= \$1\,102.50$$

In general, if m is the number of periods per year, the annual interest rate (r) will be divided by m. This in effect adjusts the interest rate to match the compounding period. However, because there are now more compounding periods, each n must be multiplied by m to adjust both future and present value equations.

For example, to calculate a future value we need to adjust Equation 4.5 as follows:

$$FV = PV \times \left(1 + \frac{r}{m}\right)^{m \times n}$$

*Equation 4.7*

Where  m = the number of compounding periods per year
n = the number of years
r = annual interest rate.

The relationship between interest rates, the number of periods that interest is earned and the future value of one dollar can be shown graphically, as in Figure 4.2.

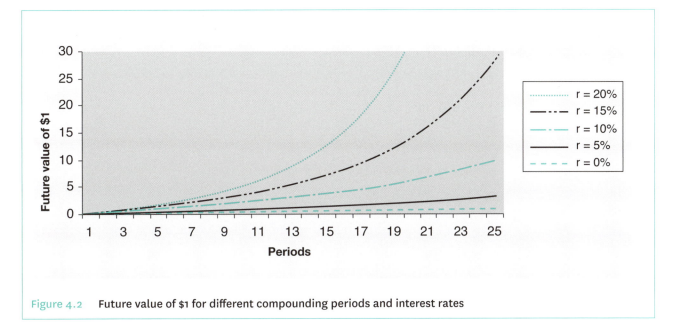

**Figure 4.2**  Future value of $1 for different compounding periods and interest rates

Two clear relationships are noted:
- firstly, the higher the interest rate, the higher the future value
- secondly, as the number of compounding periods increases, the higher the future value.

However, for an interest rate of 0%, the future value always equals the present value.

### Example 9: Frequency of compounding and future value

What is the future value (FV) after six years for $10 000 earning 12% per annum if the funds are compounded:

a quarterly?
b monthly?
c daily?

**Solution**

a $\quad FV = PV \times \left(1 + \dfrac{r}{m}\right)^{m \times n}$

$$FV = \$10\,000 \times \left(1 + \dfrac{0.12}{4}\right)^{4 \times 6}$$

$$= \$10\,000 \; (1.03)^{24}$$

$$= \$10\,000 \times 2.0328$$

$$= \$20\,328$$

b $\quad FV = \$10\,000 \times \left(1 + \dfrac{0.12}{12}\right)^{12 \times 6}$

$$= \$10\,000 \; (1.01)^{72}$$

$$= \$10\,000 \times 2.0471$$

$$= \$20\,471$$

c $\quad FV = \$10\,000 \times \left(1 + \dfrac{0.12}{365}\right)^{365 \times 6}$

$$= \$10\,000 \; (1.000\,328\,77)^{2\,190}$$

$$= \$10\,000 \times 2.0542$$

$$= \$20\,542$$

For a present value (PV) we can similarly adjust Equation 4.6 for different compounding frequencies, as follows:

$$PV = \frac{FV}{\left(1 + \frac{r}{m}\right)^{m \times n}}$$

*Equation 4.8*

### Example 10: Present value with monthly compounding

A tax-refund company offers instant tax-return refunds. If you had a $1 000 tax refund coming from the Inland Revenue (IRD) in three months and were offered an instant tax refund for a $40 dollar fee, would you take it if you could borrow $1 000 at 12%?

**Solution**

First convert the annual interest rate to a monthly rate. Do this by dividing 12% by 12 – the monthly rate is 1%. Then put the figures into Equation 4.8:

$$PV = \frac{FV}{\left(1 + \frac{r}{m}\right)^{m \times n}}$$

$$= \frac{\$1\,000}{\left(1 + \frac{0.12}{12}\right)^{12 \times \frac{3}{12}}}$$

$$= \frac{\$1\,000}{(1.01)^3}$$

$$= \$970.59$$

So your tax refund is worth $970.59 today. If you take the instant refund, you are basically selling the refund today for $960 ($1 000 – $40 = $960). As you are a wise investor, you will probably reject the tax-refund company's offer and wait three months for the $1 000.

Equation 4.8 can also be used to calculate the current value of a zero-coupon bond, as shown in the example on the next page.

> **Example 11: Current value of a zero-coupon bond**
>
> Long-term debt instruments called bonds pay interest payments based on the **coupon** rate, usually on a semi-annual basis, to the lender; whereas a single-payment bond called a **zero-coupon bond** pays no interest during its lifetime. The final repayment for a zero-coupon bond includes the interest payment at **maturity** when the bond is repaid by the borrower. Thus, today's price (i.e. the present value) of a $100 000 zero-coupon bond that has four years to maturity when the market interest rates (market yield) are 9% per annum, compounded semi-annually, can be calculated as:
>
> $$\text{Price} = \frac{FV}{\left(1 + \frac{r}{m}\right)^{m \times n}}$$
>
> $$= \frac{\$100\ 000}{\left(1 + \frac{0.09}{2}\right)^{2 \times 4}}$$
>
> $$= \frac{\$100\ 000}{(1.045)^8}$$
>
> $$= \frac{\$100\ 000}{1.4221}$$
>
> $$= \$70\ 318.54$$

**Coupon**
The interest paid to the holder of a bond, based on a percentage of a bond's face value.

**Zero-coupon bond**
A bond that makes no interest payments during its lifetime. The interest is included with the repayment of principal at maturity.

**Maturity**
The date when a security, for example, a bond, will be redeemed.

## Continuous compounding/discounting

If we increase the frequency of compounding or discounting periods for FV or PV – that is, as m approaches a very large number (infinity) – then FV approaches a limit. This limit is reached when (theoretically) the time intervals between periods reaches zero; that is, compounding and discounting take place continuously.

The general relationship is:

$$FV = PV \times e^{r \times n}$$
$$= PVe^{rn} \qquad \textit{Equation 4.9}$$

where e = a constant (equal to 2.718 281 8). Another common constant is π, which is used in finding the area of a circle.

A quick way of calculating e is to use the exponential key $e^x$ of your calculator and use x = 1 to give 2.718 281 8. The continuously compounded rate of interest (r) is expressed as a decimal, so that 9% becomes 0.09. In reality, no loans or investments are continuously compounded, but the concept is a useful one in theoretical financial models, especially ones involving growth.

> **Example 12: Continuous compounding and future value**

Find the value of an investment of $10 000 if it has continuous compounding of 6% per annum for six years.

**Solution**

$$\begin{aligned} FV &= PVe^{rn} \\ &= \$10\,000e^{0.06 \times 6} \\ &= \$10\,000e^{0.32} \\ &= \$14\,333.29 \end{aligned}$$

# Nominal and effective interest rates

You may have observed that the same annual interest rate produces different future values for different compounding frequencies. If the rate of interest for an investment or a loan is compounded more than once every year, then the quoted **nominal rate** (so called because it includes inflation) does not reflect the actual interest rate received or paid. The **effective rate ($r_e$)** is the true rate that is actually paid or received. Thus, when we include an adjustment for the frequency of compounding, the actual rate of interest on an annual basis is called the *effective annual rate*. In other words, the nominal rate that is the contractual rate charged by the lender or promised by the borrower may be misleading.

There is another interest rate called the **annual percentage rate (APR)** which results when short-term rates are annualised by multiplying the rate per period by the number of periods in a year. For example, 1.5% per month becomes the annualised percentage rate of 18% (1.5 × 12). This is not the actual interest rate as it does not take compounding into consideration.

It is important when comparing loan costs or investment returns over different compounding periods to be aware of nominal versus effective rates. We can alter the nominal percentage rate of interest to an effective rate by using the adjustment to account for non-annual periods from Equation 4.7. The nominal rate equals the effective rate when they both produce the same **rate of return**.

Thus, using the time frame of future value for one year, we have:

$$1 + r_e = \left(1 + \frac{r}{m}\right)^m$$

This equation can be rearranged to become:

$$r_e = \left(1 + \frac{r}{m}\right)^m - 1 \qquad \textit{Equation 4.10}$$

A worked example follows on the next page.

**Nominal rate**
The quoted rate that includes inflation.

**Effective rate ($r_e$)**
The actual rate of interest that includes an adjustment to the nominal rate for the frequency of compounding.

**Annual percentage rate (APR)**
The annualised interest rate that uses simple interest ratios to annualise an interest rate quoted on a fraction of a year.

**Rate of return**
The rate of increase or decrease between the present and future values of an amount over time, normally on an annual basis.

### Example 13: Application of effective interest rate

You have the choice of three accounts. In which of the following would you prefer to invest?
- Account A paying a 9.15% return compounded semi-annually.
- Account B paying a 9.05% return compounded quarterly.
- Account C paying a 9% return compounded daily.

**Solution**

Using $r_e = \left(1 + \dfrac{r}{m}\right)^m - 1$

Account A $\quad r_e = \left(1 + \dfrac{0.0915}{2}\right)^2 - 1$

$\qquad\qquad\quad = (1.04575)^2 - 1$

$\qquad\qquad\quad = 9.36\%$

Account B $\quad r_e = \left(1 + \dfrac{0.0905}{4}\right)^4 - 1$

$\qquad\qquad\quad = (1.022\,625)^4 - 1$

$\qquad\qquad\quad = 9.36\%$

Account C $\quad r_e = \left(1 + \dfrac{0.09}{365}\right)^{365} - 1$

$\qquad\qquad\quad = (1.000\,246\,58)^{365} - 1$

$\qquad\qquad\quad = 9.42\%$

As Account C's effective return is higher, it is the preferred investment.

### Example 14: Effective interest rate

What is the effective annual rate of interest charged on a one-year Mastercard debt if interest is quoted at 21% per annum but calculated on a monthly basis? Note: The 21% is an APR.

**Solution**

$$r_e = \left(1 + \dfrac{r}{m}\right)^m - 1$$

$$r_e = \left(1 + \dfrac{0.21}{12}\right)^{12} - 1$$

$$= (1.0175)^{12} - 1$$

$$= 23.14\% \text{ per annum}$$

## Solving for an unknown interest rate

Sometimes we encounter a situation where we know the present and future values of a sum of money, as well as the time between them, and we need to find out the interest rate that equates the two values. An example could be the zero-coupon bond mentioned earlier. The bond, after being issued by the borrower, is sold in the capital markets and will return a specified amount at maturity. Thus, we can find the implied rate of interest earned when both the PV and FV are known for a defined period of time.

Notice that the interest rate can be solved directly when it involves only the future value and present value of a single payment. There are several ways to solve this problem using a financial calculator. However, solving the problem directly involves the rearrangement of Equation 4.5 so that

$$FV/PV = (1 + r)^n$$

Therefore by taking the nth root of both sides and isolating r, we obtain the expression for r below:

$$r = \left(\frac{FV}{PV}\right)^{1/n} - 1 \qquad \text{Equation 4.11}$$

> **Mathematical hint**
>
>  The $Y^x$ key on an ordinary calculator can be used to find the nth root if there is no $Y^{1/x}$ key. However, any fractional x value should be changed to a decimal before using the $Y^x$ key. For example, 1/4 becomes 0.25.

The rate of return for a single cash flow can be calculated as shown in the example on the next page.

> **Example 15: Rate of return for a single cash flow**
>
> Suppose we know that $1 000 is to be deposited in the bank today and that we will be able to withdraw $1 210 at the end of two years. What rate of return or yield is this account paying?
>
> **Solution**
>
> $$r = \left(\frac{FV}{PV}\right)^{1/n} - 1$$
>
> $$r = \left(\frac{\$1\,210}{\$1\,000}\right)^{1/2} - 1$$
>
> $$= (1.210)^{0.5} - 1$$
>
> $$= 0.10 \text{ or } 10\%$$
>
> Again we use the $Y^x$ key on the calculator with 1/2 expressed as a decimal 0.5.

Example 15 can also be solved using a financial calculator. Remember to clear the calculator first, then enter PV = –1000, FV = 1 210, N = 2, PMT = 0, and press the CPT key followed by the i% key to find the interest rate of 10%. Remember some calculators will need PV or FV to be negative, so PV is negative to represent an outflow.

**Financial calculator solution**

| Inputs: | –1000 | 1210 | 2 | 0 |
|---|---|---|---|---|
| | PV | FV | N | PMT |
| Press: | CPT | i% | | |

Solution: 10%

## Solving for an unknown time period

Occasionally, we want to find the time required for a present sum to grow into a desired future value. Using Equation 4.5 and rearranging to solve for n, we have:

$$n = \frac{\ln(FV/PV)}{\ln(1+r)} \qquad \text{Equation 4.12}$$

Here we say that n is the required time for a present value to grow into a desired future value with a specified interest rate r.

### Example 16: Finding the number of periods n

Assume we have an investment with present value (PV) of $1 000, a future value (FV) of $1 450 and an interest rate (r) of 6% per annum. What length of time will this investment involve?

$$n = \frac{\ln(FV/PV)}{\ln(1+r)}$$

$$n = \frac{\ln(1\,450/1\,000)}{\ln(1+0.06)}$$

$$n = \frac{0.371\,563\,5}{0.058\,268\,9}$$

$$n = 6.38 \text{ years}$$

Example 16 can also be solved using a financial calculator. First remember to clear the calculator. Enter: PV = –1000; FV = 1450; i% = 6; PMT = 0. Then press the compute (CPT or COMP) key followed by the n key to find the period. Remember some calculators will need PV or FV to be negative, so we have made PV –1000 as an outflow.

**Financial calculator solution**

Inputs:  | –1 000 | 1 450 | 6 | 0 |
|---|---|---|---|---|
| | PV | FV | i% | PMT |

Press: | CPT | n |

Solution: 6.38 years

Note that on the calculator there is a key for payments (PMT) during the period. As shown in the solution above, we make PMT zero.

Spreadsheet programs exist for finding interest rates. Following is Example 16 solved using an Excel program.

**Spreadsheet solution**

The number of time periods n can be calculated by using the Excel financial function called NPER. Following the previously described instructions for using $f_x$ and clicking on the NPER financial function, we have the following three-step solution:

= NPER(Rate,Pmt,PV,FV,Type)
= NPER(0.06,0,–1 000,1 450,0)
= 6.38 years

## Conclusion

In this chapter we have introduced the important concept of the time value of money. The key idea is that because we can invest money and receive interest on it, money received today is worth more than the same amount at some future date. Interest is a cost for a borrower and a reward for a lender, and can be calculated in many ways.

First we looked at simple interest that is calculated only on the principal, and then at applications of the simple interest formula. For example, the simple interest formula can be rearranged to find the price of a short-term money market instrument. Next we considered compound interest where interest of one period is added to the principal, and this new total becomes the new principal for the following period. We learned how to calculate future and present values through the use of formulae and a calculator or spreadsheet. Thus, as a consequence of these concepts, we can value cash flows at points in time other than the present.

After considering single payments, we looked at the effect of changing the frequency of compounding and its impact on the future and present values of cash flows and interest rates. Last, we considered how to work out an interest rate when the present and future value is known.

### SELF-TEST QUESTIONS

1. Samantha Wise has $20 000 that she can deposit in any of three banks for a two-year period. Bank A compounds interest on an annual basis; Bank B compounds interest semi-annually (twice a year); and Bank C compounds interest quarterly. All three banks have a quoted annual interest rate of 5%.
   a  What amount would Samantha have at the end of two years, leaving all interest paid on deposit in each bank?
   b  What effective interest rate would she earn at each of the banks?
   c  Based on your findings in a and b, which bank should Samantha deal with? Why?

2. Hamish Hardy has a choice of buying either an investment that offers the cash flows shown in the table alongside, or an investment that offers a lump sum of $2 500 immediately. Assuming a 8% opportunity cost, which investment opportunity would he prefer?

| Year | Cash flow |
|---|---|
| 1 | $1 200 |
| 2 | $ 800 |
| 3 | $ 700 |

### ANSWERS TO SELF-TEST QUESTIONS

1  a  Bank A: $FV_2 = \$20\,000\,(1.05)^2$
            $= \$20\,000\,(1.1025)$
            $= \$22\,050$

      Bank B: $FV_2 = \$20\,000 \left(1 + \dfrac{0.05}{2}\right)^{2 \times 2}$

            $= \$20\,000\,(1.025)^4$
            $= \$20\,000\,(1.10381)$
            $= \$22\,076.26$

Bank C:  $FV_2 = \$20\,000 \left(1 + \dfrac{0.05}{4}\right)^{2 \times 4}$

$= \$20\,000\,(1.0125)^8$
$= \$20\,000\,(1.10448)$
$= \$22\,089.72$

**b** Bank A:  $r_e = \left(1 + \dfrac{0.05}{1}\right)^1 - 1$

$= 1.05 - 1$
$= 5\%$

Bank B:  $r_e = \left(1 + \dfrac{0.05}{2}\right)^2 - 1$

$= (1.025)^2 - 1$
$= 5.06\%$

Bank C:  $r_e = \left(1 + \dfrac{0.05}{4}\right)^4 - 1$

$= (1.0125)^4 - 1$
$= 5.09\%$

**c** Samantha Wise should deal with Bank C: the quarterly compounded interest at 5% will result in the highest future value.

**2** Current value $= \dfrac{1\,200}{(1.08)^1} + \dfrac{800}{(1.08)^2} + \dfrac{700}{(1.08)^3}$

$= \$1\,111.1111 + \dfrac{\$800}{1.1644} + \dfrac{\$700}{1.25971}$

$= \$2\,352.66$

Hamish Hardy would prefer the lump sum of $2 500.

**QUESTIONS AND PROBLEMS**

Note: Assume that interest is compounded if it is not stated. However, when dealing with money market instruments with short-term maturities, interest can be assumed to be simple interest unless otherwise stated.

1. What is the future value of a $2 500 investment if it earns simple interest of 11% for five years?

2. A company borrows $225 000 for 120 days at 8.5% simple interest from the short-term money markets. How much must it repay?

3. Suppose, as a company treasurer, you borrow funds for 90 days with the current market yields at 7.6%, assuming simple interest. At the end of 90 days you have to pay $500 000 to the lender. How much did you actually borrow in the beginning?

4. What is the future value of a $4 500 investment if it earns 8.8% (compounded annually) for three years?

5. If you deposit $3 300 into an account that earns compound interest of 8.2% per annum, how much will you have in total after 2.5 years?

6. As an investor, if you had a choice, would you prefer a shorter or a longer compounding period?

7. If the compound discount rate is 9%, what is the present value of a payment of $11 000 to be received in three years' time?

8. You invest an amount today; that is, a present value. As time goes on, will the amount to be received become larger or smaller?

9. You are expecting a future payment. Will today's value – that is, the present value of this future payment – increase or decrease as time goes on?

10. Calculate today's price of a debt security that does not pay any interest during its term of three years, but at maturity with the principal repays $100 000 with an annual yield of 8.2% (assume compounded).

11. If $7 000 is required in five years from now and money is worth 7% compounded annually, find the present value.

12. What initial outlay will accumulate to $500 000 in 20 years at 9% compounded annually?

13. Find the compounded future amount in each of the following:
    a. $5 000 for two years at 10% per annum compounded semi-annually
    b. $2 300 for one year at 8% per annum compounded quarterly
    c. $1 150 for six months at 11% per annum compounded monthly
    d. $2 000 for one year at 9% per annum compounded daily
    e. $3 000 for 1.5 years at 7.5% per annum compounded monthly
    f. $9 000 for 2.5 years at 12% per annum compounded semi-annually
    g. $10 000 for three years at 8.8% per annum compounded every two months.

14. Find the compound amount when $10 000 is invested at 6% per annum compounded continuously for three years.

15  What is the present value of a payment of $11 000 to be received in four years if the discount rate is:

   a  8%, assuming semi-annual discounting?

   b  8%, assuming monthly discounting?

   c  11%, assuming semi-annual discounting?

   d  11%, assuming monthly discounting?

16  What is the present value of a payment of $12 000 to be received:

   a  in three years?

   b  in ten years, if the discount rate is 7%, and assuming semi-annual discounting?

17  Jane Saver has $10 000 in her savings account at the end of three years. The interest rate is 12% compounded monthly. How much did she deposit in the account three years ago?

18  What principal will accumulate to $7 500 in six years at 9% compounded quarterly?

19  Find the price of a $500 000 zero-coupon bond which has four years to run, when the market yield is 10% per annum compounded semi-annually.

20  David Debtor borrowed some money for five years. When the debt was due, he paid $12 500 for the money borrowed, and the interest charged. The interest rate was 9% compounded quarterly. How much did he borrow?

21  What is the effective rate of interest on a loan if the stated rate is 12% and the principal is compounded monthly?

22  If $1 000 is invested at 8% compounded quarterly for one year, what is the effective rate?

23  Find the effective rate if money invested at 10% is compounded quarterly in the money market.

24  Bank A offers its depositors an interest rate of 7% compounded monthly, while Bank B gives its depositors an interest rate of 7.5%, compounded semi-annually. Which of the two banks makes the better offer?

25  Jessica's goal is to become a millionaire. Today, her portfolio is worth $110 000. If she believes she can get 9% per annum on these funds without adding or withdrawing funds, how long will she have to wait before these funds grow into a million dollars?

26  Lisa examined her first Visa card statement, for February. The statement listed the periodic rate of this month as 1.5%, and the corresponding annual percentage rate as 18%. Calculate her effective annual interest rate.

27  Suppose you can delay your $1 500 tax payment now and pay tax of $1 800 in one year plus a penalty of $50. What interest rate must you earn to make it worthwhile to delay paying your tax for a year?

28  You are offered a choice of receiving $1 500 now, or $2 200 in three years' time. What interest rate would make you indifferent as to whether you chose this present value or the future value?

29  You then negotiate your choice of $2 000 in two years or $1 600 now. What interest rate does this imply? Which would you choose if you can invest at 14% annual interest?

30  You can pay tax of $1 100 now or $1 150 in one month. What interest rate does this choice imply? What choice should you make if you can earn 12% for one year in your savings account?

# CHAPTER 5  Time value of money – Multiple payments

### Learning objectives
By the end of this chapter, you should be able to:
- calculate the future and present value of multiple cash flows
- calculate the present and future values of an ordinary annuity
- calculate the regular payment for an annuity from both present and future values
- value an infinite stream of equal cash flows
- calculate the price of a fixed-interest bond
- prepare a repayment schedule for a reducible loan with annual payments.

## Introduction
In Chapter 4, we considered future and present value problems involving a single cash flow. Most real-world situations will involve many cash flows over time.

## Multiple cash flows
Many investments or loans involve a stream of cash flows occurring at different points in time. These cash flows can be equal, or can be different amounts. In the previous chapter, we explained how to calculate the present and future values of a single amount. Now we show how to calculate the future and present values of more than one cash flow.

### Future value of multiple cash flows
The future value of multiple cash flows is found by summing the individual future value cash flows for different periods.

The future value at time n of a multiple cash flow stream can be shown as:

$$FV = C_1 \times (1 + r)^{n-1} + C_2 \times (1 + r)^{n-2} + \ldots + C_{n-1} \times (1 + r)^1 + C_n \times (1 + r)^0$$

*Equation 5.1*

where  n  = the time period of the future cash flows
$C_1$ = cash flow in year 1, and so on.

It is useful to draw a time line and mark the cash flows on it as a guide. To illustrate what a time line is, consider the following diagram:

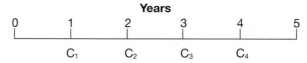

Time 0 represents today; time 1 is one period from today; time 2 is two periods from today; and so on. Note that we usually assume time 1, 2, 3 and so on are end-of-period values; that is, time 1 is at the end of period 1. The cash flows occurring at the end of each period (in this case years) are shown below the line, with positive values indicating cash inflows or cash being received at the end of each year ($1 000 inflow at the end of the first year, $3 000 inflow at the end of the second year, and $2 000 inflow at the end of the third year). Time lines are useful tools to visualise cash flows being received (positive cash inflows) or paid out (negative cash outflows). So for problems to find the value of a series of cash flows at some future time, calculate the future value of each cash flow and then sum all of these cash flows for the answer.

Example 1 on the next page shows how to calculate the future value of multiple cash flows.

## Present value of multiple cash flows

We can calculate the present value of a series of cash flows to be received in the future by summing the present value of each cash flow. The following formula solves for the present value of a stream of cash flows.

$$PV = \frac{C_1}{(1+r)^1} + \frac{C_2}{(1+r)^2} + \ldots + \frac{C_n}{(1+r)^n} \qquad \text{Equation 5.2}$$

or

$$PV = \sum_{t=1}^{n} \frac{C_t}{(1+r)^t}$$

The symbol $\Sigma$ stands for 'sigma' and is a mathematical symbol meaning 'to find the sum of' (in this case) n terms beginning with the first term when $t = 1$.

When dealing with present value problems, we often refer to r as a discount rate, where r can be used to represent rates such as market interest rates or the opportunity cost of funds.

Example 2 shows how to calculate the present value of multiple cash flows.

> **Example 1: Future value of multiple cash flows**

Suppose you are saving for a holiday in five years, and you save $1 000 at the end of year 1, $3 000 at the end of year 2, $2 000 at the end of year 3, and $1 500 at the end of the fourth year. What will the account balance be at the end of year 5 if you can earn 5% per annum over the period?

First, draw a time line to help visualise the cash flows. As the time line shows, we grow the cash deposit by the interest rate to the future date. So using Equation 4.5, $FV = PV(1+r)^n$, we work out each deposit as a lump-sum payment and then simply add the four different deposits (with their accumulated interest) to the end of the fifth year. This way we bring the different cash deposits to the same point in time.

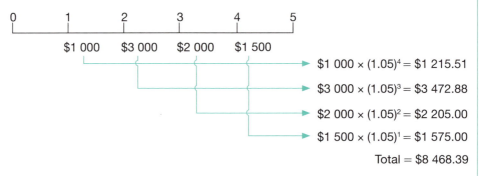

FV of cash flow for year 1 = $1 000 × $(1.05)^4$ = $1 215.51
FV of cash flow for year 2 = $3 000 × $(1.05)^3$ = $3 472.88
FV of cash flow for year 3 = $2 000 × $(1.05)^2$ = $2 205.00
FV of cash flow for year 4 = $1 500 × $(1.05)^1$ = $1 575.00
Total = $8 468.39

By looking at the time line closely, we can see that the first deposit earns interest over four years, the second deposit earns interest over three years, the third deposit earns interest over two years, and the last deposit earns interest for one year. Then we value all of the deposits as future dollars at the end of the fifth year and can sum all the multiple cash flows to that point.

> **Example 2: Present value of multiple cash flows**
>
> Find the present value of the following cash flow stream where r equals 8%. Assume year-end cash flows.
>
> | Year | Cash flow |
> |---|---|
> | 1 | $ 500 |
> | 2 | $ 700 |
> | 3 | $11 000 |
>
> **Solution**
>
> Draw a time line and note the number of years each cash flow is discounted. These become the power for the relevant cash flow.
>
> ```
>   0      1      2       3      4      5
>   |      |      |       |      |      |
>        $500   $700   $11 000
> ```
>
> $500 × 1/1.08
>
> $700 × 1/(1.08)$^2$
>
> $11 000 × 1/(1.08)$^3$
>
> $$PV = \frac{C_1}{(1+r)^1} + \frac{C_2}{(1+r)^2} + \ldots + \frac{C_n}{(1+r)^n}$$
>
> $$PV = \frac{\$500}{(1+0.08)^1} + \frac{\$700}{(1+0.08)^2} + \frac{\$11\,000}{(1+0.08)^3}$$
>
> $= \$500 \times (1.08)^{-1} + \$700 \times (1.08)^{-2} + \$11\,000 \times (1.08)^{-3}$
>
> $= \$500 \times (0.92593) + \$700 \times (0.85734) + \$11\,000 \times (0.79383)$
>
> $= \$462.96 + \$600.14 + \$8\,732.13$
>
> $= \$9\,795.23$
>
> The amount of $9 795.23 is the maximum price you should be willing to pay in order to receive these cash flows.

# Level cash flows: Annuities and perpetuities

Often we have a series of periodic payments or receipts, usually made in equal amounts, called an **annuity**. Examples include insurance premiums, rent and most loan repayments, such as hire purchases or mortgages. Originally, the term 'annuity' referred to annual payments, but now it applies to payment intervals of any length of time.

There are two basic types of annuity. When an annuity payment occurs at the end of each period, it is referred to as an **ordinary annuity**. An ordinary annuity

> **Annuity**
> A regular stream of payments over a fixed time.
>
> **Ordinary annuity**
> An annuity with a first payment that occurs one period hence. Sometimes referred to as a simple annuity or an annuity in arrears.

is a series of regular payments that are made at the end of each annuity period. For example, we might be depositing an equal sum of money at the end of each year in order to buy a new car. So we would need to know how much our savings have grown by some date in the future.

An **annuity due** is less common – it differs in that its payments occur at the beginning of each period. Sometimes an annuity due may have an additional payment. Examples are lease payments and rent. In addition, because an annuity due provides the payments at an earlier stage, i.e. at the beginning of the period, it has a larger present value than an ordinary annuity. However, in this book, we mainly consider ordinary annuities.

The **term** of an ordinary annuity is equal to the number of payments over its lifetime. This is found by counting the number of payments over the period. For example, a two-year loan with fortnightly payments is a 52-period annuity.

Future amounts (compounding) and present amounts (discounting) for annuities can be calculated by the methods already discussed in the previous chapter. The amount of the annuity is found by summing the compound amounts of the individual periodic payments. However, this can be time-consuming, so modified formulae have been developed and will be covered in this chapter.

> **Annuity due**
> An annuity with a payment made immediately; that is, the first payment is at time zero.
>
> **Term**
> The time between the beginning of an annuity's first payment and the end of its last payment.

### Future value of an annuity

The future value of an ordinary annuity is the sum of the regular payments and the interest that has been paid on each payment. To illustrate the calculation of the future value of an ordinary annuity, we set up a four-year annuity with $1 payments. These are drawn on the time line below:

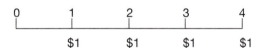

The future value of an annuity is the sum of the future value of each annuity payment where each payment is compounded according to the period in which it falls. Thus, the future value of the annuity at the end of year 4, as shown in the above time line, could be calculated as the sum of the following quantities:

First dollar = $1(1 + r)^3$
Second dollar = $1(1 + r)^2$
Third dollar = $1(1 + r)^1$
Fourth dollar = $1(1 + r)^0 = 1$

The first dollar is compounded forward by three periods, because only three periods will occur after the first payment is made. Similarly, the second dollar is compounded forward only two periods, and the third by one period. The final fourth dollar payment is made when the annuity finishes at the end of year 4 and is included in the sum. This process of finding individual sums for each annuity payment is unwieldy, and so a formula for finding the future value of an ordinary annuity has been derived algebraically from the sum of a geometric series.

For an ordinary annuity of regular payments (PMT) for n number of annuity periods and an interest rate of r% per annum, the future value of an annuity (FVA) is given by:

$$FVA = PMT \left[ \frac{(1+r)^n - 1}{r} \right]$$

*Equation 5.3*

Using the previous example, and assuming that the interest rate of 5% per annum remains constant over the period, the future value of an ordinary annuity of $1 payments at the end of each of the next four periods is found by:

$$FVA = PMT \left[\frac{(1+r)^n - 1}{r}\right]$$

$$FVA = \$1 \left[\frac{(1+0.05)^4 - 1}{0.05}\right]$$

$$= \$1 \left[\frac{1.21551 - 1}{0.05}\right]$$

$$= \$1 \left[\frac{0.21551}{0.05}\right]$$

$$= \$4.31$$

**Example 3: Future value of an annuity**

If we deposit $1 250 in a bank at the end of each year for the next five years, and assuming that we earn 7% per annum over the period, how much will we have saved – including interest – by the end of year 5?

**Solution**

$$FVA = PMT \left[\frac{(1+r)^n - 1}{r}\right]$$

$$FVA = \$1\,250 \left[\frac{(1+0.07)^5 - 1}{0.07}\right]$$

$$= \$1\,250 \left[\frac{1.402552 - 1}{0.07}\right]$$

$$= \$1\,250 \left[\frac{0.402552}{0.07}\right]$$

$$= \$1\,250 \times 5.75074$$

$$= \$7\,188.42$$

Example 3 of the future value of an annuity can be solved using a financial calculator. In addition to previously used keys, the key PMT is used for ordinary annuities. As before, first make sure to clear the calculator. Enter –1 250 and press the PMT key, enter 7 and press i%, then enter 5 and press the N key and then enter 0 for PV. Finally, press the CPT (or COMP) key followed by the FV key to find the FVA of $7 188.42. Because this example involves a periodic outflow of $1 250, most calculators will need the payment to be entered as a negative number to solve for a positive FVA.

**Financial calculator solution**

| Inputs: | −1250 | 7 | 5 | 0 |
|---|---|---|---|---|
| | PMT | i% | N | PV |
| Press: | CPT | FV | | |
| Solution: | $7 188.42 | | | |

Note that for this case the PV is 0.

Spreadsheet programs exist for calculating the future value of an annuity. Following is Example 3 of an ordinary annuity solved using an Excel spreadsheet program and its function $f_x$.

**Spreadsheet solution**

We solve for the future value of an annuity as follows:

= FV(Rate,Nper,Pmt,PV,Type)
= FV(0.07,5,−1250,0,0)
= $7 188.42

| | A | B |
|---|---|---|
| 1 | Use *fx* to find future value of an ordinary annuity | |
| 2 | Rate | 0.07 |
| 3 | Nper | 5 |
| 4 | Pmt | -1250 |
| 5 | Pv | 0 |
| 6 | Type | 0 |
| 7 | Fv | $7,188.42 |

B7   $f_x$   =FV(0.07,5,-1250,0,0)

### Present value and annuities

Recall from the previous chapter that the present value of a future payment is calculated by discounting (i.e. dividing) the payment by its interest factor. Thus, as for the future value of an annuity, the present value of an ordinary annuity can be found by discounting each payment by its interest factor and summing these present values. Again, the process is laborious and is usually done by using a formula, a financial calculator or an Excel spreadsheet.

The present value of an annuity (PVA) for an ordinary annuity of regular payments (PMT) for n number of annuity periods using an interest rate of r% per annum is given by the expression:

$$PVA = PMT \left[ \frac{1 - (1+r)^{-n}}{r} \right]$$

*Equation 5.4*

where the term inside the square brackets is the present value factor for an ordinary annuity (PVIFA$_{r,n}$). The term outside the brackets is the regular payment PMT.

If a financial asset promises to pay regular cash flows at the end of n future years, then the present value of these annuity payments represents its market price from the point of view of the investor. In the United States, many retired people buy annuities from insurance companies as a way of having a steady income payment.

### Example 4: Present value of an annuity

A company offers you an annuity that will pay you $5 000 per year for the next ten years. Assuming that interest rates over the period will average 9% per annum, how much would you expect to pay for the annuity?

**Solution**

$$PVA = PMT \left[ \frac{1 - (1 + r)^{-n}}{r} \right]$$

$$PVA = \$5\,000 \left[ \frac{1 - (1 + 0.09)^{-10}}{0.09} \right]$$

$$= \$5\,000 \left[ \frac{1 - 0.42241}{0.09} \right]$$

$$= \$5\,000 \left( \frac{0.57759}{0.09} \right)$$

$$= \$5\,000 \times 6.417676$$

$$= \$32\,088.29$$

Example 4 of the present value of an annuity can also be solved using a financial calculator. The result for the ten-year PVA annuity can be verified. Enter –5000 and press the PMT key. Enter 9 and press i%, then enter 10 and press the N key. Enter 0 for FV. Finally, press the CPT (or COMP) key followed by the PV key to find the PVA of $32 088.29. Since this example involves a periodic outflow of $5 000, most calculators will need the payment to be entered as a negative number to solve for a positive PVA. If you omit the negative sign, then the PV appears as –32 088.29.

**Financial calculator solution**

| | | | | |
|---|---|---|---|---|
| Inputs: | –5 000 | 9 | 10 | 0 |
| | PMT | i% | N | FV |
| Press: | CPT | PV | | |
| Solution: | $32 088.29 | | | |

Spreadsheet programs exist for finding present value of an annuity. Following is Example 4 solved using an Excel spreadsheet program.

**Spreadsheet solution**

Using the previously described present value financial function $f_x$ of Excel, we have:

$$= PV(Rate, Nper, Pmt, FV, Type)$$
$$= PV(0.09, 10, -5\,000, 0, 0)$$
$$= \$32\,088.29$$

> **Example 5: Future value of an annuity**
>
> Suppose an investor invests $1 200 for the next six years in order to provide themselves with some funds. Assuming that they can invest their funds at 8% per annum compounded annually:
>
> a how much will they have at the end of six years?
>
> b how much would they have to invest in one lump sum now to build up these funds in six years?
>
> **Solution**
>
> a The future value can be calculated as:
>
> $$FVA = PMT \left[ \frac{(1+r)^n - 1}{r} \right]$$
>
> $$FVA = \$1\,200 \left[ \frac{(1+0.08)^6 - 1}{0.08} \right]$$
>
> $$= \$1\,200 \left[ \frac{1.58687 - 1}{0.08} \right]$$
>
> $$= \$1\,200 \left( \frac{0.58687}{0.08} \right)$$
>
> $$= \$1\,200 \times 7.33593$$
>
> $$= \$8\,803.11$$
>
> b The present value of the lump sum required to be invested now is found by discounting the lump sum to be received at the end of six years:
>
> $$PV = \frac{\$8\,803.11}{(1.08)^6}$$
>
> $$= \$5\,547.45$$
>
> Note: An alternative way of finding the present value is by calculating the present value of an annuity as follows:
>
> $$PVA = PMT \left[ \frac{1 - (1+r)^{-n}}{r} \right]$$
>
> $$PVA = \$1\,200 \left[ \frac{1 - (1+0.08)^{-6}}{0.08} \right]$$
>
> $$= \$1\,200 \left( \frac{0.36983}{0.08} \right)$$
>
> $$= \$1\,200 \times 4.62288$$
>
> $$= \$5\,547.45$$

# Finding the amount of a regular payment

If a future value and regular payments are required, the regular payment (PMT) for an annuity can be calculated by simply rearranging Equation 5.3.

### Example 6: Annual payment

You may decide to set yourself a goal to save $9 000 in four years (i.e. an FV), and will do so by saving regular amounts at an interest rate of 8% per annum compounded annually. If equal payments are made at the end of each year, how much should you invest at the end of each year to reach your target?

**Solution**

In order to perform the required calculations, use Equation 5.3, the future value of an annuity formula.

$$FVA = PMT \left[ \frac{(1+r)^n - 1}{r} \right]$$

is rearranged to become:

$$PMT = \frac{FVA}{\frac{(1+r)^n - 1}{r}} = \frac{FVA \times r}{(1+r)^n - 1} \qquad \textit{Equation 5.5}$$

Therefore:

$$PMT = \frac{\$9\,000 \times 0.08}{(1 + 0.08)^4 - 1}$$

$$= \frac{\$720}{0.360488}$$

$$= \$1\,997.29$$

Example 6 of the annual payments for an ordinary annuity can be verified by using a financial calculator. As before, make sure you clear the calculator. Enter 8 and press i%, then enter 4 and press the N key. Enter 0 for PV, then enter –9000 and press the FV key. Finally, press the CPT (or COMP) key followed by the PMT key to find $1 997.29.

Since this example involves a periodic outflow of $1 997.29, most calculators will need the payment to be entered as a negative number to solve for a positive PMT.

**Financial calculator solution**

| | | | | |
|---|---|---|---|---|
| Inputs: | 8 | 4 | 0 | –9 000 |
| | i% | N | PV | FV |
| Press: | CPT | PMT | | |
| Solution: | $1 997.29 | | | |

Spreadsheet programs exist for finding annual payments of an annuity. Following is the same Example 6 solved using an Excel spreadsheet program.

> **Spreadsheet solution**
> Using the previously described financial function $f_x$ of Excel, we have:
> $$= \text{PMT(Rate,Nper,PV,FV,Type)}$$
> $$= \text{PMT}(0.08, 4, 0, -9000, 0)$$
> $$= \$1\,997.29$$

If instead you have a sum invested (PV) in the bank and need to make regular withdrawals from it for a set period of time, Equation 5.4 will have to be rearranged in order to calculate the amount of regular withdrawals to be made.

### Example 7: Payments for an annuity

Suppose you are beginning your four-year university degree with $25 000 in the bank. If you can invest your funds at 9% per annum, how much money can be withdrawn each year to provide for living expenses without exhausting your funds before you finish your studies?

**Solution**
In order to perform these calculations, Equation 5.4

$$\text{PVA} = \text{PMT}\left[\frac{1 - (1 + r)^{-n}}{r}\right]$$

is rearranged to become:

$$\text{PMT} = \frac{\text{PVA}}{\frac{1 - (1 + r)^{-n}}{r}} = \frac{\text{PVA} \times r}{1 - (1 + r)^{-n}} \qquad \textit{Equation 5.6}$$

where PVA = the sum invested today.

Therefore:
$$\text{PMT} = \frac{\$25\,000 \times 0.09}{1 - (1 + 0.09)^{-4}}$$
$$= \frac{\$2\,250}{1 - 0.70843}$$
$$= \frac{\$2\,250}{0.291574}$$
$$= \$7\,716.72 \text{ per annum}$$

This annuity payment involving a present value amount can be solved by a financial calculator or the financial function in a spreadsheet. The financial function ($f_x$) of a spreadsheet would be as follows:

$$= \text{PMT(Rate,Nper,PV,FV,Type)}$$
$$= \text{PMT}(0.09, 4, -25000, 0, 0)$$
$$= \$7\,716.72$$

## Annuity due

There are a few annuities that have payment due at the beginning of the time period. For example, when someone rents a house, the rental payment is generally due at the beginning (a pre-payment). For annuity due, the ordinary annuity formulae are modified by a factor $(1 + r)$. For example, the future value of annuity Equation 5.3 becomes:

$$\text{FV Annuity due} = \text{PMT} \left[ \frac{(1+r)^n - 1}{r} \right] (1+r)$$

*Equation 5.7*

The $(1 + r)$ effectively compounds each payment by one more year to reflect payments starting at the beginning of each period.

The present value annuity Equation 5.4 becomes:

$$\text{PV Annuity due} = \text{PMT} \left[ \frac{1 - (1+r)^{-n}}{r} \right] (1+r)$$

*Equation 5.8*

Recall Example 3, which involved a five-year annuity, annual payments of $1 250 and a 7% interest rate. Now, let's assume all payments are made at the beginning of the year, with the first payment made at the start of the first year – that is, time 0. So:

$$\text{FVA annuity due} = \text{PMT} \left[ \frac{(1+r)^n - 1}{r} \right] (1+r)$$

$$\text{FVA due} = 1250 \left[ \frac{(1+0.07)^5 - 1}{0.07} \right] (1.07)$$

$$= 1250 \left[ \frac{0.402552}{0.07} \right] (1.07)$$

$$= \$7\,691.61$$

Annuity due problems may also be solved with financial calculators. Most financial calculators have a DUE key (or a switch, for example, BGN) for shifting payments from the end of time periods to the beginning of time periods.

We now alter the previous example to become a future value of an annuity due, solved using a financial calculator. So we use the PMT key for ordinary annuities, and the key for annuity due. Enter –1250 (depending on the calculator) and press the PMT key, then enter 7 and press i%. Enter 5 and press the N key, then enter 0 for PV. Next press the DUE (or BGN) key, followed by the FV key to find the FVA of $7 691.61.

Since this example involves a periodic outflow of $1 250, most calculators will need the payment to be entered as a negative number to solve for a positive FVA due.

**Financial calculator solution**

Inputs:   −1250   7   5   0
          PMT    i%   N   PV

Press:    BGN    FV

Solution: $7 691.61

Spreadsheet programs exist for calculating the future value of an annuity. Following is the example solved using an Excel spreadsheet program.

**Spreadsheet solution**

The future value of annuity due $FVA_{due}$ is solved using Excel's financial function (FV) and adjusting for when the cash flows occur, as follows:

$$= FV(Rate, Nper, Pmt, PV, Type)$$
$$= FV(7\%, 5, -1\,250, 0, 1)$$
$$= \$7\,691.61$$

This time, the Type value was given a 1 to show that cash flows now occur at the beginning of the period; previously, we have used a 0 value to show end of period cash flows.

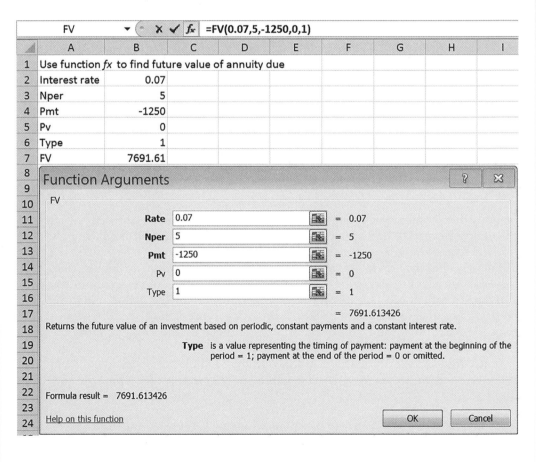

## Perpetuities

Annuity formulae are useful for many cash flow streams. The ultimate annuity carries forever. An infinite stream of cash flow is called a **perpetuity**. For example, the British Government issued securities called Consuls, the first being in 1751, that pay interest payments forever and which provide the holder with a stream of equal cash flows to infinity. Note that the symbol for infinity is ∞.

> **Perpetuity**
> A security that promises regular cash flows forever.

Interestingly, the concept of valuing each cash flow and then summing them is made simpler when an infinite stream of payments is considered. For example, if we assume that the first interest payment of the perpetuity occurs one year from now, then the present value of the perpetuity paying the cash flow amount $C each period at an interest rate of r% per period is:

$$PV = \frac{C}{(1+r)} + \frac{C}{(1+r)^2} + \ldots + \frac{C}{(1+r)^\infty}$$

However, this infinite series of payments can be reduced by algebraic manipulation to:

$$PV = \frac{C_1}{r} \qquad \textit{Equation 5.9}$$

This formula gives the present value of a perpetuity one period before the first payment, so that in order to find the present value of a perpetuity at time $t = 0$ it is assumed that the first payment will occur at time $t = 1$. It is interesting to note that the present value of a perpetuity is a simplified case of annuities.

---

**Example 8: Present value of a perpetuity**

Find the present value of an investment that promises to pay you $1 750 at the end of every year forever, when the interest rate is 11%.

**Solution**

$$PV = \frac{C_1}{r}$$

$$PV = \frac{\$1\ 750}{0.11}$$

$$= \$15\ 909.09$$

---

We can extend the idea of a perpetuity with a constant payment to one that will grow at a rate (g) indefinitely. For a constant payment that continues indefinitely and grows at a proportionate rate, the formula for the present value of a growing perpetuity can be derived as:

$$PV = \frac{C_1}{r-g} \qquad \textit{Equation 5.10}$$

where     r = discount rate and g = growth rate.

So a growing perpetuity is a stream of level cash flows, and its value is found by the value of the cash flow at the end of the first period divided by the difference between the discount rate and the growth rate. Note that the discount rate must be higher than the growth rate to use this formula.

For example, when a property investor buys a building and receives rents that grow at a fixed percentage each year, the current value of these future payments can be found using the growing perpetuity formula.

> **Example 9: Present value of a growing perpetuity**
>
> A property investor buys a commercial building that will pay him $10 000 rental cash flow at the end of the first year. The rental cash flow is then expected to grow at a constant rate of 2% per year thereafter. If the discount rate is 10%, find the present value of this growing perpetuity.
>
> **Solution**
>
> $$PV = \frac{C_1}{r - g}$$
> $$PV = \frac{10\,000}{0.10 - 0.02}$$
> $$= \$125\,000$$

## Asset valuation: Capitalisation method of property valuation

The **capitalisation approach** for the valuation of property assumes a property's net operating income continues into perpetuity. This approach is used to estimate both the value of a property to an individual investor ('subjective' value) and also the value in the market, i.e. an estimate of a property's 'objective' value.

When undertaking an objective valuation, the intention is to estimate how a 'typical purchaser' may value the property. For income producing properties, such as commercial, industrial and specialist residential rental properties (that are not able to be owner-occupied), the **capitalisation rate** approach is appropriate.

The calculation is performed by dividing **net operating income** (before debt servicing and taxes) by the required rate of return, which is referred to as the capitalisation rate or (often in industry) as just the 'cap rate'. The income to be capitalised excludes financing costs, such as the principal and the interest costs of debt, as well as taxes, as both financing and taxes are specific to an investor rather than to the property itself.

> **Capitalisation approach**
> Valuation method for determining property value by dividing income by the capitalisation rate.
>
> **Capitalisation rate**
> Yield-based rate used to estimate property value in the capitalisation approach.
>
> **Net operating income**
> Rental or lease income less relevant expenses (before debt servicing and taxes).

$$\text{Capitalisation rate valuation} = V = \frac{\text{Net operating income}}{r}$$

*Equation 5.11*

where

$V$ = value of property

$r$ = required rate of return (or capitalisation rate)

Net operating income = rental or lease income less relevant expenses (before debt servicing and taxes).

Investors may also wish to know what 'cap rate' properties have sold for in order to understand current return yields on different types of property investment, as a check of the objective valuation as evidenced by market transactions. Equation 5.11 can be rearranged to solve for the required rate of return as follows:

$$r = \frac{\text{Net operating income}}{V}$$

Equation 5.12

### Example 10: Capitalisation of income method

A property has a net income of $62 400 per annum before debt servicing costs and taxes and has a required rate of return of 6.5%. To estimate the property's subjective value, assuming the income continues each year thereafter, we would calculate:

$$V = \frac{\text{Net operating income}}{r}$$
$$= \frac{\$62\,400}{0.065}$$
$$= \$960\,000$$

This tells the investor that if they purchased the property for $960 000 and the income remained at $62 400 per annum, they would receive a 6.5% income return before their specific financing and tax costs.

Alternatively, the investor may wish to know their return each year should they pay $960 000 for the property. In which case, we would use Equation 5.12 to solve for r as follows:

$$\text{Capitalisation rate} = r = \frac{\text{Net operating income}}{V}$$
$$= \frac{\$62\,400}{\$960\,000}$$
$$= 0.065 \text{ or } 6.5\%$$

Although used in practice, this subjective valuation approach is limited as it does not allow for change to net income over time; however, it can be used as a rough 'rule of thumb' valuation technique. When calculating 'objective' capitalisation rates from market transactions, the capitalisation rate will reflect the factors considered by the parties when agreeing to the price, such as potential income growth and asset risk. We will explore other property return and evaluation techniques in Chapter 13.

Note that for residential properties a 'typical purchaser' may wish to occupy, a different valuation methodology is normally adopted.

# Asset valuation: Calculating the price of a bond

We can use the annuity formula to calculate the price of a bond. As discussed earlier (in Chapter 1), governments and large companies issue bonds to raise considerable amounts of money. A bond is a long-term debt instrument that pays regular coupon interest payments, usually every six months (semi-annually), to the lender. The principal or amount lent to the borrower will be repaid at a specified time in the future when the bond matures. We can price a bond by finding the present value of its coupon payments and the principal amount to be repaid at the **maturity date**. The normal practice in New Zealand is to base bond price calculations on a **par** or **face value** of $100 for the bond. In other countries, generally a par or face value of $1 000 is used. Therefore, in the case of a large company that raises $100 million in New Zealand by issuing three-year bonds that offer an annual coupon interest rate of 9% per annum, this means that once a year, for three years, the company will pay bond investors some multiple of the basic coupon payments of $9 (9% of $100). Then, at maturity, the company will repay the principal of $100 plus the last coupon of $9 to the bond holder. These cash flows are shown on the following time line.

> **Maturity date**
> The date at which the last bond payment is due.
>
> **Par value**
> The face value on a bond, usually $1 000 in the United States and $100 in New Zealand. The face value is normally equal to the maturity value.
>
> **Face value**
> The maturity value of a bond, usually the principal, that is repaid to the lender.

Therefore, the current price of a bond equals the sum of the present value of the future payments that the issuer is obliged to make until the bond matures. Using the previous example of the three-year, 9%-per-annum coupon interest rate bond, the value of the future three annual coupon payments and the principal can be discounted to a current value using an interest rate or a required return that depends on economic conditions such as current interest rates and various risks; for example, the risk that a company may default on its interest payments. The equation used to calculate the price (P) of a bond is shown below:

$$P = PMT \left[ \frac{1 - (1 + r)^{-n}}{r} \right] + \frac{F}{(1 + r)^n}$$

*Equation 5.13*

where    $r =$ the annual yield when the bond is bought
   $PMT =$ the coupon payment
   $n =$ the number of coupon periods remaining
   $F =$ the par or face value (usually $100 in New Zealand).

The coupon payments form an annuity and are represented by the first part of the formula, whereas the principal value is represented by the second part. It should be noted that the coupon rate (PMT) and the face value (F) of $100 are fixed and any variation in the bond's price depends on r and n. Often r is called 'the required return' by bond investors who want the interest rate to compensate them for a variety of risks. For this reason, they use the current market rates for bonds of similar risk and maturity as an investment guide.

> **Example 11: Basic bond valuation**
>
> Using Equation 5.13, we can work out the value for a three-year bond with a coupon interest rate of 9% per annum and a par value of $100 issued by a large New Zealand company when bond investors require a 9% return for current market conditions. Its value is:
>
> $$P = \text{PMT}\left[\frac{1-(1+r)^{-n}}{r}\right] + \frac{100}{(1+r)^n}$$
>
> $$P = \$9\left[\frac{1-(1.09)^{-3}}{0.09}\right] + \frac{100}{(1.09)^3}$$
>
> $$P = \$9\left[\frac{1-0.77218}{0.09}\right] + \frac{100}{1.29503}$$
>
> $$P = \$9\left[\frac{0.22781}{0.09}\right] + 77.21835$$
>
> $$= 9(2.53129) + 77.21835$$
>
> $$= 22.78165 + 77.21835$$
>
> $$= \$100$$
>
> This bond has a value of $100, and the calculation illustrates that its value will always be at par or face value when the bond's coupon rate equals the interest rate required by bond investors or by the current market environment.

However, the value of a bond is seldom equal to its par value over its lifetime, since a variety of factors – mainly the behaviour of interest rates, as previously mentioned – will cause bond prices to vary. This means that any bond holder who sells (buys) before a bond matures will face either a capital gain or a loss, depending on interest rate movements.

> **Example 12: Current price of a bond after an increase in interest rates**
>
> A bond investor who requires a 10% return is considering buying a 9%-per-annum coupon bond with a $100 face value, with two years to maturity. Using Equation 5.13, its value is given by:
>
> $$P = PMT \left[ \frac{1 - (1 + r)^{-n}}{r} \right] + \frac{100}{(1 + r)^n}$$
>
> $$P = \$9 \left[ \frac{1 - (1.10)^{-2}}{0.10} \right] + \frac{100}{(1.10)^2}$$
>
> $$P = \$9 \left[ \frac{1 - 0.82645}{0.10} \right] + \frac{100}{1.21}$$
>
> $$P = \$9 \left[ \frac{0.17355}{0.10} \right] + 82.64463$$
>
> $$= 9(1.73554) + 82.64463$$
>
> $$= 15.61983 + 82.64463$$
>
> $$= \$98.26$$
>
> At a 10% required return, the bond should sell at a discount to its face value. This reflects that its price has to drop in order for a potential investor to obtain their required return.

The example on the next page demonstrates what happens to the price of a bond when market interest rates fall below its coupon rate.

> **Example 13: Current price of a bond after a decrease in interest rates**
>
> A bond investor is considering buying a three-year bond with a 9%-per-annum coupon interest rate when comparable market instruments are yielding a 7.5% return for investors. Assuming the bond has a face value of $100 and using Equation 5.13, its price is given by:
>
> $$P = PMT\left[\frac{1-(1+r)^{-n}}{r}\right] + \frac{100}{(1+r)^n}$$
>
> $$P = \$9\left[\frac{1-(1.075)^{-3}}{0.075}\right] + \frac{100}{(1.075)^3}$$
>
> $$P = \$9\left[\frac{1-0.80496}{0.075}\right] + \frac{100}{1.24230}$$
>
> $$P = \$9\left[\frac{0.19504}{0.075}\right] + 80.49606$$
>
> $$= 9(2.60052) + 80.49606$$
>
> $$= 23.40473 + 80.49606$$
>
> $$= \$103.90$$
>
> This means that the bond's price is at a premium to its face value. This reflects that its coupon interest rate is above comparable market interest rates and any potential bond investor will need to pay a higher price to obtain the higher coupon rate.

Lastly, we consider how we adjust Equation 5.13 in order to find the price of a bond when there are semi-annual coupon payments, the common payment method for most bonds.

> **Example 14: Current price of a bond with semi-annual coupon payments**
>
> A bond holder is considering selling her 10%-per-annum coupon interest rate three-year bond of $100 par value that pays interest semi-annually at a time when bond investors require 8% per annum. This means the bond issuer will pay the bond holder coupon payments of $5 ($10 divided by two) every six months, making a total of six payments over the three years. The price of the bond can be found using a discount interest rate of 4% (8% divided by two to match the semi-annual payments):

$$P = PMT\left[\frac{1-(1+r)^{-n}}{r}\right] + \frac{100}{(1+r)^n}$$

$$P = \$5\left[\frac{1-(1.04)^{-6}}{0.04}\right] + \frac{100}{(1.04)^6}$$

$$P = \$5\left[\frac{1-0.79031}{0.04}\right] + \frac{100}{1.26532}$$

$$P = \$5\left[\frac{0.20969}{0.04}\right] + 79.03145$$

$$= 5(5.24214) + 79.03145$$

$$= 26.21068 + 79.03145$$

$$= \$105.24$$

This bond investor will make a capital gain as the bond is at a premium. It should be noted that its price is at a slighter higher premium than if it had annual coupons (for annual coupons its price is $105.15), because the semi-annual coupons mean that investors receive interest every six months rather than at the end of each year.

## Loan types

Another application of annuity formulae is for loans. There are several different types of loan. For example, an interest-only loan can either require the borrower to make interest payments over the term of the loan and at the end of the loan period repay the principal, or require the borrower to repay the loan, together with all the interest accrued, at the end of the period.

Another type of loan, sometimes called a table loan, is where principal repayments are made concurrently with the interest payments. This process, where the total amount of the loan and the interest due on it is discharged by a series of payments, is called **amortisation**. In other words, the total amount of the loan is said to be amortised over the lifetime of the loan, with the borrower making regular payments. These payments consist of the interest due since the last payment and a principal component that reduces the outstanding principal. Hence, a proportion of the outstanding principal is being repaid with each payment.

At the beginning of the loan, if it is a long-term one, the interest component makes up virtually all of the regular payment. However, over time, the interest segment decreases because the repayment of the principal reduces the amount owing and hence the amount of interest due. Therefore, at the beginning of the loan, the principal component of the regular payment is small and the interest segment large, but, over time, as the interest component falls, money is freed up to pay larger amounts off the principal. Interest rates for loans can be fixed for the life of the loan or be floating, where the rate may be adjusted after a stated period if the reference interest rate has changed.

Housing loans are typically drawn up as table loans and the payments are usually made monthly. However, in this book we will simplify the calculations by *assuming annual payments*. Such payments are usually made over a long period, say 30 years. If the interest rates don't change over the period, the regular payments will remain unaltered over the term. The majority of home loans are mortgages,

**Amortisation**
Process of discharging a debt by a set of regular and equal or unequal payments that include the amount borrowed and interest owing.

with the security for the loan being the property it finances. In this way, the lender can sell the property if the borrower defaults on the payments.

By undertaking to pay regular payments to the lender, the borrower is, in effect, selling an annuity to the lender. The price that the lender will pay for the annuity is its present value. Hence, the present value of the loan repayments will equal the principal, or capital, amount due. The regular payment is found by using Equation 5.6.

$$PMT = \frac{PVA \times r}{1 - (1 + r)^{-n}}$$

If the interest rate is fixed over the lifetime of the loan, the borrower will repay the loan by making the regular payments that include both interest and principal by the stated dates. The loan repayment schedule can be determined in a number of steps.

### Example 15: Calculation of a loan repayment schedule

Suppose you borrow $10 000 over five years with annual payments at a fixed rate of 8% per annum. Using Equation 5.6, the loan repayment schedule would be calculated as follows.

**Step 1:** Calculate the annual payments:

$$\begin{aligned}
PMT &= \frac{PVA \times r}{1 - (1 + r)^{-n}} \\
&= \frac{\$10\,000 \times 0.08}{1 - (1 + 0.08)^{-5}} \\
&= \frac{\$800}{1 - 0.68058} \\
&= \frac{\$800}{0.3194167} \\
&= \$2\,504.56
\end{aligned}$$

**Step 2:** Calculate the amount of interest due at the end of year 1 ($I_1$) by using the initial principal $P_0$:

$$\begin{aligned}
I_1 &= P_0 \times r \\
&= \$10\,000 \times 0.08 \\
&= \$800
\end{aligned}$$

▶

**Step 3:** Calculate the capital (i.e. principal) repayment ($CR_1$) part of the regular payment due at the end of year 1:

$$CR_1 = PMT - I_1$$
$$= \$2\,504.56 - \$800$$
$$= \$1\,704.56$$

**Step 4:** Calculate the amount of loan outstanding ($P_1$) or balance at the end of year 1:

$$P_1 = P_0 - CR_1$$
$$= \$10\,000 - \$1\,704.56$$
$$= \$8\,295.44$$

This process is repeated for the next four years of the loan. The results are presented in Table 5.1.

Table 5.1   Loan repayment schedule for five-year loan

| Period | (1) Balance at beginning of period | (2) Regular payment | (3) Interest component (1) × 0.08 | (4) Capital component (2) − (3) | (5) Balance at end of period (1) − (4) |
|---|---|---|---|---|---|
| 1 | $10 000.00 | $2 504.56 | $800.00 | $1 704.56 | $8 295.44 |
| 2 | $ 8 295.44 | $2 504.56 | $663.64 | $1 840.92 | $6 454.52 |
| 3 | $ 6 454.52 | $2 504.56 | $516.36 | $1 988.20 | $4 466.32 |
| 4 | $ 4 466.32 | $2 504.56 | $357.31 | $2 147.25 | $2 319.06 |
| 5 | $ 2 319.06 | $2 504.56 | $185.52 | $2 319.04 | 0.03 |

We can solve the payments for the previous example using a financial calculator or spreadsheet.

The example above is based on annual loan repayments. Typically, however, loan repayments are made each month or fortnight. As a result, using the previous example, the monthly interest rate would become $0.08/12 = 0.00667$, or $0.667\%$ per month, and the number of periods would become $5 \times 12 = 60$ resulting in 60 rows for the repayment schedule.

## Multiple payments per annum and compounding frequency

In Chapter 4 we saw how the single-lump-sum FV and PV formulae are adjusted when the frequency of compounding is more than once per year. Essentially, we adjusted the formulae to account for the number of compounding periods (rather than years) and the per-period rate of return (rather than the annual rate of return). Therefore, r and n in Equation 4.5 became r/m and n × m, respectively, as shown in Equation 4.7 (recall that m was the number of compounding periods per annum). We made the same adjustments for the single-lump-sum PV formula as shown in Equation 4.8.

In fact, any of the time value of money formulae in Chapters 4 and 5 can account for compounding frequency in the same way. So, wherever r appears in a formula it becomes r/m, and n is replaced with n × m. Example 16 below shows how we could adjust Equation 5.6 Annuity (PV) – regular payment when frequency of compounding is more than once per year. We could make exactly the same adjustments to the other equations in this chapter.

> **Example 16: Regular multiple loan payments per year**
>
> In the previous example, your loan repayments were $2 504.56 per year. If the bank also offers you the option to make quarterly repayments, what would your payment be each quarter?
>
> To calculate the quarterly payment, we would adjust Equation 5.6 as follows:
>
> $$\text{PMT} = \frac{\text{PVA} \times r/m}{1 - (1 + r/m)^{-n \times m}}$$
>
> The annual interest rate r = 8%, n = 5 and the number of compounding periods per annum m = 4. The calculation now is:
>
> $$\begin{aligned} \text{PMT} &= \frac{\$10\,000 \times 0.08/4}{1 - (1+0.08/4)^{-5 \times 4}} \\ &= \frac{\$10\,000 \times 0.02}{1 - (1+0.02)^{-20}} \\ &= \frac{\$200}{1 - 0.67297} \\ &= \frac{\$200}{0.32703} \\ &= \$611.57 \end{aligned}$$
>
> If you make quarterly payments of $611.57 then you will be paying $2 446.28 per year, which is less than the annual payment of $2 504.56 calculated in Example 15. The reason for the lower amount is that you start paying back the loan sooner (i.e. after one quarter, rather than after one year), and therefore the balance you owe the bank reduces sooner and you will be charged less interest overall. We look at the benefits of making more-frequent loan payments in Chapter 7 when discussing residential property loans.

# Conclusion

In this chapter we first examined the time series of multiple cash flows, then a series of finite, equal payments called annuities. We began by distinguishing between an ordinary annuity and an annuity due. Then we learned how to calculate the future and present value of an ordinary annuity by using formulae, financial calculators and spreadsheets.

Various applications were considered. For example, we covered the manipulation of the annuity formula to find the amount of a regular deposit required to acquire a future lump sum and had a brief look at annuities due. We ended the chapter by examining a commonly met application of a mortgage as an extension. The time value of money concept underpins much of the analysis in later chapters.

## SELF-TEST QUESTIONS

1. **a** John Trusty wishes to accumulate a deposit for a house by making equal end-of-year deposits of $8 000 over the next five years. If he can earn 6% per annum on his investment, how much will he have at the end of five years?

   **b** By his calculation in part **a**, John Trusty works out he will need a deposit of $50 000 at the end of five years. If he can earn the same 6% on his investments, how much must he deposit at the end of each year to meet this goal of $50 000?

2. Carey Industries has a $100 face-value bond with an 8% coupon rate of interest on issue. The bond has seven years remaining to its maturity date. If the interest is paid annually, what is the current value of the bond when the required return is 6%?

## ANSWERS TO SELF-TEST QUESTIONS

**1 a** $\text{FVA} = \text{PMT}\left[\dfrac{(1+r)^n - 1}{r}\right]$

$\text{FVA} = \$8\,000\left[\dfrac{(1+0.06)^5 - 1}{0.06}\right]$

$= \$8\,000\left[\dfrac{0.33822}{0.06}\right]$

$= \$8\,000\,[5.63709]$

$= \$45\,096.74$

**b** $\text{PMT} = \dfrac{\text{FVA} \times r}{(1+r)^n - 1}$

$\text{PMT} = \dfrac{\$50\,000 \times 0.06}{(1+0.06)^5 - 1}$

$\text{PMT} = \dfrac{\$3\,000}{0.33822}$

$= \$8\,869.82$

**2** $P = \text{PMT}\left[\dfrac{1-(1+r)^{-n}}{r}\right] + \dfrac{F}{(1+r)^n}$

$P = \$8\left[\dfrac{1-(1+0.06)^{-7}}{0.06}\right] + \dfrac{\$100}{(1+0.06)^7}$

$P = \$8\left[\dfrac{1-0.66505}{0.06}\right] + \dfrac{\$100}{1.50363}$

$P = \$8\left[\dfrac{0.33494}{0.06}\right] + \$66.50571$

$P = \$8\,[5.58238] + \$66.50571$

$= \$44.65905 + \$66.50571$

$= \$111.16$

Note: The price is at a premium to the original face value as it offers a higher coupon interest rate than current market rates.

## QUESTIONS AND PROBLEMS

1. Consider the cash flows on the right.

   Find the present value of this cash flow stream, assuming an interest rate of 8%.

| Year | Cash flow |
|---|---|
| 1 | $11 000 |
| 2 | $ 700 |
| 3 | $ 500 |

2. A financial asset pays its holder an annual payment of $90 for four years, and will also repay $1 000 at maturity. What is the current price of the financial asset if the market interest rates are 11%?

3   A company is offered an opportunity to receive the mixed stream of cash flows shown here over the next five years. If the firm must earn 9% per annum on its investments, what is the most the company should pay for this opportunity?

| Year | Cash flow |
|---|---|
| 1 | $4 000 |
| 2 | $8 000 |
| 3 | $5 000 |
| 4 | $4 000 |
| 5 | $3 000 |

4   Compare the future value of a four-year ordinary annuity with that of a ten-year annuity where each has:
   a   a regular payment of $500 a year and the interest rate is 8% per annum
   b   a regular payment of $1 000 a year and the interest rate is 8% per annum.

5   Lisa Prudent deposits $1 000 in a bank at the end of each year. If the money earns 8% per annum over the term, how much will she have in her account at the end of eight years?

6   What is the amount of an annuity at the end of three years if the size of each payment is $3 000, payable at the end of each year for three years, at an interest rate of 9% compounded annually?

7   What is the present value of an annuity of $1 200 paid annually over five years (with the first payment to be received at the end of the first year), and with a current yield of 9% per annum compounded annually?

8   Find the total future amount if Reg Retiring deposits $2 000 at the end of each year for 40 years and the average interest rate over the period is 10% compounded annually.

9   You hold a ten-year $100 face-value bond that pays you annual coupons of $7.25. Find the present value of the coupon stream if yields are currently 9.2% compounded annually. (*Hint*: Use only the first part of the formula.)

10   If a man wants to receive $2 000 at the end of each year for 20 years from a bank that pays 7% interest per annum over the same period, how much must he deposit in the bank now?

11   What is the cash value of a car that can be bought for a $4 000 deposit and $800 payment every year for five years if the money is worth 10% compounded annually?

12   How much should you pay the insurance company for an annuity that will pay $7 500 at the end of each year for 15 years, assuming the interest rate over the period is 8% per annum?

13   You want to save for a deposit of $25 000 on a house in five years. Given an interest rate of 7.5% compounded annually over the period, how much should you invest at the end of each year (in equal payments) to reach your target?

14   Simon Simple has saved $315 000 and is considering retiring. If he can invest his funds at 9% per annum, how much can he withdraw at the end of each year for the next 20 years without exhausting his funds?

15   What happens to the present value of a perpetuity as the interest rate gets larger?

16   Find the present value of an investment that promises to pay $15 000 each year, forever, when the interest rate is 10%.

17   What price would you pay for an 11% government bond, maturing in 10 years, if you required a yield of 9.5% per annum compounded annually (assuming a face value of $1 000)? (*Hint*: Find the sum of the present value of both the coupon stream and the face value payable at maturity.)

18. A woman purchased a house for $120 000. Her initial deposit was $20 000, and she agreed to make equal payments at the end of each year for 20 years. If the interest is 10% compounded annually, what is the size of the yearly payment?

19. Suppose you are a loans officer with a bank. You approve an application for a loan of $50 000 at 9.00% compounded annually. Assuming the client is required to make seven equal yearly payments, prepare a loan repayment schedule for the client.

20. You are a bond portfolio manager for a superannuation fund and are considering buying a five-year government bond, with a face value of $100 and paying 9% annual coupons. Given that current market yields are 8% per annum, what would the price of this bond be?

21. A large insurance company is considering selling from its bond portfolio a ten-year bond paying 7.5% per annum when current market rates are 8.5% per annum. What is the bond's current price if its face value is $1 000?

22. An investor wishes to buy a three-year bond with face value $100 that pays 9%-per-annum coupon interest rates, paid semi-annually. What is the current price of this bond if comparable market rates are 8.0% per annum?

23. A large New Zealand electricity company issues bonds that will mature to their face value of $100 in 10 years. Find the value of the bond that will pay a semi-annual coupon interest rate of 8.4% per annum if the required rate of return is (a) 7.8% and (b) 10% per annum.

24. You are evaluating small retail commercial properties and would like to determine what the required rate of return is likely to be. You have identified two recent property sales that are comparable to the ones you are evaluating. Details of each sale is shown below:

   Property A sold for $890 000 and has net operating income of $57 900

   Property B sold for $1 160 000 and has net operating income of $70 000

   a   What is the capitalisation rate (or cap rate) for each property?

   b   One of the comparable properties you are evaluating has a net operating income of $48 600. Provide an estimate of the property's value.

# PART 3

# Personal finance

This section on personal finance describes risk and return, and presents the steps in the financial planning process. It also develops the framework that forms the basis for evaluating all financial decisions.

An understanding of risk and return is required to undertake any financial planning process. As the returns offered from any investment or project increase, the risks associated also rise. These risks, however, can be reduced if diversification across a range of assets is undertaken.

In Chapter 6, the two components that constitute a return — such as the real interest return and the expected inflation premium — are described. The methods for calculating the level of return using holding period yields are explained, as are the techniques for estimating future risk and return.

Chapter 7 looks at the procedures individuals follow in making personal financial decisions. These procedures require individuals to establish goals and put strategies in place to achieve them, as well as to consider alternatives to those goals. The time value of money concepts covered in Chapters 4 and 5 will be revisited and applied to long-term financing and investment decisions. The long-term financial goals described in Chapter 7 include buying a house, saving for a specific goal such as retirement, and setting up a small business.

# CHAPTER 6

# Risk and return

### Learning objectives

By the end of this chapter, you should:
- understand the components of an expected return
- understand the difference between nominal and real rates of return
- be able to identify the shapes of yield curves
- appreciate that financial and real assets offer differing rates of return
- understand the nature and causes of risk
- understand the importance of the trade-off between risk and return
- be able to calculate holding period yields
- estimate ex-ante and ex-post risks and returns
- explain the concept of diversification.

## Introduction

This chapter will describe the concepts of risk and return. Risk-free assets are considered first, together with the components that make up the risk-free rate. The difference between a nominal and a real interest rate of return will also be discussed, together with how interest rates change over time.

We then turn our attention to risky assets. Some investment or financing decisions will incur negligible risks, whereas others will be speculative and hence possess a high level of uncertainty concerning the returns to be received.

Risk is an ever-present phenomenon whenever a decision to invest is made. A decision to take one option invariably means that another option – even the option to do nothing – has been discarded. As the benefits associated with any decision will not be known until some time in the future, it may be several years before you know whether or not the decision you made was the correct one.

First we estimate the returns earned over a discrete investment period (for example, one year), then calculate return and total risk for a single risky asset over a number of periods (i.e. many years). After measuring historical risk and return, methods for estimating future risks and returns associated with individual investments are then described.

As investors typically hold a portfolio of many different assets, the risk-reduction benefits associated with diversification will be introduced. While diversification reduces risks associated with individual assets, investors are still exposed to non-diversifiable risks, which affect the whole market. Therefore, investors with well-diversified portfolios are only concerned with the risks they cannot avoid (i.e. non-diversifiable risk). This chapter concludes by introducing the capital asset pricing model (CAPM), which uses an asset's non-diversifiable risk to estimate that asset's required rate of return.

# Risk-free assets

## The two components of a return

It is important to note that, throughout this section, the terms *nominal returns* and *nominal interest rates* will be used interchangeably. From the perspective of investors (lenders), nominal returns are the reward they require for deferring their consumption of funds between two periods. From the perspective of borrowers, nominal interest rates are the costs they incur in order to use the funds of investors. A nominal interest rate (or nominal return) is made up of two components:

- the **real interest rate**
- a premium for expected **inflation**.

We can express this in equation form as:

Risk-free interest rate = Real interest rate + Expected inflation rate   *Equation 6.1*

> **Real interest rate**
> The underlying interest rate with no inflation or uncertainty about future cash flows.
>
> **Inflation**
> Increase in the level of prices as a result of changes in demand or money supply.

## The real interest rate

In a perfect world, inflation and risk would not occur. As a result, the nominal interest rate would equal the real interest rate. In such a perfect world, borrowers and lenders of funds would not be concerned with how long their funds were lent or invested, since the outcome of any project would be known with certainty. In this situation there would be one cost of money that would compensate the suppliers of funds for deferring their consumption. This cost of money is the real interest rate, and represents the interest rate required to bring the supply of and the demand for investment funds into equilibrium. That is, it is the basic cost of funds that a borrower will have to pay in order to receive the money they require. If a situation existed where there were more funds available for investment than projects available, the real interest rate would fall. Conversely, the real interest rate would rise if the demand for funds was greater than the supply. As a result, the real interest rate will fluctuate according to changes taking place in the economy.

## Expected inflation

Unfortunately a perfect world does not exist, so the nominal interest rate includes a premium for inflation and represents the actual interest rate charged for the use of funds. It is important to note that investors require compensation for *expected* future inflation over the period of the loan or investment, and that historical rates of inflation are irrelevant.

Changes in the general level of prices are measured each quarter by the **Consumer Price Index (CPI)**. As shown in Figure 6.1 on the next page there have been some quite large variations in this index over the past 60 years. Variations in inflation may occur for a number of reasons, such as oil price rises and government policies. What is clear from Figure 6.1 on the next page is both the high level of inflation and the high variability in inflation until 1990. Other than a few small spikes relating to changes in GST, inflation was generally within the targets set by the RBNZ until 2021. This sharp rise in inflation after 2021 can be attributed to both national (high government spending, easy availability of low cost credit, and a slow RBNZ response in inflation pressures) and international (conflicts including the war in Ukraine, supply chain constraints due to Covid-19 disruptions) factors.

> **Consumer Price Index (CPI)**
> Annual index updated quarterly that reflects changes in the general level of prices.

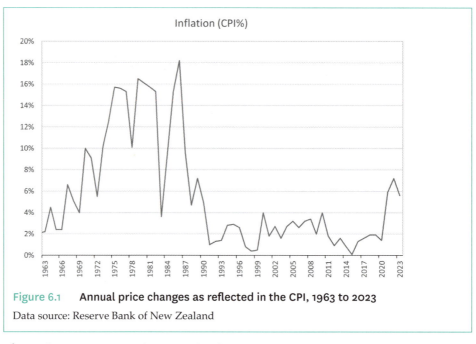

Figure 6.1    Annual price changes as reflected in the CPI, 1963 to 2023
Data source: Reserve Bank of New Zealand

**Risk-free**
Free from default risk. A government Treasury bill is regarded as risk-free.

The real interest rate and expected inflation rate can be combined to reflect a **risk-free** nominal interest rate. The New Zealand government issues a 90-day Treasury bill which is considered to be risk-free, since the likelihood of default is negligible. While the real interest rate may remain constant, the nominal interest rate will rise or fall according to fluctuations in expected inflation.

To illustrate, assume that you have deposited $1 000 in the bank at a nominal interest rate of 5% per annum. At the end of the year you will have $1 050 in your bank account. Will you be any better off than you were a year earlier? If the real rate of interest was 3.5% and you expected the price of goods to rise by 1.45% during the year as a result of inflation, then your overall purchasing power will have increased. Goods or services that cost $1 000 at the beginning of the year would now cost $1 014.50 ($1 000 × 1.0145). But given an end-of-year bank balance of $1 050, you would be better off by $35.50 (i.e. $1 050 – $1 014.50), or 3.5% ($35.50/$1 014.50 = 0.03499, i.e. 3.5%).

### Nominal interest rate

As shown by Equation 6.1, the nominal interest rate includes both the real interest rate and a premium for expected inflation. The nominal interest rate will fluctuate in accordance with changes in expected inflation, but as long as the nominal interest rate can adjust sufficiently to compensate for the level of expected inflation, the real interest rate will remain the same. Therefore, whenever the real interest rate and the expected inflation rate are known, it is possible to calculate the nominal interest rate, as follows:

Nominal interest rate  = [(1 + Real interest rate) × (1 + Expected inflation rate)] – 1

*Equation 6.2*

$$= [(1 + 0.035) \times (1 + 0.0145)] - 1$$
$$= [(1.035) \times (1.0145)] - 1$$
$$= 1.05 - 1$$
$$= 0.05 \text{ or } 5\%$$

This shows that if the nominal interest rate was 5%, an investor would be compensated both for deferring the consumption of funds and also for the expected rate of inflation during the period of investment.

Conversely, if the nominal interest rate and the expected inflation rate are known, the real rate of return can be calculated by rearranging the formula:

$$\text{Real interest rate} = \left(\frac{1 + \text{Nominal interest rate}}{1 + \text{Rate of expected inflation}}\right) - 1 \qquad \textit{Equation 6.3}$$

The nominal and real interest rates equations above are known as the Fisher equations, as a result of the work done by Irving Fisher on interest rates. However, there is also an approximation method that is often used which states that the nominal interest rate approximately equals the real interest rate plus the expected inflation rate:

$$\text{Nominal interest rate} \approx \text{Real interest rate} + \text{Expected inflation rate} \qquad \textit{Equation 6.4}$$

or alternatively,

$$\text{Real interest rate} \approx \text{Nominal interest rate} - \text{Expected inflation rate} \qquad \textit{Equation 6.5}$$

If both the real interest rate and the expected inflation rate are high, the approximation method should not be used, and the only way to calculate the nominal interest rate with any accuracy is by using Equation 6.2.

Returns on all investments will be affected by the increase or decrease in the rate of inflation. Inflationary changes will also affect investors' required rates of return from equity, fixed interest, property and other investments. So, for example, any decisions made by a company concerning the acquisition of plant or equipment or the acceptance of projects will be influenced by the nominal interest rate. Given that nominal returns are commonly quoted for a variety of investment opportunities, the formulae above may be used to determine the real interest rate prevailing at any given time.

Let's recap the material covered so far. Firstly, the real interest rate is the compensation a supplier of funds will receive for deferring the use of the funds, and is equal to the cost, or interest rate, that brings the supply and demand for investment funds into equilibrium. Secondly, the inflation component is *not* the level of inflation that has occurred in the past, but rather the level of inflation *expected* to occur in the future. Together, the real interest rate and the expected inflation rate form a risk-free nominal interest rate that is identical for *all* investments at any given point in time. The component of interest rates that varies between investments is the **risk premium** that compensates for the various forms of risk that are discussed below.

**Risk premium**
Additional return investors require for investing in risky assets.

# Term structure of interest rates

## Shape of yield curves

Figure 6.2 shows how short-term and long-term yields can change over time. A major fall in yields occurred in 2008–2009 due to the deterioration in the global economy (resulting in a GFC). Most of New Zealand's trading partners were in economic recession and the outlook for their recovery was uncertain. In order to protect the New

Zealand economy, the RBNZ reduced the official cash rate (OCR). The RBNZ also substantially reduced the OCR in 2020 in anticipation of a deteriorating economic outlook due to Covid-19, and this was followed by the fastest rise in history for the OCR over 2022 to 2023 to help ward off the inflationary pressures.

The **term structure of interest rates** relates the level of interest rates prevailing on a particular security to the time to maturity. When depicted in graphical form, these rates are called yield curves. The shape of the yield curves is shown in Figure 6.3 and can be explained by:

- expected inflation
- liquidity preferences
- supply and demand pressures.

**Term structure of interest rates**
Relationship between time to maturity and percentage yield.

**Figure 6.2** New Zealand short-term and long-term yields, 2003 to 2023
Data source: Reserve Bank of New Zealand.

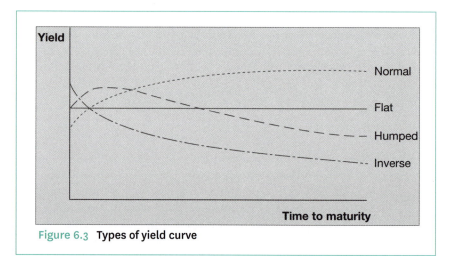

**Figure 6.3** Types of yield curve

The most common yield curve is the normal yield curve. This is an upward-sloping curve that occurs when short-term yields are low and will rise with longer maturities. The reverse of this yield curve is the inverse (or downward-sloping) yield curve, where short-term yields are high and yields on long-term maturities fall over time. This curve occurs periodically and sometimes indicates that a recession is about to begin. If the yield curve is flat, then little change in interest rates is expected to occur across all time periods, and the structure could be reflecting a move from a normal to an inverse yield curve (or vice versa). Finally, a humped yield curve indicates that the yield for, say, a one-year security is higher than those offered for on-call securities, and the rates for the longer-term bonds are lower than those for the short-term securities.

The shape of the yield curve also reflects the expectations of future interest rates, and can be used by investors in the following ways:

- if interest rates are expected to rise in the future, investors will purchase short-term securities and roll these over into more short-term securities until they are sure that the long-term rates have stabilised at a higher level
- if interest rates are expected to fall, then investors will purchase the higher-yielding long-term securities in anticipation of an inverse yield curve.

We have now learned about risk-free assets, and we turn our attention to risky assets and how risk can be reduced.

## Risky assets

Since the decision to invest in any project or security occurs **ex ante**, the uncertainty surrounding the success of the decision will be unknown for some time. Investors will seek a return greater than the returns offered by risk-free assets. In this section we cover techniques for measuring an asset's expected returns and risk. We will also show how, by adding a variety of assets to a portfolio, this risk can be reduced.

> **Ex ante**
> Before the event.

The two components of a return described above – the real interest rate and expected inflation – are the same for each investment or financing decision made by an individual or company. The risk premium, however, is the one variable that will vary across or within an investment. When considering any investment or financing decision, an individual, or a company, expects to be compensated for the risk inherent in the financial or real asset by receiving a return that corresponds to the level of risk. In this sense, risk refers to the possibility of loss, or the chance that the expected returns may not eventuate. Therefore, risk refers to the uncertainty of receiving the expected returns because a borrower may not be able to repay the principal on fixed-interest securities when required, and may become **insolvent**. Therefore, whenever any financial decisions are made, risk is involved, because the decision takes into account uncertain future activities.

> **Insolvent**
> The status of an individual or a company with insufficient assets to meet their financial commitments.

Broadly speaking, there are two types of risk to incorporate into a return: risks pertaining to the environment the firm operates in, which it has little control of; and risks associated with the operations of the firm. We will cover these two risk types further in the section on the benefits of diversification.

The formula for a nominal return becomes:

Nominal return = Risk-free return + Risk premium      *Equation 6.6*

The risk premium compensates investors for an asset's risk. Some of the risk components are described on the following page.

### Business risk

**Business risk** refers to fluctuations of cash inflows, notably sales. For example, if the sales of a business fluctuate significantly, then the amount of the firm's cash outflows to investors will be uncertain. The greater the variability associated with these cash flows, the higher the premium that will be required to compensate for these risks. Hence, a power company would have a relatively stable level of sales compared with a jewellery store, whose sales typically increase in periods of economic growth and fall when the economy contracts.

> **Business risk**
> Fluctuations in cash flows, such as sales.

### Financial risk

**Financial risk** occurs whenever the firm uses debt as well as equity to finance its operations. If the company uses equity alone to fund its investment projects, it has no financial risk, only business risk. Whenever a firm uses debt, it incurs a fixed financing charge, and has a contractual obligation to pay these charges whenever they fall due. Investors holding debt securities in the company will receive income in the form of interest on their investment before those holding equity can be paid a dividend. Consequently, high debt levels may threaten the firm's ability to pay dividends. For firms with both high business risk and high financial risk, long-term survival can be difficult.

> **Financial risk**
> Relates to the amount of debt used to fund a firm's operations.

### Liquidity risk

**Liquidity risk** refers to the risk that an investor holding equity or fixed-interest investments in a company may be unable to sell them to another investor. If an investment is liquid, then an investor should be able to transfer it to someone else at a price that does not differ significantly from the price recorded for a prior trade. Therefore, a liquid security is one that can be sold promptly with little change in price in relation to the previous price paid. The greater the uncertainty that these two requirements cannot be met, the higher the liquidity risk.

> **Liquidity risk**
> The risk that an investor holding equity or fixed-income investments in a company may be unable to sell them to another investor.

### Exchange rate risk

**Exchange rate risk** occurs due to movements in **offshore currencies** relative to the local currency. These fluctuations will affect the price of overseas goods sold within New Zealand and the price charged for New Zealand goods overseas. Therefore, the expected returns from offshore investments may vary for:

- investors with shares in domestic companies that have a large exposure to overseas trade
- investors who have acquired real or financial assets in other countries
- importers or exporters of goods or services
- companies with operations in other countries.

Adverse movements in exchange rates can erode the level of return the investor expects to receive.

> **Exchange rate risk**
> The risk associated with fluctuations in exchange rates.
>
> **Offshore currency**
> The monetary medium of exchange relating to other countries.

### Country risk

**Country risk** relates to the uncertainty of returns arising from investments in another country if the possibility exists that a major political upheaval may occur. The level of this type of risk differs from country to country. For example, the US has a low level of political risk compared with the Middle East, which is currently facing economic turmoil.

> **Country risk**
> Refers to the uncertainty of returns from investments in another country.

> **Example 1: Government vs. finance company securities**

New Zealand government securities are considered to bear no risk, whereas the securities for private-sector companies should have risk premiums that reflect a number of the risks covered above. For example, in December 2023 the RBNZ issued two-year Kiwi Bonds with an AA+ credit rating at a risk-free interest rate of 5.00%. General Finance and Liberty Financial are two finance companies in New Zealand. At the same time, General Finance had a BB credit rating and offered two-year **debenture** rates of 7.50%, while Liberty Financial's credit rating is BBB and offered 6.80% for the 2 year rate. Using Equation 6.7, the risk premiums are:

> Risk premium = Nominal return – Risk-free return          *Equation 6.7*

> General Finance risk premium  = 7.50% – 5.00%
> = 2.50%
> Liberty Financial risk premium  = 6.80% – 5.00%
> = 1.80%

Liberty Financial's BBB credit rating means it is at the lower end of the investment grade ratings given by the international credit rating agencies (Standard & Poors, Moody's, and Fitch). However, its credit rating is better than General Finance's BB rating which is considered 'junk' or sub-investment grade by the rating agencies. Liberty's better credit rating is reflected in its lower risk premium of 1.80% compared to General Finance's 2.50% risk premium.

> **Debenture**
> A medium- to long-term loan agreement secured by assets of the borrower.

# Risk and return – the trade-off

Individuals also have differing attitudes to risk, and the risk they are prepared to accept will be a function of their age, financial well-being and level of education. The economic assumption is that investors are assumed to be rational beings, and hence would rather be certain of achieving their expected returns than cope with the uncertainty of achieving a return that differs from the one they expect to receive. In the main, most investors are risk-averse: that is, they prefer less risk to more risk, given a particular expected return. However, even if they invest in projects or securities that have a high risk, they are still deemed to be rational investors as long as they are compensated for the risks undertaken by an appropriately high expected return. This is called the risk–return trade-off and refers to the direct relationship between risk and return as shown in Figure 6.4 on the following page. The risk–return line has a positive slope and depicts the increase in risk that occurs as expected returns rise. You will note that the sloping line commences above the origin (the intersection of the vertical and horizontal lines). The point where the diagonal line intersects the vertical line represents the return from a zero-risk (or risk-free) security such as 90-day Treasury bills.

Figure 6.4  Relationship between risk and expected return

In order to entice investors to accept riskier securities, they must be compensated for the risk inherent in the investment by the returns offered. Companies that offer securities must ensure that the type of product and the returns associated with them will appeal to investors. If the security has no, or few, desirable features, then investors will not purchase them and the company will be left without the funds required to finance its future operations.

As Figure 6.5 shows, returns can be generated by real and financial assets, but it is important to note that the risks and the returns associated with all types of investment assets will fluctuate over time depending on the current economic conditions that prevail at the time. In some years the returns will fall; in other years the returns may rise. The forces of supply and demand for assets are never constant and tend to move in cycles that repeat themselves over time.

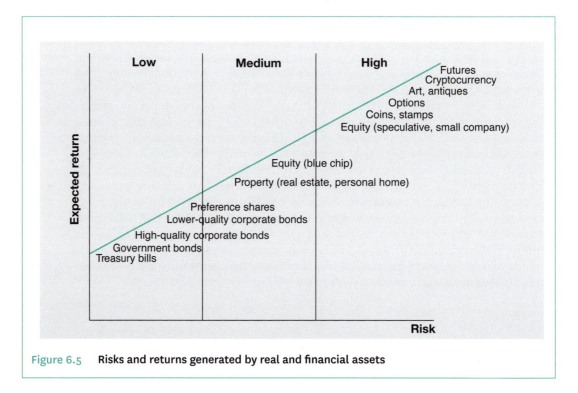

Figure 6.5  Risks and returns generated by real and financial assets

With the wide range of financial products and assets available to investors, it is possible to achieve a position on the expected return–risk line that reflects the level of risk and return they seek. Other asset classes, such as art, antiques, car plates, and stamps, are often one-off items that are not homogeneous and may not appeal to everyone. The market in these assets is not readily reported, because there is no formal transaction reporting system and the market is often illiquid. In addition, there is a lack of registered, knowledgeable valuers for some art/antiques in New Zealand and it is difficult to obtain relevant data concerning prices. This may be due to a lack of buyers operating in a small market. As a result, the prices for these assets may not be realistic and may not reflect the true value of the item in the same way as they would in a larger market. The proportion of funds placed in each type of security will differ for each investor, depending on their relative degree of **risk aversion**.

Hence, there are two rules which should be followed when investing in risky assets. Firstly, if two investments have the same expected return but one has a higher level of risk associated with it, the investment with the lower level of risk should be selected. Secondly, if two investments have the same level of risk, select the investment with the higher expected return. In doing so, expected returns will be maximised for less risk.

In order to make good decisions, it is important to estimate the ex-ante risk and return of each investment proposal. These techniques will be covered in the next section.

**Risk aversion**
The avoidance of risk.

## Measuring historical risk and return

### Returns from investment

The decision to invest funds and the expected returns (yields) from doing so always occur ex ante because the individual has made the investment in the expectation of receiving a return. However, **ex post**, the investor may find that the returns expected at the outset have not eventuated. In this section we will measure the ex-post returns.

**Ex post**
After the event.

### Holding period yields or return

Whenever the decision to forego consumption is made, a choice between alternative investments must be made. This also applies to businesses needing to evaluate proposed projects. In order to evaluate alternative investments and determine which will provide the highest return, the **holding period yield** (HPY) for each investment will be calculated. The calculation takes into account any change in price of, say, a share or property over the period being considered, as well as any income such as dividends or net rents received from the investment.

It should be noted that when calculating the HPY, any income received from the investment is assumed to be paid at the end of the holding period. If the holding period is greater than a year, the formula ignores the reinvestment of dividends or interest received in earlier periods.

**Holding period yield**
Percentage return received on an investment over the period it was owned.

> **Example 2: Holding period yield**
>
> You are comparing how two companies in your share portfolio performed. For the first company, you made your purchase one year ago for $2.11 per share. The share is currently worth $2.20, and you also received $0.09 in dividends. For the second company, you have owned the share for two years. It originally cost $10.00 and is now worth $11.65 (it paid no dividends during that time). What is the holding period yield of each share?
>
> $$\text{HPY} = \frac{(EV - BV) + C}{BV} \qquad \text{Equation 6.8}$$
>
> where  EV = ending value of investment
>   BV = beginning value of investment
>   C = income received over investment period.
>
> Therefore, the holding period yield for the two investments are as follows.
>
> *First company:*
>
> $$\text{HPY} = \frac{(\$2.20 - \$2.11) + \$0.09}{\$2.11}$$
>
> $$= 0.085 \text{ or } 8.5\%$$
>
> *Second company:*
>
> $$\text{HPY} = \frac{(\$11.65 - \$10.00)}{\$10.00}$$
>
> $$= 0.165 \text{ or } 16.5\%$$
>
> However, it is difficult to compare how well the two investments performed as the holding period was different for each. Further, an HPY earned over more than one year is often not meaningful unless it is converted to an annual yield.
>
> To convert the HPY to an annual HPY we can use the following formula, which is based on Equation 4.11, solving for an unknown interest rate:
>
> $$\text{Annual HPY} = \left(\frac{EV + C}{BV}\right)^{1/n} - 1 \qquad \text{Equation 6.9}$$
>
> where n = number of years the investment is held.
>
> The variable n is usually represented as a whole number; however, if part of a year is used then it is represented by a decimal based on the fraction of the year. For example, for a holding period of six months, n would equal 0.5. If it was held for 270 days, then it would be 270/365, i.e. 0.74 of a year.

## Example 3: Annual holding period yields

Consider the two investments described in Example 2. To compare which performed better on an annual basis, you calculate the annual HPY for each as follows.

*First company:*

$$\text{Annual HPY} = \left(\frac{\$2.20 + \$0.09}{\$2.11}\right)^{1/1} - 1$$

$$= 0.085 \text{ or } 8.5\%$$

*Second company:*

$$\text{Annual HPY} = \left(\frac{\$11.65}{\$10.00}\right)^{1/2} - 1$$

$$= 0.0794 \text{ or } 7.9\%$$

When annualising the two investments, it becomes obvious that the one-year investment has provided a higher annual yield than the two-year investment.

> **Annual holding period yield**
> The annual percentage return received on an investment.

## Example 4: Calculating company annual HPYs

The same calculations can be used to compare the prices of two shares in order to determine which would provide the largest annual returns. To illustrate this, Figure 6.6 on the next page graphs the share prices for Fisher & Paykel Healthcare Ltd (FPH) and Briscoe Group Ltd (BGR) over a period of 13 years, from 2011 to 2023. For this example, we are including the dividends that were received on these shares as well as the changes in share prices, or the **capital gains** or **capital losses** accruing to the shares, over this period.

> **Capital gain**
> Amount by which the selling price of an asset exceeds its purchase price.
>
> **Capital loss**
> Amount by which the selling price of an asset is below its purchase price.

|  | Fisher & Paykel Healthcare Corp. Ltd | Briscoe Group Ltd |
|---|---|---|
| Beginning value (2011) | $2.37 | $0.91 |
| Ending value (2023) | $21.58 | $4.70 |
| Dividends received | $3.95 | $3.55 |

Using Equation 6.9, calculate the annual HPY for each company:

FPH
$$\text{Annual HPY} = \left(\frac{\$21.58 + \$3.95}{\$2.37}\right)^{1/13} - 1$$

$$= 10.77215^{0.077} - 1$$

$$= 0.200 \text{ or } 20\%$$

BGR
$$\text{Annual HPY} = \left(\frac{\$4.70 + \$3.35}{\$0.91}\right)^{1/13} - 1$$

$$= 8.84615^{0.077} - 1$$

$$= 0.183 \text{ or } 18.3\%$$

The results show that FPH's return was slightly higher than BGR's over this period. This may be surprising when comparing the share price performance in Figure 6.6, but it is due to the higher percentage return that BGR shareholders received from dividends compared with FPH. However, the variability of returns and risks associated with the two companies has not been considered and should be brought into the analysis.

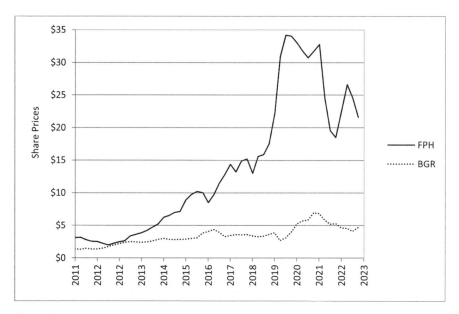

**Figure 6.6** Quarterly share prices for FPH and BGR
Data source: NZ Stock Exchange.

## Standard deviation as a measure of risk

As stated before, the decision to invest and defer the consumption of funds occurs ex ante, or before the return can be received. In other words, there is a level of uncertainty surrounding this decision due to the lack of certainty about future events. When risk-free assets are considered, their future outcomes are known with certainty; this is not the case with risky assets. A level of uncertainty exists, arising from a range of potential outcomes that may incur a loss.

The data shown below give the annual percentage returns for two assets.

| Year | Asset A returns (%) | Asset B returns (%) |
|---|---|---|
| 20X3 | 8 | 13 |
| 20X4 | 2 | 22 |
| 20X5 | 12 | −8 |
| 20X6 | 9 | 10 |
| 20X7 | 4 | 13 |

For Assets A and B we can calculate their mean return r using Equation 6.10 below:

$$\bar{r} = \frac{\Sigma r}{n}$$ 

Equation 6.10

where the mean return is equal to the sum of each period's observed return r divided by the total number of observations n.

$$\text{Asset A mean return} = \frac{0.08 + 0.02 + 0.12 + 0.09 + 0.04}{5}$$
$$= \frac{0.35}{5}$$
$$= 0.07 \text{ or } 7.0\%$$

$$\text{Asset B mean return} = \frac{0.13 + 0.22 - 0.08 + 0.10 + 0.13}{5}$$
$$= \frac{0.5}{5}$$
$$= 0.10 \text{ or } 10.0\%$$

So Asset B has a higher mean return than Asset A. However, it is also clear from the data that Asset B has a much greater level of variability in returns: Asset A returns have a range of 10%, from the lowest return 2% to its highest of 12%; in contrast, Asset B has a range of 30%, varying from –8% to 22%. Therefore, the narrower range in returns from Asset A indicates that it should be less risky. Two statistical techniques that can be used to assess the risk associated with any risky investment are **variance** ($\sigma^2$) and **standard deviation** ($\sigma$).

Variance and standard deviation measure the uncertainty of the outcome emanating from an investment.

In order to calculate standard deviation ($\sigma$), we first calculate the variance ($\sigma^2$):

$$\sigma^2 = \frac{\sum_{i=1}^{n}(r_i - \bar{r})^2}{n - 1}$$

Equation 6.11

**Variance**
The variance measures how far each return is from the mean, or average, of all returns.

**Standard deviation**
The standard deviation measures the variability of a set of values.

where
$r_i$ = the return for $i^{th}$ observation
$\bar{r}$ = the asset's mean return as calculated in Equation 6.10
n = the total number of observations.

The reason 1 is deducted from the total number of observations n is to adjust for the degree of freedom. In other words, the more data used in the calculation the greater the accuracy of $\sigma^2$.

The standard deviation ($\sigma$) is the square root of the variance:

$$\text{Standard deviation} = \sqrt{\text{variance}} = \sqrt{\sigma^2}$$

Equation 6.12

**Example 5: Calculating the variance and standard deviation for Assets A and B**

Variance for Asset A

$$= \frac{(0.08 - 0.07)^2 + (0.02 - 0.07)^2 + (0.12 - 0.07)^2 + (0.09 - 0.07)^2 + (0.04 - 0.07)^2}{5 - 1}$$

$$= \frac{(0.01)^2 + (-0.05)^2 + (0.05)^2 + (0.02)^2 + (-0.03)^2}{4}$$

$$= \frac{0.0001 + 0.0025 + 0.0025 + 0.0004 + 0.0009}{4}$$

$$= \frac{0.0064}{4} = 0.0016$$

Standard deviation for Asset A $= \sqrt{0.0016} = 0.04$ or $4.0\%$

Variance for Asset B

$$= \frac{(0.13 - 0.10)^2 + (0.22 - 0.10)^2 + (0.08 - 0.10)^2 + (0.10 - 0.10)^2 + (0.13 - 0.10)^2}{5 - 1}$$

$$= \frac{(0.03)^2 + (0.12)^2 + (-0.18)^2 + (0.00)^2 + (0.03)^2}{4}$$

$$= \frac{0.0009 + 0.0144 + 0.0324 + 0 + 0.0009}{4}$$

$$= \frac{0.0486}{4} = 0.01215$$

Standard deviation for Asset A $= \sqrt{0.01215} = 0.110$ or $11.0\%$

The calculations show that Asset B's returns, with its larger spread of returns, had a higher mean return and larger variance and standard deviation than the returns generated by Asset A. This confirms that while Asset B generates a higher return, it also has higher risk.

The calculated figures are a good representation of the information but it is not easy to visualise. If we have a large number of observations, these can be plotted and shown to follow a normal bell-shaped distribution. The shape of the bell varies depending on the standard deviation. If the standard deviation is large, then the bell will be wide.

The normal distribution shown in Figure 6.7 shows that 68% of all observations will fall within $1\sigma$ either side of the mean ($\mu$). That is, 34% of the observations will fall between −1 and 0 and 34% will fall between 0 and 1. Ninety-five per cent of all observations will fall $2\sigma$ either side of the mean, whereas nearly 99% of all data observations will fall within $\pm 3\sigma$ of the mean.

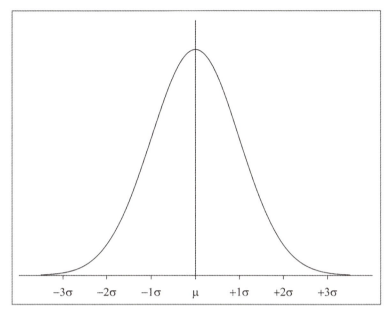

Figure 6.7    Standard (normal) 'bell-shaped' distribution

In order to illustrate this further, if Asset A's annual returns are normally distributed then approximately 68% of the time an investor could expect annual returns to be within one standard deviation (4%) of the mean return of 7% (ie within the range 3% to 11%); 95% of the time the investor could expect their returns to be within the range –1% to 15%.

However, in order to make sound investment decisions it is necessary to consider what the expected future (i.e. ex ante) returns might be. Because these returns will occur in the future, there is an element of uncertainty surrounding them. These issues will be dealt with in the following section.

## Measuring future risk and return

When considering an investment, we know what has occurred in the past but we have little idea what will happen in the future. How then do you consider these ex ante, or future, returns?

In order to do so it is necessary to estimate the probability of a future outcome, or outcomes. When examining the future of an outcome it is necessary to consider what is likely to occur within the economy, and how the industry will adapt to changes in the economy before thinking about how the company will function in that environment.

Consider, for example, an investment in a company producing a wide range of glass products. How will such a company perform in the current environment in New Zealand? Currently, there is a large demand for new houses to cope with the demand for accommodation. This demand will flow into the building industry, so that glass manufacturers will be required to provide the windows, doors and balustrading. While the expected demand is present, the company's share price should rise. If the expected demand falls due to a lower demand for houses, then the share price will fall.

How then can the expected return of such an investment be determined? This can be done by calculating the expected return as follows:

$$\bar{r} = \sum_{i=1}^{n} r_i \times \text{probability}_i$$

*Equation 6.13*

where  n = number of possible outcomes
$r_i$ = return for the $i^{th}$ outcome
probability$_i$ = the probability that the $i^{th}$ outcome will occur

Note that the sum of the probabilities should always sum to 1.

### Example 6: Wonder Windows Ltd expected return

You are analysing whether to invest in Wonder Windows Ltd. If demand for housing increases, then the expected return over the next year would be 26%. If housing demand remains at current levels, then a return of 10% is expected; whereas a –5% return is anticipated should housing demand decline. The table below summarises your expected probabilities associated with each outcome.

| Demand | Expected return | Probability of outcome occurring |
| --- | --- | --- |
| Rises | 26% | 0.5 |
| Static | 10% | 0.3 |
| Falls | –5% | 0.2 |

The expected return for Wonder Windows is:

$$\bar{r} = (0.26 \times 0.5) + (0.10 \times 0.3) + (-0.05 \times 0.2)$$
$$= 0.13 + 0.03 + -0.01$$
$$= 0.15 \text{ or } 15.0\%$$

Now that the $\bar{r}$ is known it is necessary to calculate the risk associated with the investment. The variance ($\sigma^2$) and standard deviation ($\sigma$) can be calculated using the following formulae:

and 
$$\sigma^2 = \sum_{i=1}^{n} (r_i - \bar{r})^2 \times \text{probability}_i$$

*Equation 6.14*

$$\sigma = \sqrt{\sigma^2}$$

> **Example 7: Wonder Windows Ltd risk**
>
> $$\begin{aligned}
\sigma^2 &= (0.26 - 0.15)^2 \times 0.5 + (0.10 - 0.15)^2 \times 0.3 + (-0.05 - 0.15)^2 \times 0.2 \\
&= (0.11)^2 \times 0.5 + (-0.05)^2 \times 0.3 + (-0.20)^2 \times 0.2 \\
&= 0.0121 \times 0.5 + 0.0025 \times 0.3 + 0.0400 \times 0.2 \\
&= 0.00605 + 0.00075 + 0.0080 \\
&= 0.0148
\end{aligned}$$
>
> $$\sigma = \sqrt{0.0148} = 0.122 \quad \text{or} \quad 12.2\%$$
>
> Once the risk and expected return of an asset has been ascertained, investment decisions can be made. However, such decisions should not be made in isolation but considered with regard to other investments available. This is the topic of the following section.

## The benefit of diversification

Risk is present in every decision concerning the investment of surplus funds. The level of risk deemed to be acceptable by investors will differ according to each individual's assessment of the risk–return trade-off. One method to determine the level of risk associated with each investment is to ascertain the variability of returns generated by that asset over a predetermined period of time. The larger the variability, the greater the risk associated with the investment. In finance, risk is measured using the statistical techniques of variance and standard deviation. Figure 6.8 below uses a bell-shaped curve to depict the variability of returns around a number of securities' expected, or mean, returns (E(R) in the figure).

The figure shows there is absolute certainty that the expected return from 90-day Treasury bills will be received. However, if you refer back to Figure 6.5 you will note that high-quality bonds, blue-chip equity and futures have more risk associated with them. High-quality bonds are categorised as low risk, blue-chip equity are medium-risk securities, and speculating in futures has the greatest risk because an investor could receive either extremely high or exceptionally low returns from this investment. Therefore, there is a larger variance resulting from speculating in futures, which is shown by the greater spread and dispersion of the curve.

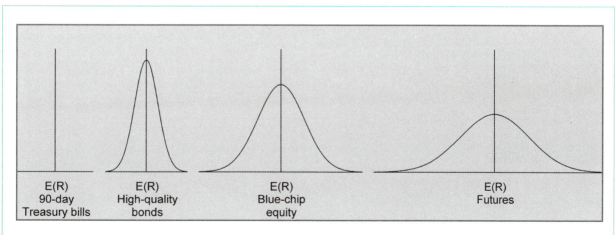

**Figure 6.8** Depicting the variability of a security's returns

**Diversify**
Place funds in a range of assets in order to spread risk.

**Diversification**
Practice of spreading risk by investing in a number of different assets.

Recall the old cliché that you should never put all your eggs into one basket. This is especially true for investments, where the objective is to **diversify** investments across a range of assets in order to reduce risk. The process associated with reducing risk by spreading investment funds over a range of different securities is called **diversification**. Diversification works to reduce risk (variability), because it is unlikely that all investment assets will perform in exactly the same way. It has been found that, over time, some investments will perform well when others are performing poorly, so that the returns on assets will not move in the same direction at the same time.

Earlier in the chapter, Figure 6.6 depicted the quarterly share prices of Fisher & Paykel Healthcare Ltd (FPH) and Briscoe Group Ltd (BGR). Over the same period, FPH had slightly higher risk (standard deviation of 13.1% compared to 12.8% for BGR) indicating the there was more variability in FPH's share price. While both had similar frequency of negative quarters, FPH had 16 quarters where its return was worse than -1% compared to 13 for BGR.

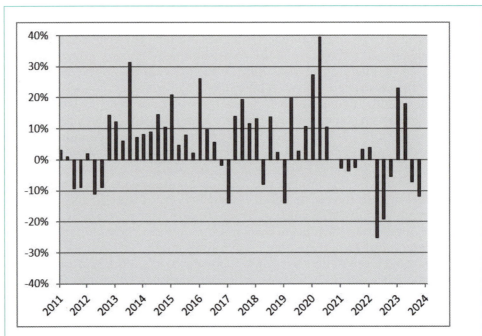

Figure 6.9   **Fisher & Paykel Healthcare Ltd quarterly returns**
Data source: NZ Stock Exchange.

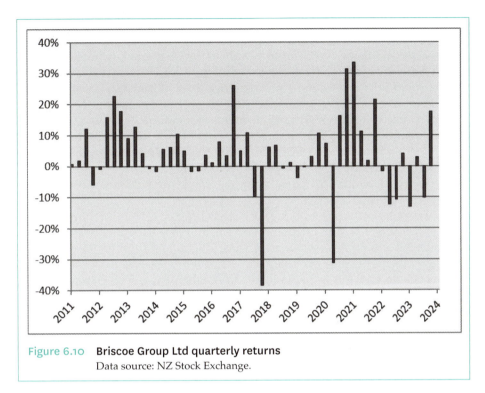

Figure 6.10   **Briscoe Group Ltd quarterly returns**
Data source: NZ Stock Exchange.

However, Figure 6.11 clearly illustrates that for a portfolio containing 50% of FPH and 50% of BGR (combined), the variability of these returns would be lower and the individual riskiness of the returns provided by both FPH and BGR is reduced.

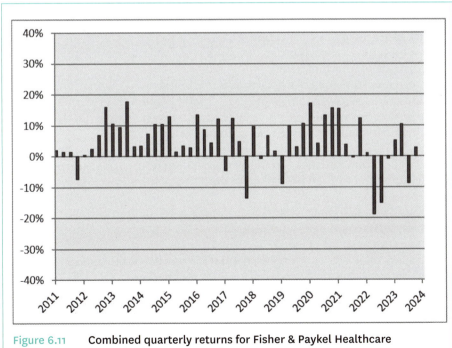

Figure 6.11   **Combined quarterly returns for Fisher & Paykel Healthcare Ltd and Briscoe Group Ltd**
Data source: NZ Stock Exchange.

Figure 6.11 shows that investing in both FPH and BGR would provide better risk reduction than investing in only one of the companies. FPH operates in the healthcare sector and has a significant exposure to the US market, whereas BGR is primarily a domestic company in the retail sector. As the sectors' cost and revenue drivers differ and FPH has foreign-exchange risk through sales and costs, while BGR has foreign-exchange risk primarily through purchase of goods, the returns would not be expected to move in the same direction over time. As shown in Figure 6.11, combining the two companies reduces the variability of the returns. In fact the standard deviation is reduced to 8.2% for the 50/50 portfolio, compared to 13.1% and 12.8% for FPH and BGR respectively. This indicates that the two companies' returns are likely to exhibit low **correlation** (i.e. the returns do not move in the same direction over time).

> **Correlation**
> A measure of the relationship between two sets of variables.

While the correlation coefficient for most assets is positive, it is rarely perfectly positively correlated (+1). The correlation between FPH and BGR is –0.14, which confirms that the companies' share prices had a tendency to move in different directions over the period shown in Figure 6.11.

We have considered two companies from different business sectors, but if more companies from a wider range of sectors were added to the portfolio the risk would be reduced further. However, it is not possible to eliminate risk completely, because when the economy is performing strongly most companies will also perform well. If the economy is stagnating then only a few, if any, will perform satisfactorily.

The risk that can be diversified by holding a portfolio of shares is called **unsystematic risk**, or the risk that can be minimised by diversification. Unsystematic risks, such as lawsuits, strikes or losing a key customer, affect a single firm (or sector) but not all firms. As a rule of thumb, a portfolio containing approximately 25 shares should achieve a low level of unsystematic risk and be considered a well-diversified portfolio.

> **Unsystematic risk**
> Risk that can be diversified away.

There is, however, a risk that cannot be diversified away. This is called **systematic risk**, or non-diversifiable risk; it pertains to the market and relates to the uncertainty surrounding future economic conditions that may affect all companies operating within the economy. Systematic risks such as war, international incidents and inflation are likely to affect all firms.

> **Systematic risk**
> Risk that cannot be diversified away because it pertains to the market.

Therefore, if investors can create portfolios to eliminate unsystematic risk, their only relevant risk is systematic risk. It is systematic risk that investors will wish to be compensated for when investing; the higher the systematic risk, the higher the return investors will demand to be compensated for that risk.

Systematic risk can be measured by **beta** ($\beta$), which is the co-movement of a single asset or portfolio returns with the overall market returns. Hence systematic risk is the risk inherent in the overall economic and political forces operating in the marketplace.

> **Beta**
> Beta measures the volatility of an individual security or portfolio in relation to the market.

On average $\beta = 1$, so that if a share has a $\beta$ of 1 it is considered to have the same systematic risk as the market as a whole (i.e. the $\beta$ for the market portfolio is 1). A $\beta$ greater than 1 means that the share is riskier than the market; conversely, if the share has a $\beta$ less than 1 it has a lower risk than the market. If the security or asset has a $\beta$ of zero then it has no co-movement with the market.

Figure 6.12 depicts the unsystematic and systematic risk of a portfolio. The diagram shows that systematic risk is stable no matter how many shares are contained in the portfolio. The portfolio risk curve highlights how, as more shares are added to the portfolio, the level of unsystematic risk falls, until the point is reached where adding more shares will not reduce it any further.

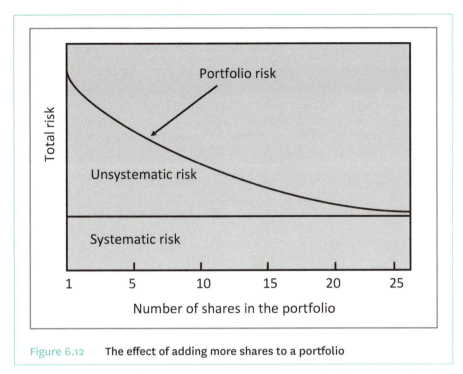

Figure 6.12   The effect of adding more shares to a portfolio

To summarise, we have looked at two measures of risk associated with financial assets: σ and β. An asset's total risk (both systematic and unsystematic) is measured by σ, whereas β measures systematic risk or the risk that cannot be diversified away. Assuming that investors hold a well-diversified portfolio, β is the relevant risk measure. The next section outlines how β is used to estimate an investor's required return.

## The capital asset pricing model and the security market line relationship

The **capital asset pricing model (CAPM)** calculates the required rate of return for risky assets. The CAPM formula is similar to Equation 6.6, where the required return on an asset is equal to the risk-free rate plus an additional premium for investing in risky assets.

The **market risk premium (MRP)** is the additional return (premium) investors require to compensate them for investing in the **market portfolio**. The MRP is adjusted for an asset or portfolio's specific systematic risk as shown in the CAPM formula below:

$$r_i = r_f + \beta_i(MRP) \qquad \text{Equation 6.15}$$

where
$r_i$ = the required return on asset i
$r_f$ = risk-free rate of return
$\beta_i$ = systematic risk of asset i
MRP = market risk premium.

**Capital asset pricing model (CAPM)**
The CAPM calculates the required rate of return for any risky asset.

**Market risk premium (MRP)**
The additional return investors must earn to compensate them for investing in the market portfolio.

**Market portfolio**
The portfolio containing all risky assets.

> **Example 8: Using CAPM to estimate required return**
>
> You wish to estimate the required return of investing in FPH and BGR, assuming their β values are 1.2 and 0.8, respectively. If long-term government bonds (risk-free rate) have a required return of 3.5% and the market risk premium is 5.5%, the required return can be calculated as follows.
>
> $$r_{FPH} = 0.035 + 1.2(0.055)$$
> $$= 0.101 \text{ or } 10.1\%$$
>
> $$r_{BGR} = 0.035 + 0.8(0.055)$$
> $$= 0.079 \text{ or } 7.9\%$$
>
> Note that we could also estimate the required return ($Er_m$) on the market portfolio. As the market has a β value of 1, then the return on the market will be $0.035 + 1(0.055) = 0.09$ or 9.0%. Therefore the return on the market portfolio is equal to the risk-free rate plus the market risk premium ($r_f$ + MRP).
>
> By now it should be clear that there is a special relationship between the expected return and risk of an asset as measured by β. The higher an asset's β, the higher the additional risk premium and required return the asset must earn to compensate investors. Figure 6.13 graphically represents the CAPM equation by depicting the relationship between risk, as shown by $β_i$ on the x-axis and the securities' $r_i$ on the y-axis. The graph is similar to Figure 6.5 which graphed the risk and return for assets. The line is called the **security market line (SML)**.
>
>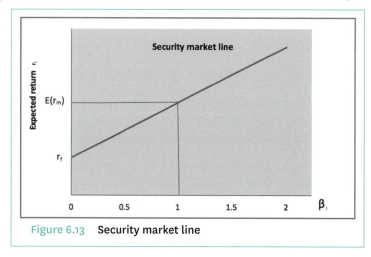
>
> Figure 6.13   Security market line

**Security market line (SML)**
The SML displays the expected return of an individual security or portfolio in relation to its systematic, non-diversifiable risk.

The graph shows that any investment without risk will have a return equal to the risk-free rate $r_f$, and this rate will be sufficient to compensate the investor for inflation and the time the funds are invested. The SML shows that as β increases, the expected return rises to compensate the investor for the higher risk, consistent with the trade-off between risk and return described in Figure 6.5. Risk-seeking investors will invest in assets with a β greater than 1 in order to obtain the higher returns that will compensate them for the additional risk in the investment.

According to CAPM theory, if the asset's risk and expected return are on the SML, then its risk and expected return is said to be correctly valued in relation to its risk. If an asset's expected return and risk are plotted above the SML, then it is undervalued and the investor should receive a greater return for the risk associated with the investment. If the asset is below the SML, it is considered to be overvalued and the investor will receive a lower return for the level of risk associated with the asset. The concept of CAPM will be used again in Chapter 10, where we will estimate the required return shareholders may expect from an investment in a firm.

## Conclusion

This chapter has introduced the concepts of risk and return. Firstly, assets without risk were introduced, and the two components comprising the risk-free rate – the real interest rate and expected inflation – were described. These components have a significant effect on interest rates and, therefore, on the shape of the yield curve for any particular class of securities.

The two components of a return – the real return and expected inflation – are the same for every investment or financing decision, but an element of risk is also present. Risk is the one uncertain factor investors require compensation for. We have looked at methods of calculating ex-post and ex-ante risks and returns, and introduced the concept of diversification, which is the practice of spreading risk by investing in a wide range of real and financial assets. Finally CAPM, a linear equation that calculates the risk and return for any asset or portfolio, was described. Once the values are obtained they can be plotted on the SML in order to show whether the returns from the investment justify the risks associated with it.

**SELF-TEST QUESTIONS**

1. Calculate the annual holding period yields for Colonial Fruit Company Ltd (CFC) and Turangi Timber Mills Ltd (TTM) using the following information:

   |  | CFC | TTM |
   |---|---|---|
   | Beginning share price 31/12/20X5 | $1.95 | $1.75 |
   | Ending share price 30/6/20X7 | $2.30 | $2.21 |
   | Dividends received | $0.25 | $0.15 |

2. An investment company has a number of portfolios available for clients to invest in. The financial assets contained in three of these portfolios are listed below.
   - Portfolio 1: Futures, property (retail), speculative shares, high-quality corporate bonds.
   - Portfolio 2: Government bonds, equity (blue chip), property (industrial), high-quality corporate bonds, preference shares.
   - Portfolio 3: Equity (blue chip), equity (speculative), high-quality corporate bonds, property (industrial), preference shares.

   Which portfolio would suit:
   a a young career professional person aged 25?
   b a family person with three dependent children, aged 45?
   c a professional person aged 62?
   Justify your answers.

3. When we introduced mean returns and standard deviations earlier in this chapter, we showed the annual returns and risks for Asset A and Asset B. This information is reproduced below:

   | Year | Asset A returns (%) | Asset B returns (%) | 50/50 portfolio returns (%) | 75/25 portfolio returns (%) |
   |---|---|---|---|---|
   | 20X3 | 8 | 13 | 10.5 | 9.25 |
   | 20X4 | 2 | 22 | 12.0 | 7.0 |
   | 20X5 | 12 | –8 | 2.0 | 7.0 |
   | 20X6 | 9 | 10 | 9.5 | 9.25 |
   | 20X7 | 4 | 13 | 8.5 | 6.25 |

   a Calculate the mean return and standard deviation of the portfolio containing 50% invested in Asset A and 50% in Asset B.
   b Calculate the mean return and standard deviation of the portfolio containing 75% invested in Asset A and 25% in Asset B.
   c In a table, summarise the mean return and standard deviations for Assets A and B and the two portfolio combinations calculated above. Compare and contrast the risk and return of each.
   d How is it possible that the returns for the two portfolio combinations are both greater than Asset A but have lower risk than Asset A?

4 The dairy industry is important to the New Zealand economy. Unfortunately, it is very difficult for farmers to predict the price they can expect to receive from Fonterra. The dairy industry has estimated that the following scenarios may occur over the coming year:

|  | Return on milk solids | Probability |
| --- | --- | --- |
| Increase | 15% | 0.4 |
| Stable | 9% | 0.35 |
| Decrease | 3% | 0.25 |

a Calculate the expected returns the farmers may expect to receive in the coming year.
b Calculate the standard deviation of these returns.

## ANSWERS TO SELF-TEST QUESTIONS

1

$$
\begin{aligned}
&\text{CFC} &&\text{TTM} \\
\text{Annual HPY} &= \left(\frac{\$2.30 + \$0.25}{\$1.95}\right)^{1/1.5} - 1 &&= \left(\frac{\$2.21 + \$0.15}{\$1.75}\right)^{1/1.5} - 1 \\
&= 1.30769^{0.6667} - 1 &&= 1.34857^{0.66667} - 1 \\
&= 0.1958 \text{ or } 19.58\% &&= 0.2206 \text{ or } 22.06\%
\end{aligned}
$$

2 Portfolio 1 contains securities such as futures and speculative equity that are categorised as high risk and hence would suit the 25-year-old career professional. This person should have 30–40 years in the workforce, and therefore has sufficient time to make up any losses that may arise from risky investment decisions.

Portfolio 2 contains primarily low-risk securities and as a result would suit the 62-year-old professional person. Due to the age of the investor, they are usually cautious regarding their investment decisions because their ability to recoup any investment losses is low.

Portfolio 3 contains some low-risk financial assets as well as some speculative shares to permit a higher return to be generated. This portfolio should suit the 45-year-old family person who could have a cautious attitude to risk while at the same time wanting to receive the benefit of the higher returns generated by riskier financial securities.

3 a 50/50 portfolio

| Year | Asset A returns (%) | Asset B returns (%) | 50/50 portfolio (%) |
|---|---|---|---|
| 20X3 | 8 | 13 | 10.5 |
| 20X4 | 2 | 22 | 12.0 |
| 20X5 | 12 | −8 | 2.0 |
| 20X6 | 9 | 10 | 9.5 |
| 20X7 | 4 | 13 | 8.5 |

$$\bar{r} = \frac{\sum r}{n}$$

$$50/50 \text{ Portfolio mean return} = \frac{0.105 + 0.12 + 0.02 + 0.095 + 0.085}{5}$$

$$= \frac{0.425}{5}$$

$$= 0.085 \text{ or } 8.5\%$$

$$\sigma^2 = \frac{\sum_{i=1}^{n}(r_i - \bar{r})^2}{n - 1}$$

$$\sigma^2 = \frac{(0.105 - 0.085)^2 + (0.12 - 0.085)^2 + (0.02 - 0.085)^2 + (0.095 - 0.085)^2 + (0.085 - 0.085)}{5 - 1}$$

$$= \frac{(0.02)^2 + (0.035)^2 + (-0.065)^2 + (0.01)^2 + (0)^2}{4}$$

$$= \frac{0.0004 + 0.00123 + 0.00423 + 0.0001 + 0}{4}$$

$$= \frac{0.00596}{4}$$

$$= 0.00149$$

$$\sigma = \sqrt{0.00149} = 0.0386 \text{ or } 3.86\%$$

**b** 75/25 portfolio

| Year | Asset A returns (%) | Asset B returns (%) | 75/25 portfolio (%) |
|---|---|---|---|
| 20X3 | 8 | 13 | 9.25 |
| 20X4 | 2 | 22 | 7.0 |
| 20X5 | 12 | −8 | 7.0 |
| 20X6 | 9 | 10 | 9.25 |
| 20X7 | 4 | 13 | 6.25 |

$$75/25 \text{ Asset mean return} = \frac{0.0925 + 0.07 + 0.07 + 0.0925 + 0.0625}{5}$$

$$= \frac{0.3875}{5}$$

$$= 0.0775 \text{ or } 7.75\%$$

$$\sigma^2 = \frac{(0.0925 - 0.0775)^2 + (0.07 - 0.0775)^2 + (0.07 - 0.0775)^2 + (0.0925 - 0.0775)^2 + (0.0625 - 0.0775)^2}{5 - 1}$$

$$= \frac{0.00023 + 0.00006 + 0.00006 + 0.00023 + 0.00023}{4}$$

$$= \frac{0.00081}{4} = 0.0002$$

$$\sigma = \sqrt{0.0002} = 0.01414 \text{ or } 1.4\%$$

**c**

| | Asset A | Asset B | 50/50 portfolio | 75/25 portfolio |
|---|---|---|---|---|
| Mean return | 7.0% | 10.0% | 8.5% | 7.75% |
| Standard deviation | 4.0% | 11.0% | 3.86% | 1.4% |

The table above shows that Asset B provides the highest return and greatest risk of all investments. By diversifying and holding some of the less risky Asset A, the investor is able to reduce the risk inherent in Asset B (and Asset A) significantly. The two portfolio returns provide a higher return but lower risk than simply investing in the lowest risk Asset A. This shows the benefits derived from diversification.

**d** The objective of diversification is to find assets with returns that vary over time. The returns for Asset A and Asset B differ each year, which indicates that the returns from each asset are not perfectly correlated. When this situation occurs, the variability of the annual returns in a portfolio will be reduced.

4a
$$\bar{r} = \sum_{i=1}^{n} r_i \times \text{probability}_i$$
$$= (0.15 \times 0.4) + (0.09 \times 0.35) + (0.03 \times 0.25)$$
$$= 0.06 + 0.0315 + 0.0075$$
$$= 0.099 \text{ or } 9.9\%$$

b
$$\sigma^2 = \sum_{i=1}^{n} (r_i - \bar{r})^2 \times \text{probability}_i$$
$$= (0.15 - 0.099)^2 \times 0.4 + (0.09 - 0.099)^2 \times 0.35 + (0.03 - 0.099)^2 \times 0.25$$
$$= (0.051)^2 \times 0.4 + (-0.009)^2\times 0.35 + (-0.069)^2 \times 0.25$$
$$= 0.0026 \times 0.4 + 0.00008 \times 0.35 + 0.00476 \times 0.25$$
$$= 0.00104 + 0.00003 + 0.00119$$

$\sigma = \sqrt{\sigma^2}$  $\quad = 0.00226$

$$= \sqrt{0.0026}$$
$$= 0.04754 \text{ or } 4.75\%$$

The dairy farmers should expect a return of 9.9% on their milk solids for the coming year. They will need to consider whether the risk of 4.75% is acceptable by comparing it with the risk associated with other primary products.

## QUESTIONS AND PROBLEMS

1. Define risk and return.

2. Two years ago you purchased shares in AB Supreme at $4.76 per share. Today their price is $7.10. During the period, dividends of 18 cents per share were received. Compute the holding period yield and annual holding period yield on your investment.

3. Refer to question 2 above. The returns computed for this question are nominal rates of return. If the expected inflation rate was 1.2%, compute the real rate of return.

4. A risk-free asset comprises two components. List these two components, and describe each one.

5. Five components make up the risk premium. List them, and describe each one.

6. Describe the four forms of term structure of interest rates.

7. The objective of diversification is to reduce the risk of a portfolio. Describe systematic and unsystematic risk in the context of diversification.

8. Fluctuations in the New Zealand dollar and petrol prices have affected the operations of Trans Tasman Tourism (TTT) over the past few years. The Chief Financial Officer considers that if tourist numbers increase in the coming year, the company's expected return would be 30%. If the level of tourism remains the same, a return of 15% would be expected. If tourist numbers fell during this time, however, she considers the company will receive an expected return of –10%. The table below provides the returns and probabilities for TTT:

| Demand | Expected return | Probability of outcome occurring |
|---|---|---|
| Rises | 30% | 0.4 |
| Static | 15% | 0.25 |
| Falls | –10% | 0.35 |

   a. Calculate the expected return for TTT.

   b. Calculate the variance and standard deviation of these returns.

   c. Assume TTT has a β of 1.3, the $r_f$ is 3% and the MRP is 5.3%. Calculate TTT's expected return using CAPM.

# CHAPTER 7

# Personal financial management

### Learning objectives

By the end of this chapter, you should be able to:

- describe the process of making personal financial decisions
- establish personal financial goals and use appropriate techniques to ensure their attainment
- use money-management techniques
- describe the range of savings options which can be used to finance retirement
- describe how to manage the financing of a house
- outline the areas to investigate when preparing the preliminary evaluation of a business opportunity
- be familiar with the types of property ownership and rights, as well as common legal aspects relating to property.

## Introduction

This chapter introduces the processes and procedures to help individuals with their short-term and long-term personal financial decision-making. This involves setting goals, determining the financial opportunity costs associated with these goals, and then selecting the strategies to achieve them. We then study how money management aids in this process.

After determining how to set and attain personal short-term goals, we next consider those goals to be required in the long-term. For example, the level of home ownership in New Zealand is high compared with that in other countries, so at some stage most people will need to make a decision whether to rent an apartment or house or purchase some form of residence. In addition, we need to plan for our personal well-being in retirement; that is, how much money will be required to fund an enjoyable quality of life that permits the pursuit of leisure activities. Finally, we investigate the process of starting or buying a business.

## The personal financial planning activity

The **goal** of personal financial planning is to enhance one's financial well-being and consequently one's standard of living. If done properly, it should be possible to obtain and retain the basic necessities of life, as well as the comforts and luxuries desired for a 'good life'.

In order to achieve these goals, a number of decisions or choices must be made which are directly related to each individual's choice of lifestyle. For example, the level of education individuals attain, the type of career, friends, accommodation and their level of self-sufficiency will all be affected by the financial goals that they have set at different times. The quality of an individual's life will thus be affected by decisions associated with the level of their personal finances.

> **Goal**
> The object (or aim) of a person's ambitions or efforts.

**Personal financial planning** is the process of setting financial goals to satisfy a need. It is an ongoing activity, which should be constantly updated, revised and amended to take into account the changes that occur as people move through life. The process involves managing money in order to maximise the benefits and attain a desired level of personal economic well-being. In order to achieve this objective, some form of financial planning and control is required.

> **Personal financial planning**
> Process of setting financial goals in order to satisfy a need.

The following are a number of activities that are undertaken to assist the financial planning process, as shown in Figure 7.1.

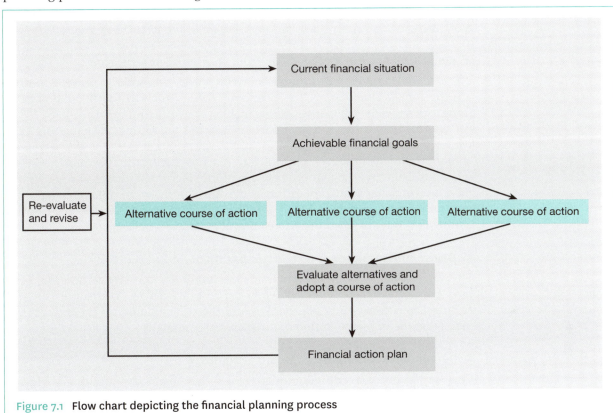

Figure 7.1 **Flow chart depicting the financial planning process**

## 1 Determine your current financial situation

This involves assessing how much income is received on a regular basis, the amount spent on living expenses, how much money can be saved, and the amount of debt owed to others.

## 2 Establish achievable financial goals

It is important that people know themselves and their attitude to money; that is, their degree of risk aversion and the amount of care they take with their money. Once this has been determined, then it is possible to categorise an individual's **needs** and separate them from their **wants**. Needs will be incorporated into the financial goals, and the selection will be made independently, depending on each individual's current household and financial situation. The goals should be realistically stated in an easy-to-understand way, be measurable, and be linked to a time frame. These components will be discussed in more detail below.

> **Needs**
> Items of necessity.
>
> **Wants**
> Items of desire.

### 3 Identify alternative course(s) of action to achieve the required goals

This will ensure that all possibilities have been considered. The alternatives may be to:

- continue as before and maintain the status quo
- expand on the current situation by increasing savings or increasing debt repayments
- make changes to the current situation by using EFTPOS or internet banking rather than cheques to pay for items
- do something entirely different, such as using savings to repay credit card debt.

### 4 Evaluate possible alternatives from your current situation

Possible alternatives will be influenced by each individual's present lifestyle and personal values, as well as economic factors such as the likelihood of an improvement in the job market, falling interest rates and a buoyant economy. When considering these aspects it is important to assess the risks of each alternative as well as the impact of the time value of money on any strategies devised. Whenever choices are made, however, opportunity costs are incurred. These costs relate to what has been given up in order to make the decision, and are not necessarily measured in dollar terms. For example, the opportunity costs could refer to the cost of the alternative direction to be taken, or to the time taken to make the decision – time that could be used in a more enjoyable pursuit.

### 5 Devise and implement a realistic financial action plan

This can be done once the current financial situation is known and financial goals have been established. It is only when the groundwork has been done carefully and decisions concerning alternatives and the risks inherent in them have been made that the implementation of the plan can commence.

### 6 Re-evaluate and update the plan regularly

This should be done annually unless major changes to an individual's lifestyle occur. Whenever lifestyle changes occur, the financial plan will need to be promptly revised. These changes may be personal, social or economic. In the process of revising your financial goals, new alternatives may arise which will require analysis and further decisions to be made.

The process of monitoring a financial plan ensures that targets can still be reached or the plans revised to achieve more realistic goals. The six steps listed above may be used by individuals to plan their finances, and is the same procedure that can be used for any small or large company operating anywhere in the world.

The process described above forces consideration of what the short-term, medium-term and long-term financial requirements are, and what steps need to be set in place in order to achieve these requirements. These requirements will differ depending on the age, sex, cultural background, employment category, living arrangements, etc. of the individual. Other factors, such as the economic situation and government policy currently in existence, will also affect financial plans and may cause a re-evaluation of the plans.

## Money management

Once financial goals have been established, it is important to develop strategies for managing money so that a successful outcome can be achieved. It helps to remember Charles Dickens's Mr Micawber, who described the desired outcome of managing one's money by observing that if income equalled £100.00 and expenses equalled £99.95, the result was happiness, but if income was £100.00 and expenses were £100.05, then the outcome was misery.

The **strategies** used to aid the management of scarce resources such as income are **budgeting** and the development of **personal financial statements** which list those assets owned personally and those liabilities owed to other people. These strategies will be described more fully below, and can be used by individuals and the owners of small, medium and large businesses, although they are referred to as 'balance sheets' by firms. If budgets and financial statements are not used, then even though the level of income earned may seem high, expenditure, if not controlled, may be even higher – with the end result being bankruptcy! Control of spending will ensure that bankruptcy does not occur and that financial goals can be met.

However, in order to implement the required strategies, conflicting situations will almost certainly arise. That is, if any income has been spent, it will no longer be available to meet long-term savings and investment goals. When money is invested, it can no longer be used for spending, which can in turn create other problems. For example, the desire to acquire an item may be so great that the decision to buy on credit or use a credit card today may override the choice of paying cash a little later. It should be remembered that there is a cost associated with the use of funds belonging to another person or organisation. At some point in time, items which have been bought on credit must be paid for, and the amount to be paid for the goods will include their cost as well as the charges associated with borrowed funds. Hence, the trade-off, or opportunity cost, of using credit means that the item(s) purchased will be more expensive than if cash was paid at the outset. Some items, such as houses, will almost always be acquired using loan funds. However, there are ways to reduce the costs associated with borrowing money, and these will be covered in more detail later in this chapter.

The development of personal financial statements involves three activities:

- the gathering of financial information
- preparing an **income statement**
- developing a personal balance sheet.

These activities are discussed below.

> **Strategy**
> A plan of action designed to achieve a goal.
>
> **Budgeting**
> Process of allocating income and expenditure over a future period.
>
> **Personal financial statement**
> Statement listing the items an individual owns (assets) and the amount of debt they owe to someone else (liabilities). (Similar to a balance sheet.)
>
> **Income statement**
> Statement showing the income/deficit resulting from income and expenditure over a period.

## Gathering financial information

This involves recording all sources of income that have been received during the year. Examples may be employment earnings, interest earned from funds invested in fixed interest, or dividends received from monies invested in company shares. Household and personal expenses are deducted from income so that a surplus or deficit for the year can be ascertained. This can be shown in equation form as:

$$\text{Income} - \text{Expenses} = \text{Surplus (Deficit)} \qquad \textit{Equation 7.1}$$

Surplus funds are available to be put away for investment purposes or to achieve financial targets. Examples of household and personal expenses may be food, electricity, insurance, clothing, student loan repayments, travel, etc.

Documentation of the above income and expenses provides a basis for the compilation of personal financial statements in the form of an income statement and balance sheet. These are detailed below.

## Preparing an income statement

The income statement lists the income received and spent by a household during the year and reflects their financial well-being. If a surplus is made, then some funds can be saved so that longer-term financial goals can be met. However, if a deficit is incurred, then the statement provides timely information that expenses should be more strictly controlled. In this case, steps must be put in place to eliminate the deficit. One way of doing this is to develop a budget for the coming year, based on details contained in the income statement and after considering any amendments expected in the coming year.

## Budget preparation

Budgeting is undertaken in order to ensure that all financial goals can be met within the predetermined time frame. Although a number of expense items will remain the same each month, the budget will indicate those periods when a shortage of cash may occur so that steps can be taken to make sure that funds are on hand to meet the shortfall. As mentioned earlier, if a loan has to be obtained to achieve financial goals, then the cost associated with these goals will be higher. Therefore, budgets enable individuals to make sure they:

- spend less than they earn
- make wise financial decisions regarding spending their money
- reach their predetermined financial goals
- have funds put aside to meet financial emergencies
- develop sound financial management habits.

## Developing a personal balance sheet

To obtain a fuller picture of an individual's financial position, a balance sheet can be developed. The balance sheet has two sides: one half depicts what the individual owns (their assets), and the other half shows how much they owe (their liabilities), with any balance representing positive or negative **net worth** as shown by the formula below.

$$\text{Assets} - \text{Liabilities} = \text{Net worth} \qquad \textit{Equation 7.2}$$

For example, if they have items of value of $12 500 and they owe others $7 250 then their net worth is $5 250, that is:

$$\$12\,500 - \$7\,250 = \$5\,250$$

The formula can be stated another way, to show that all assets are financed with either liabilities (debt) or net worth (equity).

$$\text{Assets} = \text{Liabilities} + \text{Net worth} \qquad \textit{Equation 7.3}$$

The balance sheet provides information as at a particular date. This should be distinguished from the income statement, which measures income and expenses between two dates. The assets and liabilities categories are broken down further, as follows.

- Financial assets can be divided into two groups: current and long-term assets. Current assets are those that can be readily converted into cash within one year, such as money in a cheque or savings account. Long-term financial assets

> **Net worth**
> Net worth represents the amount of money a person would have left over if all their assets were sold to pay off their debts.

represent the market value of retirement funds that have been invested in shares or fixed-interest securities, KiwiSaver funds, etc. These cannot be readily converted into cash, and in many cases the only reason to liquidate them would be when no other alternative exists.

- **Fixed assets** have an expected life greater than one year, and usually include real estate in the form of a house, bach or any other land. They are included in the balance sheet at the current government valuation figure. Alternatively, a value determined by an independent valuer or by comparison with similar properties which have recently been sold can be used. Arriving at a value for household possessions, artworks, jewellery, etc. is more difficult, because although the price may be known at the time of purchase the value will alter over time. Therefore, the values of these items should be revised periodically so that the current (or market) value can be incorporated into the balance sheet. It is possible to obtain an estimated value of specific items by either looking in second-hand shops or advertisements in the paper to see what price comparable items are selling for. Alternatively, the services of an appraiser can be used.

> **Fixed assets**
> Assets that are real (for example, buildings, equipment, vehicles).

- Liabilities are sums that are owed to another person(s) whereby a benefit has been gained that has given rise to a debt. Liabilities exclude future commitments that are not due at the moment, such as a golf subscription or next week's rent. Liabilities also fall into current (short-term) and long-term categories. **Current liabilities** are due within a short period of time (usually within a year) and include tax payments, insurance premiums, rent and electricity. Long-term liabilities are debts that do not require payment in full within a year. Examples include a house mortgage, a student loan and a car loan.

> **Current liabilities**
> Debts that are due to be paid within the year.

## Financial planning for life

Once financial goals have been set, the following questions should be asked.

- Are the goals realistic?
- Can they be measured?
- Are they achievable with a set time frame?

Financial needs do change over an individual's lifetime and pass through three phases.

- **The accumulation phase**
  This phase occurs during the early and middle years of an individual's working life. During this phase, assets are accumulated to satisfy immediate needs, such as the acquisition of a car and work-related clothing, the setting-up of a flat or accumulating the deposit on a house. In the longer term, a goal may be to fund children's education in order to minimise their student loans.

  During this phase, an individual's net worth is small and could even be negative. However, because retirement is a long way off at this stage and the potential exists for increasing their level of earnings, these people are prepared to take more risks and will assume more debt than older individuals. In many cases, the level of debt owed by people during this phase will be greater than their earnings, and any investments they make may earn greater returns due to the extra associated risks.

- **The consolidation phase**
  This phase occurs when people are entering the middle of their working life and they are starting to think about their retirement. As a result, the dollar value of debt and mortgage balances are probably low or non-existent and there may be sufficient funds available to assist with children's education requirements. Income should exceed expenses, thereby freeing up the funds required to provide for retirement. Because the length of time to retirement is shorter than during the accumulation phase, people in this group become more cautious where risk is concerned and tend to be more careful with their investments. In order to protect the value of their assets at this stage, people avoid high-risk securities in favour of those with more moderate risk. This is because people have less time to recoup any losses incurred as a result of bad investment decisions.

- **The spending phase**
  This occurs once retirement is reached. Living expenses decline and so does the level of income coming into the household. Income will take the form of investment and/or superannuation/pension income. Some people may seek part-time or consultancy work to supplement their income and to ensure their capital is protected. Because the average life expectancy is increasing steadily, reliance on savings will be required for a longer period of time. This may cause a conflict for those people reliant on investment income for their well-being. For example, while their savings must be protected so that they have sufficient income during their retirement, they will also require the higher returns that will be generated from investments in at least some risky assets to protect their nest egg from being eroded by inflation.

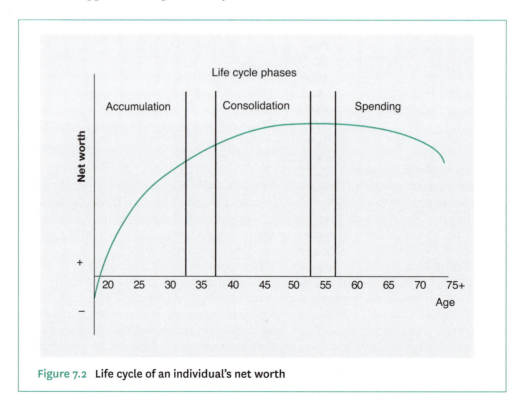

Figure 7.2  Life cycle of an individual's net worth

The three phases are shown in Figure 7.2 and depict the current and expected phases that you will pass through during your working life. At the outset most people commence their working life with negative net worth (liabilities exceed assets). However, over time assets are acquired and debts reduced so that net worth becomes positive. The level of net worth rises during the accumulation phase and, to a lesser extent, during the consolidation phase, before starting to decline. Note that there is a transition period between each phase which reflects the fact that some people will enter each phase earlier than others.

Figure 7.3 illustrates the risk preferences of people as they move through their life cycle. Note that the life cycle phases are reversed as compared with Figure 7.2. Risk and return preferences are lowest during the spending phase, moderate through consolidation, and highest during accumulation. The pattern depicted in the figures may be changing slowly as people now enter the workforce, marry and have families at an older age. In addition, redundancies and time out of the workforce in order to retrain will also affect the pattern shown.

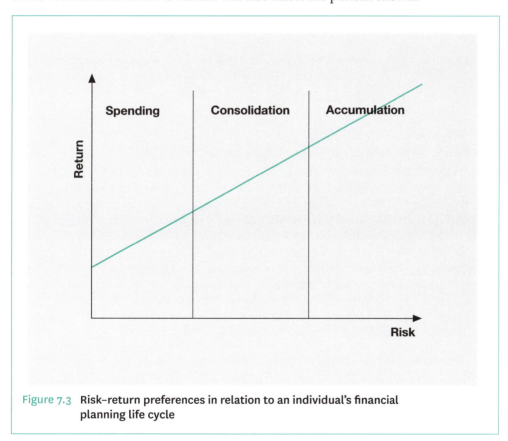

Figure 7.3   Risk–return preferences in relation to an individual's financial planning life cycle

# Financial goal attainment

In order to reach a goal of having sufficient funds to enjoy retirement, individuals must use the financial resources that are being accumulated sensibly. This requires the integration and co-ordination of a number of components. For instance, if a person is employed, careful planning is needed to make sure that earnings are not wasted. The earnings are used to partly fund immediate living requirements; any surplus is saved so that future financial goals can be met. It is important to consider the timing of these goals and to make sure that savings are available for use at the right time. This means that sufficient liquid funds should be available when they are required. Liquid funds are savings that can be converted into cash when required, without incurring a penalty that would result in a reduction in the value of the investment.

Sometimes it becomes necessary to borrow funds in order to purchase a more expensive asset, such as a house or a car, and in these cases the goals which have been set can often be met more quickly by obtaining a loan. However, a loan increases the effective cost of the item, because consumption is being accelerated and a charge must be paid for the use of other people's money. Borrowing money in these circumstances is not a problem, but it is important to use credit carefully so that earnings are used for enjoyment and not merely to service debt. Therefore, in order to achieve their financial goals, people need to identify their goals and then prioritise them.

## Funding a retirement plan

Planning for retirement and committing funds towards this objective are fraught with difficulties, especially when income seems to be fully committed during the accumulation phase of the life cycle. During this phase very few people would be able to answer the following questions with any degree of certainty.

- How old will you be when you retire?
- How much money do you think you will need to save in order to be able to live comfortably in retirement?
- When should the saving activity commence?

During the accumulation phase it may not be possible to answer the above questions with any degree of confidence.

For example, the decision concerning how much income is required at retirement could strongly influence the decision of when to retire, especially if no savings plan has been implemented. It is important to realise that if people retire at 65 years of age they can expect to have approximately 20 years of retirement to enjoy. The length of time spent in retirement is increasing all the time, as is the quality of life of retirees. As a result it is becoming more important to ensure that sufficient funds will be available to finance the spending phase of one's life comfortably. However, over time, people may become less active, so that funds previously spent on leisure activities may be spent on health-related needs.

Table 7.1 **Level of demand on earnings over an individual's life cycle**

| Expense items | Individual life cycle phases | | |
| --- | --- | --- | --- |
| | Accumulation | Consolidation | Spending |
| Mortgage payments | High | Low–medium | Nil–low |
| Household possessions | High | Low–high prior to retirement | Low |
| Living expenses | High | Medium–high | Low (no work-related expenses) |
| Children | High | Medium–high | Nil–low |
| Entertainment/travel | High | Medium–high | Low–medium |
| Health | Low–medium | Low–medium | Medium–high |
| Savings | Low | Medium–high | High |

Table 7.1 shows how the demand for funds changes over the three phases of an individual's life cycle. It is an illustration only, due to the large number of factors that need to be taken into account. For example, decisions concerning buying or renting accommodation, whether to have children, the level of entertainment or travel to be undertaken, etc., will all depend on individual choice.

Although there are a great many decisions to make concerning a person's retirement, it is important to remember that the level of enjoyment to be experienced will depend, to a large extent, on the level of funds that have been allocated to this period. In order to determine the level of savings required for retirement, two estimates are required to be undertaken:

- **target annual retirement income** (after-tax income)
- **annual retirement income** (after-tax income).

Once these estimates have been made the **retirement income gap** can be calculated.

> **Target annual retirement income**
> Amount of income required to cover estimated retirement expenses.
>
> **Annual retirement income**
> The various sources of income that can be used to fund retirement.
>
> **Retirement income gap**
> The surplus or deficit in income required to fund one's retirement.

## Retirement income gap

The retirement income gap highlights any shortfall in income required to fund one's retirement lifestyle. One method used to calculate the retirement income gap is to compile a Retirement Expense Worksheet so that the level of annual expenditure expected during this time can be calculated. The worksheet depicted on the next page has been compiled for a married couple. The amounts contained in the worksheet will differ depending on each individual's needs and wants.

The first estimate in the retirement income gap calculation is the target annual retirement income (after tax). This estimate is based on the income required to cover the estimated costs of the lifestyle desired. Naturally, a number of work-related expenses, such as transportation costs, will no longer be required, but these expenses may be replaced by hobby or health-related costs. A rule-of-thumb estimate to use for the target annual retirement income (after tax) is 70% of your estimated annual income (after tax) just prior to your retirement. Nevertheless this estimate is very difficult to determine if the time to retirement is 30 or more years away.

| Retirement Expense Worksheet | |
|---|---:|
| **Expenses (per month)** | |
| Electricity / Telephone | $ 400.00 |
| Insurance – house | $ 165.00 |
| – contents | $ 85.00 |
| – car | $ 50.00 |
| – health | $ 480.00 |
| Car registration | $ 9.00 |
| Rates | $ 262.00 |
| Clothes | $ 550.00 |
| Food | $ 820.00 |
| Entertainment | $ 400.00 |
| Travel – holidays | $ 450.00 |
| – car (plus maintenance) | $ 400.00 |
| Miscellaneous | $ 500.00 |
| Monthly expenses | $ 4 571.00 |
| Annual expenses | $54 852.00 |
| | |
| Therefore income target (after-tax) | $54 852.00 |
| *Minus* New Zealand superannuation (after-tax)[1] | $41 557.00 |
| | $13 295.00 |
| Other income | $1 185.40 |
| Retirement income gap (per annum) | $12 109.60 |

[1] As at 2024 this sum represents weekly payments of $799.18 for a couple who qualify.

From the information provided in the worksheet above, we see that $54 852.00 is required annually in order for the couple to meet their needs.

The other estimate required to calculate the retirement income gap is the annual retirement income (after tax). This estimate takes into account the various types of income available during this time. These funds may come from a variety of sources, such as those listed below.

- *Employment*
  This may be from part-time work or consultancies, or a new venture undertaken at retirement.
- *Savings*
  Many people will have a private pension/superannuation scheme, investments or KiwiSaver.
- *New Zealand superannuation*
  This is available to all New Zealand permanent residents providing residency and age requirements have been met. The 2024 after-tax income that can be expected from this source is $799.18 per week for a couple who have reached

the qualifying age of 65; $519.46 per week for a single person living alone; and $479.52 per week for a single person sharing accommodation.

- *Others*
  Inheritances, gifts, etc.

## KiwiSaver

KiwiSaver was introduced by the New Zealand government on 2 July 2007 as a voluntary long-term savings scheme. Its main purpose was to encourage New Zealanders to commence a savings programme to fund their retirement. Younger participants, however, can use their KiwiSaver funds towards a deposit for their first home.

Any New Zealand citizen with residency aged 64 or younger can join the scheme, while those under 18 require parental permission to do so. At the time of writing, employees can choose to contribute 3%, 4%, 8% or 10% of their gross wages or salary to a fund, while their employers are required to contribute at least 3% (less tax) of each contributing employees' gross salary or wage into the employee's KiwiSaver account.

There are a number of benefits that accrue to participants. These are:

- the KiwiSaver contribution comes out of the employee's pay before they see it in their bank account so there is no opportunity to spend it
- participants save an additional sum over and above their salary from their employer's contribution
- the government pays an annual member tax credit of $521.00 into each KiwiSaver account of contributing members over 18 years of age who qualify
- KiwiSaver provides an opportunity for contributors to save for their retirement or to save for their first home through a KiwiSaver HomeStart programme
- KiwiSaver accounts are transportable should contributors change jobs or leave the workforce.

## Choosing a KiwiSaver fund

A number of providers, such as banks and investment companies, offer KiwiSaver schemes. (Note that it is important to realise that the government does not guarantee any KiwiSaver scheme or their investment funds.) Each provider offers a range of schemes – each with a different mix of financial and real assets – at varying levels of risk. For example, people entering the workforce have a long, productive working life ahead of them, so they may decide that an aggressive, high-risk fund would be the most appropriate for them. These funds invest primarily in growth assets, which can be volatile and, as a result, may produce high returns some years and negative returns in others. Over the long run these funds usually earn a higher return to compensate for their higher risk. At the other end of the spectrum, employees at the end of their working lives are more likely to switch their KiwiSaver money into defensive, low-risk funds to better protect their savings.

> **Example 1: Calculating the retirement income gap**

From the information above, the retirement income gap that will satisfy the needs of this couple at retirement is estimated to be $12 109.60; that is,

$$\begin{matrix} \text{Annual retirement} \\ \text{income target} \\ \text{(after tax)} \end{matrix} - \begin{matrix} \text{Annual retirement} \\ \text{income (after tax)} \end{matrix} = \text{Retirement income gap}$$

$$\$54\ 852.00 - \$42\ 742.40 = \$12\ 109.60$$

The time line below portrays the situation for the couple. The time line shows that they have 18 years in which to save a sum of money that should provide the additional funds they require once they have retired.

| Time 0 | Retirement | End of 20 years |
|---|---|---|
| Time to retirement = 18 years | Income of $12 109.60 per annum for 20 years | |

- Equation 5.4 is used to calculate the sum they need to save that will provide them with 20 payments of $12 109.60 per annum:

$$PVA = PMT \left[ \frac{1 - (1 + r)^{-n}}{r} \right]$$

$$= \$12\ 109.60 \left[ \frac{1 - (1 + 0.03)^{-20}}{0.03} \right]$$

$$= \$12\ 109.60 \left[ \frac{1 - 0.55368}{0.03} \right]$$

$$= \$12\ 109.60 \left[ \frac{0.44632}{0.03} \right]$$

$$= \$12\ 109.60 \times 14.87733$$

$$= \$180\ 158.52$$

Therefore, based on a life expectancy of 20 years and a 3% real rate of return, they would need to save $180 158.52 by the time they retire in 18 years' time. This calculation has solved the problem of the target level of savings required; that is, the right-hand side of the time line above. Now all that needs to be done is to solve the left-hand side of the time line.

- Using Equation 5.3, calculate how much should be saved each year for 18 years to reach the target level of savings of $180 158.52.

$$PMT = \frac{FVA \times r}{(1 + r)^n - 1}$$

$$= \frac{\$180\ 158.52 \times 0.03}{(1 + 0.03)^{18} - 1}$$

$$= \frac{\$5\ 404.76}{1.70243 - 1}$$

$$= \frac{\$5\ 404.76}{0.70243}$$

$$= \$7\ 694.38$$

In order to achieve this target level of savings, using a 3% real rate of return, the couple would have to save $7 694.38 per annum. The completed time line is shown below.

Because the retirement income gap was a positive figure, additional funds were required in order to achieve the desired level of income after retirement. However, herein lies a source of conflict – if it is found that the gap is large, then it will be necessary to do one of the following:
- revise the target set for retirement
- work as long as possible so that the target level of funds is achieved
- consider some form of consultancy or part-time work in retirement.

Therefore, the earlier some form of savings plan to fund retirement is developed, the less likely these problems are to arise. Once debts (including mortgages) have been reduced or eliminated, then these funds can be transferred to a savings plan to finance retirement savings.

In addition, if a budget is compiled of the current income and expenses for the household, then it is easy to see whether or not there are sufficient surplus funds on hand to meet this monthly expense, which can then be included in the regular savings pattern of the household. Alternatively, lump-sum payments, such as bonuses, prizes, etc., can be invested for the balance of the time to retirement, and funds released after debt and/or mortgage reduction activities have been completed can also be used as additional savings. Much can be achieved by small sacrifices, but it is important to ensure that the savings programme does not become so onerous that the hard work brings no reward for the effort expended.

Finally, decisions concerning the type of accommodation to be used in retirement are important. For example, a home owned without any debt is likely to cost less per year compared to renting accommodation during retirement. Therefore, a decision to rent a residence during retirement will require more money to fund the rental outlays.

## Residential property and mortgages

As noted above, at some point in time most people will make the decision whether to live in rented accommodation or purchase some form of **residential property**. This decision differs from country to country. For example, in many countries the thought of owning your own home simply does not arise, because the means of saving the deposit and being able to pay a mortgage are beyond the financial ability of most people. This differs markedly from the situation in Australia and New Zealand, where the rate of home ownership is very high and where many people strive to own their own home.

**Residential property**
Property in which people live.

There are a number of advantages associated with renting a house or an apartment rather than owning a house. For instance:

- funds otherwise tied up in a house can be invested elsewhere
- repairs and maintenance on rental property are normally the responsibility of the **landlord**
- if it becomes necessary to move to another town, all that the tenant needs to do is serve the landlord the required notice – by contrast, selling a house can often take a long time, which means that relocation may bring with it additional problems.

However, there are also a number of advantages to owning a house. For example:

- the security of having control over the property and knowing you cannot be evicted at any time (unless there are arrears in mortgage payments)
- the ability to make changes to the house and/or the garden to satisfy your own lifestyle
- the potential of a capital gain on the property when it is sold
- homes are considered a safe investment for protecting **capital** (money).
- freehold interests represent the highest form of property ownership, and therefore afford the greatest set of rights afforded to the owner.

> **Landlord**
> Person who owns or leases property.

> **Capital**
> Wealth that is available to be used to produce more wealth.

## Property investment: Rights and ownership

The biggest financial decision many people make during their lives is whether to buy a residential property, either to occupy themselves or as an investment. Property often has a large weighting in the overall portfolio of assets a person may own and is typically acquired through extensive use of debt financing. Therefore, to make the best decision and achieve long-term financial success, understanding the rights and obligations of property, along with debt financing, is critical.

An essential part of researching a property investment is to investigate the ownership and property rights (and obligations) attached to the property. These rights can be identified from two sources: the record of title (formerly certificate of title), and the relevant District Plan, both discussed later in the chapter.

### Property concepts

In Chapter 2 we introduced some important land and property concepts. These are revised in Table 7.2 on the following page and some additional important property definitions have been added.

Table 7.2 **Key land and property concepts**

| | |
|---|---|
| Land | Land is a permanent asset. This permanence means that it will normally be expected to outlast uses and improvements, which have a finite life. |
| Improvements | Improvements are work done or material used, the benefits of which are unexhausted. They may have substance, such as a dwelling or a concrete drive, or they may be hidden, such as underground drainage or fertiliser application. They form an integral part of the land they are attached to. |
| Real property | Real property includes all the rights, interests and benefits related to the ownership of real estate. |
| Bundle of rights | The bundle of rights concept likens property ownership to a bundle of sticks with each stick representing a distinct and separate right of the property owner, for example the right to use, to sell, to lease, to give away, or to choose to exercise all or none of these rights. |
| Chattels | Personal property capable of complete transfer by delivery. Examples include light fittings, curtains, electric oven and carpets. |
| Plant and machinery | May include both chattels and fixtures and is a term normally associated with an industrial process. |
| Intangibles | Those aspects of real estate that do not have substance; you cannot physically see them or handle them. This includes rights associated with land use, such as an easement or a right of way, and with business operation, such as goodwill. |
| Lessor | The party who grants a lease, usually the property owner (though leases may also be subleased, creating a 'sub-lessor' status of a lessee). |
| Lessee | The party who accepts a lease, referred to as a tenant (or sub-tenant or a sub-lessor). |

## Definition of land and land ownership

The following extract from Jefferies describes how land is legally defined and described.[1]

> For land to be dealt with in property transactions it needs to have a clear definition as to its location, dimensions, area, and sometimes the natural features such as streams, foreshore, and road access. This is facilitated by land being surveyed and given a *legal description*. This legal description is unique for each separate parcel of land. All crown land when defined for grant, lease, or reservation is given a section number and in general these are Sections of a Block of a Survey District. The whole of New Zealand is covered by various surveys districts which are broken up into various blocks.

Various forms of ownership or legal estates in land exist to suit the differing requirements of land occupation and use. As discussed in Chapter 2, the real estate market deals in rights – not directly in the land and buildings that are property

---

1  Rodney Jefferies, *Urban valuation in New Zealand*, vol. 1, 2nd edn. (Wellington: New Zealand Institute of Valuers, 1991), chapter 4, p. 6.

objects. The various forms of ownership and legal estates in land confer various rights over the land and buildings. It is for this reason that ownership of real estate may be referred to as ownership of a bundle of rights.

The ownership of property is in principle the ownership of a bundle of rights relating to a particular parcel of land. The two-dimensional (plan view) definition of the land parcel can be extended to include a number of rights within the dimensions above and below the physical ground level, as shown in Figure 7.4, giving a three-dimensional view of the associated rights.

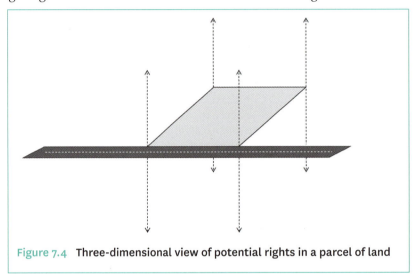

Figure 7.4  Three-dimensional view of potential rights in a parcel of land

In addition to the ownership of the two-dimensional land parcel, property (e.g. apartments) is also commonly held by way of a strata title under the Unit Titles Act 2010. Under this form of ownership there are exclusive rights to a defined three-dimensional space, and rights over the common areas which service the space. The land on which the property is situated is held in shared ownership by the owners of the units, as shown in Figure 7.5.

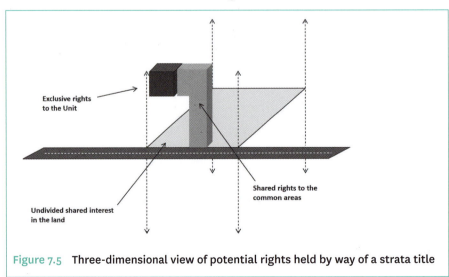

Figure 7.5  Three-dimensional view of potential rights held by way of a strata title

There are limitations to the bundle of rights, and the rights are not unlimited within the three-dimensional space. There are Acts which confer certain rights on the Crown or other agencies, such as the Resource Management Act or the Crown Minerals Act.

## Forms of ownership

Two common forms of ownership include freehold and leasehold ownership. Freehold is the highest form of ownership in common law. The person holding the **freehold interest** is the absolute owner of all rights to the property and can do anything with it subject only to the law of the land and the rights of others. The owner of the freehold estate owns the title to the land and the exclusive rights to its possession, use and occupancy. The ownership is a perpetual one in that it continues indefinitely.

A **lease interest** is a contractual relationship between a lessor (the property owner) and a lessee or tenant. The lessee typically has a non-permanent right to use the lease property in return for rental payments and observance of covenants. A **ground lease** is a long-term lease of land with the lessee permitted to improve or build on the land, and is often able to be extended indefinitely by the lessee (referred to as 'perpetually renewable'), thereby creating a separate leasehold interest that can be held in the manner of a title.

Understanding the advantages and disadvantages of lease interests and ground leases, described in Table 7.3, is important for determining whether the property being evaluated is fit for the investor or owner's intended use and investment criteria.

> **Freehold interest**
> Absolute ownership of real property with no time constraints; considered the highest form of ownership.
>
> **Lease interest**
> Non-permanent right to use the lease property in return for rental payments and observance of covenants.
>
> **Ground lease**
> Lease of land for a specified period, with the lessee permitted to improve or build on the land.

Table 7.3    Advantages and disadvantages of lease interests and ground leases

| Advantages | Disadvantages |
| --- | --- |
| There can be a saving of capital that can be devoted to other purposes. | The lessee holds the premises subject to varying limitations according to the terms and conditions of the lease agreement |
| The lessee may be able to secure premises that might otherwise have been unaffordable. | Planning for the future may be difficult with short-term leases. |
| The lessee enjoys the benefit of increases in land value between rent reviews. If the land value reduces, there is an opportunity to have the rent lowered at the end of the term. | The lessee only benefits temporarily from land value increases, until there is a rent review. |
| With renewable ground leases the lessee usually pays a rent that is a lower percentage of the land value than the current rates of interest for a first mortgage. | If the interval between rent reviews is small there may be high administration and legal costs. |
|  | Lessees do not have the intangible satisfaction of ownership. |
|  | Future plans can be dependent upon the lessor's consent. |

Other less common forms of ownership include cross-leases, life estate and timeshares.

**Record of title**
Official document detailing property ownership and rights.

## Land registration and record of title

In New Zealand, land is grouped into either Māori land or land where the **record of title** (previously referred to as computer registers or certificates of title) proves the ownership of land and the rights and restrictions that apply to the land. Here we look at records of title that are registered under the Land Transfer Act 1952 and later amendments, in particular the Land Transfer Act 2017.

The Land Transfer Act is the principal act dealing with registration of interests in land. The registration system provides for the keeping of a Computer Freehold Register (CFR), formerly, and still often, referred to as a 'certificate of title' or simply 'CT'. This system facilitates dealings in land and provides security of title, under what is known as the Torrens system, which is used in a number of other Commonwealth countries. Any dealings relating to a parcel of land are recorded on the register and any memorial – record – provides conclusive evidence of a dealing connected with that piece of land.

By way of background, it is worth reviewing the recent history of titles under the Land Transfer Act 2017. In May 2002, Land Information New Zealand (LINZ) issued the last paper-based certificate of title in New Zealand. Records of titles are now held in a digital register, rather than as a physical certificate, via a system called Landonline. The website is www.linz.govt.nz. When a land transaction occurs, registration (in the absence of fraud) gives an **indefeasible (undisputed) title** to the estate or interest, or in the case of easements, to the right created. Figure 7.6 provides an example highlighting the key features of a record of title.

**Indefeasible title**
Undisputed ownership rights providing legal certainty.

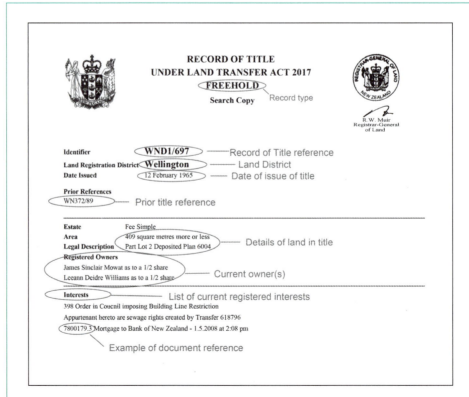

**Figure 7.6**    **Example of a record of title**

Source: www.linz.govt.nz/products-services/land-records/types-land-records/record-title-current, reproduced with permission of the owners

When searched, the electronic register shows only the current instruments registered against the parcel (unlike the previous paper CTs, which showed all transactions). Land professionals can conduct remote searching of the Landonline survey and title database. If you wish to search a title, you can use an agent to conduct the search on your behalf. All records of title have an identifier, and this should be quoted when requesting a title search. If the number is not known, the legal description or street address is needed to find the property identifier number. Table 7.4 highlights key information contained on the registry of a record of title. [2]

Table 7.4    Information commonly included in a record of title

| | |
|---|---|
| **Search date** | The date the search was obtained is printed on the bottom right-hand corner of the CFR. It is important to have the search done as close to the required date as possible, to minimise the risk of further unknown memorials being registered against the title. |
| **Property identifier** | Formerly known as the CT reference, this is shown in the top section of the document. Quoting this number when requesting a register search speeds up the response substantially. |
| **Proprietors** | Shows the current registered owner. Note that historical titles show the original proprietor, and to determine the current owner the most recent transfer must be located on the document. |
| **Estate** | Shows the type of tenure, such as freehold, leasehold or stratum. |
| **Area** | The land area, as per the digital plan. |
| **Legal description** | The full individual legal description is given. This sets the land aside from any other parcel of land. |
| **Interests** | Any current legally registered dealing in the land is recorded on the CFR. These dealings may include caveats, easements, leases, mortgages, transfers (Table 7.5 over the page contains an extract from Jefferies [1991] who defines some of these most frequently found 'interests' on record of titles). An historical search will be required to ascertain any non-current charges. Further, it is LINZ's policy that the benefits of land covenants are no longer recorded on the beneficiary's title. Land covenants are now only recorded on the title of the grantor of the land covenant. It is therefore necessary to undertake both an historical title search and a search of historical interests to determine whether or not a title has the benefit of a land covenant. |
| **Deposited plan** | An accurate (but not to scale) diagram of the property is digitally held and linked to the title. This shows the area and dimensions of the property. Stratum estate titles include sufficiently detailed plans and cross-sections of the property to enable the three-dimensional interest to be defined. |

---

2    'Record of title – current', Toitū Te Whenua Land Information New Zealand, accessed 27 March 2024, www.linz.govt.nz/products-services/land-records/types-land-records/record-title-current

Table 7.5  Definition of common 'interests' found on records of title[3]

| | |
|---|---|
| **Transfers** | When the land is transferred from the original owner, the new purchaser's name(s) is shown together with the date and actual time when the transfer document and title was produced for registration. To obtain further details, particularly regarding the price paid, including any noted figure for chattels, and the actual date of signing of the transfer it is necessary to peruse the memorial itself. |
| **Leases** | Any leases of the fee simple to a lessee or from a lessee to a sub-lessee that are registered are shown, giving the name of the lessee, the term and usually an indication of whether there are any further rights of renewal or fencing or other covenants. From the lease document itself the valuer can obtain the rental paid, the provision for rent reviews or renewals and all the detailed covenants such as limitations on use, or rights of purchase. |
| **Mortgages** | Only the name of the mortgagee together with the maximum sum that is protected by the instrument and the date and time the mortgage is presented for registration is noted on the title. All details in connection with the mortgage such as the principal sum, principal reductions, interest rate, term and other conditions must be obtained from the loan document. Where there is more than one mortgage registered, the order of registration will determine the order in which proceeds from sale are used to satisfy the mortgagee's claim. |
| **Easement** | Where any easement such as a right-of-way, drainage easement, light and air easement, party wall or other important encumbrance affecting the value of a property is noted on the title, usually only the type of easement, names of the parties and date registered appear on the titles. Again, the actual document needs to be searched to obtain the full details and reference to the Deposited Plan or a Deeds Plan separately to note the location and the size of the easement. |
| **Restrictive covenants** | These are agreements which restrict the use and enjoyment of the land, sometimes placed on a property, and are sometimes called negative easements. Some examples would be: a vendor restricting the purchaser as to the height of a building that can be built on a section protecting the view of the vendor; the minimum costs and restrictions as to the type of building in a new subdivision imposed by a subdivider when selling sections; or where a vendor prohibits the cutting down of certain specimen trees, etc. |
| **Encumbrances** | This includes charges, licences and transmissions. These are other miscellaneous memorials which are placed against a title either as a result of providing security for the performance of a debt or personal covenant; a charge made by the High Court or under certain legislation such as The Rating Powers Act 1988 for unpaid rates; a licence to occupy or to have access to part of a property; and lastly recording the transfer of a property under a will. |
| **Caveats** | A caveat is a document which may be lodged forbidding certain dealings against the land as specified in the caveat. A typical use of a caveat would be when a person buying a property under a long-term sale and purchase agreement wishes to ensure that no other dealing is made with the land without his or her consent. |

3  Jefferies, *Urban Valuation in New Zealand*, chapter 4, pp. 5–6.

## Resource Management Act 1991

The Resource Management Act (RMA) 1991 is the governing Act that local and regional authorities use to develop district plans. The purpose of the RMA is to help us look after the environment; it is based on the idea of sustainable management of resources. It is an overarching act that attempts to encourage involvement in decisions related to our environment and leave the decisions about how to manage our environment in the hands of the local community (through local councils).

The primary touch-point for property investors is the district plan that is drawn up by the Territorial Local Authority (commonly referred to as a TLA or a 'city council') that controls the use, development and protection of land within the context of promoting sustainable management. The district plan covers the rules and stipulations for land use for each area of a city, including permitted uses, height restriction, site coverage, services, landscaping, etc. If you intend to undertake any form of property investment (especially development, including subdividing or extending a property), it is essential that you have a thorough knowledge of the local district plan.

One of the primary purposes of the district plan is to enable the public to determine whether a particular activity can be undertaken at a particular site. This is one of the most important purposes from the point of view of the property investor. There are six categories of activity provided for by the Resource Management Act 1991 with which the district plan has to comply, ranging from 'permitted' activities to 'prohibited' activities. These can be seen as a continuum. Permitted activities are allowed as of right and the council is unable to not approve a use that is permitted on that site. At the other end of the continuum, the council cannot approve a prohibited activity. Between these two ends of the continuum are increasing levels of conditions and uncertainty that an investor must take account of. An investor will need to investigate the district plan carefully to ensure the current or proposed activity is allowed on the property that is to be developed.

Depending on the size of the area under control of the TLA, there may be both a district plan and a regional plan that is under the authority of a regional council. These regional plans are less to do with specific properties but rather with the natural environment (land, water and air). District plans are undertaken while recognising the requirements of any regional plan.

It is clear that the Resource Management Act 1991 has a significant impact on land use, and therefore on property investment. While these impacts are numerous and wide-reaching, two key areas are compliance and strategy.

### Compliance

It is imperative that the RMA is complied with in all property matters. This applies to day-to-day property management, redevelopment, and purchasing and disposal. Many legislative requirements can be financially costly if not complied with. The key to success is information – both being aware yourself of the Act and the local planning environment, and knowing when to pay for specialist planning advice.

A mechanism commonly used by property investors is to obtain a Land Information Memorandum (LIM). This is a document (or parcel of documents) prepared by a TLA in respect of a property. It is essentially a copy of all the information that the TLA has for that property, which may be useful to a person who has an interest in the property. The LIM should identify any areas of non-compliance.

It should be noted that the RMA relates to the use of land and properties, but TLAs also administer the Building Act which covers the requirements for the built environment and the building consent process.

### Strategy

The planning environment is rarely static. Planning regulations change over time, and plans allow for the changing economic patterns of the community. These changes represent both opportunities and threats to investors. By way of example, the re-zoning of fringe rural land to residential can increase the value of that land significantly. Similarly, the value of industrial or commercial land can be diminished should planning regulations begin to restrict the types of uses to protect adjoining land occupiers. Again, the key to success is being informed.

## Financing the purchase of residential property

One of the biggest unknown variables that must be taken into consideration when buying a house is interest rates. New Zealand interest rates are volatile, and this volatility has serious repercussions for the rate being charged by banks for housing loans. If interest rates rise and the house is financed by a **floating-rate mortgage**, then the funds required to service this loan will also rise. Conversely, if the interest rates fall, then fewer funds will be needed to service the mortgage. Some of this uncertainty can be removed by taking a **fixed-rate mortgage** where the interest rates are fixed at a particular level for the term of the mortgage.

The purchase of any item will always depend on the financial resources that are available for its acquisition. Sufficient surplus funds will be required up front to pay the deposit on a property. The minimum deposit banks require is guided by RBNZ policy. However, banks prefer a deposit of 20% of the purchase price of a property to be paid, but will accept a minimum deposit of between 5% and 10%. Agreement to proceed will only occur when the bank knows that sufficient disposable funds are available to meet the mortgage repayments, which could continue for a period of 20 years. Remember that the deposit is not the only expense relating to the acquisition of property – legal fees, valuation fees, property insurance and bank fees for establishing the mortgage facility will also be incurred.

> **Floating-rate mortgage**
> Mortgage where the interest rates rise and fall.
>
> **Fixed-rate mortgage**
> Mortgage where the interest rate is set at the beginning of the period and does not change.

**Example 2: Financing residential property**

If a bank requires, say, a 20% deposit to be paid on a property, it means it is willing to lend 80% of the purchase price. Therefore, if a property was priced at $1 100 000, the deposit would be $220 000, which means that the bank would lend the balance of $880 000 providing the purchaser's ability to repay was proven. The term of the loan would be agreed to by the purchaser and the bank, but it is commonly set at 30 years.

The purchaser will also be given the option of having a mortgage with a fixed or floating interest rate, or a mixture of the two. For example, some people like to have the security of a fixed interest rate because the monthly outgoings are known with certainty. On the other hand, others may expect interest rates to fall and therefore will decide on a floating interest rate to take advantage of future interest rate declines.

▶

Continuing our house example, and assuming that the purchaser paid a deposit of $220 000 on a $1 100 000 house, then the mortgage loan would cover the difference of $880 000. Assuming that the bank has agreed to lend this sum for a period of 30 years at an annual interest rate of 5.25% then monthly repayments can be calculated using Equation 5.6 from Chapter 5, as follows:

$$\begin{aligned} \text{PMT} &= \frac{\text{PVA} \times r/m}{1 - (1 + r/m)^{-n \times m}} \\ &= \frac{\$880\,000 \times 0.0525/12}{1 - (1 + 0.0525/12)^{-30 \times 12}} \\ &= \frac{\$880\,000 \times 0.004375}{1 - (1.004375)^{-360}} \\ &= \frac{\$3\,850}{1 - 0.20772} \\ &= \$4\,859.39 \end{aligned}$$

The monthly mortgage payment is $4 859.39 However, if the monthly mortgage repayment is instead halved to $2 429.70 to allow for 26 fortnightly installments rather than 12 monthly installments, then two extra repayments will be made each year which will reduce the term of the loan from 30 years to 25 years. Furthermore, the total amount of interest paid over the life of the mortgage will fall by over $166 000. Alternatively, if the loan is paid off more quickly by increasing the fortnightly dollar repayments, then the term of the mortgage and amount of interest paid will reduce even further.

The decision of how quickly to repay personal debts such as credit card debt, student loans, mortgages or car loans is not straightforward. From a purely mathematical viewpoint, the following general rules give the best financial outcome:

- if the after-tax interest rate on your savings is less than the interest rate on debt, repay debt as fast as possible
- if the after-tax interest rate on your savings is greater than the interest rate on debt, repay debt at the minimum amount required.

This is a useful rule of thumb for repaying short-term debts, but for most people, a strategy of accumulating an emergency nest egg and/or saving for retirement while paying off a long-term mortgage is generally prudent.

While buying a house is an activity that can be undertaken at any time during an individual's working life, the decision to retire is generally the culmination of one's work activities. At some stage during the accumulation or consolidation phase of the life cycle, a decision may be made to become self-employed, with all the responsibilities for work-related decisions and their consequences. The next section will consider the inputs into such a decision, and also the components of a business plan.

## Starting or buying a business

The decision to become self-employed usually follows a lot of planning and soul-searching and is never taken in isolation. Figure 7.7 on the next page illustrates the steps that should be followed, commencing with the time someone first becomes aware of a business opportunity through to the development of a business plan.

Sometimes the business opportunity may simply arise; in other cases it may develop out of a hobby that starts to grow into a larger operation. A business opportunity can occur in four ways: by commencing a venture from scratch; by purchasing a firm from another person; by buying a franchised operation such as McDonald's; or by expanding a hobby, invention or small business into something larger and more defined. Planning a new business venture involves many of the activities described earlier so that realistic goals are set, alternative courses of action are considered and the necessary plans to achieve these goals are put in place.

In many instances, the end result of becoming self-employed is a very satisfying one, but in other cases it can be fraught with difficulties and may end in failure. For most people, one of the main advantages of being self-employed is being able to make their own decisions and be responsible for their own successes and failures. If they are successful, they will receive recognition for their own efforts. However, these advantages can come at a cost; for example, when starting up a new business working between 9 am and 5 pm is often not possible. Many business owners will work irregular, and often very long, hours in order to get the job done – without being fully compensated financially for their efforts. In the early stages of a business there is also little or no security and no business perks. Not everybody is willing to accept the uncertainties, time commitment and fluctuating pay packet that may come with being self-employed.

In this section we will investigate:
- the personality traits of the self-employed
- the factors required for a preliminary evaluation of a business opportunity
- the components of a business plan.

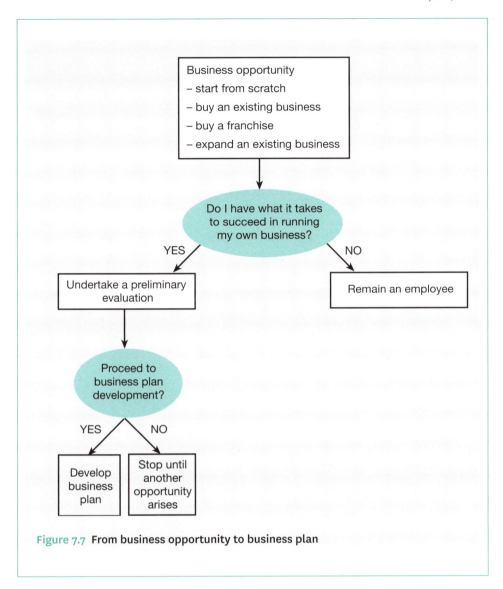

Figure 7.7 **From business opportunity to business plan**

## Personality traits

If you have the right personality traits to survive self-employment, then your answer to each of the following should be 'yes'.

- Do you have the drive and commitment to manage the business indefinitely?
- Do you have the confidence and ability to communicate with banks, clients and suppliers and achieve a successful outcome?
- Do you have the ability to solve problems, which will arise persistently?
- Do you have the ability to plan, to set goals to achieve certain objectives and then achieve those goals?
- Are you able to guess how much risk is acceptable to all participants (banks, clients, suppliers and employees)?
- Can you think outside the square?
- Do you have the knowledge and experience to undertake the venture?

- Could you cope with failure?
- Are you receptive to feedback even when it is negative?
- Do you have the ability to take the initiative when an exciting opportunity presents itself?
- Are you able to use resources efficiently in order to minimise waste?
- Are you able to cope in situations of uncertainty?
- Are you the right type of person to operate the business venture you have identified?

### Preliminary evaluation

If this stage is done properly, it will ensure that the potential owner of the business has the required level of experience and knowledge to lead a successful venture. It is important to note that no New Zealand firm can operate in isolation – all firms must function as part of a global economy and also as part of an industry within New Zealand. Being a small country, New Zealand is affected quite significantly by the activities of its larger trading partners. Therefore, when these countries experience high economic growth, the demand for New Zealand goods tends to be high. Unfortunately, the reverse occurs when these countries move into **recession**, and company cash flows can be seriously affected. Therefore, when starting any new venture, a lot of thought must be given to issues facing the New Zealand economy and to how these problems will affect the supply and demand for goods, the domestic currency and interest rates. These, in turn, affect the industry and the company's trading operations.

> **Recession**
> An economic decline or a contraction in business activity.

Answers to questions such as those below will aid the decision-making process and provide the groundwork for the development of a business plan.

- Is the economy and industry in a growth or a decline phase, and how long will the current phase continue?
- What are the issues facing the economy, and how will these affect the industry and the companies operating within it?
- How strong will competition be within the industry, and who are your competitors?
- Is the industry prone to fads and fashions and, if so, how will this affect operations?
- Does the industry have a strong technological base, and how will new technology changes affect the business?
- What is the firm's commitment to research and development, and how does this compare with that of its competitors?
- How will the business be affected by foreign competition, exchange rate fluctuations and offshore political activities such as trade barriers?
- What are the skills and knowledge requirements for employees, and is there a sufficient pool of people to meet the firm's requirements?
- How much capital investment will be required now and in the future in order to maintain (or improve) the current level of competition?

The above list of questions highlights many of the matters to be considered by a potential business owner, and is by no means all-inclusive. Other areas to consider pertain to problems within the industry itself, how these problems can be resolved, and the costs involved in solving these issues. In addition, the supply of materials and the type of customer to be serviced also require thought. Any problem areas associated with these factors should be resolved before the decision to proceed with the new venture is made.

It is clear that this part of the analysis includes consideration of both strategic factors requiring resolution and uncontrollable factors which may not be able to be resolved, but which may affect business operations. Some knowledge of these uncontrollable factors will provide information as to whether or not they are favourable to the business. A number of controllable factors should also be considered – these usually involve staff, goods, markets and financial issues. The information obtained from the preliminary evaluation will provide the foundation for the development of the business plan.

## Business plan

The answers to the questions posed in the preliminary evaluation of the new business venture, along with the results of research undertaken, will be incorporated into the business plan. A business plan is essential for business operations to function successfully, and is required by prospective suppliers of capital (i.e. money). For example, relatives, banks and finance organisations will want information concerning the business and its proposed current and future operations; **SWOT** analyses of the industry, business, market and labour; as well as financial forecasts, or projections, of the proposed operations.

In order to produce financial forecasts for the firm, it is necessary to know the current level and past growth of sales in the industry, and the expected market share the business expects to achieve. Therefore, information on the cost of the products, the prices that competitors are charging for similar goods, and the competitors' marketing strategy should be obtained. It is essential that this research is accurate, because if customers resist the prices to be charged, then the proposed level of sales will not be achieved.

If the business plan has been constructed properly, it will highlight the benefits and problems associated with the business. Once completed, the plan remains operational throughout the life of the business. It should be updated regularly so that it becomes a living document.

> **SWOT**
> Analysis of a venture in order to determine its Strengths, Weaknesses, Opportunities and Threats.

### Components of a business plan

The components of a business plan are described below.

#### Introduction

The introduction sets out the objectives of the plan. If the objective of the plan is to seek financing, then details concerning the person seeking the funds, the amount required, the reason for the request for funds, and the benefits to be derived by the firm from receipt of the money should be included.

#### Economic and industry overview

This overview provides details of the current and future status of both the economic and industry environments in which the business will operate. The overview should include a discussion of new products, technologies, competitors, and local and overseas markets which may affect the firm's operations.

#### Business or company

All details concerning the organisation and operation of the proposed venture, including the location and facilities should be provided. Data regarding availability of suppliers, financiers and others in the industry should be included.

### Product or service

The product or service to be provided by the firm should be described. Any unique features differentiating the product from others currently on the market should be emphasised. New market opportunities arising from this business venture should also be indicated.

### Marketing plan

The plan provides information about the customer, the size of the market, the proposed market share, details of any competitors, and how the firm intends to capture their market share. An estimation of sales figures for the next three years should also be provided. Most of the information provided in this component will provide the basis for estimates incorporated into the income section of the financial forecast.

### Marketing strategy

This section flows from the marketing plan and indicates the target market and the strategies required in order to obtain the desired market share. Details include pricing policy, advertising campaigns, and promotion of the product or venture.

### Management team

This section provides details of the team who will lead the operation. It should include managers' qualifications and employment history, and should explain how their previous work experience relates to the new venture. Details of their role and responsibilities in the organisation, as well as their salaries, should be included. Names of external advisers such as a lawyer, accountant and banker should also be supplied.

### Staff

The number of staff expected to be employed should be specified, along with the skill level required, and the availability of full-time, part-time or seasonal workers. Any costs associated with obtaining and training staff should be included.

### Supporting documents

Documents should be provided to support all components of the plan, and may include demographic data, property and/or equipment valuations, credit information, managers' curricula vitae, etc.

### Financial forecasts

A business plan commonly provides financial forecasts for the first three years of operations. For an existing firm with a track record, information pertaining to its current financial situation will be used to assist with the forecasts for the next three years. For a new venture it will be more difficult to make financial forecasts, as there are no historical financial statements. Nevertheless, success in obtaining financing from banks and other equity partners requires that forecasts be as comprehensive as possible, and this includes preparing a forecast income statement, forecast **cash flow statement** and forecast balance sheet.

> **Cash flow statement** Statement showing the inflows and outflows of cash over a defined period of time.

# Conclusion

This chapter has discussed the process of personal financial planning. Personal financial goals that will satisfy the requirements of individuals or households should be set. These goals may be amended as individuals move through various life phases. We have introduced the process of budgeting to show how an income statement can be used as a basis for forecasting income and expenses over the coming year.

Long-term personal financial planning involves setting a long-term strategy to achieve one's financial goals. One of the biggest quandaries facing many people during their working lives is how much money they should save in order to ensure an enjoyable retirement. In order to help resolve this problem, we have shown a method of calculating the retirement income gap.

Another long-term personal financial decision is whether or not to purchase a house. This is the largest asset that most people will own during their lives. We have described the procedures related to buying a house, outlined the types of and rights associated with property, as well as common features in the Record of Titles, before examining how property transactions could be financed.

Finally, we have described the evaluation of a business opportunity and the development of a business plan. Any new business requires sufficient capital to support its operations. In other words, funds are required to purchase fixed assets (such as equipment, buildings, etc.), finance operating needs (rent, wages, material, etc.) and pay creditors (people who are owed money by the firm). This in turn raises questions about the type of funding the business will use. For example, will the business be financed solely by the owner, or will the firm take out a loan or some other form of financing? This question will be answered in Chapter 10, where the different sources of financing for a firm are described.

## SELF-TEST QUESTION

Gareth and Rhonwen Davies plan to retire in 25 years' time when they are both 65 years of age. They have estimated their living expenses and retirement income as follows.

| Income (annual) | |
|---|---:|
| New Zealand superannuation (after tax) | $16 930.16 |
| Fixed interest (after tax) | $ 2 760.00 |
| Dividends (after tax) | $ 4 620.00 |
| **Expenses (per month)** | |
| Electricity/gas | $ 160.00 |
| Telephone/internet | $ 120.00 |
| Food | $ 420.00 |
| Insurance | |
| – House | $ 40.00 |
| – Contents | $ 32.00 |
| – Cars | |
| • Gareth | $ 32.00 |
| • Rhonwen | $ 26.00 |
| – Health | $ 180.00 |
| Car running expenses | $ 220.00 |
| Clothes | $ 250.00 |
| Entertainment | $ 280.00 |
| Medical | $ 50.00 |
| Rates | $ 210.00 |
| Car registration | |
| – Gareth | $ 24.00 |
| – Rhonwen | $ 21.00 |
| Holidays | $ 300.00 |
| Miscellaneous | $ 250.00 |

Assume a 25-year retirement period and a 2.5% real rate of return.

Calculate:

a Gareth and Rhonwen's retirement income gap
b the additional sum they will need to save to cover any shortfall in funds
c the annual savings required to reach their target level of savings.

## ANSWER TO SELF-TEST QUESTION

a

**Gareth and Rhonwen Davies**

**Retirement Expense Worksheet**

| Expenses (per month) | | |
|---|---|---|
| Electricity/gas | | $ 160.00 |
| Telephone/internet | | $ 120.00 |
| Food | | $ 420.00 |
| Insurance – House | | $ 40.00 |
| – Contents | | $ 32.00 |
| – Car | | |
| • Gareth | | $ 32.00 |
| • Rhonwen | | $ 26.00 |
| – Health | | $ 180.00 |
| Car running expenses | | $ 220.00 |
| Clothes | | $ 250.00 |
| Entertainment | | $ 280.00 |
| Medical | | $ 50.00 |
| Rates | | $ 210.00 |
| Car registration | | |
| – Gareth | | $ 24.00 |
| – Rhonwen | | $ 21.00 |
| Holidays | | $ 300.00 |
| Miscellaneous | | $ 250.00 |
| Monthly expenses | | $ 2 615.00 |
| Annual expenses | | $31 380.00 |
| | | |
| Therefore income target (after tax) | | $31 380.00 |
| Minus New Zealand superannuation (after tax) | | $16 930.16 |
| | | $14 449.84 |
| Other income | | $ 7 380.00 |
| Retirement income gap (per annum) | | $ 7 069.84 |

**b** Calculate the sum required to be saved that will provide the Davies with $7 069.84 for 25 years.

$$PVA = PMT \left(\frac{1-(1+r)^{-n}}{r}\right)$$

$$= \$7\,069.84 \left(\frac{1-(1+0.025)^{-25}}{0.025}\right)$$

$$= \$7\,069.84 \left(\frac{0.46061}{0.025}\right)$$

$$= \$7\,069.84\,(18.42438)$$

$$= \$130\,257.39$$

**c** Calculate the annual savings required for the Davies to reach their target level of savings of $130 257.28.

$$PMT = \left[\frac{FVA \times r}{(1+r)^n - 1}\right]$$

$$= \left[\frac{\$130\,257.39 \times 0.025}{(1.025)^{25} - 1}\right]$$

$$= \left(\frac{\$3\,256.43475}{0.85394}\right)$$

$$= \$3\,813.41$$

**QUESTIONS AND PROBLEMS**

1. What is the goal of personal financial planning?
2. Describe the activities associated with the financial planning process. What are the benefits associated with these activities?
3. Describe the phases individuals pass through during their lifetime. Are the financial goals established during these phases static? Justify your answer.
4. What strategies can be used to help manage scarce resources such as money? Describe how these strategies make it possible for people to achieve their objectives.
5. What is the difference between an *asset* and a *liability*?
6. List the advantages associated with:
    a  renting a house or an apartment
    b  owning a house or an apartment.
    Which form of accommodation do you think is more advantageous?
7. What is one of the biggest unknown variables associated with buying property? Why is it a problem?
8. What is the importance of the retirement income gap?
9. What are some of the problems associated with estimating the annual retirement income target (after tax)?
10. What sources of funds may be available to you in your retirement?
11. You have a life insurance policy that will be worth $100 000 when you retire in 40 years' time. If the funds are discounted back at 9%, what is the present value of this policy?
12. When talking about a retirement fund with friends, one said he had been advised to set a target of $1 million. If you decided to aim for the same target for when you retire in 35 years, how much should you place in the fund now? Assume an 8% interest rate.
13. You have an opportunity to acquire a business for $250 000, but will require a loan from the bank for 65% of the purchase price. The bank has agreed to lend you the money you require at an interest charge of 9.75%. How much interest would you be required to pay at the end of year 1?
14. What is the purpose of a business plan?
15. What information is contained on the Computer Freehold Register?
16. How do you obtain a copy of the Computer Freehold Register?
17. Define each of the following terms:
    - Easement
    - Caveat
    - Restrictive covenant
18. Explain the difference between a freehold and a leasehold interest.
19. What is the highest form of ownership in land?
20. What are the implications for investors of the Resource Management Act?

# PART 4

# Financial management

Part 4 of this book deals with the subject of financial management within the context of a business firm. Financial management is primarily concerned with making financial decisions that will maximise the wealth of the firm's owners. Many of the concepts and tools discussed earlier in this book, such as the time value of money, risk and return, and the financial market processes, will be important considerations in achieving this goal. We will use these concepts and tools to help us manage the firm's current asset and liquidity position, make financial forecasts, plan for suitable financing and make long-term investment decisions.

People involved in all facets of business need some knowledge of financial management, as they are all affected by it to some degree. Unit managers need to set budgetary targets, which in turn affect the human, physical and financial resources of the unit and the organisation. Much of the information needed for the forecasts comes from the operating units themselves, such as sales projections from the marketing staff. Production staff must have some input into financial decisions that affect their unit, such as maintenance of sufficient stocks and purchases of new equipment. Consequently, some knowledge of finance will benefit all those who plan to work in the business sector.

Chapter 8 commences this section with an introduction to the objective and role of financial management. It describes the three principal functions of financial management: financial forecasting and planning, financing the firm, and investment in assets; and discusses how the business environment and decisions of the risk–return trade-off affect the firm and its owners.

Chapter 9 applies the risk–return principles to the management of net working capital, for which we will focus primarily upon cash, accounts receivable, inventory and accounts payable. Given that a large proportion of a firm's assets are tied up in net working capital, a variety of tools and techniques are discussed to assist the efficient management of this particularly important and time-consuming task.

In Chapter 10 we further develop our fictitious company from Chapter 7, Technability Ltd, in order to follow the financing of a firm through its life cycle of start up, growth and maturity. The different sources of debt and equity funds that are available to businesses are discussed, and the important issues that affect the financing of the firm are examined.

Chapters 11 and 12 cover the topic of investment in long-term assets. Long-term investments, such as the purchase of new equipment and facilities, the development of new products and the establishment of new business ventures, often have a serious effect on the financial success of a business. Chapter 11 describes the process of determining, evaluating and implementing investment projects, and the measurement of the net benefits. Chapter 12 then demonstrates how such investment evaluation techniques can be applied in order to assess the financial acceptability of a proposed investment.

Finally, Chapter 13 explores property investments, which are a critical asset class, as a way of drawing together concepts and investment and financing techniques from across the entire textbook.

# Financial management

**CHAPTER 8**

◼ **Learning objectives**

By the end of this chapter, you should be able to:
- understand the objective and the role of financial management, and the nature of financing and investment decisions
- describe the three principal functions of financial management
- explain why financial management is important both to businesses and to the economy as a whole
- describe the financial objective of wealth maximisation
- discuss the environmental factors of key importance in financial decision-making
- describe the relationship between risk and return.

## Introduction

Chapters 8 to 12 will focus on financial management and its importance to an organisation. You will recall from Chapter 1 that the organisational segment consists of three levels: sole proprietor, partnership and corporation. At all levels, business organisations function within the financial system, raising funds through the financial markets in order to invest in real and financial assets. This process was depicted in Figure 1.1 and is reproduced below in Figure 8.1. From the organisational perspective, individuals transact on behalf of sole proprietors and partnerships, while managers represent shareholders' interests in corporations. All of these organisations engage in financial management activities, although their goals and procedures may differ slightly.

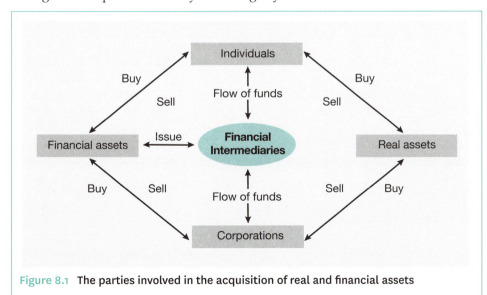

Figure 8.1 The parties involved in the acquisition of real and financial assets

This chapter will introduce the process of financial management, describing the types of decision made, the functions undertaken, and where the process fits in an organisational setting. To ensure that financial decisions are optimal, it is necessary for the objective of financial management to be explicitly defined. Most finance literature agrees that maximisation of shareholders' wealth is the most appropriate objective. The tools and techniques developed for financial management should therefore be consistent with the wealth maximisation objective.

The process of financial management does not occur in isolation. The financial markets, regulatory bodies and government authorities all have an influence. It is through financial markets that firms raise funds, and the market price of the firm's shares is set by buyers and sellers. Regulatory bodies and government authorities impose a constraint on business activities through taxes, business laws and regulations. Financial managers must consider these external factors and assess the expected risk and return of outcomes as part of the decision-making process.

## Role of financial management

The finance function is described by a variety of titles such as financial management, business finance, corporate finance and managerial finance. For the most part, these titles are interchangeable as they all relate to the subject of finance. In this section of the book, the term *financial management* will be used.

### Financial management

**Financial management** Activities and decisions undertaken with regard to the financing and investment requirements of an organisation.

**Financial management** can be described as the activities and decisions undertaken with regard to the financing and investment requirements of an organisation. This definition allows us to classify the activities and decisions into three principal functions:

- financial forecasting and planning
- financing the firm
- investment in assets.

These functions are particularly important as the decisions made can have a significant effect on the value of the organisation.

### Financial forecasting and planning

**Financial forecasting and planning** An ongoing process that involves forecasting financial performance, planning the sources and uses of funds, and monitoring cash flows.

**Financial forecasting and planning** is an ongoing process of forecasting financial performance, planning the sources and uses of funds, and monitoring cash flows. It forms the necessary foundation for decisions concerning the investment and financing activities of the firm, and involves planning the funding requirements of the operational activities given the availability of funds from internal and external sources.

**Bank overdraft** A short-term loan whereby a bank gives permission to a borrower to have a negative bank balance up to a pre-arranged limit.

### Financing the firm

Financing the firm involves obtaining funds for use in the business. Funds can be raised internally through the profits and excess cash flows generated by the business, to the extent that they have not already been paid out to shareholders as dividends. Alternatively, financing can be obtained externally via the financial markets. External sources include debt funds such as **bank overdrafts**, loans and debentures, and equity funds such as owners' **contributed capital**. The proportion of debt versus equity funding affects not only the cost of financing but also the profitability and risk of the business, so the debt–equity mix must be carefully managed. For example, the excessive reliance by firms on debt financing was a major factor contributing to the sharemarket crash of 1987. Chapter 10 will further discuss the various sources of financing and the costs of using them.

> **Contributed capital**
> Funds contributed to a business by the owner(s). Represents a portion of owners' or shareholders' equity.

### Investment in assets

The investment function involves deciding how funds can be used to achieve the most benefit to the firm and its owners. Some alternative investments are to purchase inventory, invest in Treasury bills or buy new equipment. Such decisions have a major influence on the liquidity, profitability, risk and value of the organisation. Decisions and techniques relating to investment in **current assets** will be dealt with in Chapter 9, while investment in **long-term assets** will be covered in Chapters 11 and 12.

> **Current assets**
> Cash, or assets which are expected to be converted to cash within one year.
>
> **Long-term assets**
> Assets which are expected to provide benefits over more than one accounting year.

### Organisational context

Financial management decisions are not made in isolation. Rather, there is much interaction between the finance unit and other main functional units within an organisation. By examining Figure 8.2, it can be seen that marketing, manufacturing, purchasing and warehousing activities provide information which is summarised via the accounting information system and then used for financial planning. Production, investment and funding plans will also provide information needed for the financial planning process. Conversely, financial factors such as the types of investment undertaken will affect the activities of the different organisational units.

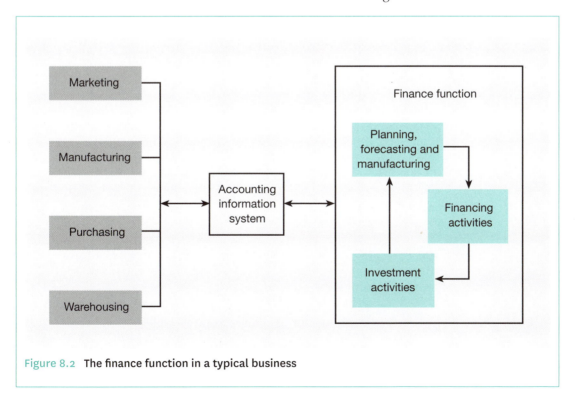

Figure 8.2  The finance function in a typical business

> **Inventory**
> Goods for resale, or to be used in production of goods for sale. Also known as stock in trade.
>
> **Accounts receivable**
> Short-term debt due from a customer, on account of goods sold in the normal course of business. Also known as debtors.
>
> **Economic life**
> The useful life of a business asset.

An increase in sales necessitates an additional investment in the form of increased **inventory** and **accounts receivable**. Further credit and debt collection activities will ensue. If sales increase sufficiently, it may be necessary to invest in more plant and equipment.

Plant and equipment are the major capital requirements to support manufacturing and production activities. Existing equipment must be replaced at the end of its **economic life**, and during good business conditions may be upgraded. Furthermore, research and development activities may reveal new opportunities to expand business operations, which may require additional fixed assets.

In order to produce and sell goods, it is necessary to buy raw materials and to store inventory. The quantity of materials to be purchased with each order to a supplier must be determined, as there is a trade-off between cost and preventing stock-outs. Holding excessive inventory is costly and impairs a firm's liquidity by tying up funds. However, stock-outs can cause production stoppages and lost sales due to the inability to meet customer demands. Consequently, there must be close contact between staff in the purchasing, warehousing and financing functions to optimise the level of inventory.

Financial management is of considerable importance in assisting the firm to achieve its goals and objectives. However, all of the functional units of an organisation must work together to ensure that the defined goals are attained. Firms must find a niche for their goods and/or services, and efficiently bring together human and financial resources in order to serve the needs of their customers.

## Objective of financial management

We have stated that financial management plays an important part in ensuring that the goals and objectives of a firm are met. However, what these objectives should be has not yet been defined. In current finance literature, it is generally accepted that the objective of a firm and financial management should be to maximise the wealth of the firm's owners. In a **private-sector** company, it is the shareholders who own the firm, and so it is their wealth that the firm should aim to maximise.

But what is wealth? For individual shareholders, it is the market price of their ordinary shares. Shares represent the shareholders' claim to the future earnings (and dividends) of a firm. Consequently, the objective of the firm and financial management should be to maximise shareholders' wealth by increasing the market price of the firm's shares. Thus, the goal of a firm is shareholder **wealth maximisation**.

What about proprietorships and partnerships? Is wealth maximisation a suitable goal? We can answer 'yes' to this question, although the definition of wealth will change. For proprietorships and partnerships, wealth is defined in terms of the market value of the owners' investment, respectively known as **owners' equity** and **partnership capital**.

Note that wealth maximisation is not necessarily the only goal that business firms may have. Other goals may relate to innovation, employment, customers, sustainable environmental management and other non-financial criteria. An interesting case in point is Aotearoa Fisheries Limited (AFL). AFL was created as a result of the Māori Fisheries Act 2004 to manage Māori commercial fishing assets on behalf of all iwi (who, together with Te Ohu Kaimoana, are the shareholders of AFL). AFL is the world's largest Māori-owned fisheries business, and holds a number of subsidiaries, including Moana Pacific Fisheries, Prepared Foods and Pacific Marine Farms, as well as owning 50% of Sealord Group Limited. AFL's vision is to 'maximise the value of Māori fisheries assets . . . delivering growth in

> **Private sector**
> The business sector of the economy. Excludes government departments and state-owned enterprises.
>
> **Wealth maximisation**
> Represents the goal of financial management. Refers to maximising the wealth of the firm's owners. For a company, this is achieved by maximising the market price of the company's shares.
>
> **Owners' equity, partnership capital**
> A residual claim by the owner(s) on the assets of the business, after payment of all liabilities.

shareholder wealth to iwi' (afl.maori.nz). However, in addition to AFL's goal to maximise value and grow shareholder wealth, the Māori Fisheries Act 2004 requires AFL to use its best endeavours to work co-operatively with iwi on commercial interests. As such, there may be additional goals, such as generating employment for iwi through joint commercial interests for the benefit of all Māori.

However, for **public-sector** and other not-for-profit organisations, wealth maximisation may not be a suitable objective, as many social benefits are qualitative in nature. In the public sector, it is necessary to refine the financial objectives to ensure that social objectives are also met. Similarly, the objectives of other organisations such as charitable trusts, incorporated societies and Māori Trust Boards focus less on **commercial** activities and more on charitable, social, educational and cultural purposes. For example, Māori Trust Boards administer the assets and manage the cash flows for the benefit of their hapū (sub-tribe) or iwi (tribe). Yet public-sector and non-commercial organisations still need to make financial plans, arrange financing and undertake investments in order to meet their obligations to their stakeholders. So although the wealth maximisation principles may not apply in these cases, most of the financial management techniques discussed in this book are equally relevant to public-sector and non-commercial organisations.

**Public sector**
Government departments and state-owned enterprises.

**Commercial**
Relating to commerce; profit-oriented.

## What about profit maximisation?

If a firm shows a profit each year, then it is generally considered to be in good health. Profit (also known as net income) is measured as the difference between income and expenses, while a **loss** will arise if expenses exceed income. **Earnings per share** are another profit-related measure, calculated as the net profit after taxes divided by the total number of ordinary shares issued by the firm.

$$\text{Net profit after taxes} = \text{Income} - \text{Expenses} \qquad \textit{Equation 8.1}$$

$$\text{Earnings per share} = \frac{\text{Net profit after taxes}}{\text{Number of ordinary shares on issue}} \qquad \textit{Equation 8.2}$$

**Loss**
A negative 'profit' arising when expenses exceed income.

**Earnings per share**
Net profit after taxes divided by the number of ordinary shares on issue.

Investors in large corporations eagerly await quarterly or semi-annual announcements of profit, and business newspapers report daily not only on share prices but also on profits and earnings per share. Managers also put great emphasis on profitability. In fact, an analysis of profits may be extremely useful for many applications, yet profit maximisation is inappropriate as a long-term objective for the firm. Profit maximisation is deficient for the following reasons:

- it fails to account for the time value of money
- it does not represent cash flow
- it ignores risk.

## Time value of money

The time value of money means that, if all else is equal, earlier returns are preferred over later returns. Funds received earlier can be reinvested to earn additional returns in the future. Profit maximisation does not recognise this, while wealth maximisation does.

> **Example 1: Time value of money**
>
> Arnold N. Investor is seeking to purchase shares in either Company A or Company B. The companies are equal in risk, and both pay out all annual earnings as dividends. Table 8.1 reveals the forecast earnings per share (EPS) for the next 20 years.
>
> Table 8.1 EPS of Companies A and B
>
> | Company | Earnings per share (EPS) | | |
> |---|---|---|---|
> | | Years 1–19 | Year 20 | Years 1–20 (average) |
> | A | $1.00 | $ 1.00 | $1.00 |
> | B | $ 0 | $20.00 | $1.00 |
>
> The forecast EPS (a profit-based measure) for Company A is $1.00 for each of the next 20 years. This gives an average of $1.00 per share for Company A over the 20-year period. For Company B the forecast EPS is zero for Years 1–19 and then $20.00 per share in Year 20. This also gives an average EPS of $1 over the 20-year period.
>
> If Arnold is concerned only with profit maximisation, then he will be indifferent about which of the two investments he chooses, because on average, they result in identical EPS. Yet Company A is the better investment because most of the earnings will be received earlier and Arnold will be able to reinvest these earnings to result in higher total earnings. This can be seen more clearly if we use the time value of money techniques from Chapters 4 and 5 to value the EPS to be earned over the next 20 years. Assuming a discount rate of 12%, the present value of the EPS is $7.47 for Company A and $2.07 for Company B. As the EPS stream for Company A is more valuable, Arnold should place a higher value on the shares of Company A.

Similarly, managers must recognise that investors prefer to receive returns earlier rather than later. So while profit is a useful short-term measure of performance, it is inadequate as a basis for long-term decisions. Wealth maximisation does not suffer from this deficiency, because share prices implicitly consider the time value of money.

## Cash flows

Another deficiency of profit maximisation as an objective of the firm is that it does not reflect cash flows. Cash flows are measured as cash receipts less cash expenditures. Recall from the cash flow statement introduced in Chapter 7 that net cash flow is different from the net profit after tax in the income statement. Consequently, non-cash items such as **depreciation** and accruals are excluded from cash flow calculations. Cash flows are very important for long-term decisions for the following reasons.

**Depreciation**
The allocation of the cost of a long-term asset to the periods benefiting from its use. Represents a non-cash expense. Relates only to assets that decline in value over time.

- **Owners' returns are measured using cash flows**

    Owners of firms receive their returns from two sources: dividends and share price appreciation. A firm may experience an increase in EPS and yet this may not result in increased dividend payments, as there may not be sufficient cash available to pay shareholders. Similarly, a one-off increase in EPS may not affect share prices, particularly if the increase is at the expense of long-term growth in EPS.

- **Cash flows are more objective**

    Cash flows can be measured without any need to refer to accounting rules. The cash balance and cash flow can be observed directly from the firm's banking records, whereas the measurement of profits and EPS can vary depending on the particular accounting practice employed.

- **Cash flows determine liquidity and solvency**

    In order to maintain the liquidity and **solvency** of an organisation, it is necessary to monitor cash flows. Sufficient funds must be on hand to pay bills and meet obligations as they become due.

> **Solvency**
> The ability of a person or an organisation to meet their financial commitments as they come due.

## Risk

The third shortcoming of profit maximisation is that it ignores risk, or the uncertainty of an outcome. Recall from the earlier discussion of risk in Chapter 6 that rational investors require a risk premium to compensate for the level of risk of an investment. Wealth maximisation correctly takes risk into consideration through the market forces which set share prices.

### Example 2: Risk assessment

A New Zealand sheep farmer is considering an expansion that would involve the acquisition of additional land. In this fictitious example, the farmer has $2.5 million to spend and has identified two alternative courses of action. He could invest the $2.5 million to improve and expand his sheep herd. Alternatively, he could use the funds to develop an exotic fruit orchard.

The expected profits from the alternative investments are similar, although the range and standard deviation of outcomes differs considerably. An investment in the exotic fruit orchard is subject to more uncertainty, depending on the success of the production system and the future demand for the fruit. We will assume that the forecast annual profits from the alternative investments are as indicated in Table 8.2.

Table 8.2 Forecast annual profits

| Investment | Annual profit under forecast market conditions | | |
|---|---|---|---|
| | Poor | Normal | Good |
| Herd upgrade | $100 000 | $200 000 | $300 000 |
| Fruit orchard | $ 0 | $200 000 | $400 000 |

Given an initial investment of $2.5 million, the herd expansion may result in a narrow range of outcomes ($100 000 to $300 000), whereas the development of an exotic fruit orchard may result in a wider range of annual profits ($0 to $400 000).

Further, if we assume there is an equal probability of the three forecast market conditions (poor, normal and good) occurring, then we can use the standard deviation from Chapter 6 to measure total risk. The standard deviation of annual profits for the fruit orchard is $163 299, double that for the herd upgrade at $81 650. Recall that the higher the standard deviation the greater the risk, so we can conclude that the orchard development is riskier than upgrading the herd.

If the farmer considered only expected profits and ignored risk, then the herd expansion and orchard development would be equally attractive as they are both likely to generate an annual profit of $200 000.

▶

However, most investors are averse to risk. That is, if all else is equal, they prefer less risk to more risk. Wealth maximisation recognises this, while profit maximisation does not. So in this example, if the farmer is risk-averse then the herd expansion would be the preferred investment, as the possible outcomes are more certain. That is, there is less chance of earning very large profits and less chance of earning very little.

In summary, wealth maximisation is a particularly appropriate objective for a business, as it incorporates many important considerations. Wealth maximisation considers the time value of money, the magnitude of cash flows and risk. Simply maximising the profits earned by an organisation does not take such factors into account.

### Managers as agents

So far, we have observed that it is the responsibility of managers to represent the interests of shareholders through the wealth maximisation objective. The shareholders, who are the owners of the firm, appoint a board of directors whose role is to devise the firm's constitution; this defines the strategic objectives and rules for governing the management of the firm. The specific policies and procedures that direct and control how a company conducts its business are collectively known as the firm's **corporate governance**. In a sense it is the eco-system which directs how the board of directors, managers and employees interact with each other, with the owners, and with external parties such as suppliers, customers and the wider community.

The board of directors appoints a managing director or chief executive officer (CEO) whose job is to oversee the firm's operations, ensure that the defined policies are carried out, and report periodically to the board of directors. The CEO, often in consultation with the board of directors, will hire managers to fulfil the finance, operations and marketing functions. As shown in Figure 8.3, although the shareholders are the owners of the firm, there is a separation between the owners and the managers. There are several reasons why it may be better to have managers rather than the shareholders running the business.

- Managers may have better skills, abilities and expertise.
- It is more efficient to run a business with a small number of professional managers. To have a large number of shareholders managing the business would be unwieldy, while the costs of gathering information would be high.
- It allows for more continuity of business activities. The sale of a company's shares from one investor to another will have no effect on the company's operations. Although managers can and do resign, the disruption to the business should be minor as they will normally be replaced by another manager with comparable experience.
- It allows shareholders to diversify by investing in several companies in different industries so that risk is reduced. If owners all managed their own businesses, they would have to limit their investment to a small number of companies.

> **Corporate governance**
> The set of policies and procedures that direct and control how a company conducts its business.

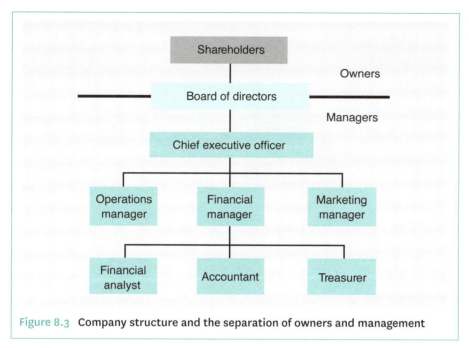

Figure 8.3 Company structure and the separation of owners and management

Note that up until now, no mention has been made as to whether managers' activities are truly consistent with the wealth maximisation objective. In fact, much evidence has been brought forward to suggest that managers frequently do not act to maximise owners' wealth. Rather, they are often rewarded on the basis of short-term profitability, and so they may attempt to enhance their own personal wealth, security or prestige, or undertake other actions that are not consistent with maximising owners' wealth.

Nevertheless, this does not negate our entire discussion. Wealth maximisation has been suggested as an appropriate guide for how managers should act. It is recognised that the actions of managers will not always be consistent with this objective.

However, there exist some market forces that help to reduce this problem. The threat of dismissal for poor performance provides managers with an incentive to behave appropriately. Furthermore, poor performance may cause the company's share price to fall, thereby providing an opportunity for outside investors to take over the company by acquiring a significant proportion of shares. The new investors may use the opportunity to replace management.

Owners can encourage managers to act consistently with shareholder wealth maximisation by incurring **agency costs**. Agency costs include the costs incurred to monitor management and the costs associated with offering financial incentives. Auditing and other monitoring costs are incurred to encourage managers to act in the best interests of the shareholders. Remuneration packages can be structured to reward managers for an increase in the company share price through **share options** and other incentives. Share options give managers the opportunity to buy shares at a set price. If the share price increases, the value of the options will rise. This links managers' remuneration to changes in the share price, giving managers considerable incentive to maximise shareholder wealth.

**Agency costs**
Costs incurred to monitor management and costs associated with offering financial incentives to act consistently with shareholder wealth maximisation.

**Share options**
A financial asset that gives the holder the right to purchase shares at a given price.

## Economic implications of wealth maximisation

In the pursuit of shareholder wealth maximisation, the firm's activities can be of benefit to many stakeholders, such as management, employees, creditors and the government. Each stakeholder has a claim on the company's earnings, as demonstrated in Figure 8.4.

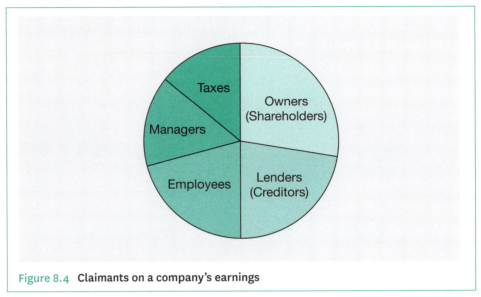

Figure 8.4 **Claimants on a company's earnings**

The diagram illustrates how the earnings of the firm may be divided among the various claimants. Shareholders receive a return on their investment through dividends and/or the change in share price. Management and employees are paid salaries, wages and benefits, while creditors receive payment for the goods and services that they have provided. The government also has a claim in the form of taxes.

Consequently, the wealth maximisation objective not only affects individual businesses but can also have a positive effect on the national economy. In undertaking investment activities consistent with this objective, managers seek to raise funds through the financial markets. Those businesses with the most attractive investment opportunities should be able to promise suppliers of capital the highest return for the degree of risk undertaken; hence, funds should be channelled to their most efficient use. Several benefits may ensue:

- investment in research and development, new technologies and new products can increase revenues, decrease costs and increase employment
- customers can benefit from new or improved products and services
- as the business becomes more successful, additional income taxes may be paid, which are then used for the benefit of society as a whole.

Many large organisations support community projects. Examples are McDonald's (Ronald McDonald House), ANZ Bank (Cancer Society's Daffodil Day) and Westpac Bank (rescue helicopters). Hence, an entire economy can prosper when funds are committed to their most productive use.

Researchers, the media, the public and businesses are now questioning whether firms have moral or ethical obligations to invest their resources in a socially responsible manner. Furthermore, it is unclear how such obligations may comfortably coexist with an organisation's responsibilities to its investors. For example, could a voluntary investment in environmental protection compromise a company's financial obligations to its shareholders in comparison with the behaviour of its less socially conscientious competitors? We have no clear answers to these issues. In the airline industry, many companies are attempting to offset their emissions through the purchase of carbon credits. While this is costly, it is possible that ignoring sustainability may be even more expensive in terms of lost tourism opportunities. Also, companies that participate in socially responsible corporate activities are likely to attract investors who are increasingly seeking ethical investments.

The media, environmental groups, political parties and other socially minded groups tend to be vocal when they perceive that a company is not acting as a good corporate citizen. For example, moves by New Zealand companies to relocate call-centre operations to overseas locations tend to be perceived negatively by traditional and social media and the public because of the consequential loss of local jobs.

In what is considered to be one of New Zealand's first social media-driven campaigns, Cadbury faced a huge backlash from Kiwi consumers in 2009 when it replaced cocoa butter with the cheaper alternative of palm oil as a cost-saving measure. Social media rapidly turned the spotlight on palm oil's association with deforestation in Southeast Asia and the resulting negative impact on wildlife, including the endangered orangutan. For the previous six years, Cadbury had held firmly to the title of 'New Zealand's most-trusted brand', according to the Reader's Digest Trusted Brands survey, but by 2010 the company had plummeted out of the top 20. In their place, Whittaker's – Cadbury's main New Zealand competitor – claimed the top spot in 2010. In 2023 Whittaker's was again named New Zealand's most trusted brand, and Cadbury has still not reappeared in the top 20 most trusted brands. Reputational damage wasn't Cadbury's only concern; it also lost significant market share to Whittaker's, whose sales grew by 60% in the year following the palm-oil debacle, and continued to grow at rates faster than industry growth in subsequent years. Cadbury's cost-saving decision to use palm oil highlights the need to consider not only the economic but also the social impacts of decisions. Near-sighted behaviour, such as focusing on short-term gain, can lead to longer-term pain for investors.

However, the objective of wealth maximisation is not sufficient to ensure that a business will fulfil its social responsibilities. Social and ethical issues such as tax evasion, insider trading and environmental concerns must be addressed by laws and regulations to ensure that businesses conform to the expectations of society.

## Corporate governance and business ethics

Contemporary businesses are increasingly considering the importance of stakeholder rights when setting their corporate objectives. Stakeholders are a broad group, encompassing a wider social perspective than previously expressed by narrow financial definitions. Coming to grips with stakeholders' rights is an important topic currently under debate in the finance discipline. Two alternative approaches to stakeholder rights are discussed below: **corporate social responsibility (CSR)** and creating shared value (CSV).

Some businesses have attempted to address stakeholder rights through CSR goals. Tench[1] argues that transparency of business practices, adopting ethical policies and acting responsibly through sustainable management all contribute to adding value to both stakeholders and society. Tench asserts that to be credible, these CSR policies and practices must be legitimate – and not simply **greenwashing**,

**Corporate social responsibility (CSR)**
Business practice integrating ethical, social and environmental concerns into goals and operations, contributing to sustainable development and stakeholder well-being.

**Greenwashing**
Misleading or deceptive marketing to create a false impression of a company's environmental responsibility.

---

1   Ralph Tench, 'The role of corporate social responsibility in the financial crisis', in William Sun, Jim Stewart and David Pollard (eds), 'Reframing corporate social responsibility: Lessons from the Global Financial Crisis', *Critical Studies on Corporate Responsibility, Governance and Sustainability*, vol. 1 (2010): 43–56.

where an organisation spends more time and money on marketing itself as environmentally friendly than on actually minimising its environmental impact.

Social and news media both undertake an important role of monitoring and publicising business activities, so business communications with stakeholders will increasingly need to build trust – both functional and ethical – in order to restore public confidence in the decision making and actions of business managers. Ultimately, success will be determined by how well CSR and financial goals are able to be reconciled.

Porter and Kramer[2] argue that the traditional view of firm value creation is too narrow, as it tends to focus on the internal benefits to the firm and ignores external costs to the communities in which it operates. The authors propose that the traditional view should be redefined as **creating shared value (CSV)**, and that this should replace CSR. Specifically, shared value involves 'creating economic value in a way that also creates value for society by addressing its needs and challenges'.[3] Therefore, shared value focuses on the connections between societal and economic progress. To unlock shared value, firms can address social harms through technological, process and management innovations which could lead to reconceiving products and markets, redefining productivity in the value chain and enabling local cluster development.

**Creating shared value (CSV)**
Business strategy aligning corporate success with societal progress, aiming to address social issues while achieving economic goals.

### Reconceiving products and markets

Through assessing and exploring community and societal needs, firms will find new opportunities for product differentiation and open new markets that were previously overlooked. In his work for the Fred Hollows Foundation, Sir Ray Avery (2010 New Zealander of the Year), developed novel low-cost, high-quality intraocular lenses. The lenses (and the surgical techniques developed) disrupted the cataract surgery industry worldwide by collapsing the cost per operation to the point where surgery is now accessible to almost everyone. By commissioning state-of-the-art intraocular lens manufacturing facilities in Eritrea and Nepal, the Fred Hollows Foundation provides local training, skilled employment and valuable export revenue for developing countries that also have some of the world's highest incidence of cataracts.

### Redefining productivity in the value chain

A firm's value chain represents the activities the firm undertakes in order to deliver its product or service for the market. A narrow perspective of the firm's value chain might simply consider the direct activities the business is involved with, whereas a shared-value perspective would take the entire chain into account. For example, a sheep and beef farmer might consider what arrives at their farm gate (e.g. livestock, fertiliser, feed), what activities are conducted on the farm (e.g. stock handling, fencing) and consider their value chain complete when the animals leave their gate. Companies like Silver Fern Farms now consider the entire supply chain from farm gate to customer plate. In working closely with both the farmers (for consistency in product) and international supermarkets, companies like Silver Fern Farms have been able to attract premium prices from this strategy, through carefully considering how it procures its product from suppliers and delivers this to its customers.

---

2    Michael Porter and Mark Kramer, 'Creating shared value: How to reinvent capitalism – and unleash a wave of innovation and growth', *Harvard Business Review* 89 (January–February 2011): 62–77.
3    Ibid., 64.

## Enabling local cluster development

No firm is an island: every firm relies heavily on supporting businesses and the infrastructure around it. Innovation and productivity are strongly influenced by clusters of related businesses, suppliers and logistical infrastructure that support an industry. For example, the filming of the *Lord of the Rings* movies led to a cluster of supporting businesses in Miramar, Wellington, including Wētā Workshop, that continue to attract international projects.

## Ethical considerations in property

Within the property sector, there are additional ethical considerations. The two most often encountered are the provision of residential accommodation and the agency–principal relationship. There is also increased awareness of the impact of the built environment on emissions, energy consumption and carbon footprint.

Residential investment differs from most other investment types in that it impacts on the most inherent of human needs: shelter and social cohesion. From an ethical perspective, any investor in residential property should be aware that their product can have a considerable impact on the well-being of its occupants. This relates not only to physical condition but also to the contractual relationship with the occupants and their certainty of tenure in the location (such as linkages to schools and community). For this reason, there is considerable public interest in housing, especially for vulnerable communities, and this is reflected in the scope of the Residential Tenancies Act 1986, which provides a comprehensive regulatory framework specifically for this asset class.

The property market, more than most others, is dominated by agents undertaking transactions on behalf of principals and therefore this creates 'agency risk'. The use of agents occurs throughout the sector, but is most commonly encountered with the outsourcing of property management and the use of real estate agents for both leasing and sales transactions. This, combined with the widespread use of commission-based remuneration, can lead to conflicts of interest between the principal and the agent. For this reason, the real estate agency sector is regulated by statute and monitored by a Crown entity, the Real Estate Authority.

# The external environment

A business does not operate in isolation. The financial management decisions and activities that concern the operations of a business must take into account environmental factors external to the organisation. The operations of the financial markets and the effects of government regulations and taxes are, for the most part, beyond the control of the firm's managers. Nevertheless, these external factors will have a pronounced effect on the financial decisions made within the firm.

## Financial markets

It is through the financial markets that the value of ordinary shares and other financial instruments is set. Market participants buy and sell securities and, in the process, assign a monetary value or price to these securities. The value of any asset depends on the benefits expected to be received by virtue of owning the asset. The expected timing, magnitude and risk of the benefits will therefore have an effect on the value placed on the assets. The longer one must wait before receiving the benefits, and the more uncertainty there is about the magnitude of the future benefits, the lower will be the present value of the assets. Consequently, shareholders consider the timing, magnitude and risk of future dividend income and share price changes when they value the shares of a company. Likewise, lenders assess the timing, magnitude and risk of future interest income and principal repayments when they value a debt instrument or consider a loan application.

The relationship between the expected timing, magnitude and risk of future benefits and value has important implications for most businesses. Recall that the objective of financial management is to maximise the wealth of the owners by maximising the value or price of the firm's shares. In order to work towards this goal, it is critical for managers to understand the variables that influence the price of the firm's shares.

## Regulatory environment

Many financial decisions require managers to keep abreast of the business laws and regulations for those countries in which the company conducts its business. There are myriad constraints on business activities imposed by regulatory bodies in order to protect stakeholders such as consumers, investors, employees and suppliers. Some of the activities that are affected by these constraints are summarised below:

- trade practices – promoting competition in markets and protecting consumers
- provision of credit – regulating disclosure in credit, hire-purchase, lay-by and similar contracts
- employment practices
- issuing shares or other securities to the public
- company formation, administration and winding-up
- business acquisitions
- activities affecting health, safety and the environment
- income taxes.

Financial decisions will frequently need to take into account the laws and regulations that affect the above-mentioned activities.

## Risk and return

Almost all financial decisions are affected by risk, being the uncertainty of an outcome. If too much inventory is produced, then excessive labour and inventory-holding costs will be incurred. However, if too little inventory is produced, then potential sales may be lost. Our farmer in Example 2 had to forecast the future returns from the alternative investments, and these returns could vary depending on his expertise, the success of the production systems and future prices.

Despite the presence of uncertainty, managers must make financial decisions; otherwise, organisations would cease to function. However, the tendency for managers to be risk-averse leads to an important observation – *the higher the risk, the higher the required return*.

This was described in Chapter 6 as the risk–return trade-off. Before managers make financial decisions, they assess the expected risk. If the risk is expected to be high, then a high return is required. If the risk is expected to be low, then a lower return is acceptable. Figure 8.5 depicts the risk–return trade-off.

The slope of the line reflects the degree of risk aversion for the business and, hence, the minimum required return. A steeper slope implies a higher degree of risk aversion. For a project to be acceptable, the expected return must be on or above the risk–return line.

The risk–return trade-off has an important effect on financial decision making. If the expected (or forecast) return is less than the required return, then a 'no-go' decision will be made. If the expected return exceeds the required return, then the proposal will go ahead.

In Figure 8.5 and Table 8.3, proposal T carries little risk, so the required return is low (8%). As the expected return of 10% exceeds the required return of 8%, proposal T is financially acceptable. In contrast, proposal W is riskier, so the required return is higher (16%). However, the expected return of 13% is lower than the required return of 16%, so proposal W would be rejected.

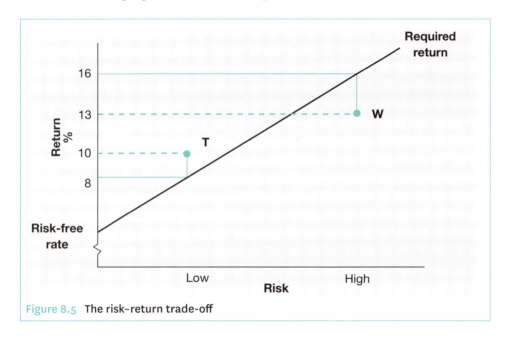

Figure 8.5 The risk–return trade-off

Table 8.3 Decision making and the risk–return trade-off

|            | Risk | Required return | Expected return | Decision |
|------------|------|-----------------|-----------------|----------|
| **Proposal T** | Low  | 8%              | 10%             | Accept   |
| **Proposal W** | High | 16%             | 13%             | Reject   |

The assessment of the risk–return trade-off is critical to many financial decisions, and assists decision-makers to meet the firm's objective of maximising owners' wealth. The following example illustrates how poor corporate governance led to unethical decision-making that went undetected, and how this in turn impacted on the firm's risk and the returns demanded by investors. We shall see that the ultimate result was the collapse of the firm's value through wealth destruction.

> **Example 3: Ethics, risk, return and value**
>
> Unethical behaviour on the part of a firm's managers can result in severe wealth destruction for investors. An example of how destructive unethical behaviour can be is the Volkswagen emission scandal. On 18 September 2015 Volkswagen admitted having designed and installed emissions-cheating software in as many as 11 million vehicles. The sole purpose of the software was to mislead regulators about the level of pollution emissions from the diesel engines. In fact the vehicles were emitting up to 40 times the maximum limit levels of nitrogen dioxide.
>
> The market impact was swift. Within two days Volkswagen's preference share values fell by more than a third, and the yield demanded on the company's bonds more than doubled, from 2.3% to over 4.6% as investors demanded higher returns to compensate for the perceived higher risk. The higher returns demanded by new investors purchasing Volkswagen bonds meant that existing Volkswagen bond investors felt the pain of sharply falling bond values.
>
> As Volkswagen's ordinary shares are not publicly traded, it is difficult to fully quantify the extent of wealth destroyed by the unethical practice. However, one of the company's largest shareholders, Qatar's Sovereign Investment Fund – which owned almost 13% of Volkswagen's preference shares and 17% of its ordinary shares – is reported to have lost over $6 billion in the two days following the news of the scandal. Therefore the unethical practice destroyed shareholder wealth on a massive scale.
>
> While the impact on share and bond values was immediate, there were also longer-term concerns for both Volkswagen's financial performance and the company's reputation. Aside from the tens of billions of dollars' worth of fines and the cost of putting the problem right, reputational damage can negatively affect sales for a long time afterwards. As we will see in Chapter 10, the higher risk-adjusted return demanded by both shareholders and bond holders substantially increased Volkswagen's cost of financing; as its weighted average cost of capital rises, the value of the firm's current and future investments falls.
>
> Questions were raised about Volkswagen's corporate governance structure, given that it enabled such an unsound decision to occur and go undetected by the board of directors for so long. The CEO stated that he had no knowledge of the cover-up, and, after initially resisting calls for his resignation, he subsequently resigned on 23 September 2015.

The assessment of the risk–return trade-off should consider both internal and external factors. The financial decisions that result from this assessment will affect the timing, magnitude and risk of the firm's cash flows. The financial markets' perceptions of the risk and return characteristics of the firm will in turn influence the firm's share price and value. These relationships are shown graphically in Figure 8.6.

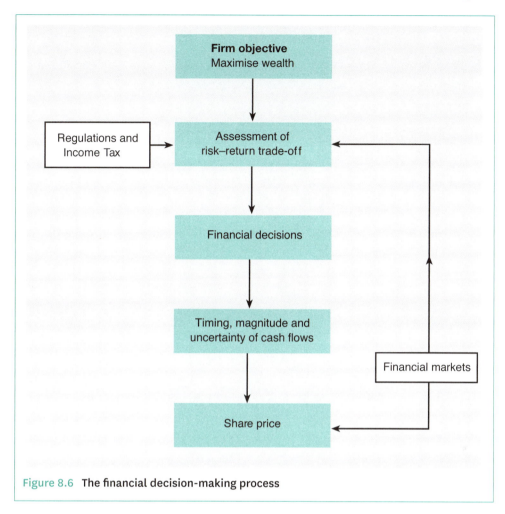

Figure 8.6 The financial decision-making process

# Conclusion

Financial management refers to the activities and decisions undertaken with regard to the financing and investment requirements of an organisation. The three principal functions of financial management are *financial forecasting and planning, financing the firm* and *investment in assets*. While all functional areas within an organisation influence financial decisions, marketing, manufacturing, purchasing and warehousing activities provide particularly valuable information for financial forecasting and planning. Financial management is an important part of the managerial planning process that ensures that the goals and objectives of the firm are being met.

The financial objective of a firm should be to maximise owners' wealth. Profit maximisation is inappropriate as a long-term objective, as it fails to account for the timing, magnitude and risk of cash flows.

The process of financial management is an interactive one involving the movement of funds between business organisations, the financial markets and the government. Financial markets set asset and share values according to the expected timing, magnitude and risk of future benefits. Other environmental influences, such as business and income tax laws, will also have a substantial impact on financial decision-making.

## SELF-TEST QUESTIONS

1. Which of the following goals are consistent with the wealth maximisation objective?
   a  Maximise the market price of the firm's ordinary shares.
   b  Maximise the market value of owners' equity.
   c  Maximise earnings per share.
   d  Maximise net profit.
   e  Maximise the value of the firm's assets.

2. The owner-manager of Whiz-Bang Panelbeaters is considering two alternative equipment purchases, A and B. They both have a five-year life and will cost about $40 000. Different scenarios result in forecast annual profits as follows:

| Equipment | Scenarios | | |
|---|---|---|---|
| | Pessimistic | Expected | Optimistic |
| A | $5 000 | $10 000 | $15 000 |
| B | $ 0 | $10 000 | $20 000 |

If the owner-manager of Whiz-Bang is risk-averse, which piece of equipment should he purchase? Explain why.

## ANSWERS TO SELF-TEST QUESTIONS

1. Maximising either the market price of ordinary shares (**a**) for a company, or the market value of owners' equity (**b**) for an unincorporated business, is consistent with the wealth maximisation objective.

   While not strictly equivalent to shareholder wealth maximisation, a goal of maximising the value of the firm's assets (**e**) may be considered acceptable from an operational point of view. Given that total assets equal debt plus equity, if debt levels remain unchanged then any increase in the value of the assets will also increase the value of owners' equity.

   Net profit (**d**) and earnings per share (**c**) are accounting-related measures that will not necessarily maximise owners' wealth because:
   - they fail to consider the time value of money
   - they do not represent cash flow
   - they ignore risk.

2. We normally assume that managers and investors are risk-averse. This implies that, if all else is equal, more return is preferred for a given level of risk, and less risk is preferred for a given level of return. In this context, risk is considered to be variability of returns. Both pieces of equipment are expected to earn a return of $10 000. The risk-averse owner-manager of Whiz-Bang Panelbeaters will choose Equipment A because there is less risk of an unfavourable outcome – that is, a zero profit. In fact, being risk-averse, the owner-manager is willing to forego the possibility of earning a very high profit in the optimistic scenario with Equipment B, in return for a more certain outcome by purchasing Equipment A.

## QUESTIONS AND PROBLEMS

1. What is financial management?
2. Describe the three principal functions of financial management.
3. What should be the objective of financial management?
4. Define *wealth* with respect to:
   a the shareholders of a firm
   b the owner of a sole proprietorship
   c the owners of a business partnership.
5. Give three reasons why profit maximisation is inappropriate as a long-term objective for financial management. Explain each of the three.
6. What is risk?
7. Why are most investors considered to be risk-averse?
8. Which external environment factors most directly affect the financial decisions of a business?
9. Describe the process by which the value of ordinary shares and other financial instruments is set in the marketplace.
10. In what way will the expected timing, magnitude and risk of future benefits affect the value of an asset?
11. What are some of the financial activities affected by regulatory constraints?
12. What is meant by the expression 'risk–return trade-off'?
13. Why is it necessary for financial decisions to consider information from other functional areas within an organisation?
14. Some managers hold significant shareholdings in the companies that they manage. What are the potential benefits of this situation to the firm's other shareholders? Are there any potential disadvantages?
15. In some countries, union officials are represented on the board of directors of many public companies.
    a Do you see any potential conflict between the objectives of the union and those of the firm?
    b Would the potential conflict be diminished if a significant proportion of union members were also shareholders in the company?
16. Alec Smart, a first-year varsity social work student, and Lee Brier, a first-year business studies student, are debating the merits to society of business investment. Alec presents the following argument:

    > Business investment in plant and equipment only benefits the capitalist élite in our society. If a business prospers, then the wealthy shareholders prosper. The business managers who have increased their shareholders' wealth also gain, as they receive extravagant salaries and fringe benefits as their reward. As always, the rich get richer and the poor get poorer.

    Lee understands the point Alec is making, but she feels that the issues are not quite as black and white as Alec is portraying. What points could Lee raise to demonstrate to Alec that benefits from business investment accrue not only to shareholders and managers but also to society as a whole?

17  If the wealth maximisation objective benefits both investors and the national economy, then why are regulatory constraints imposed on businesses?

18  Two banks offer similar five-year term deposits, but Bank A pays 8% annual interest while Bank B pays 12% annual interest. What would you conclude about the relative risks of each bank? What would you conclude about the respective risk attitudes of the two banks' depositors?

19  In what ways might the shareholder wealth maximisation objective:

   a  be of benefit to some stakeholders?

   b  be inappropriate as a goal in some organisations?

   c  be insufficient to ensure that a business will fulfil its social responsibilities?

20  Dynamic Dinghies Ltd, a major manufacturer of small boats, is considering two alternative investment opportunities, Q and R. They both have a five-year life. As a result of these opportunities, earnings per share are expected to be as follows:

| Investment | Earnings per share (EPS) in year | | | | | Total EPS Years 1–5 |
|---|---|---|---|---|---|---|
| | 1 | 2 | 3 | 4 | 5 | |
| Q | $1.00 | $1.00 | $1.00 | $1.00 | $1.00 | $5.00 |
| R | $0.10 | $0.40 | $0.50 | $1.00 | $3.10 | $5.10 |

   a  Based on a profit maximisation objective of maximising total EPS, which investment would be preferred?

   b  Find the present value of the five-year EPS stream for each of Q and R, assuming a discount rate of 14%.

   c  Explain why the decision reached in **a** may be deficient.

21  Shock Electrical Ltd is deciding between three investments, each with an investment cost of $100 000. The forecast annual profits from the alternative investments, given three different economic scenarios, are as follows:

| Investment | Scenarios | | |
|---|---|---|---|
| | Poor | Normal | Good |
| A | $ 20 000 | $50 000 | $ 80 000 |
| B | –$200 000 | $50 000 | $200 000 |
| C | $ 40 000 | $50 000 | $ 60 000 |

If the managers of Shock Electrical are risk-averse, which investment should be selected? Explain why.

22  TLC Toy Manufacturing Ltd is considering several investment opportunities that have different levels of risk. The financial controller has set the following criteria for evaluating the proposals:

| Risk | Required returns (%) |
|---|---|
| Very low | 8 |
| Low | 10 |
| Average | 12 |
| High | 15 |
| Very high | 20 |

The expected risks and returns for the investments are as shown in the table on the right.

Assuming that TLC will accept all desirable projects, which ones should it accept?

| Investment | Risk | Expected returns (%) |
|---|---|---|
| F | High | 12 |
| G | Average | 14 |
| H | Low | 9 |
| I | Average | 10 |
| J | High | 15 |
| K | Very high | 18 |
| L | Very low | 8 |
| M | Average | 12 |
| N | Low | 10 |

23  Liz Biz, a wealthy retired actress, is looking at investing in the ordinary shares of several companies. Her sharebroker has provided details of the expected returns of each company, and graphed them along with Liz's risk–return line. The risk–return line indicates Liz's required return for each level of risk. Assuming that Liz wishes to purchase all desirable shares, which ones should she buy? Explain why.

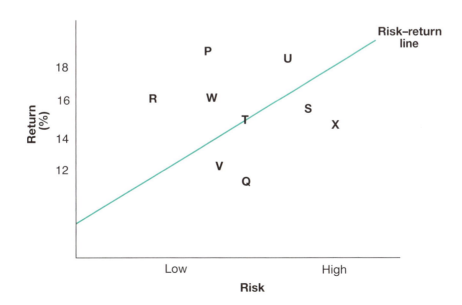

24 AppTrap makes gaming apps for smartphones and tablets. It is currently evaluating two alternative investments. The first proposed game, Lolly Scramble, would be based around a current top-selling game, while the second, Pied Pie, is an entirely new gaming idea. The investment costs are expected to be similar, but AppTrap only has enough funding to develop one new game. Lolly Scramble is likely to have a much narrower range of market demand and annual profit than Pied Pie, as shown below.

| Investment | Annual profit under forecast market demand conditions | | |
|---|---|---|---|
| | Low | Normal | High |
| Lolly Scramble | $150 000 | $200 000 | $250 000 |
| Pied Pie | $ 0 | $300 000 | $600 000 |

a  Assuming that there is an equal probability of each forecast market demand occurring, calculate the expected return and standard deviation for each app alternative.

b  Recalculate each app's expected return and standard deviation assuming that there is a 40% probability of low market demand, a 40% probability of normal market demand and a 20% probability of high market demand.

c  Which app has the highest risk? Why?

# Investment in net working capital

**CHAPTER 9**

### Learning objectives

By the end of this chapter, you should be able to:
- understand the relationship between the components of working capital
- define 'net working capital', and explain how, by balancing profitability and risk, a suitable goal for the management of net working capital can be established
- describe three motives for holding cash balances
- prepare a forecast cash flow statement
- describe the three major components of credit policy
- list the major costs of inventory
- calculate the cost of foregoing a discount on an account payable, and assess whether to take or forego the discount
- explain three strategies for managing the cash conversion cycle.

## Introduction

This chapter will introduce working capital management. The importance of managing current assets and current liabilities should not be overlooked by organisations, as current assets may represent a large proportion of total assets. Consequently, the amount, type and financing of current assets can significantly affect the profitability and risk of an organisation. In this chapter we will focus on the management of net working capital.

## Net working capital

**Net working capital** is the difference between current assets and current liabilities, and is one measure of the liquidity of an organisation. The investment in net working capital can be very significant, affecting the profitability and risk of the organisation.

Recall that the objective of a firm should be to maximise the value of owners' wealth. From a short-term perspective, profitability and wealth are complementary, such that increased profits will contribute to increased wealth. Since net working capital is a short-term concept involving assets and obligations that are due within a year, profitability is a suitable measure to evaluate the management of net working capital.

The following goal can therefore be established for the management of each of the current asset and current liability **accounts** affected by net working capital:

- *to achieve an optimal balance between profitability and risk that maximises owners' wealth.*

> **Net working capital**
> Current assets minus current liabilities.

> **Accounts**
> Items accounted for on a balance sheet, income statement or cash flow statement.

## Risk–profitability trade-off

Just as there is a trade-off between risk and return, there is also a trade-off between risk and profitability. One comes at the expense of the other, and the task of a manager is to balance these trade-offs. These trade-offs are illustrated in the following scenario.

> **Example 1: Risk–profitability trade-off**
>
> Technability Ltd is a new surfboard and windsurfer manufacturer and has completed financial projections for its first year of operations. As shown in Table 9.1, Technability Ltd expects to have net working capital equal to $49 763, which is calculated as current assets of $64 794 less current liabilities of $15 031.
>
> Table 9.1    Net working capital position, Technability Ltd
>
> | Current assets | | Current liabilities | |
> |---|---|---|---|
> | Accounts receivable | $59 105 | Trade accounts payable | $ 3 220 |
> | GST refund due | $ 1 689 | Sundry accounts payable | $11 811 |
> | Inventory | $ 4 000 | | |
> | Total | $64 794 | Total | $15 031 |
>
> Technability Ltd's financial manager must decide on the appropriate balance in each of the current asset and current liability accounts. If the balance of the current asset accounts increases by $40 000, then net working capital will increase by the same amount. This will decrease the risk of being unable to pay the $15 031 in current liabilities. However, the increased investment in current assets will decrease the firm's overall rate of return (the profit relative to assets employed). Furthermore, if the increase in current assets is due to slow collection of accounts receivable and excessive inventory levels, then the level of profits could decrease due to increased bad debts, damage to inventory and increased costs of financing the current assets. So, increasing the investment in net working capital can decrease risk, but at a cost of decreased profitability.
>
> Conversely, if the net working capital balance of $49 763 falls by $40 000 to $9 763 (current assets of $24 794 less current liabilities of $15 031), there will be an increased risk of failing to meet the liabilities as they become due. This increases the risk of financial distress, and the firm could become insolvent. However, profits could actually improve if the decrease in net working capital was attributable to faster collection of accounts receivable, better inventory management and slower payment of **accounts payable**. So decreasing the investment in net working capital can increase profitability, but it will also increase risk.

**Accounts payable**
Current debts arising from the purchases of goods and services.

## Management of net working capital

Keeping in mind the risk versus profitability trade-off, we will next examine in more detail the management of three particularly significant current assets: cash and near-cash, accounts receivable and inventory. We will then consider the management of current liabilities and how they can be used to reduce the amount of funds tied up in net working capital.

## Managing cash

Cash management involves planning for cash inflows and outflows and determining the optimal balances of cash and near-cash accounts. Cash management regularly features as the top priority of CFOs and treasurers in the biannual PwC Global Treasury Survey. The 2023 PwC Survey revealed that CFOs were 'laser focused on optimizing cash efficiency' as firms exited from the Covid-19 affected years, and firms also ranked cash and working capital management among their highest priorities. Irrespective of their size or industry sector, all organisations can benefit from planning and controlling net cash flows – consequently, this will be our focus here. However, the calculation of optimal cash balances is beyond the scope of this text.

### Cash and near-cash

In our definition of cash we include cash-on-hand, cash-in-bank and near-cash such as **marketable securities**. Marketable securities are short-term interest-earning financial claims that can be quickly converted to cash without any significant loss of value. Examples are Treasury bills, certificates of deposit and commercial bills.

### Motives for holding cash

There are three motives for firms to hold at least some cash balances.

- **The transactions motive**

    Some cash balances are needed to pay for certain predictable obligations as they fall due, such as employees' wages, suppliers' bills and taxes.

- **The safety motive**

    As not all day-to-day payments are predictable; some additional cash balances are needed to allow for unforeseen cash needs. These funds could be invested in interest-earning marketable securities, which are transferred into cash as the need arises.

- **The speculative motive**

    A few firms may maintain additional funds in interest-earning marketable securities in order to take advantage of unexpected investment opportunities as they arise.

Transactions balances are maintained to meet expected operating cash needs; safety balances relate to unforeseen operating and financing needs; and speculative balances are held to take advantage of potential, unexpected investments.

### Forecast cash flow statement

The forecast cash flow statement is an important tool in **cash management** that estimates the future cash balances of an organisation through forecasting cash receipts and cash disbursements. By highlighting future deficiencies and surpluses of cash, a forecast cash flow statement can be useful in the following ways:

- it allows time to arrange additional financing

---

**Marketable securities**
Short-term interest-earning financial claims that can be quickly converted to cash without any significant loss of value.

**Transactions motive**
Maintaining additional cash balances to pay for predictable day-to-day cash needs.

**Safety motive**
Maintaining additional cash balances for unforeseen day-to-day cash needs.

**Speculative motive**
Maintaining additional cash balances in interest-earning marketable securities in order to take advantage of unexpected investment opportunities.

**Cash management**
The management of cash-on-hand, bank balances and marketable securities.

- the amount and timing of surplus cash available for investment is revealed
- the timing of debt repayments can be planned
- it is a supporting document required to accompany most loan applications
- it shows the amount of cash available for dividend payments – the directors of a company would refer to a forecast cash flow statement as one step in the process of applying the solvency test required by the Companies Act 1993 (New Zealand) prior to authorising a distribution (such as a dividend) to shareholders.

Forecast cash flow statements are used for both short-term and medium-term planning. Short-term forecast cash flow statements may forecast the week ahead and are broken down on a daily basis in order to plan for daily changes in the cash balance. Medium-term forecast cash flow statements tend to forecast for the next 6–12 months, revealing monthly changes in cash balances. Monthly cash balances may vary considerably, particularly in businesses subject to seasonal sales demand or variable production requirements. The following discussion will focus on medium-term forecast cash flow statements.

The preparation of a medium-term forecast cash flow statement requires a detailed forecast of **cash receipts** and **cash disbursements**. The first step is to obtain a monthly forecast of sales, which will be prepared with the assistance of marketing staff. Given information on the collection pattern for credit sales, monthly cash receipts from sales can be predicted.

Other cash receipts are then added to cash receipts from sales, to arrive at total cash receipts. Cash disbursements then must be forecast and totalled for **operating cash flows** and **financing** as well as investment needs. Table 9.2 gives some examples of common cash receipts and cash disbursements. Note that **goods and services tax (GST)** received from sales and GST paid with expenses are included in cash receipts and cash disbursements, respectively. The difference between GST collected and GST paid must be remitted periodically to the Inland Revenue Department (IRD). Although GST does not 'belong' to the firm, it affects the cash flows and should be included in a forecast cash flow statement.

Net cash flow is then calculated as total cash receipts minus total cash disbursements. The opening cash balance is next added to net cash flow to arrive at the closing cash balance. If the closing cash balance is positive, then excess cash may be invested in marketable securities. If the closing cash balance is negative, then additional financing will be required. The following example illustrates the process of preparing a forecast cash flow statement.

> **Cash receipts**
> Cash inflows received.
>
> **Cash disbursements**
> Cash payments.
>
> **Operating cash flows**
> Cash inflows received and outflows incurred as a result of the firm's day-to-day operating activities.
>
> **Financing cash flows**
> Cash inflows received and cash outflows incurred as part of the firm's financing activities.
>
> **Goods and services tax (GST)**
> A type of value-added tax collected by suppliers of goods and services on behalf of the government.

Table 9.2 **Examples of cash receipts and cash disbursements**

| Cash receipts | Cash disbursements |
| --- | --- |
| Cash sales | Cash purchases |
| Collections of accounts receivable | Payments of accounts payable |
| Interest and dividends received | Rent payments |
| Proceeds from sale of fixed assets | Payments for salaries, wages, overheads and administration |
| New loan proceeds | |
| GST received from sales | Tax payments |
| Capital contributions from owners | Interest, principal and dividend payments |
| | Purchases of fixed assets |
| | GST paid with expenses |
| | Net GST remittance to the IRD |

### Example 2: Forecast cash flow statement

International Operations Limited (IOL) is a large, diversified multinational company with its head office in Auckland. One division of IOL operates a timber yard that sells timber and wood products to building contractors. After consultations with the marketing department, the financial controller has prepared a forecast of sales for August to December. Past experience has shown that 10% of sales are for cash, 50% are collected in the month following the sale, and 40% are collected two months after the sale. There are no other cash receipts, except for the **salvage value** to be received in November from the sale of equipment. Table 9.3 is a simplified version of the total forecast cash receipts.

Purchases are estimated to be 60% of the next month's sales. All purchases are on credit and are paid for in the following month. Other outlays will be made for wages and salaries, rent, other operating expenses, interest, tax and the purchase of equipment. Table 9.4 calculates the total forecast cash disbursements.

The forecast cash flow statement takes forecast cash receipts and deducts forecast cash disbursements. A simplified forecast cash flow statement for IOL is shown in Table 9.5 on the next page.

**Salvage value**
The price received from the sale of a fixed asset at the end of its useful life.

**Table 9.3** Schedule of forecast cash receipts ($000)

|  | August | September | October | November | December |
|---|---|---|---|---|---|
| Projected sales | $200 | $400 | $400 | $400 | $600 |
| Cash sales (10%) | $ 20 | $ 40 | $ 40 | $ 40 | $ 60 |
| *Collections:* | | | | | |
| From sales one month previous (50%) | | $100 | $200 | $200 | $200 |
| From sales two months previous (40%) | | | $ 80 | $160 | $160 |
| Sale of equipment | | | | $ 10 | |
| **Total cash receipts** | | | **$320** | **$410** | **$420** |

**Table 9.4** Schedule of forecast cash disbursements ($000)

|  |  |  |  |  |  |
|---|---|---|---|---|---|
| Projected purchases[1] | | $240 | $240 | $360 | $300 |
| Payments of accounts payable[2] | | | $240 | $240 | $360 |
| Wages and salaries | | | $ 50 | $ 60 | $ 50 |
| Rent | | | $ 10 | $ 10 | $ 10 |
| Payments for operating expenses | | | $ 6 | $ 8 | $ 8 |
| Interest payments | | | $ 4 | $ 4 | $ 4 |
| Tax payments | | | $ 2 | $ 12 | $ 2 |
| Outlay for purchase of equipment | | | | $110 | |
| **Total cash disbursements** | | | **$312** | **$444** | **$434** |

[1] 60% of next month's sales. Projected sales for January are $500.
[2] All purchases are paid for in the following month.

Table 9.5   Forecast cash flow statement ($000)

|  | October | November | December |
|---|---|---|---|
| Total cash receipts | $320 | $410 | $420 |
| Less: Total cash disbursements | $312 | $444 | $434 |
| Net cash inflow (outflow)[1] | $ 8 | ($ 34) | ($ 14) |
| Add: Opening cash balance | $ 15 | $ 23 | ($ 11) |
| Closing cash balance | $ 23 | ($ 11) | ($ 25) |
| Surplus cash to invest | $ 23 |  |  |
| Cumulative financing required |  | $ 11 | $ 25 |

[1] Parentheses denote negative numbers.

The net cash flow is positive $8 000 in October, negative $34 000 in November and negative $14 000 in December. Given an opening cash balance at 1 October of $15 000, the closing cash balance is positive $23 000 in October, negative $11 000 in November and negative $25 000 in December. Consequently, although $23 000 is available for investment in marketable securities in October, this will have to be liquidated in November and a further amount borrowed of $11 000. Another $14 000 will need to be borrowed in December, for cumulative financing needed of $25 000 ($11 000 + $14 000).

A forecast cash flow statement is a forecast of the future cash flows and cash balances, yet the actual figures may deviate from those expected. Large discrepancies between the actual and forecast balances may signal possible problems that need to be investigated, such as declining sales, a slowing of collections on accounts receivable, or poor planning. The forecast cash flow statements are updated and extended intermittently as part of the continuing process of managing cash.

## Management of accounts receivable

Most firms would prefer to have cash sales only and therefore hold no accounts receivable. This would eliminate bad debts expense and avoid interest costs for financing the investment in accounts receivable. However, for competitive reasons, firms must generally offer customers the opportunity to buy on credit. Otherwise, they could lose sales. Accordingly, accounts receivable management attempts to minimise the costs of bad debts and financing while maximising sales.

### Setting credit policy

**Credit policy** involves setting standards and guidelines that govern the management of accounts receivable. It comprises three major components:

**Credit policy**
Setting standards and guidelines that govern the management of accounts receivable. Consists of credit standards, credit terms and collection policy.

- credit standards
- credit terms
- collection policy.

These policies are set by the senior financial manager after a careful analysis of the applicable costs, benefits and risks. However, it is up to the credit manager to ensure that the policies are properly implemented.

**Credit standards** are the criteria used to evaluate the creditworthiness of customers who seek to purchase goods or services on credit. The goal is to minimise the likelihood of the customer defaulting on payments. To assess this risk, the customer's past payment history, available cash resources, income stream and financial strength – including ownership of assets – are established. External credit references will also be obtained, and other competitive and unique conditions assessed in order to come to a final decision on how much credit, if any, to extend to the customer.

**Credit terms** specify the repayment requirements for all customers. The length of the credit period will be stated on the monthly statement to each customer. Terms such as net 20 days or net 30 days are common, meaning payment is required within 20 (or 30) days from the date of the statement. Occasionally, credit terms will apply to the invoice date rather than the statement date. This is particularly the case where discounts are offered for early payment. The credit terms must be set carefully, as they can affect not only customers' payment dates but also the level of sales, investment in accounts receivable and bad debts.

> **Credit standards**
> Criteria used to evaluate the creditworthiness of customers who are seeking to purchase goods or services on credit.
>
> **Credit terms**
> The time-frame requirements for customer repayments of trade credit.

---

**Example 3: Credit terms**

Invoice A:     1 September
Invoice B:     8 September
Invoice C:    22 September

Statement date:         30 September
**Credit terms:**       **Net 20 days**
Last day for payment:   20 October

---

**Collection policy** refers to the procedures adopted to collect accounts receivable. Prompt attention to collecting overdue accounts can minimise bad debts, although over-zealous action may hamper future sales. Normally the rigour of collection action increases with the age of the overdue account, beginning with reminder letters and telephone calls, progressing to personal visits, referral to collection agencies and finally legal action.

> **Collection policy**
> Procedures adopted to collect accounts receivable.

## Management of inventory

Many firms have a significant portion of their funds tied up in inventory. The higher the investment in inventory, the higher the holding and financing costs, and the lower the profits. Yet too low an investment in inventory can also be costly. Insufficient levels of **raw material** and **work-in-process inventories** may lead to production bottlenecks, while low levels of **finished goods inventory** carry the risk of stock-outs and lost sales. So inventory management attempts to balance these trade-offs by minimising total costs. A summary of the major costs of inventory is presented in Table 9.6 on the next page.

> **Raw materials inventory**
> Unprocessed materials inventory held while awaiting production.
>
> **Work-in-process inventory**
> Partly completed goods that are still in production.
>
> **Finished goods inventory**
> Fully completed goods available for sale.

Table 9.6    Inventory costs

| Holding costs | Order costs | Stock-out costs |
| --- | --- | --- |
| Financial costs | Clerical ordering costs | Lost sales |
| Storage and handling costs | Production set-up time | Production bottlenecks |
| Insurance | Shipping and receiving costs | |
| Deterioration and obsolescence | | |

Inventory management aims to minimise the total inventory costs of holding costs, order costs and stock-out costs.

Several models and techniques have been developed that attempt to reduce the various inventory costs. These include:

- the economic order quantity model
- computerised inventory control systems
- just-in-time inventory systems.

### Economic order quantity model

> **Economic order quantity (EOQ)**
> The optimal order quantity that minimises total holding and ordering costs.

A well-known model called the **economic order quantity (EOQ)** model seeks to determine the order quantities that minimise total holding and ordering costs, while considering usage rates. For raw materials and work-in-process inventories, usage rates are determined by production requirements. The usage rates for finished goods inventory are forecast as the number of units to be sold. Once the optimal order quantity has been established, average inventory levels and reorder points can be determined.

### Computerised inventory control system

Computerised inventory control systems are becoming more common as part of computerised accounting information systems, particularly among firms that have numerous lines of inventory. A system will normally document quantity and value, but may also specify reorder points and order quantities. Retail systems can use scanners to read inventory bar codes at the point of sale, record a reduction in inventory and, if necessary, place an order with the supplier to reorder.

### Just-in-time system

> **Just-in-time system**
> An arrangement with suppliers for inventory to be delivered at the time when it is needed for production.

Both large and small firms are increasingly using a **just-in-time system** in which arrangements are made with suppliers to deliver goods as they are needed for production. The idea is to maintain a minimal raw materials inventory in order to minimise the associated holding costs. Successful implementation of this system requires careful co-ordination of delivery times between the firm and its suppliers, and good-quality control systems.

## Management of current liabilities

The assets of a firm can be financed either by short-term obligations, known as current liabilities, or by permanent sources such as long-term debt or equity. For most firms, current liabilities are a major source of financing, and the management of current liabilities can affect the firm's profitability. Earlier, in Example 1, when we considered the investment in net working capital by Technability Ltd, we saw that current assets exceeded current liabilities by $49 763 ($64 794 – $15 031). This implies that the current assets of $64 794 have been financed in part by current liabilities of $15 031, and the balance by long-term funds of $49 763. As a firm increases its investment in net working capital, more of the firm's current assets are being financed with long-term funds (e.g. shareholders' equity), which lowers the risk of financial distress. However, as we will see in Chapter 10, long-term funds have a greater cost of financing compared with current liabilities, such as accounts payable. Therefore, by using long-term funds to finance more of a firm's current assets, the firm's risk and return (profitability) will be reduced. In contrast, decreasing investment in net working capital can improve profitability, but it increases the risk of financial distress.

Current liabilities commonly include accounts payable, accruals, bank overdrafts and short-term loans. Accounts payable arise when businesses that supply goods and services allow their customers to purchase on account, known as **trade credit**. Trade credit can be an important source of finance as it is spontaneous finance with no **explicit interest cost**. It is spontaneous because, once credit has been granted and a credit limit established from a particular supplier, there is no need to make any further applications for credit unless a higher credit limit is desired. Accounts payable will increase spontaneously as purchases are made. Furthermore, trade credit has no explicit interest cost. By deferring payment for purchased goods to a later point in time, the customer essentially receives an interest-free loan for those goods. Consequently, when it is offered, businesses should certainly take the opportunity to use trade credit.

Suppliers may offer their customers a discount for early payment of accounts. If the account is not paid early, then the full account must be paid by the end of the credit period.

> **Trade credit**
> The purchase of goods or services on account, for payment at a later date.
>
> **Explicit interest cost**
> A stated interest charge.

### Example 4: Supplier's discount

Frisky Freight Forwarders offers its credit customers the following terms that are detailed on each invoice:

**Payment terms: Net 30 days from invoice date;
1% cash discount if paid within 10 days.**

This means that customers may take a discount equal to 1% of the invoice value if the account is paid within 10 days of the invoice date (**interest-free period**). Otherwise, the full value of the invoice must be paid within 30 days of the invoice date (**credit period**).

Although trade credit has no explicit interest cost, when a supplier offers a discount for early payment of accounts there is an **implicit interest cost** if the customer foregoes the discount.

So if Frisky Freight Forwarders sends a customer an invoice for $1 000 on the credit terms mentioned above, then the customer has two options:

**Option 1: Take discount**
The customer could pay the discounted price on day 10:
$1 000 × (1 – 0.01) = $990

> **Interest-free period**
> The period over which a supplier will extend credit to a customer with no explicit or implicit interest charge.
>
> **Credit period**
> The period ending with the final date for payment of an invoice.
>
> **Implicit interest cost**
> An implied, but unstated, interest charge.

**Option 2: Forego discount**
The customer could pay the full $1 000 on day 30. This payment represents two components:

Full price = Discounted price + Implicit interest charge
$1 000   =      $990        +        $10

Essentially, the customer obtains a loan from the supplier, Frisky Freight Forwarders, equal to the discounted price of the invoice of $990. Free credit is extended for the first 10 days from the invoice date. The extra $10 is essentially a financing charge paid by the customer to defer payment for another 20 days (day 30 minus day 10). These relationships are shown in Figure 9.1.

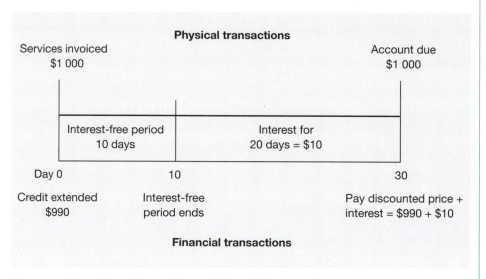

Figure 9.1 Foregoing a discount from Frisky Freight Forwarders

The cost of foregoing a discount can be calculated as an annual interest rate, which allows the customer to compare the costs of financing from different sources. The formula is shown below:

$$CD = \frac{D}{100\% - D} \times \frac{365}{N} \qquad \text{Equation 9.1}$$

where CD = cost of foregoing a discount
      D = discount as a percentage of invoice value
      N = difference in days between credit period and interest-free period.

In Equation 9.1, the interest rate for N days is equivalent to the N-day interest rate as a percentage of the discounted value of the invoice. Then the N-day interest rate is multiplied by the number of N-day periods in a year to arrive at the corresponding annualised interest rate. Annualising the interest rate makes it easier to compare alternatives.

When a discount is offered, customers must evaluate whether to settle the account early in order to take the discount, or to pay later and use their short-term funds in another way, such as to invest in marketable securities. This decision is depicted in Figure 9.2 on the following page.

- If the customer has excess funds invested at an annual holding period yield of HPY, and if the CD is greater than the HPY, then they should accept the discount and pay the account by the last day of the interest-free period. In this case, there is no point borrowing from the supplier at an interest rate greater than the return on excess funds invested, which is in fact an opportunity cost. It would be best to liquidate some of the low-returning investments to pay the invoice early and avoid the high cost of borrowing from the supplier.
- If, however, the CD is less than the HPY, then the customer should forego the discount and pay the full invoice price by the last day of the credit period. There is no point in liquidating high-yielding investments if the supplier will extend credit at a lower interest rate.

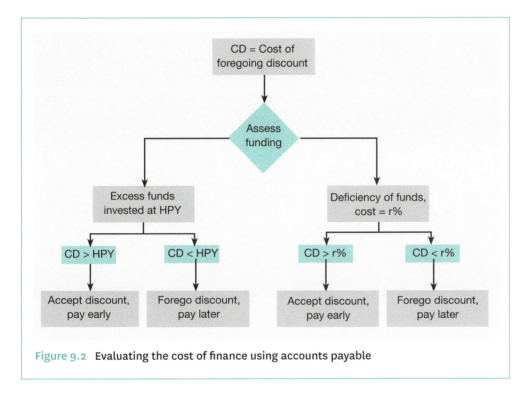

Figure 9.2 **Evaluating the cost of finance using accounts payable**

Alternatively, if the customer lacks short-term funds, then the decision may instead be how to finance the purchased goods and services. The customer can borrow either from the bank at r%, or from the supplier at CD. The best financing decision is the one with the least interest cost.

- If the CD is greater than r%, then the customer should borrow funds more cheaply from the bank in order to pay early and accept the discount to avoid the high cost of credit from the supplier.
- In contrast, if the CD is less than r%, then the customer is better off borrowing funds from the supplier rather than the bank by foregoing the discount and paying the full invoice price at the end of the credit period.

These alternatives can be summarised as follows:

If CD > opportunity or finance costs → accept discount, pay early.
If CD < opportunity or finance costs → reject discount, pay full amount later.

> **Example 5: Cost of foregoing a discount**
>
> Continuing our example, Frisky Freight Forwarders is effectively charging its credit customers an interest rate of 1% per 20 days or 18.4% per annum.
>
> $$CD = \frac{1\%}{100\% - 1\%} \times \frac{365}{30 - 10}$$
> $$= 0.0101 \times 18.25$$
> $$= 0.184$$
> $$= 18.4\% \text{ per annum}$$
>
> To borrow from Frisky Freight Forwarders by delaying payments on account to the end of the credit period costs 18.4% per annum. Customer A can borrow funds against a bank overdraft at an annual interest rate of 16%. Customer B, however, can only borrow funds at an annual interest rate of 20%. Customer A and Customer B should attempt to borrow funds at the lowest cost possible.
>
> **Customer A:**    CD    > opportunity or finance costs
>                      18.4% > 16%
>
> → **Borrow from the bank, accept discount and pay supplier early.**
>
> Customer A should borrow funds from the bank at an annual rate of interest of 16%, and pay Frisky Freight Forwarders the discounted invoice price by the discount date. To forego the discount would not be wise, as it would cost 18.4%.
>
> **Customer B:**    CD    < opportunity or finance costs
>                      18.4% < 20%
>
> → **Forego discount, pay full invoice amount later.**
>
> Customer B is better off foregoing the discount, as borrowing from the supplier costs 18.4% which is cheaper than borrowing from the bank at 20%.

If payment is made within the interest-free period, or if no discount is offered, then trade credit has no interest cost. However, trade credit can be an expensive source of short-term funds when a discount is offered but not consistently taken. A firm with sufficient cash balances will normally take a cash discount, as the cost of foregoing the discount is often much higher than the interest income earned on marketable securities. Alternatively, a firm with a deficiency of cash will often find it cheaper to borrow from a bank than to borrow by foregoing a supplier's discount.

Trade credit from business firms is not the only source of short-term funds to arise spontaneously in the course of business. Accrued salaries and wages payable to employees and accrued taxes payable to the IRD are also spontaneous sources of credit, representing expenses owed that have yet to be paid. Although they do not supply an inflow of cash, they result in the deferral of cash outflows. As with trade credit, accruals are a cost-free source of funds.

As you will have observed from the previous discussion, the use of accounts payable and early payment discounts can affect the cost of financing for a firm, and therefore judicious management is important in order to minimise costs. A full discussion of the management of other short-term sources of funds such as bank overdrafts and short-term loans is beyond the scope of this textbook, but as a general rule we can observe that firms will attempt to use those sources of short-term funds that will minimise financing costs.

## Cash conversion cycle

We have pointed out that it is costly to have funds tied up in current assets, and that efficient management of current assets and current liabilities is necessary in order to define the appropriate level of investment in net working capital. To the extent that cash is invested in accounts receivable and inventory, it is unavailable for other uses within the organisation. The length of time (typically stated in number of days) that cash is tied up in net working capital is known as the **cash conversion cycle (CCC)** which is estimated as:

$$CCC = AAI + ACP - APP \qquad \textit{Equation 9.2}$$

The length of the cash conversion cycle is influenced by the investment in inventory between the time of purchase of the inventory to when it is sold (**average age of inventory, AAI**), the receipt of cash from the customer (the **average collection period, ACP**), as well as the time taken to pay suppliers (**average payment period, APP**). Holding inventory and granting credit to customers ties up money within an organisation. A firm that purchases goods for resale or for production will often have to pay suppliers and employees before the goods are sold to the customer. If the goods have been sold on credit, then many days may elapse before cash is actually received from the customer. Each of these three components (AAI, ACP and APP) can be calculated using data available from the **accounting system**.

> **Cash conversion cycle (CCC)**
> Average length of time that cash is tied up in net working capital. Calculated as AAI + ACP − APP.
>
> **Average age of inventory (AAI)**
> Average length of time between the purchase and sale of inventory.
>
> **Average collection period (ACP)**
> Average length of time between the sale of inventory and the receipt of cash for payment from the customer.
>
> **Average payment period (APP)**
> Average length of time to pay for materials and labour consumed.
>
> **Accounting system**
> A method of recording financial transactions.

**Example 6: Cash conversion cycle**

Recall our earlier example of Technability Ltd, a surfboard and windsurfer manufacturer. On average, Technability pays its suppliers 40 days after a purchase, while employees are paid weekly. Overall, Technability calculates its average payment period (APP) for goods and labour to be 25 days. Technability maintains a minimum of raw materials inventory, and, because it manufactures goods to order, finished goods inventory is nil. Consequently, the average time that it takes to produce and sell the finished goods is 10 days. This is its average age of inventory (AAI). Technability has found that once the finished goods are sold, accounts from its customers are on average received (ACP) within 50 days of the sale. These relationships are depicted graphically on a timeline in Figure 9.3 on the next page.

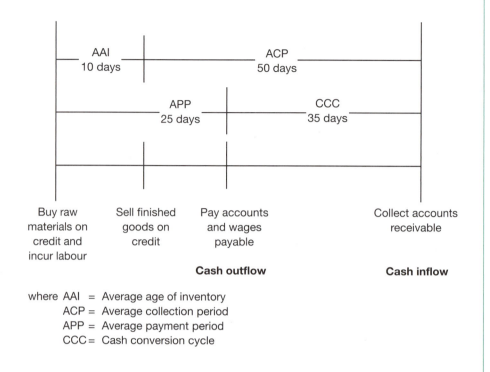

Figure 9.3  **Cash conversion cycle, Technability Ltd**

The time from the cash outflow for payment of accounts and wages (day 25) to the cash inflow from collection of customers' accounts (day 60) is, on average, 35 days. Therefore, Technability has a cash conversion cycle of 35 days. Mathematically, the cash conversion cycle can be determined as the average age of inventory plus the average collection period minus the average payment period. For Technability, this is calculated as follows:

$$CCC = AAI + ACP - APP$$
$$CCC = 10 + 50 - 25 = 35 \text{ days}$$

A bank overdraft is often arranged to finance the cash conversion cycle, so a longer cycle will incur more interest expense than a shorter cycle. Consequently, minimising the cash conversion cycle will minimise the financing costs and enhance profitability. If we incorporate risk into the analysis, then three policies can be devised for managing the cash conversion cycle.

- **Minimise the average age of inventory**

    This can be achieved by increasing sales relative to inventory levels, by reducing production time, or by reducing inventory (for example, through a just-in-time system). However, it is important to avoid stock-outs that can result in lost sales.

- **Minimise the average collection period**

    Collect accounts receivable as quickly as feasible. However, avoid using overly harsh collection tactics that may jeopardise future sales.

- **Maximise the average payment period**

    Pay accounts payable as late as possible. However, do not pay so late as to jeopardise the future supply of goods, or to damage the firm's credit reputation. When credit and trading conditions are difficult, average payment periods tend to lengthen as businesses attempt to manage their cash flows. Once established, slow payment practices can be hard to break, yet may impair a firm's ability to operate efficiently.

These strategies represent an attempt to achieve a balance between profitability and risk, and this theme should be kept in mind when considering the management of cash, accounts receivable, inventory and current liabilities.

# Conclusion

Financial decisions must ensure that returns are commensurate with the risk taken. This principle applies to most financial decisions, including those with a short-term focus, such as the management of net working capital. In this case, the goal is to achieve an optimal balance between profitability and risk, to maximise owners' wealth. Net working capital is the difference between current assets and current liabilities, reflecting the liquidity of an organisation. This chapter looked at the management of current assets (particularly cash, accounts receivable and inventory) and current liabilities.

The aim of cash management is to achieve an optimal balance of cash assets. The forecast cash flow statement is an important tool for planning the cash flow of a business through a forecast of cash receipts and cash disbursements. The statement reveals the timing of cash surpluses and deficiencies, and allows the business to plan for its financing requirements.

Carrying accounts receivable incurs costs, and businesses can reduce these costs by carefully setting their credit policy. Businesses need to establish: credit standards to evaluate the creditworthiness of customers; credit terms for repayment; and collection policies.

Inventory management aims to minimise the holding, order and stock-out costs associated with inventory. Inventory management techniques include the EOQ model, computerised inventory control, and just-in-time systems.

Considering the management of current liabilities, we find that accounts payable and early payment discounts can materially affect the cost of financing to a firm. In general, the goal is to select those sources of short-term funds that have the lowest financing costs.

The concept of the cash conversion cycle is introduced as a useful technique for liquidity planning. Businesses should aim to minimise the average age of inventory, minimise the average collection period, and maximise the average payment period.

**SELF-TEST QUESTIONS**

1. Splotch'n' Stuff is a craft dealer that supplies art and craft materials to schools and other groups. The owner-manager wishes to prepare a forecast cash flow statement for the months of July to September.

   Half of all sales are for cash, 40% are collected in the next month, and 10% are collected in the second month following the sales. Actual sales in May and June were $60 000, while projected sales are $100 000 in July, $60 000 in August, and $80 000 in each of September and October.

   Purchases are equal to 60% of next month's sales, and are paid for in the month following the purchase. Rent is $4 000 per month, power and telephone are $500 per month, and other administrative expenses are $1 000 per month. Salaries and wages are $12 000 per month, loan repayments are $4 500 per month, goods and services tax (GST) of $1 000 is due in August, and provisional tax of $6 000 is due in September. At 1 July, the firm has a bank overdraft of $3 000.

   Prepare a forecast cash flow statement for the months of July, August and September. Indicate how much financing will be required, or excess funds available for investment, for July, August and September.

2. Tess Fashions has received an electricity bill of $300 due for payment in 30 days' time. The electricity supplier has offered a 2% discount if the bill is paid within 7 days.

   a If Tess currently has a bank overdraft incurring an interest rate of 14%, should she take or forego the cash discount?

   b If Tess currently has excess funds earning an interest rate of 6%, should she take or forego the cash discount?

**ANSWERS TO SELF-TEST QUESTIONS**

1.

| Splotch'n' Stuff<br>Schedule of Forecast Cash Receipts | | | | | |
|---|---|---|---|---|---|
| | May | June | July | Aug | Sept |
| Projected sales | $60 000 | $60 000 | $100 000 | $60 000 | $80 000 |
| Cash sales (50%) | | | $ 50 000 | $30 000 | $40 000 |
| Collections: | | | | | |
| From sales one month previous (40%) | | | $ 24 000 | $40 000 | $24 000 |
| From sales two months previous (10%) | | | $  6 000 | $ 6 000 | $10 000 |
| Total cash receipts | | | $ 80 000 | $76 000 | $74 000 |

### Splotch'n' Stuff
### Schedule of Forecast Cash Disbursements

|  | June | July | Aug | Sept |
|---|---|---|---|---|
| Projected purchases | $60 000 | $36 000 | $48 000 | $48 000 |
| Payments of A/P |  | $60 000 | $36 000 | $48 000 |
| Rent |  | $ 4 000 | $ 4 000 | $ 4 000 |
| Power and telephone |  | $  500 | $  500 | $  500 |
| Other administrative expenses |  | $ 1 000 | $ 1 000 | $ 1 000 |
| Salaries and wages |  | $12 000 | $12 000 | $12 000 |
| Loan repayments |  | $ 4 500 | $ 4 500 | $ 4 500 |
| GST |  |  | $ 1 000 |  |
| Provisional tax |  |  |  | $ 6 000 |
| Total cash disbursements |  | $82 000 | $59 000 | $76 000 |

### Splotch'n' Stuff
### Forecast Cash Flow Statement

|  | July | Aug | Sept |
|---|---|---|---|
| Total cash receipts | $80 000 | $76 000 | $74 000 |
| Less: total cash disbursements | $82 000 | $59 000 | $76 000 |
| Net cash inflow (outflow) | ($ 2 000) | $17 000 | ($ 2 000) |
| *Add:* Opening cash balance (overdraft) | ($ 3 000) | ($ 5 000) | $12 000 |
| Closing cash balance | ($ 5 000) | $12 000 | $10 000 |
| Surplus cash to invest |  | $12 000 | $10 000 |
| Cumulative financing needed | ($ 5 000) |  |  |

2  $CD = \dfrac{D}{100\% - D} \times \dfrac{365}{N}$

$CD = \dfrac{2.0\%}{100\% - 2.0\%} \times \dfrac{365}{30 - 7} = 0.324 = 32.4\%$

a  Tess should take the discount by going further into overdraft at an interest rate of 14%, as to forego the discount would cost 32.4%.

b  If Tess has excess funds earning 6% interest, then it would be best to liquidate enough investments to pay the supplier early and take the discount. To forego the discount would cost 32.4% whereas to forego interest income will cost only 6%.

**QUESTIONS AND PROBLEMS**

1. Define *net working capital,* and explain how, by balancing risk and profitability, a suitable goal for the management of net working capital can be established.
2. What is the effect on risk and profitability of an increase in net working capital?
3. Describe three motives for holding cash balances.
4. What is a forecast cash flow statement, and how is it useful?
5. Describe the three major components of credit policy.
6. List the major costs of inventory.
7. Given that owner wealth maximisation is the most appropriate objective of financial management, why does net working capital management focus on profits rather than share value?
8. What could cause actual cash balances to be consistently lower than forecast cash balances over a six-month period? What problems could result from this situation?
9. In what ways could credit policy have a negative effect on sales?
10. What problems can arise if sales staff are authorised to grant credit to customers?
11. How can the credit terms that are set for customers who purchase on credit influence the level of sales, investment in accounts receivable and bad debts?
12. How could inventory costs increase with declining levels of stock?
13. Inventory management attempts to minimise the total costs of holding and ordering inventory, and stock-outs. How might this goal conflict with the attitudes of managers of production, purchasing and sales departments?
14. List three spontaneous sources of finance. Why are they considered to be spontaneous?
15. In relation to trade credit, define the terms *interest-free period* and *credit period*.
16. Explain why trade credit incurs no explicit interest cost, while foregoing a discount for early payment of accounts incurs an implicit interest cost.
17. Describe the components of the formula for calculating the cost of foregoing a discount for the early payment of accounts.
18. Summarise the criteria used in a decision of whether to accept or forego a discount for the early payment of accounts.
19. Describe the factors that must be considered by a customer who has a substantial investment in marketable securities when she assesses whether to take or forego a discount for early payment of accounts.
20. Describe the factors that must be considered by a customer who has a deficiency of cash and marketable securities, when he assesses whether to take or forego a discount for early payment of accounts.
21. What is the cash conversion cycle? Describe three strategies for managing the cash conversion cycle.
22. In what circumstances would it be possible to have a negative cash conversion cycle? Is this desirable?

23 How will each of the following affect the investment in net working capital, profitability and risk? Answer either 'increase', 'decrease' or 'no change'.

  a  Convert $100 000 of current assets into fixed assets.

  b  Extinguish a short-term loan of $50 000 by liquidating marketable securities.

  c  Pay accounts payable more quickly.

  d  Decrease inventory by improved inventory management.

24 Cheeky Clothing Ltd expects sales of $500 000 in January, $600 000 in February and $800 000 in each of March, April and May. Generally customers have paid in the following pattern:

| Payment pattern | Percentage of sales |
|---|---|
| Cash sales | 10% |
| Month following sale | 50% |
| Second month following sale | 40% |

What are Cheeky's forecast cash receipts for March, April and May?

25 Smudge Paint Products Ltd expects to purchase raw materials for paint processing in the following amounts:

| Month | Purchases |
|---|---|
| October | $100 000 |
| November | $120 000 |
| December | $ 80 000 |
| January | $ 80 000 |
| February | $100 000 |
| March | $120 000 |

Given past payment patterns, 15% of purchases are for cash, and the balance is paid for in the month following the purchase. Calculate Smudge's forecast payments for purchases for November to March.

26 The new assistant financial manager of Marmud Food Company Ltd, John Spread, has been asked to examine the financial records of the company (shown on the next page) and to report on the sufficiency of cash available to finance the purchase of a new microcomputer and printer. The total cost will be $5 000, with the purchase to be made in one month's time on 1 July.

| | |
|---|---|
| Cash in bank, 1 June | $ 1 000 |
| **June financial information** | |
| Cash sales | $ 5 000 |
| Credit sales | $56 000 |
| Collections of May accounts receivable | $65 000 |
| Cash expenses | $ 9 000 |
| Accounts and wages payable, 30 June | $55 000 |
| Payments on May accounts and wages payable | $46 000 |
| Loan payment | $ 5 000 |
| Depreciation expense | $20 000 |

Credit sales arising in June will be collected in July. Accounts and wages payable as at 30 June will be paid in July. The loan payment of $5 000 arises every month.

a  Calculate the expected cash balance of Marmud Food Company as at 30 June. Is there expected to be sufficient cash available for the purchase of the new equipment?

b  Do you foresee any potential liquidity problems for Marmud within the next two months?

27  Wendy Widgets Ltd has gathered the following data in order to prepare a forecast cash flow statement for July, August and September.
- Sales in May and June were $120 000 and $135v000, respectively. Forecast sales for July, August and September are $140 000 per month. Twenty per cent of sales are for cash, 50% are collected in the next month, and 30% are collected two months after the sale.
- Purchases in June were $70 000. Forecast purchases for July, August and September are $70 000, $75 000 and $80 000, respectively. All purchases are paid for in the month following the purchase.
- Rent is $7 200 per month, power and telephone are $2 000 per month, and other administrative expenses are $1 800 per month.
- Salaries and wages are $15 000 per month.
- A loan repayment of $40 000 is due in July.
- Equipment costing $43 500 in July must be paid for in August.
- Taxes are expected to be $4 000 per month.
- The opening cash balance on 1 July is $10 000.

a  Prepare a forecast cash flow statement for the months of July, August and September.

b  How much additional financing will be required, or excess funds available for investment, for July, August and September?

28 In late June of each year Cath Office Supplies prepares a forecast cash flow statement for the next six months.

Actual sales for May and projected sales for the following months are:

| May (actual) | $20 000 | October | $94 000 |
| June | $28 000 | November | $74 000 |
| July | $24 000 | December | $52 000 |
| August | $26 000 | January | $40 000 |
| September | $50 000 | | |

Approximately 25% of sales are for cash and 75% are on credit. Past experience has shown that of the 75% credit sales, two-thirds are collected in the first month following sales and the remaining one-third is collected in the second month following the sales.

The firm estimates purchases as 70% of the next month's projected sales, so that June's purchases are 70% of July's estimated sales, and so on. This ensures that the goods needed to support sales are acquired in the preceding month. All purchases are paid for in the month following the purchase. Other disbursements are expected to be:

| July | $7 100 | October | $10 400 |
| August | $7 100 | November | $11 200 |
| September | $7 500 | December | $7 200 |

On 1 July, a cash balance of $8 400 is expected.

a   Prepare a forecast cash flow statement for the six months ended 31 December.

b   How much additional financing will be required, or excess cash available for investment, for the six months ended 31 December?

29 Determine the last date for payment for an invoice dated 15 January, under each of the following credit terms:

a   net 15 days from invoice date

b   net 20 days from invoice date

c   net 30 days from invoice date.

30 Determine the last date for payment within the (i) interest-free period and (ii) credit period for an invoice dated 31 August under the following credit terms:

a   net 15 days from invoice date; 1% cash discount if paid within 7 days

b   net 20 days from invoice date; 0.5% cash discount if paid within 10 days

c   net 45 days from invoice date; 2% cash discount if paid within 15 days.

31 Calculate the implicit interest cost of foregoing the cash discount for each of **a** to **c** in Question 30.

32 Determine the last date for payment within the (i) interest-free period (if applicable) and (ii) credit period for an invoice dated 28 April, under each of the following credit terms:

a  net 30 days from invoice date

b  net 20 days from invoice date; 1% cash discount if paid within 7 days

c  net 60 days from invoice date; 2% cash discount if paid within 10 days.

33 Refer to Question 32. Determine the last date for payment assuming the invoice was dated 2 April.

34 On the last day of each month a supplier sends to each customer a monthly statement of account that summarises the monthly transactions and outstanding balance to date. Determine the last date for payment within the (i) interest-free period (if applicable) and (ii) credit period for an invoice dated 2 April, under each of the following credit terms:

a  net 30 days from statement date

b  net 20 days from statement date; 1% cash discount if paid within 7 days from statement date

c  net 60 days from statement date; 2% cash discount if paid within 10 days from statement date.

When the credit terms indicate that the credit period commences from the statement date, on which day of the month should customers attempt to purchase goods or services in order to maximise the use of free credit?

35 Calculate the implicit interest cost of foregoing the cash discounts from each of the following suppliers.

| Supplier | Credit terms |
| --- | --- |
| A | Net 20 days from invoice date; 1% cash discount if paid within 10 days |
| B | Net 30 days from invoice date; 1% cash discount if paid within 20 days |
| C | Net 20 days from statement date; 0.5% cash discount if paid within 7 days |
| D | Net 30 days from statement date; 0.5% cash discount if paid within 7 days |

36 Oscar's Takeaways has the opportunity to purchase supplies on credit terms of net 20 days from invoice date; 0.5% cash discount for payment within 10 days. If Oscar's bank account is currently in overdraft at an interest rate of 15%, should Oscar's take or forego the discount? Explain why. Alternatively, if the overdraft interest was 20%, what should Oscar's do?

37 Felix Pet Supplies has been offered the following credit terms from its suppliers.

| Supplier | Credit terms |
| --- | --- |
| A | Net 30 days from statement date; 1% cash discount if paid within 7 days from statement date |
| B | Net 60 days from statement date; 1.5% cash discount if paid within 10 days from statement date |

Felix has a reserve of marketable securities invested at an interest rate of 8% per annum and can borrow funds from the bank at 13.5%. Assuming the supplier's statements are dated the last day of each month, should Felix take or forego either (or both) of the cash discounts? Explain why.

38  Calculate the cash conversion cycle for the following firms.

| Firm | Average age of inventory | Average collection period | Average payment period |
|---|---|---|---|
| Q | 20 | 10 | 35 |
| R | 60 | 45 | 25 |
| S | 90 | 30 | 45 |
| T | 120 | 25 | 15 |

39  Slick Leather Goods Ltd currently holds 90 days of inventory, collects accounts receivable in 30 days and pays accounts payable in 20 days.

  a  Calculate the length in days of the current cash conversion cycle.

  b  What would be the length of the cash conversion cycle if the average age of inventory decreased by 10 days, the average collection period decreased by 5 days, and the average payment period increased by 15 days?

40  Pesky Pet Foods Ltd is seeking to reduce costs by shortening its cash conversion cycle. Currently, inventory is held for an average of 80 days, accounts receivable are collected 60 days after sales, and accounts payable are paid 35 days after purchases.

  a  Calculate the length in days of the current cash conversion cycle.

  b  What would be the length of the cash conversion cycle if the average age of inventory decreased by 10 days, the average collection period decreased by 15 days, and the average payment period increased by 5 days?

  c  Why is it that drastic reductions in the cash conversion cycle may result in lost sales?

41  Greenie Paper Products Ltd is examining alternative plans affecting its cash conversion cycle.

| Plan | Average age of inventory | Average collection period | Average payment period |
|---|---|---|---|
| Current | 110 | 40 | 50 |
| A | 100 | 30 | 60 |
| B | 90 | 35 | 50 |

  a  Which plan – Current, A, or B – results in the shortest cash conversion period?

  b  Is the shortest cash conversion cycle always the best alternative? Why, or why not?

# CHAPTER 10

# Financing the firm

**Learning objectives**

By the end of this chapter, you should be able to:
- compare and contrast the major features of debt and equity finance
- describe the major sources of debt and equity funds available to a firm throughout its life cycle
- explain the issues involved in choosing an appropriate financing mix
- describe and calculate the component costs of capital, and calculate the weighted average cost of capital.

## Introduction

This chapter will focus on financing the firm, which has been described in Chapter 8 as one of the three principal functions of financial management. Irrespective of size, all businesses need to finance their assets, either with equity or with a combination of debt and equity. There is a great variety of financing alternatives, yet the accessibility and appropriateness of many sources of funds vary according to the size and nature of the business. Furthermore, the costs and risks of the funding sources might differ considerably. Consequently, there are several decisions that must be made concerning the financing of the firm. In this chapter we will discuss the different sources of debt and equity funds available to businesses, and examine the important issues that affect the financing decision.

## Features of debt and equity

Most firms are financed using a mixture of debt and equity. Debt funds are supplied by lenders, whereas equity funds represent owners' capital.

With debt finance, interest and principal payments must be made on specified dates. Interest represents a fixed financial expense that must be met before owners can take drawings or receive dividends. Suppliers of debt funds do not participate in the management of the firm unless it defaults on interest or principal repayments, in which case the lenders may have the power (under statute or security deeds) to appoint a manager or a liquidator to wind up the firm. In liquidation, lenders have a priority claim over the earnings and assets of the firm. Due to these rights, debt is considered by lenders to be of lower risk than equity. The result under the risk–return trade-off is that lenders will require a lower return than owners, and this reduces the cost of debt to the firm.

Equity finance is a long-term source of funds that has no fixed date for repayment. You will recall from Chapter 8 that in a large firm the shareholders elect a board of directors, which appoints managers. In a small firm, the owners tend to manage the firm, or select the managers themselves. Owners can only take drawings or receive dividends after debt commitments have been met.

However, the failure to pay drawings or dividends will not directly threaten the survival of a firm. In the event of liquidation, owners are entitled to any residual assets remaining after payment of all debt commitments. Equity finance is more expensive than debt, as owners require a higher rate of return to compensate for the additional riskiness of the investment.

The major features that distinguish debt from equity are summarised in Table 10.1.

Table 10.1  **Features of debt and equity finance**

| Features of debt | Features of equity |
| --- | --- |
| • Lenders have no say in management. | • Owners directly or indirectly select management. |
| • Lenders have a priority claim on earnings and assets. | • Owners have a residual claim on earnings and assets. |
| • The loan must be repaid at maturity. | • Owners' capital has no maturity date. |
| • Interest is a fixed commitment. | • Drawings/dividends are optional. |

In American textbooks, the point is often made that debt finance is cheaper than equity finance because the interest expense on debt is tax-deductible to the company, whereas dividend payments to shareholders are not. In contrast, equity earnings are taxed twice: once when profits are earned, and again when the profits are distributed to the shareholders as dividends. This leads to a bias in favour of debt finance. However, in countries such as New Zealand and Australia, taxation imputation systems minimise the incidence of double taxation of dividends. Under dividend imputation, company profits are taxed but the tax paid by the company is, in effect, treated as a **withholding tax** on behalf of shareholders. The shareholders report the dividends received as income on their personal tax returns, but may claim a **tax credit** for the tax paid by the company. Consequently, equity earnings are taxed only once between the company and the shareholder. This greatly reduces the relative tax advantage of financing using debt compared with financing using equity sources. However, even without its relative tax advantage, debt financing is still cheaper than equity, as the providers of debt finance (e.g. banks, bondholders) face less risk than providers of equity finance (shareholders) in the same firm.

**Withholding tax**
Tax deducted from a payment and remitted to the IRD on behalf of a recipient who receives the after-tax payment.

**Tax credit**
A deduction from taxes payable.

# Funding a firm's life cycle

A firm's financing needs will change over time, according to the scale of operations, asset acquisition or replacement requirements, variability and predictability of cash flows and competitive conditions.

The impact of these changes upon sales and net operating cash flow on the firm as it goes through the stages of start-up, growth, maturity, and possibly decline, is depicted in Figure 10.1 on the next page.

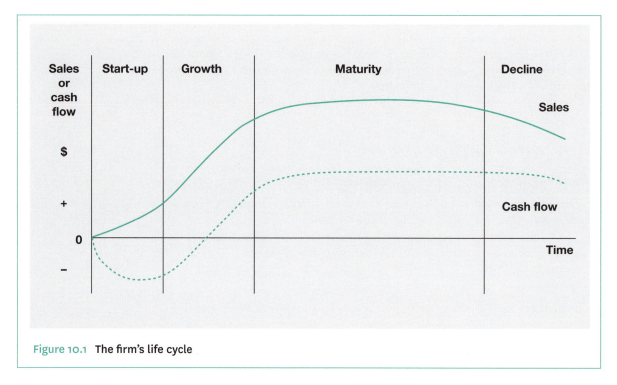

Figure 10.1 **The firm's life cycle**

Net operating cash flow is negative during the start-up stage, as a result of investment and operating costs. However, once sales begin and the firm experiences growth, net operating cash flow increases. Competition or other factors may cause sales and net operating cash flow to level off during the maturity stage. Product redevelopment or expansion of operations may be necessary to prevent an eventual decline in sales and net cash flow. Note that the relationship depicted in Figure 10.1 between sales and net operating cash flow is not necessarily typical, as in practice the relationships vary considerably between firms, and fluctuate over time. The changes in a firm's financing requirements throughout its life cycle, and how the different sources of finance are used, are discussed in the following sections.

### Start-up stage

Although a business may begin on a small scale, numerous outlays may be required before any sales can be generated: legal costs of setting up the organisational structure; capital expenditures for land, buildings and equipment; research and development costs; outlays for the purchase of inventory; and advertising and promotion expenses are all examples of expenditures that may precede cash inflows from sales. The start-up phase is characterised by significant cash outflows and an absence of operating cash inflows. Funding for this negative cash flow may come from several different sources, including the owners, friends and relatives, banks and finance companies, suppliers, crowdfunding and venture capital organisations. These alternatives, which will be developed as we consider the stages of growth and financing in later sections of this chapter, are summarised in Table 10.2.

Table 10.2  Sources of finance – Start-up stage

| Source of finance | Stage of firm's life cycle | | |
| --- | --- | --- | --- |
| | Start-up | Growth | Maturity |
| Owners' personal investment | ✓ | | |
| Friends' and relatives' personal investment | ✓ | | |
| Banks and financial institutions | ✓ | | |
| Suppliers | ✓ | | |
| Crowdfunding and venture capital | ✓ | | |

### Owners' personal investment

During the start-up stage, a primary source of finance will be the owners' personal investment. Depending on whether the business is a proprietorship, partnership or company, the owners' personal investment may take the form of owners' equity, partners' capital or share capital, respectively. Other sources of financing are difficult to attract unless the owners have a significant personal investment, and it is this constraint that prevents many aspiring entrepreneurs from starting their own businesses.

### Friends' and relatives' personal investment

In a small new business the entrepreneur will often seek out family and friends who may be willing to supply equity or debt funds. Equity funding could result in a partnership arrangement or, for a company, the issue of additional ordinary or preference shares. Active partners and ordinary shareholders in closely-held companies often have a voice in the management of the business, whereas silent partners and preference shareholders do not. Personal debt funds can take many forms, although loans are the most common. In some cases, the borrower may be required to offer some security against the loan or, alternatively, to personally guarantee the loan.

### Banks and financial institutions

Banks and other financial institutions can provide a variety of debt funds in the start-up stage of the firm's life cycle, although there are generally stringent conditions governing the nature and amount of funding.

### Overdrafts and loans

Short-term debt, being debt with a maturity of less than one year, can be provided as a bank overdraft or short-term loan. In Australasia, the bank overdraft is a particularly important source of short-term debt. A bank overdraft gives the borrower permission to have a negative cheque account balance, up to a pre-arranged overdraft limit. Various fees, including interest, will be charged by the bank for granting the availability and use of the overdraft facility. An overdraft will often be arranged to finance an investment in accounts receivable, although it is also used to cover general operating expenses. Both banks and finance companies may grant short-term loans to purchase inventory. However, in the start-up and growth stages, the lender will seek substantial security such as a **floating debenture** secured by a charge over the entire assets of the business.

> **Floating debenture**
> Medium-term or long-term debt funds secured by a charge over all otherwise unsecured assets.

Medium-term loans for periods from one to five years are offered by banks and finance companies to businesses to finance the purchase of fixed assets. The assets will normally be used as security against the loan, although additional security may also be required. Banks, finance companies and life insurance companies also supply medium- and long-term mortgage loans that are secured over land and buildings.

Some finance companies and equipment dealers offer businesses hire-purchase loans as a means of financing the purchase of plant and equipment. With a hire-purchase loan, the borrower gains the use of the asset immediately upon purchase. However, title to the asset does not pass to the purchaser/borrower until all of the loan repayments have been made.

### Leases

> **Financial lease**
> A lease contract whereby the lessee acquires the use of an asset over a period approximately equal to the useful life of the asset.

Another means of acquiring the use of a long-term asset is by a **financial lease**. Banks, finance companies, life insurance companies or other organisations may act as the lessor, requiring the lessee (borrower) to make lease payments that are equivalent to interest and principal payments on debt. Effectively the lessee is acquiring the long-term use of the asset and receiving 100% funding from the lessor over a period approximately equal to the useful life of the asset. A financial lease is treated for income tax purposes as a debt-financing arrangement for the purchase of an asset. Although it is very similar to a hire-purchase loan, a financial lease does not necessarily allow for the title to the asset to pass to the borrower. Should the borrower wish to acquire the asset, they may usually do so by paying the lessor a nominal price at the end of the lease.

> **Lease interest**
> A contractual relationship between a tenant (lessee) and a property owner (lessor), where the tenant has the right to use the land for the period specified in the lease agreement in return for rental payments and other obligations.
>
> **Operating lease**
> A short-term, cancellable lease where the lessee gains the use of an asset without ever buying the asset.

Many businesses require land and buildings to conduct their business activities, but most start-up businesses will not have sufficient funds to acquire suitable property. Instead, the business (lessee) will sign a deed of lease (lease agreement) with the property owner (lessor) to obtain a property **lease interest**. A property lease interest is typically a medium- to long-term contract where the lessee has the right to use the lease property for the term of the agreement. The deed of lease will state the rental payments required and other obligations of both the lessee and the lessor. In addition, the lessor will typically require a person or entity to act as guarantor of the lease agreement. This protects the lessor should the lessee not fulfil their obligations. In the event the lessee defaults on their rent payments, the guarantor is legally required to take over the lease obligations.

Alternatively, if a business requires the use of fixed assets over a relatively short period of time, an **operating lease** may be more appropriate. An operating lease is a short-term lease that can be cancelled, whereby the lessee gains the use of an asset without ever buying it. Operating leases are available from dealers of cars, trucks, office equipment, computers, machinery and other fixed assets.

New businesses in the start-up stage of a firm's life cycle tend to have difficulties in obtaining debt funds from banks or other financial institutions, particularly if the owners' investment is modest. Even when the borrower is a company, the owner-manager of a new business will generally be required to personally guarantee any overdraft, loan or debt from a financial institution. Consequently, if the borrower defaults, the lender will require the owner-manager to repay the business debt personally.

> **Example 1: Property lease interest**
>
> Joan and John have established a home goods retail store featuring locally made and imported products. They have found suitable premises for their store in Palmerston North's main street and their company, Jays Jumble Ltd, will enter into a 6-year lease for $36 000 per year. The lease carries an additional 6-year right of renewal. While Jays Jumble Ltd is the tenant, the lessor will require Joan and John to both sign the deed of lease as guarantors. As such, Joan and John are both personally guaranteeing to pay the landlord all remaining lease payments plus other obligations, such as local government rates, building insurance and health and safety related costs. Assuming these costs are $6 000 per annum, John and Joan are personally guaranteeing $42 000 per annum for the 6-year lease, or $252 000 in total. Should Jays Jumble Ltd become insolvent then Joan and John will have to personally pay any balance remaining of the 6-year lease to the landlord.

## Suppliers

Businesses that supply goods and services to other firms will often allow their customers to purchase on account. This is known as trade credit. However, it is not easy for a new business to obtain trade credit. The credit manager for the supplier will evaluate the creditworthiness of the customer, decide whether to extend credit, how much credit, if any, and what credit limit to set. Given that a new venture lacks a credit history and carries a high risk of default, many suppliers will refuse to extend credit during a customer's start-up stage. In such a case, the customer either has to pay 'cash on delivery' or purchase elsewhere.

## Crowdfunding and venture capital

**Crowdfunding** is a relatively new, cost-effective means by which companies can raise funds for business ventures or projects from the general public. It is typically facilitated through a crowdfunding service providers' online platform. Start-up businesses are able to choose between two options: equity crowdfunding or reward-based crowdfunding. Companies are able to raise funds in both forms, but in equity crowdfunding investors receive shares in the company, while reward-based backers only receive a pledge from the company to receive a product or service.

The first equity-crowdfunding offer in New Zealand was in late 2014, when Renaissance Brewing raised $700 000 in less than a two-week period. In New Zealand, the Financial Markets Authority regulates equity-crowdfunding service providers (i.e. the online platforms) and enforces the rules governing the fund-raising process. Under these rules, in any 12-month period small and established companies may raise up to $2 million in equity finance from the public relatively quickly and with considerably fewer disclosure requirements than are otherwise imposed on public companies seeking to raise money from the public. Investors can potentially benefit financially from owning shares in early-stage and rapidly growing private businesses; however, these benefits must be carefully weighed against the significantly higher risks. Investors need to be aware of the reduced regulatory controls on this form of fund-raising, and must be mindful that many of these start-up firms can and will fail.

> **Crowdfunding**
> Crowdfunding is a means of raising relatively small amounts of funds from the public to finance a business venture or project.

> **Venture capital**
> Funds (usually equity) provided to relatively new businesses by public companies or government-sponsored enterprises.

Toward the end of the start-up stage, **venture capital** funds may become available to successful businesses through venture capital organisations. These may be public companies or government-sponsored enterprises which act as intermediaries, obtaining funds from investors who seek a speculative investment, and providing funds to early-stage business ventures. Although equity funding is most commonly provided, occasionally debt funds may be available. Venture capital organisations fill a void in equity funding for businesses that lack the asset backing and credit strength to successfully sell shares to the general public or to institutional investors.

In summary, during the start-up stage of a firm's life cycle, the largest portion of funds may come from the owners. However, a variety of other equity and debt sources may be available from friends, relatives, banks and other financial institutions, suppliers, crowdfunding and venture capital organisations.

## Growth stage

Many businesses start out on a small scale, but, if successful, may experience rapid growth in assets, sales and profitability. At the beginning of the growth stage, the build-up of inventory and accounts receivable can result in liquidity problems whereby there is insufficient cash to finance the continued growth of the firm. If additional finance cannot be found, then it may be necessary to take drastic steps to prevent insolvency. These include deliberately slowing the growth in sales, limiting product lines and/or reducing inventory levels. There is a very high failure rate at this stage of a firm's development owing to a lack of financial management expertise.

During the initial growth phase, firms may rely on the sources of finance that were available during the start-up phase. Equity and debt funds will be provided by the various sources mentioned earlier. However, towards the end of the growth phase, when the firm has enjoyed a prolonged period of profitability and the scale of operations has expanded beyond that of a small business, additional sources of new finance may become available. **Retained earnings** may provide an internal source of equity funding, private placements of debt and equity may be possible, and further bank finance may be available.

Table 10.3 summarises the various sources of finance that may be utilised during the growth phase.

> **Retained earnings**
> Profits retained and reinvested in assets of the firm. Represents an internal source of equity finance.

Table 10.3  **Sources of finance – growth stage**

| Source of finance | Stage of firm's life cycle | | |
| --- | --- | --- | --- |
| | Start-up | Growth | Maturity |
| Owners' personal investment | ✓ | ✓ | |
| Friends' and relatives' personal investment | ✓ | ✓ | |
| Banks and financial institutions | ✓ | ✓ | |
| Suppliers | ✓ | ✓ | |
| Crowdfunding and venture capital | ✓ | ✓ | |
| Retained earnings | | ✓ | |
| Private placements | | ✓ | |

### Retained earnings

When the net profits of a business exceed the owners' drawings or dividends, the earnings retained within the business provide an internal source of equity funding. Retained earnings can be invested in any assets, although they are normally invested in permanent assets such as the permanent portion of inventory or fixed assets.

During the start-up stage of a business, retained earnings are not normally sufficient to provide a substantial source of funds, as the owners usually need to take salaries, drawings or dividends to support their personal expenses. However, sometime during the growth stage, retained earnings may become large enough to provide a moderate source of funds. Nevertheless, during this stage most firms still require more funds for expansion than are available from retained earnings.

### Private placements

Given a history of success, a medium-sized business may be able to sell large parcels of shares or debt securities to financial institutions, such as life insurance companies, superannuation trusts and investment companies. These financial institutions invest and deal in securities on a continuing basis. To arrange a **private placement**, the business seeking funds contracts with an investment bank which acts as an intermediary to find suitable institutional investors.

Equity finance can be arranged in the form of ordinary or preference shares, while debt finance would normally be of a secured nature such as debenture stock. A debenture is a secured note, usually with a medium- to long-term maturity. Debentures may be secured by specific assets such as property (mortgage debentures), or there may be a floating charge on all **unpledged assets**. If the business defaults, holders of debenture notes secured by specific assets will have first claim over those assets and can demand that they be sold to satisfy the debt. The holders of debentures that are secured by a floating charge on the unpledged assets have second priority, but will receive the proceeds from the sale of unpledged assets (and any surplus from the prior securities) before any distribution is made to unsecured creditors or equity holders.

> **Private placement**
> A placement of shares or debt offered only to selected investors.
>
> **Unpledged assets**
> Assets that have not been used as security for a loan.

### Banks and financial institutions

Banks and other financial institutions offer a wide range of debt facilities to successful medium-sized businesses. Although overdraft facilities, loans, factoring, hire purchase, leases and mortgages may be available to new businesses, these finance sources are more readily available to well-established firms. However, additional sources of debt, such as a line of credit, revolving credit and loans secured by accounts receivable and inventory, may be available to firms in the latter part of the growth phase.

### *Credit facilities*

A **line of credit** is an informal arrangement whereby a bank allows a firm to borrow up to a maximum specified amount over a set period of time. It is similar to a bank overdraft, although the line of credit is a loan account separate from the firm's cheque account. The firm draws on its line of credit by issuing short-term unsecured notes. Before extending further credit, the bank will require the firm to pay back at least part of the cumulative amount borrowed. This reinforces the

> **Line of credit**
> An informal arrangement with a bank to allow a firm to borrow up to a maximum specified amount over a set period of time.

short-term nature of the facility. This form of finance is most suitable for seasonal businesses or to finance a specific short-term project.

If a longer-term arrangement is required, then a **revolving credit facility** can be negotiated. Although it is similar to a line of credit, revolving credit is a legal commitment by the bank to provide credit to the firm when requested. It is generally extended for up to three years and incurs higher financing charges than a line of credit.

> **Revolving credit facility**
> A legal commitment by a bank to provide credit to a borrower up to a maximum specified amount when requested. Similar to a line of credit.

### Secured loans

Successful firms that have a substantial investment in accounts receivable and/or inventory may be able to use these assets as collateral for a short-term bank loan. A firm can **pledge** its accounts receivable if the accounts are judged by the bank to be sufficiently high in amount and quality. The loan will be for less than the face value of the accounts, so that in the event of default by the borrower the bank can fully recover the funds from collections on accounts receivable. Finished goods inventory and raw materials of high unit value can also be used as **collateral** for a short-term loan, as long as the goods are readily marketable. Examples are stocks of consumer durables such as washing machines, television sets and motor vehicles. The loan will be for less than the cost of the pledged inventory so that if the borrower defaults, the inventory will be liquidated to extinguish the loan. In general, collateral loans can be costly due to the administrative expenses associated with the registration of liens or chattel securities.

**Factoring** is another method of financing accounts receivable whereby accounts receivable are sold to a factoring company or another financial institution. The factor buys the existing and subsequent accounts receivable from a business firm for an agreed commission, being a percentage of the debts. The factor provides credit-checking facilities, mails monthly statements of account to the firm's customers and collects the payments on account. When the factoring arrangement is on a **non-recourse basis**, the factor also takes on the risk of bad debts. The factor normally pays the firm a percentage of the invoice value immediately and the balance (less commission) upon collection from the customer. Although the commissions may be as high as between 2.5% and 5% of collections, the firm gains from reduced costs of investment in accounts receivable, credit approval and debt collection. A similar alternative to factoring is **invoice discounting**, whereby the firm selling the accounts receivable retains and continues the collection function.

> **Pledge**
> To put up assets as security for a loan.
>
> **Collateral**
> Assets, such as inventory, that are pledged as security for a loan.
>
> **Factoring**
> The discounted sale of accounts receivable to a factoring company or financial institution in return for immediate receipt of funds. Credit and collection activities are undertaken by the factor.
>
> **Non-recourse basis**
> With respect to the sale of accounts receivable, when the factor takes on the risk of bad debts.
>
> **Invoice discounting**
> The discounted sale of accounts receivable to a factoring company or financial institution in return for immediate receipt of funds. Unlike factoring, credit and collection activities are retained by the seller of the accounts.

To summarise, a firm in the growth stage of its life cycle will draw on the same sources of funds as in the start-up stage, but will be able to access additional equity through:

- retained earnings
- private placements
- lines of credit
- revolving credit
- loans secured by accounts receivable or inventory
- factoring and invoice discounting.

## Example 2: Funding business growth

Assume Technability Ltd, a surfboard and windsurfer manufacturer, has entered its seventh year of operations. The research and development activities undertaken by the firm have resulted in valuable patents for its unique manufacturing process, such that Technability now enjoys an excellent worldwide reputation for high-quality products. Recently, Technability has also successfully entered the market for the manufacture of small yachts. However, the high demand for its products has put pressure on the production facilities that Technability purchased seven years earlier. It has become evident that new funding will be required to allow the firm to grow further. Technability is still heavily reliant on suppliers and banks for short-term finance, but new long-term debt funds are now being raised in the form of a debenture over new land and buildings. In order to maintain an optimal balance between debt and equity funds, a private placement of ordinary shares has been negotiated. The funding section of the balance sheet for Technability has been reproduced in Table 10.4.

Table 10.4 Liabilities and equity section, balance sheet, Technability Ltd

| Technability Ltd<br>Partial Balance Sheet<br>Year ended 31 March, Year 7 | | | |
|---|---|---|---|
| **Current liabilities** | | | |
| Trade accounts payable | | $ 58 000 | |
| Sundry accounts payable | | $ 145 000 | |
| Notes payable | 1 | $ 62 000 | |
| Accrued wages payable | | $ 38 000 | |
| Accrued taxes payable | | $ 75 000 | |
| Secured bank term loan | 2 | $ 230 000 | $ 608 000 |
| **Long-term liabilities** | | | |
| Debenture loan | 3 | | $ 820 000 |
| **Total liabilities** | | | $1 428 000 |
| **Shareholders' equity** | | | |
| Issued and paid-up capital | 4 | $ 420 000 | |
| Retained earnings | | $1 558 000 | $1 978 000 |
| **Total liabilities and equity** | | | $3 406 000 |

**Notes:**
1. The notes payable are drawn against a $300 000 line of credit.
2. The short-term loan is secured by accounts receivable and inventory valued at a cost of $1 300 000.
3. The debenture matures in 20 years and is secured by land and buildings valued on 31 March at $1 200 000.
4. On 31 January, 210 000 fully paid ordinary shares of $1.00 each were issued by private placement.

## Maturity stage

After becoming well established in the marketplace, a firm may enter a maturity stage, during which assets stabilise and sales plateau. During this stage, there may be no growth or a slight decline in profitability due to competition or other market changes. Unless further product development or geographical expansion is undertaken, the firm will eventually experience declining sales and profits.

The range of financing alternatives available to a large firm during the maturity stage is fairly diverse, as shown in Table 10.5. The firm will still rely heavily on funding from financial institutions but can also utilise spontaneous sources such as trade credit from suppliers and accruals.

Table 10.5 Sources of finance through the firm's life cycle

| Source of finance | Stage of firm's life cycle | | |
| --- | --- | --- | --- |
| | Start-up | Growth | Maturity |
| Owners' personal investment | ✓ | ✓ | |
| Friends' and relatives' personal investment | ✓ | ✓ | |
| Banks and financial institutions | ✓ | ✓ | ✓ |
| Suppliers | ✓ | ✓ | ✓ |
| Crowdfunding and venture capital | ✓ | ✓ | |
| Retained earnings | | ✓ | ✓ |
| Private placements | | ✓ | ✓ |
| Public offerings | | | ✓ |
| Offshore securities | | | ✓ |

Retained earnings may also provide a substantial source of funds if profitability can be maintained. Private placements of ordinary and preference shares, debentures, loans and unsecured notes may be made on a frequent basis to obtain small to moderate quantities of equity and debt funds.

However, to fund major expansion projects, large firms need access to substantial financial resources. Working capital and other short-term requirements can be met, not only through the previously mentioned sources but also from the issue of bank bills and commercial bills. To obtain a large amount of long-term funds, a large, well-established company can issue shares, debentures and bonds to the public through the financial markets. Alternatively, large amounts of debt funds can be raised via syndicated loans and offshore securities.

### Banks and financial institutions

Large, well-established companies in the maturity stage may use the services of a variety of financial institutions. Investment banks (or merchant banks) are intermediaries that specialise in servicing the funding needs of medium and large companies. Some large commercial banks, such as ANZ and Westpac Banking Corporation, have a separate investment banking division, while other institutions specialise only in investment banking. Their role is to act as an intermediary, bringing large-scale borrowers and lenders together.

Commercial banks, investment banks and finance companies can assist in obtaining short-term funds in the form of **commercial bills** and bank bills. Commercial bills and bank bills are short-term marketable securities that are sold in large denominations to investors. Given that they are marketable, they can be resold by the lender or holder to other investors until the maturity date. However, a bank bill is a type of commercial bill that has been accepted by a commercial bank, meaning that a particular bank has agreed to be liable to repay the bill upon maturity. To compensate the bank, the borrower makes a payment to the bank upon maturity equal to the face value of the bill plus a fee. The acceptance process assures investors that the bill will be repaid. In contrast, commercial bills may or may not carry the acceptance of a financial institution. Given that commercial bills and bank bills are **unsecured,** only firms of high financial integrity can successfully issue non-accepted bills themselves.

Investment banks can grant substantial short-term or medium-term loans to large companies through syndication. A **syndicate** is formed of several (often international) banks that directly or indirectly, through a 'lead bank', lend funds to a borrower. The syndicate results in a pooling of loan funds, so that exposure to default risk is limited to the contribution of each participating bank. This enables large multinational companies to borrow more than they could otherwise obtain from one single bank.

> **Commercial bills**
> Unsecured short-term marketable securities issued either by companies or by banks.
>
> **Unsecured**
> When no collateral is offered as security against a loan.
>
> **Syndicate**
> A group of lending institutions which pool funds on a one-off basis to lend to a very large borrower. Limits risk exposure for any one given lender.

## Public offerings

A **public offering** is an issue of securities by a company to the public. An investment bank or sharebroking firm will normally assist in the issue in the following ways.

- Expert advice is given regarding:
  - the type of securities to offer
  - what selling price to set
  - how many securities to issue.
- A prospectus is developed to advise potential investors of the financial position of the company. This document is required by law to advise potential investors of the financial position of the company intending to issue securities to the public.
- The investment bank or sharebroking firm **underwrites** the issue by agreeing to take up any securities that are not **subscribed** by the public. The company may pay a fee to have the investment bank underwrite the issue, which guarantees the sale of the entire issue.

The advantage of a public offering is that large parcels of securities can be sold to a large number of investors. When shares are sold to the general public, it is called a flotation. However, the issue costs can be very high, due to the extensive preparation required to issue shares to the public and due to the underwriting fees.

If funding requirements are not great then a rights issue may be undertaken, whereby the company offers to sell securities to existing shareholders in proportion to their current holdings. The company benefits by avoiding the high issue costs of a flotation to the general public. Existing shareholders have the choice either to retain their proportionate interest in the company by purchasing additional shares, or to sell their rights to other investors.

> **Public offering**
> Issue of securities by a company to the public.
>
> **Underwriting**
> The agreement by an investment bank to purchase any securities that are not subscribed by the public in a new issue.
>
> **Subscribe**
> To agree to purchase a security, often shares.

> **Convertible securities**
> Securities that begin their life in one form (usually debt) and that may be converted to another form (usually equity) at a later date. Includes convertible notes, capital notes and convertible preference shares.

Several securities can be sold by flotation or rights issue. Equity capital can be raised using ordinary shares, preference shares or **convertible securities**, while debt funds may be sold as debentures, unsecured notes or bonds. Ordinary and preference shares were discussed earlier. Convertible securities begin their life in one form (usually debt) and may convert at a later date to another form of securities (usually equity). Most convertible securities are considered to be deferred equity finance, and include convertible notes, capital notes and convertible preference shares. Debt funds may be secured, as with debentures, or unsecured, as with unsecured notes and bonds.

### Offshore securities

Large, reputable companies have increasingly turned to foreign markets to fund substantial requirements for equity and debt. The foreign markets have become popular in part due to the large volumes, low costs and high flexibility of **offshore finance**. In particular, the **Euromarket** has experienced rapid growth as it is subject to little government regulation. The Euromarket is an international financial market that facilitates the trading of debt and equity securities outside the country of origin. The security is denominated in a currency foreign to the country where the issue is made. Euromarket deposits and loans are with eurobanks that are generally branches of international banks, located in a major offshore centre such as London, Hong Kong (China), etc.

> **Offshore finance**
> Capital raised overseas.
>
> **Euromarket**
> An international financial market that facilitates the trading of debt and equity securities outside the country of origin.
>
> **Eurocurrency loans**
> Loans issued by an international bank, denominated in a major currency other than the legal currency of the country in which it is issued.
>
> **Foreign bonds**
> Bonds issued in a foreign country, denominated in the currency of that foreign country.
>
> **Eurobonds**
> Bonds issued outside the country of the currency in which they are denominated.
>
> **Euroequities**
> Equity funds issued in offshore centres to achieve a wider distribution of ownership and greater capital than would otherwise be possible.

A variety of short-term funds are available through the offshore markets. Two major sources are commercial bills and **eurocurrency loans**. Large, creditworthy companies may sell commercial bills in the United States at favourable interest rates. Eurocurrency loans are another alternative, being loans issued by a eurobank, denominated in a major currency other than the legal currency of the country in which it is issued. For example, Fonterra Co-operative Group Limited could obtain a loan via a Hong Kong (China) eurobank, denominated in US dollars. Three-month to six-month loans are available, although with the permission of the lender they may be 'rolled over' several times by the borrower to extend the term.

For medium-term and long-term funds, offshore markets facilitate the issue of **foreign bonds**, **eurobonds** and **euroequities**.

- Foreign bonds are bonds issued in a foreign country, denominated in the currency of that foreign country. So an issue of bonds in Canada, denominated in Canadian dollars, by a New Zealand or Australian multinational company would be a foreign bond. These issues can be private placements or public issues.

- Eurobonds are bonds issued outside the country of the currency in which they are denominated. An issue of bonds in London, denominated in US dollars, by a New Zealand company is an example of a eurobond. Note that if the issue had been sold primarily in New York, it would be a foreign bond rather than a eurobond. Eurobonds are frequently denominated in US dollars, called *eurodollars*, while those that are denominated in New Zealand dollars are more commonly referred to as *eurokiwis*.

- For large companies that need more equity funding than can be raised domestically, the euroequities market may be utilised. This permits the company to raise equity funds through an issue of ordinary shares in offshore centres, resulting in a wider distribution of ownership and a greater amount of capital than would otherwise be possible.

In summary, a firm in the maturity stage may have access to a great variety of financing instruments. No longer will one or two owners, friends and family supply the majority of the company's financing. Short-term debt will be provided by suppliers, domestic and international banks, and other financial institutions. Other funding may be via domestic or international markets, consisting of a wide variety of debt and equity sources, including bank bills, commercial bills, syndicated loans, euroloans, ordinary and preference shares, and convertible securities. This situation is illustrated by the following example of Technability Ltd.

**Example 3: Funding business maturity**

Now assume that 15 years after setting up Technability Ltd, the owners sold all shares in the company to JRP Ltd, a large publicly listed company. JRP Ltd is a mature company involved at all levels of the value chain in the sporting goods industry. The owners are pleased to remain involved in the operations of Technability Ltd in their respective capacities as research and development manager and chief executive officer. As a result, Technability Ltd is a **subsidiary** of JRP Ltd, and for financial reporting purposes the balance sheets of the **parent company** and all its subsidiaries must be **consolidated**. Table 10.6 on the next page shows the funds section of the consolidated balance sheet of our fictitious multinational company, JRP Ltd. As can be seen in the table, JRP Ltd relies primarily on suppliers and commercial bills for short-term financing. A wide variety of long-term debt instruments is employed, with major reliance being placed upon bank loans. Most of the equity funds are from ordinary shares and retained earnings, although some preference shares have been issued. Preference shareholders are not entitled to vote in the selection process for the board of directors, but they do have a priority claim on profits before ordinary shareholders.

**Subsidiary**
A company owned and controlled by another company.

**Parent company**
A company that owns and controls another company.

**Consolidated**
The combined financial accounts of a group of companies, composed of a parent and its subsidiaries.

Table 10.6  Liabilities and equity section, consolidated balance sheet, JRP Ltd

**JRP Ltd**
**Partial Balance Sheet**
**Year ended 31 March, Year 15**

| Current liabilities | | '000 | '000 |
|---|---|---|---|
| Trade accounts payable | | $185 400 | |
| Sundry accounts payable | | $110 600 | |
| Notes payable | | $ 1 000 | |
| Commercial bills | | $ 22 000 | |
| Accrued expenses payable | | $ 4 300 | |
| Dividends payable | | $ 2 800 | |
| Secured bank term loan | 1 | $ 8 000 | |
| Current portion of term debt and lease | | $ 54 000 | $ 388 100 |
| | | | |
| **Long-term liabilities** | | | |
| Unsecured bank term loans | 2 | | $ 347 300 |
| Unsecured capital notes | 3 | | $ 15 200 |
| Capitalised finance lease | 4 | | $ 11 500 |
| Debenture loans | 5 | | $ 62 500 |
| **Total liabilities** | | | $ 824 600 |
| | | | |
| **Shareholders' equity** | | | |
| Issued and paid-up capital | | | |
| Ordinary shares | 6 | $592 000 | |
| Preference shares | | $ 22 000 | |
| Retained earnings | | $273 800 | $ 887 800 |
| **Total liabilities and equity** | | | $1 712 400 |

**Notes**
1 The short-term loan is secured by inventory valued at a cost of $12 000 000.
2 The unsecured bank term loans mature as follows:
   within two years   $42 000 000        four years         $163 000 000
   three years        $117 000 000       after four years   $25 300 000
3 The capital notes are long-term fixed-rate unsecured subordinated notes that are convertible in ten years' time into ordinary shares of JRP at 98% of the then current market price of JRP ordinary shares. JRP may, at its option, redeem the capital notes in ten years' time for cash at the principal amount plus any accrued interest.
4 The capitalised finance lease terminates in eight years' time.
5 The debentures mature in 15 years' time and are secured by land, buildings and equipment valued on 31 March at $97 500 000.
6 In accordance with the constitution, 92 000 fully paid ordinary shares were issued under approved employee share-purchase schemes.

# Choosing the financing mix

Notwithstanding the constraints imposed by the availability of funds set by the stage in the firm's life cycle, there are several important decisions that owners or senior managers must make concerning the financing of the firm.

- What proportions of short-term versus long-term funding should be employed?
- To what extent should internal versus external sources of funds be used?
- What proportions of debt and equity will maximise the value of the firm?

The strategic policy decisions that deal with these issues will be examined next.

## Short-term or long-term sources?

In the last section we examined many short- and long-term financing alternatives that may be available to businesses. A strategic policy decision must be made concerning the extent to which short- or long-term sources of finance are to be relied on. This is of major importance, as such a decision will affect the risk–profitability profile of the business.

Recall that risk and profitability tend to move together. The higher the expected risk, the higher the expected profits, and vice versa. Using a high proportion of short-term finance increases the risks of being unable to pay obligations as they come due and of being unable to refinance. However, using short-term finance enhances profits as it typically costs less than long-term funds. Long-term finance carries less risk, but is less profitable. The extent of risks and profits inherent in short-term and long-term financing are summarised in Table 10.7.

Table 10.7 **Risk and profitability of short-term and long-term financing**

| Source of financing | Risk | Profitability |
|---|---|---|
| Short-term | High | High |
| Long-term | Low | Low |

Short-term financing tends to be riskier than long-term financing for two reasons.

1. The use of a high proportion of short-term finance minimises the net working capital or liquidity of a business. Recall that net working capital is equal to current assets less current liabilities. If current liabilities are high, then net working capital will be low. A low level of net working capital is risky as it increases the likelihood of the business being unable to meet its obligations as they come due. Conversely, financing with a high proportion of long-term funds is less risky, as net working capital and liquidity would be higher.
2. It may be difficult to refinance during periods of recession and/or tight monetary conditions. During the height of the 2008 global financial crisis, many businesses were unable to refinance existing loans as the banks themselves could not obtain sufficient funds. In times of recession, banks may have excessive bad debts and be reluctant to risk further losses. If property prices fall, then some properties may carry debt liabilities greater than their land values. Businesses that have financed their properties with short-term debt may need to refinance at increasingly higher interest rates, leading them to experience financial distress. Even worse, a firm that cannot refinance its short-term loans may face insolvency

and bankruptcy. However, with long-term funds there is less need for frequent refinancing, thereby reducing the refinancing risk.

Despite the inherent risks, however, a strategy of using a high proportion of short-term finance tends to yield higher profits than a strategy of long-term finance. Again, there are two reasons for this.

1. Short-term sources of finance normally cost less than long-term sources. By using suppliers' credit, for example, a business incurs no explicit interest cost as long as accounts are paid on time. Furthermore, banks and financial institutions normally charge a lower interest rate on short-term loans than on similarly secured long-term loans. The lower the financing costs, the higher the firm's profits.

2. Financing with long-term funds means that at times when finance requirements are low, excess liquidity will result. This situation is depicted graphically in Figure 10.2. Financing requirements may be low when inventory and accounts receivable are low due to a seasonal drop in sales. Yet, if only long-term funding was to be employed, the firm would need to obtain sufficient funds to cover the periods of high demands on funds. Therefore, at times of low seasonal demand, excess cash will be on hand. While this excess cash could be reinvested in marketable securities to earn interest income, the interest rate received would be much lower than the cost of financing with long-term funds. Consequently, higher costs and lower profits result from using long-term funds.

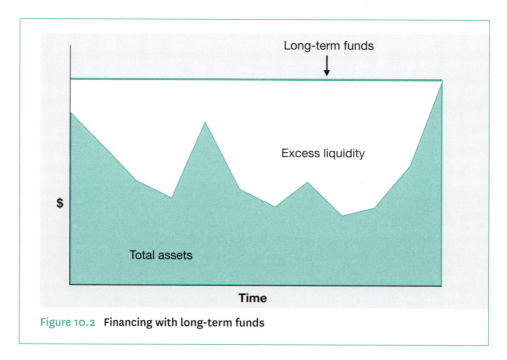

Figure 10.2 **Financing with long-term funds**

Financial decision-makers attempt to employ that mix of short-term and long-term funds that maximises profits within an acceptable level of risk. Small businesses often find that short-term sources of external funds are more accessible than long-term sources. Lenders are generally reluctant to lend long-term funds to small businesses due to the perception that investing in small businesses is riskier than investing in larger businesses. Consequently, small businesses tend to rely more heavily on trade credit and short-term bank finance than large firms do. As mentioned above, heavy reliance by small businesses on short-term finance has the effect of increasing not only their profitability but also their risk.

Lenders' perceptions and lending policies can become self-fulfilling prophecies. As mentioned earlier, heavy reliance by small businesses on short-term finance has the effect of increasing not only their profitability but also their risk. Small businesses may fail due to a lack of long-term finance and as a result of high interest costs due to perceived high risk. In larger firms, strategic corporate guidelines are frequently provided on the proportions of short-term and long-term funding to be achieved.

## Internal or external funding?

A strategic decision must be made concerning the extent to which financing should be obtained from internal or external sources. The major internal source of funds is earnings retained within the business, whereas external funds are from owners and lenders who are external to the operations of the firm.

The amount of retained earnings available for reinvestment will be affected by the firm's **dividend policy**. Profits can either be paid out to the owners as drawings or dividends, or can be retained as an internal source of equity finance. The higher the proportion of profits paid out as dividends, the lower the retained earnings and the larger the amount of external finance required. Dividend policy is set at the strategic level of management decision-making, and considers both the needs of the firm for retained earnings and the preferences of investors for the amount and consistency of dividends.

> **Dividend policy**
> A strategic policy that considers the need for profits to be retained within the firm for reinvestment and the preferences of shareholders for the amount and consistency of dividends.

Normally, when equity funds are required for investment purposes a firm will utilise retained earnings before raising new external sources of equity funds. This is because retained earnings are normally the cheapest source of equity finance as there are no issue or underwriting costs.

## Debt or equity finance?

Another strategic decision involves the attempt to set the optimal mix of debt and equity that will maximise the value of the firm. An assessment is needed of the risk and return to owners from each source of finance. Recall that earlier the major features of debt and equity were examined. Debt finance was found to be cheaper than equity finance. This is because debt is considered by lenders to be of lower risk than equity, and therefore lenders require a lower return than owners.

Consequently, using low-cost debt finance can increase earnings per share (EPS). However, from the firm's point of view, the higher the proportion of debt relative to total finance (debt plus equity), the greater the financial risk. Financial risk is a consequence of the contractual nature of debt. If the borrower defaults on interest or principal repayments, the firm may be liquidated. Since creditors have first claim on business assets in the event of liquidation, the business owners risk being unable to recover their invested capital. Therefore, debt finance increases both EPS and risk.

In contrast, using a high proportion of equity finance often results in lower EPS, but with less risk to the firm. Owners require a higher rate of return than lenders to compensate for the riskiness of their investment, so equity finance tends to be more costly. However, from the point of view of the business, equity finance is not as risky as debt finance, as a failure to pay a return in the form of dividends will not directly affect the survival of the firm. Table 10.8 summarises the risks and returns attributable to debt and equity finance from the point of view of the firm and its owners.

Table 10.8  Risk and return of debt and equity finance

| Source of financing | Risk to firm | Return to owners |
|---|---|---|
| Debt | High | High |
| Equity | Low | Low |

**Debt ratio**
A measure of the proportion of debt relative to total financing; or, alternatively, the proportion of assets financed by debt.

**Debt–equity ratio**
A measure of the proportion of long-term debt relative to shareholders' equity.

To achieve an optimal mix of debt and equity, managers attempt to balance the risk–return trade-off, setting an acceptable level of financial risk to generate a desirable level of returns. As part of this process, the financial manager of the firm will examine the financial measures of debt. The **debt ratio** measures the proportion of debt relative to total finance or, alternatively, the proportion of assets financed by debt. The **debt–equity ratio** measures the proportion of long-term debt relative to shareholders' equity. These ratios are calculated as follows:

$$\text{Debt ratio} = \frac{\text{Total liabilities}}{\text{Total assets}} \qquad \text{Equation 10.1}$$

$$\text{Debt–equity ratio} = \frac{\text{Long-term debt}}{\text{Shareholders' equity}} \qquad \text{Equation 10.2}$$

Firms in industries that experience fluctuating or unpredictable cash flows tend to limit their exposure to risk by using less debt finance. In less volatile industries where business risk is lower, businesses can afford to accept the risk of using more debt in order to gain the benefit of higher returns.

---

**Example 4: Debt ratio**

As happens in the case of many new start-ups, the debt ratio for Technability Ltd was high at 65.5%. By year 7, as shown in Table 10.4, the decline in the debt ratio, to 41.9%, had reduced the firm's financial risk exposure to a more moderate level.

|  | Year 7 |
|---|---|
| $\text{Debt ratio} = \dfrac{\text{Total liabilities}}{\text{Total assets}}$ | $\dfrac{\$1\,428\,000}{\$3\,406\,000} = 41.9\%$ |

---

**Cost of capital**
The cost of raising and using funds.

**Optimal capital structure**
The best mix of debt and equity that minimises the cost of capital and maximises the value of the firm.

**Capital structure**
The proportionate mix of debt and equity used to finance a firm.

## Cost of capital

From the point of view of a firm, the **cost of capital** represents the cost of raising and using finance. It also represents the rate of return required by the firm's investors; therefore, the cost of capital is the return the firm must earn in order to maintain the firm's value. Consequently, the cost of capital is an appropriate benchmark used by management to evaluate proposed investments. Only those investments that earn a return greater than, or equal to, the cost of capital will be undertaken.

The appropriate mix of debt and equity finance for a firm is known as the **optimal capital structure**. By maintaining an optimal **capital structure**, a firm will achieve a balance of costs and risks that both minimises the overall cost of financing and maximises the value of the firm. To achieve such a balance, it is important to know the costs of using each source of funds. The costs can vary widely between different instruments and according to the economic climate. The costs of debt and equity finance in New Zealand can be sourced from various places including the RBNZ, Treasury, bank and finance company websites and the NZX.

In general, government financing costs, as evidenced by Treasury bills and government bonds, tend to be low relative to private-sector financing costs, due to the low risk of the government defaulting on its obligations. As discussed earlier, in normal conditions we expect long-term rates to exceed short-term rates. Generally, the higher the risk, the higher the financing costs.

These various costs can be described in four broad categories – the cost of:

- debt capital
- ordinary shares
- retained earnings
- preference shares.

## Cost of debt capital

The after-tax **cost of debt** to a firm has three components:

- interest paid to lenders/debt holders
- issue costs
- the interest tax shield.

> **Cost of debt**
> The cost of financing with debt. Composed of interest and issue costs, less any interest tax shield.

### Interest cost

Lenders require a return or yield on their investment to compensate them for the time value of money and risk. On a bank loan, the compensation to the lender is the interest rate charged. For a debt instrument, such as a bond that is issued to the public, the return will be the expected holding period yield.

### Issue costs

**Issue costs** will increase the effective cost (or true cost) of debt. For a bank loan, the lenders may impose additional administrative charges in excess of the interest charge. Similarly, with a public issue of debentures or bonds, the investment bank or sharebroking firm that advises and sells the issue will charge fees. These fees, or issue costs, increase the cost of debt to the borrower.

> **Issue costs**
> Administration, selling and underwriting costs associated with the issue of a new security.

### Interest tax shield

The interest cost incurred by business borrowers is reduced by the **interest tax shield**; that is, the savings the business makes due to the tax-deductibility of interest payments. The after-tax cost of debt ($r_d$) is calculated by multiplying the pre-tax cost of debt ($r_i$) by one minus the tax rate $(1 - t)$. The formula is given below:

> **Interest tax shield**
> The savings a business makes due to the tax-deductibility of interest payments.

$$r_d = r_i \times (1 - t)$$

*Equation 10.3*

> **Example 5: Calculating the after-tax cost of debt**
>
> JRP Ltd has taken out a long-term bank loan that carries an interest rate of 6%. The tax rate is 30%. Using Equation 10.3, the after-tax cost of debt is calculated as follows:
>
> $$r_d = 0.060 \times (1 - 0.30)$$
> $$= 0.042 \text{ or } 4.2\%$$
>
> The difference between the before-tax and after-tax cost of debt represents the interest tax shield. In this example, the savings due to the tax-deductibility of interest is $6.0\% - 4.2\% = 1.8\%$.

## Cost of equity capital

**Cost of equity**
The cost of financing with equity. Composed of dividends and issue costs.

The **cost of equity** capital is the cost of financing with equity. It is a long-term source of finance and the major source of risk capital that is provided by the owners. Each of the components of equity carries a cost that must reflect the period and risk of the investment. Among the major components of company equity funds are ordinary shares, retained earnings and preference shares. Their costs are discussed in the following sections.

### Ordinary shares

Equity financing with ordinary shares results in two costs to the firm:
- dividends paid to ordinary shareholders
- issue costs.

Ordinary shareholders receive dividend payments at semi-annual intervals, usually expressed as cents per share. Cash dividends plus issue costs paid on the issue of new ordinary shares represent the total cost to the firm of ordinary share financing.

Ordinary share dividends are not tax-deductible to the firm, so there is no explicit tax shield. Nevertheless, in many countries – including Australia and New Zealand – a system of dividend imputation operates whereby equity income is taxed only once. Consequently, when a company distributes dividends out of earned (taxed) income, the dividend income is essentially taxed once only at the marginal tax rate of the shareholder. This is similar to the tax implications of debt, where interest income is taxed only in the hands of the lender. So, although a company gains no explicit tax shield by virtue of paying dividends, an implicit recognition of the effect of dividend imputation is included in the price of ordinary shares.

### Retained earnings

Many businesses maintain large working capital balances in the form of liquid assets, such as cash and marketable securities, in readiness to undertake investment opportunities. These liquid balances result from retained earnings; that is, the business cash inflows which have been reinvested in the business.

Unlike the other sources of long-term finance, the use of retained earnings does not result in the payment of interest or dividends. Nevertheless, the use of retained earnings is not cost-free. The alternative to retaining earnings is to pay out dividends to shareholders, so when earnings are retained, shareholders forego some dividend income. Shareholders who receive dividends can reinvest those funds in other investments and earn a return. Consequently, there is an opportunity cost of using retained earnings. This opportunity cost is equal to the cost of financing with ordinary shares, with an absence of issue costs. Issue costs are equal to zero, as there is no need to incur issue costs in order to use retained earnings.

Given that retained earnings essentially 'belong' to shareholders, retained earnings are considered an internal source of equity financing. While there are a number of methods used to estimate the cost of equity, in practice the most common method for estimating the cost of retained earnings (and ordinary shares before issue costs) is the CAPM. This was discussed earlier in Chapter 6.

> **Example 6: Calculating the cost of retaining earnings**
>
> JRP Ltd has a policy of paying out 60% of its profits each year as dividends, retaining the remaining 40% for investment in new projects. JRP Ltd shares have a β of 1.3, while the risk-free rate is 4% and the equity market risk premium (MRP) is 5%. Using the CAPM Equation 6.15 from Chapter 6, the cost of retained earnings is calculated as follows:
>
> $$r_e = r_f + \beta_i(MRP)$$
> $$= 0.04 + 1.3(.05)$$
> $$= 0.105 \text{ or } 10.5\%$$

### Preference shares

Firms that finance some of their assets with preference shares will incur two costs:
- dividends paid to preference shareholders
- issue costs.

Preference shareholders are generally paid a constant dollar dividend, often expressed as a percentage of the face value. The dividends, plus any issue costs paid to investment banks on the issue of new shares, represent the cost to the firm of financing with preference shares.

Note that, as with ordinary shares, there is no explicit tax shield attributable to financing with preference shares, although there may be an implicit tax benefit as a consequence of dividend imputation credits.

Like ordinary shares, there is no maturity date for preference shares. Given that preference dividend payments are the same each year in perpetuity, we can determine the cost of preference share using the perpetuity formula Equation 5.9 from Chapter 5, as shown below.

$$PV = \frac{C_1}{r}$$

We can then rearrange the formula to solve investors' required return $r_p$ (or the cost of preference shares from the company's perspective) as follows:

$$r_p = \frac{C_1}{PV}$$

*Equation 10.4*

where  $r_p$ = the cost of preference shares
$C_1$ = the total dollar value of the dividend cash flow at the end of year 1 (and each year thereafter)
PV = the current value of the preference share.

> **Example 7: Calculating the cost of preference shares**
>
> JRP Ltd has preference shares that last traded for $12.50 per share. If the preference shares pay $1.00 in dividends per year then, using Equation 10.4, the cost of preference shares is calculated as follows:
>
> $$r_p = \frac{\$1.00}{\$12.50}$$
>
> $$= 0.080 \text{ or } 8.0\%$$
>
> If JRP Ltd were to issue new preference shares, they would also incur issue costs, meaning the final cost of the new preference shares would be greater than 8%.

## Weighted average cost of capital

**Weighted average cost of capital (WACC)**
The overall cost to a firm of all long-term sources of finance.

The overall cost to the firm of all long-term sources of finance can be computed as the **weighted average cost of capital** (**WACC** or $r_{cc}$). To find this, we need to know the cost of each source of financing and their percentage weight in the firm's capital structure. These weights should ideally be calculated based upon the market values of the financing sources, and not on accounting book values. The WACC is calculated by weighting the cost of each source of capital by its respective proportion in the firm's capital structure as follows:

$$r_{cc} = (r_d \times w_d) + (r_p \times w_p) + (r_e \times w_e) \qquad \textit{Equation 10.5}$$

where
$w_d$ = the proportion of long-term debt in the firm's capital structure
$w_p$ = the proportion of preference shares in the firm's capital structure
$w_e$ = the proportion of ordinary share equity in the firm's capital structure.

The weights ($w_d$, $w_p$ and $w_e$) must sum to 1.0. For ease of calculation and interpretation of WACC, the weights are converted into decimals as shown in Example 8.

> **Example 8: Determining WACC**
>
> JRP Ltd attempts to finance 30% of the market value of total assets with debt, at an after-tax cost of 4.2%, 10% with preference shares at a cost of 8.0%, and 60% with retained earnings at a cost of 10.5%. Using Equation 10.5, the weighted average cost of finance is calculated as follows:
>
> $$r_{cc} = (0.30 \times 0.042) + (0.10 \times 0.08) + (0.60 \times 0.105)$$
> $$= 0.0836 \text{ or } 8.4\%$$
>
> Note that in practice WACC is typically rounded to the nearest tenth of a per cent, e.g. 8.4%.

The WACC represents the overall return required by all suppliers of finance to maintain their level of investment in the firm. If the firm is able to invest in projects that will earn a return greater than, or equal to, the WACC, then all suppliers of finance will be compensated at their respective required rates of return.

## Conclusion

This chapter looked at how firms are financed and the financing decisions that firms must make. Most firms are financed with a mixture of debt and equity. Debt funds are supplied by lenders, whereas equity funds represent owners' capital.

A firm's financing needs will change over the firm's life cycle. During the start-up stage, new businesses will finance their investment and operating expenditures from several sources, including owners, friends and relatives, suppliers, banks and finance companies, crowdfunding and venture capital organisations. The capital structure should include a significant proportion of equity capital, otherwise debt funds may be difficult to obtain. Furthermore, the owners and/or directors of a new business may have to personally guarantee the business debts before lenders will provide debt funding.

During the growth stage, the expansion of sales can lead to a significant investment in accounts receivable and inventory. Firms will rely on the same sources of finance that were available during the start-up stage, but as profitability and assets increase then other funding options will become available. Additional equity in the form of retained earnings, private placements of debt and equity with financial institutions, and further debt, such as lines of credit, revolving credit and secured short-term loans, may be alternative sources of finance.

A large, successful, well-established firm is likely to be in the maturity stage, when sales and profits are stable. Short-term debt will be available from suppliers, domestic and international banks, and other financial institutions. Local and international markets will be used to obtain medium-term and long-term finance in many different forms, such as syndicated loans, euroloans, ordinary and preference shares, and convertible securities.

Other important financing decisions involve choosing an appropriate proportion of short-term to long-term funds, internal to external sources, and debt to equity. These decisions involve balancing the financial risk and costs of funds relative to the stability of the anticipated returns.

A firm can calculate the overall cost of all sources of long-term finance as a weighted average of the cost of each individual source. Known as the weighted average cost of capital, it represents the minimum return required to be earned by the firm in order to compensate all suppliers of finance at their respective required rates of return. This cost of capital may be used as a benchmark in accepting projects for investment, or as a discount rate in calculating the present value of estimated future cash flows.

The use of a required rate of return, including the weighted average cost of capital, in making long-term investment decisions will be explained in the following two chapters.

## SELF-TEST QUESTIONS

1. Mo-Debt Ltd is considering repurchasing its own shares and issuing debt. The firm currently has total assets of $500 000, financed with 20% debt and 80% equity. The annual interest cost of debt is 10%, and there are 400 000 shares on issue. Operating income (earnings before interest and taxes) is $100 000 and the firm's tax rate is 30%. The proposed share repurchase would involve buying back 100 000 of Mo-Debt Ltd shares and cancelling them. Then additional debt capital of $100 000 would be raised at an interest rate of 10%.
   a. Calculate Mo-Debt's earnings per share under the current and proposed capital structures.
   b. What financial impact would you anticipate that the firm may experience as a consequence of the increase in debt?

2. NZ Communications Ltd is evaluating the following independent investment opportunities:

| Project | Expected return |
|---|---|
| A | 20% |
| B | 17% |
| C | 14% |
| D | 12% |

The financial manager has determined the firm's optimal capital structure and finance costs to be:

|  | Amount | Finance cost |
|---|---|---|
| Long-term debt | $2 200 000 | 11.43% |
| Ordinary share equity | $2 800 000 | 18.80% |
| Total liabilities and equity | $5 000 000 | |

   a. Calculate the after-tax cost of debt, assuming a tax rate of 30%.
   b. Calculate the firm's weighted average cost of capital.
   c. Which projects are expected to earn a return sufficient to cover the overall costs of financing?

3. You work at Nepal Apparel Company's head office and have been asked by your manager to calculate the minimum return the firm must earn on new investment projects. You decide to first calculate Nepal Apparel Company's current weighted average cost of capital (WACC), where 35% of Nepal Apparel Company's total assets are financed with debt, 15% with preference share equity, and 50% with ordinary share equity.

   Nepal Apparel Company has a long-term bank loan with a nominal interest cost of 6.90% per annum. The preference shares pay annual dividends of $0.75 per share and last traded on the NZX for $8.25 per share. Nepal Apparel Company's ordinary shares have a β of 1.10. The applicable risk-free rate is 4.2% and the equity market risk premium (MRP) is 5.5%.
   a. Calculate the after-tax cost of debt assuming a 30% tax rate.
   b. Calculate Nepal Apparel Company's cost of preference shares.
   c. Calculate Nepal Apparel Company's cost of ordinary share equity using the capital asset pricing model (CAPM).

d Calculate the WACC for Nepal Apparel Company.
e Assuming that Nepal Apparel Company must sell new preference and ordinary shares to finance new investment projects, is the firm's WACC likely to be higher or lower than what you calculated above? Why?

**ANSWERS TO SELF-TEST QUESTIONS**

1 a

|  | Current | Proposed |
|---|---|---|
| Total assets | $500 000 | $500 000 |
| % debt | 20% | 40% |
| Book value of debt | $100 000 | $200 000 |
| % equity | 80% | 60% |
| Book value of equity | $400 000 | $300 000 |
| Operating income | $100 000 | $100 000 |
| Interest expense (10% × debt) | $ 10 000 | $ 20 000 |
| Profit before tax | $ 90 000 | $ 80 000 |
| Taxes at 30% | $ 27 000 | $ 24 000 |
| Profit after taxes | $ 63 000 | $ 56 000 |
| Ordinary shares on issue | 400 000 | 300 000 |
| EPS | $0.158 | $0.187 |

b An increase in debt normally results in an increase in earnings per share (EPS) and increased variability of EPS. Financial risk is increased because debt is a fixed commitment that increases the likelihood of default and financial distress.

2 a $r_d = r_i \times (1 - t)$

$= 0.1143 \times (1 - 0.30)$

$= 0.08$ or $8\%$

b $r_{cc} = (r_d \times w_d) + (r_p \times w_p) + (r_e \times w_e)$

Weight of debt $= \dfrac{\$2\,200\,000}{\$5\,000\,000} = 44\%$

Weight of equity $= \dfrac{\$2\,800\,000}{\$5\,000\,000} = 56\%$

$r_{cc} = (0.44 \times 0.08) + (0.56 \times 0.188) = 0.1405$ or $14.05\%$

c Projects A and B are expected to earn returns sufficient to cover the costs of financing, and therefore should be accepted. Projects C and D will not cover the overall financing costs, and should be rejected.

3 a $r_d = r_i \times (1 - t)$

$= 0.069 \times (1 - 0.30)$

$= 0.0483$ or $4.83\%$

b  $r_p = \dfrac{C}{PV}$

$= \dfrac{\$0.75}{\$8.25}$

$= 0.0909$ or $9.09\%$

c  $r_e = r_f + \beta(MRP)$

$= 0.042 + 1.10(0.055)$

$= 0.1025$ or $10.25\%$

d  $r_{cc} = (r_d \times w_d) + (r_p \times w_p) + (r_e \times w_e)$

$= (0.35 \times 0.0483) + (0.15 \times 0.0909) + (0.50 \times 0.1025)$

$= 0.0169 + 0.0136 + 0.0513$

$= 0.0818$

Note that typically the WACC is rounded to the nearest tenth of a per cent (i.e. 8.2% for the above answer). As the CAPM formula contains estimates of both the firm risk ($\beta$) and equity market risk premium (MRP), the cost of ordinary share equity is an estimate. Therefore the WACC is also an estimate, and having precision of answers to many decimals places is not meaningful.

e  The cost is likely to be higher due to the issues costs associated with selling new shares.

## QUESTIONS AND PROBLEMS

1. Why is it that debt is considered by lenders to be of lower risk than equity?
2. Why is it that the cost of debt to a firm is less than the cost of equity?
3. List the major features that distinguish debt from equity.
4. Describe the changes in sales and operating cash flow over a firm's life cycle.
5. List the major sources of finance available during the start-up stage of a firm's life cycle. Identify each source as *debt*, *equity* or *either debt or equity*.
6. What are *venture capital funds*, and how do venture capital organisations fill a void in equity funding for businesses?
7. List and define the various debt instruments available from banks and financial institutions in the start-up stage of a firm's life cycle.
8. Discuss the major financing problems of a firm during the start-up stage of its life cycle.
9. What types of debt instrument would be suitable to finance the purchase of major equipment by a firm in the start-up stage of its life cycle?
10. Explain the major features that distinguish a financial lease from an operating lease.

11 List the major sources of finance available during the growth stage of a firm's life cycle. Identify each source as *debt*, *equity*, or *either debt or equity*.

12 Define the terms *line of credit*, *revolving credit*, *pledge* and *factoring*.

13 What financial problems could cause the failure of a young, profitable, growing business?

14 Describe the alternative debt instruments available to finance the accounts receivable of a firm in the growth stage of its life cycle.

15 List the major sources of finance available during the maturity stage of a firm's life cycle. Identify each source as *debt*, *equity*, or *either debt or equity*.

16 Distinguish between bank bills and commercial bills.

17 What is the advantage of a syndicated loan from the point of view of:

 a a borrower?

 b the lenders?

18 What is an investment bank?

19 Distinguish between a private placement and a public offering.

20 Describe three different ways for a public company to raise external equity funds using ordinary shares.

21 Why are convertible securities often considered to be deferred equity finance? What circumstances would lead a company to prefer to issue convertible securities that convert to ordinary shares in three years' time, rather than issue ordinary shares immediately?

22 What is the difference between a foreign bond and a eurobond?

23 Why is it that many large, successful companies choose to raise a portion of their debt and equity funds in foreign markets?

24 Define the terms *Euromarket* and *eurocurrency loans*.

25 How does a strategy of using a high proportion of short-term finance affect the profits and risks of a firm?

26 Wally has financed the purchase of a small-town hotel with short-term debt. Do you foresee any potential problems with this?

27 Twin Hills Ski Shop expects monthly inventory levels over the next year to range from $100 000 to $700 000. Would you recommend the use of mostly short-term or long-term funds to finance the purchase of inventory? Explain why.

28 Differentiate between internal and external sources of funds.

29 In what way are investment, dividend and financing strategies interdependent?

30 It has been said that 'debt is a double-edged sword'. What is meant by this expression?

31 What are the risks and returns attributable to debt and equity finance from the point of view of the firm?

32 Ruth purchased a corner dairy for $200 000. The vendor took $120 000 immediately as part-payment, a sum which Ruth had obtained as a long-term loan from her aunt. The balance of the

purchase price was due in four consecutive monthly instalments of $20 000 each. Ruth paid this from the cash flow of the business; however, this meant that most of Ruth's suppliers' accounts could not be paid. Assuming that the dairy generated no profit in the first four months of operations, effectively what proportions of debt and equity did Ruth use to finance the purchase? Do you foresee any potential problems for Ruth?

33  Wendell wants to purchase his first home, but has been unable to save enough money for a deposit. The house will cost $220 000, but the maximum mortgage loan Wendell can obtain is for $176 000. Wendell plans to borrow the remaining $44 000 required as a deposit from his parents. Effectively what proportion of debt and equity is Wendell planning to use to finance the purchase? What are the potential problems with Wendell's strategy?

34  Belinda Fine Foods Ltd is a successful medium-sized firm with total assets of $3 200 000. Due to the conservative nature of the managing director, who owns 51% of the issued capital, the firm is financed with 90% equity and 10% debt. The profits and cash flows of the firm are consistent and highly predictable. Could the firm's shareholders benefit from an increase in the proportion of debt in the firm's capital structure? Explain why.

35  Name the three components of the after-tax cost of debt. For each component, describe whether the effect is to increase or decrease the cost to the firm.

36  What costs does a firm incur with respect to financing with ordinary shares?

37  Explain why the use of retained earnings involves a cost to a firm.

38  What is the weighted average cost of capital to a firm, and how is it relevant in the evaluation of potential investment projects?

39  Teddy Toys Ltd is examining its mix of short-term and long-term finance. The relative costs of each are as follows:

| Source of financing | Dollar value | Average cost |
| --- | --- | --- |
| Short-term | $18 000 | 4% |
| Long-term | $34 000 | 14% |

   a  Calculate the total annual financing cost for the firm, given the current financing mix.
   b  Calculate the revised annual finance cost for the firm assuming that:
      i   $4 000 of short-term funds were converted to long-term
      ii  $4 000 of long-term funds were converted to short-term.

40  James Fishing Supplies currently has the following assets, liabilities and owners' equity:

| Assets | | Liabilities and owners' equity | |
| --- | --- | --- | --- |
| Current assets | $50 000 | Current liabilities | $40 000 |
| Fixed assets | $32 000 | Long-term debt | $16 000 |
| | | Owners' equity | $26 000 |
| | $82 000 | | $82 000 |

Short-term funds have an average finance cost of 6%, while long-term funds cost approximately 15%.

a  Calculate the current level of net working capital and the total annual finance cost for the firm.

b  Calculate the revised level of net working capital and the revised total annual finance cost for the firm assuming that:

  i   $6 000 of short-term funds were converted to long-term.

  ii  $6 000 of long-term funds were converted to short-term.

c  Comment on the relative risks and profits of the alternative financing strategies.

41 Fiona Swimwear Manufacturing Ltd's total assets for each month next year are forecast as follows:

| January | $30 000 | July | $45 000 |
|---|---|---|---|
| February | $32 000 | August | $52 000 |
| March | $32 000 | September | $56 000 |
| April | $32 000 | October | $60 000 |
| May | $35 000 | November | $55 000 |
| June | $35 000 | December | $40 000 |

a  Graph the total assets of Fiona Swimwear for each month through the year.

b  Indicate on your graph the excess liquidity that the firm would have if the assets were financed solely by $60 000 of long-term funds.

c  Calculate the total finance cost for the firm if its long-term funds cost an average of 16%.

42 New-U Cosmetics Ltd is attempting to balance its policy variables with respect to its investment, financing and dividend requirements. The firm wishes to undertake new investments costing $100 000 over the next year. To maintain a consistent dividend policy, $80 000 will be needed to pay next year's dividends. The firm wishes to retain its current capital structure of 50% debt and 50% equity. New equity funds in the form of retained earnings of $90 000 are available for investment and dividend requirements.

a  How can the firm's investment, financing and dividend requirements best be met?

b  What action could the firm undertake if the investment needs totalled $150 000 rather than $100 000?

43 Best Buy Supermarkets Ltd has total assets of $800 000. The current capital structure comprises 50% debt and 50% equity. The annual interest cost of debt is 12%, and there are 500 000 shares on issue. Operating income (earnings before interest and taxes) is $100 000 and the firm's tax rate is 30%.

a  Calculate Best Buy's profit after taxes and earnings per share (EPS).

b  Calculate Best Buy's profit after taxes and EPS, assuming a capital structure of 40% debt and 60% equity. Assume that there are now 600 000 shares on issue.

c Calculate Best Buy's profit after taxes and EPS, assuming a capital structure of 60% debt and 40% equity. Assume that there are now 400 000 shares on issue.

d Which capital structure will give the best return to shareholders?

44 Kiwi Kids Shops Ltd intends to finance its future investments with 30% debt and 70% equity. The pre-tax interest cost of debt is 8%, while the after-tax cost of new ordinary shares is 18%. Calculate the weighted average cost of capital.

45 Taylor Ltd has determined its optimal capital structure and finance costs to be as follows:

|  | Amount | After-tax cost |
|---|---|---|
| Long-term debt | $500 000 | 7% |
| Preference shares | $100 000 | 13% |
| Ordinary share equity | $400 000 | 20% |
| Total liabilities and equity | $1 000 000 |  |

Calculate Taylor Ltd's weighted average cost of capital.

46 Fast Paced Entertainment Ltd is evaluating the following (independent) investment opportunities:

| Project | Expected return |
|---|---|
| A | 19% |
| B | 16% |
| C | 15% |
| D | 13% |

Fast Paced has determined its optimal capital structure and finance costs to be:

|  | Amount | After-tax cost |
|---|---|---|
| Long-term debt | $1 200 000 | 7.5% |
| Capital notes | $ 800 000 | 14.0% |
| Ordinary share equity | $3 200 000 | 18.6% |
| Total liabilities and equity | $5 200 000 |  |

a Calculate Fast Paced's weighted average cost of capital.

b Which projects will earn a return sufficient to meet the overall costs of financing?

47 Big Oak Furniture Ltd is considering two alternative capital structures:

|  | 50% debt | 75% debt |
|---|---|---|
| **Long-term debt** | | |
| 12% annual interest | $100 000 | $100 000 |
| 14% annual interest | | $ 50 000 |
| **Ordinary shares** | | |
| 100 000 issued | $100 000 | |
| 50 000 issued | | $ 50 000 |
| | $200 000 | $200 000 |

The firm's tax rate is 30%.

a Calculate Big Oak's profit after taxes and earnings per share (EPS) at three alternative levels of operating income (earnings before interest and taxes) for each alternative financing plan, using the following format:

| | 50% debt | | | 75% debt | | |
|---|---|---|---|---|---|---|
| Operating income | $19 000 | $26 000 | $33 000 | $19 000 | $26 000 | $33 000 |
| − Interest expense | | | | | | |
| Profit before tax | | | | | | |
| − Taxes (30%) | | | | | | |
| Profit after taxes | | | | | | |
| Ordinary shares on issue | 100 000 | 100 000 | 100 000 | 50 000 | 50 000 | 50 000 |
| Earnings per share | | | | | | |

b Which capital structure would be preferred at each level of operating income?

c What is the range of EPS over the three levels of operating income for each alternative structure?

d If risk is defined as variability of EPS, which structure is riskier?

48 Several years ago Trentham Ltd issued 10% preference shares at their face value of $100 per share.

a Calculate the cost of preference shares, assuming that they are currently selling for $120 per share.

b Assuming that the preference shares are currently selling for $100 per share, what is the investors' required return?

c If investors in Trentham's preference shares are currently buying and selling the shares for $80 per share, what is the current return the investors are demanding?

d Based on your answers above, what is the relationship between the investors' required return (or the cost of Trentham Ltd's preference shares) and the current value of preference shares?

49  You are working as an investment analyst and have been asked to estimate the cost of ordinary share equity for several companies. The current risk-free rate is 4.5% and the equity market risk premium (MRP) is 5%. The companies and their respective β values are shown below.

| Company | β |
|---|---|
| Trentham Ltd (TL) | 1.00 |
| Avon River Networks (ARN) | 0.60 |
| Tukituki Winery Company (TWC) | 1.40 |

a   What is the expected equity market return?

b   Calculate the cost of ordinary share equity using the capital asset pricing model.

c   Explain the relationship between β and cost of ordinary share equity.

# Investment in long-term assets – Concepts

**CHAPTER 11**

### Learning objectives

By the end of this chapter, you should be able to:
- describe the steps of determining, evaluating and implementing long-term investment projects
- calculate the investment outlay for an investment proposal
- explain the concept of depreciation, and calculate the annual depreciation allowed for taxation purposes on an asset using the diminishing value method
- calculate the annual operating cash flows for an investment proposal
- calculate the tax effects arising from the sale of a long-term asset
- determine the terminal value for an investment proposal.

## Introduction

Previously we have discussed the concept of value and the process by which share prices (values) are set by buyers and sellers in the financial markets. These share prices reflect investors' expectations concerning the future prosperity of the firm. When value is added to a firm, share prices and shareholders' wealth will increase. This has important implications for managers, because if they are able to maximise the value of the firm, then the firm's owners will benefit and the firm will be in a strong position to raise further finance for expansion.

Achievement of the goal of shareholder wealth maximisation will be greatly dependent on the determination, evaluation and implementation of proposed long-term projects. Long-term investments involve substantial financial, physical and human resources that commit the firm to a course of action for a considerable period of time. Usually it is not easy to profitably terminate a poorly performing investment project. Consequently, it is vital that the best available means are used to establish strategic policy guidelines that will be followed with regard to long-term investment evaluation.

The next two chapters will provide an introduction to the financial evaluation of long-term investments. We will begin by discussing the **capital budgeting** process and the measurement of investment cash flows. Then, in the following chapter, we will apply investment evaluation techniques to the cash flows in order to assess the financial acceptability of a proposed investment.

**Capital budgeting**
The process of determining, evaluating and implementing long-term investment opportunities.

## Capital budgeting process

Capital budgeting is the process of determining, evaluating and implementing long-term investment opportunities. In a business situation, the successful implementation of investment projects is critical to the prosperity of the organisation. Long-term investments can include the purchase of fixed assets to replace or expand current facilities, the development of new products, establishing new business ventures, conducting long-range advertising campaigns, and acquiring the shares of another company. Projects such as these may be evaluated through a sequence of the following steps:

- identification of opportunities
- financial evaluation
- qualitative analysis
- investment decision-making
- project implementation
- conducting a post-audit.

The capital budgeting process is initiated when senior managers from production, marketing, finance and other areas bring forward ideas for long-term investment. While several different projects may be proposed, only those that are consistent with the commercial and financial goals of the organisation will be considered further.

Once the feasible alternatives have been identified, the financial evaluation process begins. This starts with a forecast of the benefits and costs of each proposal. Then quantitative techniques are applied to decide on the financial desirability of each project. It is preferable that the evaluation technique used should be consistent with the financial objective of shareholder wealth maximisation.

The next step requires an assessment of qualitative factors relating to the firm, its stakeholders and its environment. Qualitative factors are positive or negative outcomes that cannot be measured easily, but which may affect the decision to accept or reject a project. Qualitative factors may include:

- the firm's ability to better serve its customers
- the effect on competitors
- the reliability of supply of raw materials
- dependence on suppliers
- non-quantifiable environmental effects
- distribution issues
- impacts upon the firm's reputation.

As a result of this quantitative and qualitative analysis, a decision will be made to accept or reject each proposal. A discussion of the evaluation techniques for long-term investments will follow in the next chapter.

Once a decision has been made as to which projects to undertake, the implementation process begins. Financing must be arranged, assets purchased and/or constructed, staffing changes implemented and various plans carried out. The implementation process should be followed by a **post-audit** that examines the actual success of the project. If results are not up to expectations then, if possible, corrective action may be undertaken or, at a minimum, the information should be used to improve future financial decision-making.

For the balance of this chapter, we will examine the financial evaluation process, which involves measuring the costs and benefits of long-term investment proposals.

**Post-audit**
An investigation, after the implementation of a project, to compare the actual and expected financial results.

## Measuring the costs and benefits

The measurement of the costs and benefits of an investment proposal may not be straight-forward. While it may be possible to determine the immediate outlay with a fair degree of accuracy, it may be quite difficult to estimate future costs and benefits.

The costs and benefits of most investment proposals can be classified into one of three categories:

- investment outlay
- operating cash flows
- terminal value.

These categories refer to operating and investment cash flows only, and not to financing cash flows such as interest and dividends. As will be discussed later, financing cash flows are more commonly included in the cost of capital (we calculated weighted average cost of capital in the previous chapter), which is incorporated separately into the analysis. Note that this analysis emphasises cash flows rather than accrual-based revenues and expenses. The analysis is concerned with total results from the project rather than the results as they are recognised for financial reporting purposes.

## Investment outlay

The **investment outlay** is normally considered to be the net cash outflow to be paid out now (at time zero) in order to undertake the project. The most common cash flows included in the investment outlay are the cost of the asset being purchased, and any installation costs.[1]

$$\begin{aligned}&\quad\text{Cost of new asset}\\&+\ \underline{\text{Installation costs}}\\&=\ \text{Investment outlay}\end{aligned}$$

In the case of projects that have potentially negative environmental effects, regulatory **compliance costs** are incurred prior to commencement of the project. These compliance costs are added to the cost of the new asset and include the expenses of undertaking an assessment of the environmental impact and obtaining **resource consents** from government authorities.

**Investment outlay**
The net cash outflow normally paid out at time zero in order to undertake a project.

**Compliance costs**
Costs incurred to comply with laws, regulations or standards.

**Resource consent**
Formal permission by a government authority to allow an individual or an organisation to undertake a specified activity that may otherwise contravene environmental laws.

## Operating cash flows

The operating cash flows are the annual operating revenues less the annual operating costs of the project, calculated on an after-tax basis. Variables such as selling price and sales volume must be estimated to arrive at a forecast of revenue. Costs to be estimated may include the cost of materials, labour, overheads, selling and administrative costs, taxes and other costs.

### Identifying the relevant cash flows

The relevant revenues and costs are those that affect the value of the firm and include direct contractual, legal and regulatory compliance costs incurred by the

---

[1] We have assumed here that we are dealing with an expansion rather than a replacement decision. Note that if the project involves the replacement of old assets, then the after-tax proceeds from selling the old assets should be deducted from the cost of the new asset. Also, to avoid complicating the analysis, changes in net working capital are assumed to be immaterial. Normally an increase in net working capital is added to the investment outlay. Further annual changes in net working capital should be added to the annual operating cash flows. As the investment in net working capital is not normally permanent, a recovery of net working capital is usually added to the terminal value in the last year of the project.

firm in addressing stakeholders' interests. An example of incremental regulatory compliance cash flows lies in the 2008 New Zealand Emissions Trading Scheme (ETS). The world's first comprehensive ETS means producing sectors may incur costs to purchase New Zealand units to pay for their carbon emissions unless they are able to reduce carbon output and use carbon-friendly technologies. Surplus carbon credit permits could potentially be earned through environmentally friendly practices and then traded to earn revenue. For example, landowners of forests planted since 1989 have the opportunity to receive an additional revenue stream through selling New Zealand emission units. However, if the landowner subsequently decides to convert the forest to dairy farming, then the landowner must buy New Zealand emission units to compensate for the resulting carbon emissions from deforestation.

All future cash flow costs and benefits that are directly identifiable with a specific investment proposal are relevant to the analysis. The analysis should only include those **incremental** benefits and costs that result from undertaking the project. They are incremental only if they are directly attributable to the project. If they do not arise as a consequence of the project, then they are irrelevant to the analysis. For example, if overhead expenses such as power and telephone are not expected to change as a result of implementing the project, then they should not be included in the analysis.

Depreciation is not a cash flow, but rather an allocation of the cost of an asset to the period benefiting from its use. The cash outflow relating to the cost of an asset arises at the time that cash is outlaid for its purchase, and not at the time that depreciation is charged. However, for tax-reporting purposes, depreciation is an allowable deduction, thereby reducing the taxes paid by the business. Given that taxes *do* represent an incremental cash flow, we must first calculate the allowable depreciation expense in order to correctly calculate income tax expense.

> **Incremental**
> Directly relevant; additional; over and above the status quo.

### Example 1: Determining incremental cash flows

Technability Ltd is investigating the possibility of acquiring new equipment that would enable it to manufacture land yachts. The equipment would be installed in an unused section of the building. The finance manager is trying to determine whether each of the following should be included as incremental cash flows.

   a  The CEO suggests that a proportion of the annual lease and rates costs equivalent to the building space used should be allocated to the new project.
   b  Technability Ltd will need to hire an additional part-time employee if the project is approved.
   c  Last year Technability Ltd commissioned a marketing plan to determine the potential size and scope of the land-yacht market. The report cost $2 800 and was paid last year.

After deliberating, the finance manager correctly decides that (b) is an incremental cash flow but (a) and (c) are not.

For (a), her reasoning is that Technability Ltd will have to pay the same amount for the lease and rates irrespective of whether the project is approved or not. Consequently, the lease and rates costs are not incremental to the proposed purchase.

For (b), future cash outflows will increase if the acquisition is approved because an extra employee will be hired. Therefore the additional part-time employee's wages are considered to be an incremental cash flow.

With respect to (c), the $2 800 cost incurred last year for a marketing plan relates directly to this project. However, the $2 800 is not a future cash flow; it has already been paid and can't be reversed even if they decide not to manufacture land-yachts. Costs that have already been paid are called **sunk costs**. Incremental cash flows are future cash flows that arise as a consequence of the decision to accept a project. Therefore, from the perspective of Technability's decision today, the $2 800 cost incurred in the past for the marketing report is not an incremental cash flow.

**Sunk costs**
Cash outflows that have occurred and cannot be reversed irrespective of whether the project is accepted or rejected.

## Calculating depreciation expense

Accountants do not deduct the purchase price of long-term assets as expenses on the income statement. Rather, they **capitalise** the purchase as an asset on the balance sheet, because the asset is expected to provide benefits for several years. However, **depreciable assets** have a limited life, so, in order to recognise the consumption of the asset in the income-earning activities of the business, the cost of the asset may be expensed over its useful life. The Income Tax Act 1994 dictates the allowable depreciation methods and rates for income tax purposes. These are relevant to investment decisions as they affect the amount of tax paid by a business, and tax is an incremental cash flow. Note that we are not concerned here with the alternative depreciation methods and rates used in financial accounts for investors and other financial statement users, as they do not affect cash flows.

**Capitalise**
To treat an outlay as a long-term asset on the balance sheet, and not as an expense on the income statement.

**Depreciable asset**
A long-term asset that has a limited life, such as buildings and equipment.

## Depreciation methods and rates

The **depreciable value** of an asset is calculated as the purchase price plus any costs incurred to install the asset. In contrast to financial reporting applications, income tax regulations do not require an adjustment to the depreciable value for any potential salvage value from selling the asset at the end of its useful life.

Two alternative depreciation methods are allowed for income tax purposes: straight-line and diminishing value. Under **straight-line** depreciation, depreciable assets are expensed by equal annual deductions, while the **diminishing-value** method allows for higher depreciation expense in the early years of an asset's life in order to better reflect the economic reality of the decline in usefulness. Most New Zealand firms use the diminishing-value method, as it allows for a greater deferral of income taxes in the early years of an asset's life. In this textbook we will focus on the diminishing-value method.

The Inland Revenue Department publishes in a bulletin the maximum allowable rate of depreciation that can be claimed on each type of asset according to the industry in which it is used. Each year, the amount of depreciation claimed is deducted from the value of the asset. The undepreciated balance is the book value for tax purposes, and is also known as the **adjusted tax value**. Under the diminishing-value method, the amount of depreciation that can be expensed for income tax purposes is calculated as the adjusted tax value of the asset multiplied by the allowable depreciation rate. As a consequence of using this method, the amount of depreciation expense will decline each year.

The example on the next page demonstrates how depreciation is calculated using the diminishing-valve method.

**Depreciable value**
The value of an asset that is to be depreciated. Includes the purchase price plus installation costs.

**Straight-line**
A method of depreciation that expenses an asset by equal annual deductions.

**Diminishing-value (d.v.)**
A method of depreciation that allows for higher depreciation expense in the early years of an asset's life.

**Adjusted tax value**
For income tax purposes, the undepreciated balance of the depreciable value of an asset (also known as an asset's book value for tax purposes).

> **Example 2: Calculating depreciation expense using the diminishing-value method**
>
> Technability Ltd is investigating the possibility of acquiring new equipment that would enable it to manufacture land-yachts. The new equipment will cost $120 000 plus $10 000 in installation costs. The company intends to claim the maximum diminishing-value (d.v.) rate of 20%.
>
> The depreciable value of the asset is calculated as the cost of the new equipment plus the installation costs. The annual depreciation expense is shown in Table 11.1.
>
> | | |
> |---|---|
> | Cost of new equipment | $120 000 |
> | Installation costs | $ 10 000 |
> | Depreciable value | $130 000 |
>
> Table 11.1 **Depreciation expense, Technability Ltd**
>
> | Year | Adjusted tax value, beginning of year | Depreciation expense 20% d.v. | Adjusted tax value, end of year |
> |---|---|---|---|
> | 1 | $130 000 | $26 000 | $104 000 |
> | 2 | $104 000 | $20 800 | $ 83 200 |
> | 3 | $ 83 200 | $16 640 | $ 66 560 |
> | 4 | $ 66 560 | $13 312 | $ 53 248 |
> | 5 | $ 53 248 | $10 650 | $ 42 598 |
>
> For the first year, the allowable depreciation expense is calculated as $130 000 × 20% = $26 000. The depreciable value less the depreciation expense gives the adjusted tax value at the end of year 1, being $130 000 − $26 000 = $104 000. For all subsequent years, depreciation expense is calculated as the opening adjusted tax value multiplied by the d.v. rate of 20%.

### Calculating operating cash flows

The format for calculating the annual operating cash flows is given on the next page. The estimates of operating revenue and operating expenses include all cash flows attributable to the operating activities of the project.

$$
\begin{aligned}
&\quad \text{Operating revenue} \\
&- \text{Operating expenses (excluding depreciation)} \\
&- \text{Depreciation} \\
&= \text{Profit before taxes} \\
&- \text{Taxes} \\
&= \text{Profit after taxes} \\
&+ \text{Depreciation} \\
&= \text{Operating cash flow}
\end{aligned}
$$

Depreciation expense for tax-reporting purposes should be temporarily deducted from operating revenue to arrive at profit before taxes, even though it is a non-cash expense. Recall the point made earlier that depreciation is not a cash flow but it affects taxes, which are a cash item. It is included only because it is an allowable deduction to calculate taxes. Once taxes have been calculated, depreciation must be added back to profit after taxes to arrive at operating cash flow. By this action, depreciation is correctly removed from the analysis, while the tax effects of the deductibility of depreciation have been correctly incorporated.

## Terminal value

It is often difficult to forecast the life of a project under consideration. Many firms set a finite period, such as five years, beyond which the forecast cash flows are considered to be too uncertain to warrant inclusion in the analysis. In such a case, the analysis should not extend beyond this cut-off point. In other circumstances, the project's expected life may be shorter than this cut-off point, in which case the analysis will be for the life of the project.

The **terminal value** is an estimate of the value to the firm of the assets at either the end of the life of the project or at a predetermined cut-off point. It is calculated as the estimated salvage value of the assets, less any tax consequences from the disposal. The terminal value, or after-tax proceeds of selling the new asset, is included as a cash inflow in the final year of the analysis.[2]

> **Terminal value**
> An estimate of the value to the firm of a long-term asset at either the end of the life of the project or at a predetermined cut-off point.

Proceeds, sale of new asset
± Tax on sale of new asset
= Terminal value

**Example 3: Measuring benefits and costs**

Recall our earlier example of a proposal by Technability Ltd to purchase new equipment for manufacturing land-yachts. The new equipment will cost $120 000 plus $10 000 in installation costs. By virtue of the acquisition, cash-based revenues and expenses are expected to increase as follows:

|  | End of year | | | | |
|---|---|---|---|---|---|
|  | 1 | 2 | 3 | 4 | 5 |
| Revenue | $80 000 | $96 000 | $96 000 | $96 000 | $96 000 |
| Expenses | $44 000 | $52 800 | $52 800 | $52 800 | $52 800 |

The expenses exclude depreciation and taxes. Depreciation for tax purposes is calculated at 20% diminishing value. At the end of five years, it is expected that the firm will sell the equipment at a price equal to the adjusted tax value calculated in Table 11.1 as $42 598 at the end of year 5. Tax on the sale of the equipment is expected to be zero. The firm pays tax at a rate of 30% of net profits.

---

[2] We are assuming here that the disposal of all assets arises at the end of the life of the project or at the predetermined cut-off point, and that the assets have been depreciated over this same period. New Zealand tax laws prohibit any deduction for depreciation in the year of the disposal of an asset. However, if we assume that the assets are sold immediately on the first day of the year following the final year of the asset's use, then from a time value of money point of view, that is the same as a disposal on the last day of the year of final use. So from a practical point of view, our treatment here does not differ in any significant manner from that allowed by income tax laws.

The investment outlay, operating cash flows and terminal value attributable to the purchase of new equipment can be summarised as shown in Table 11.2.

Table 11.2  Measuring cash flows, Technability Ltd

### Investment outlay

| | |
|---|---|
| Cost of new equipment | $120 000 |
| Installation costs | $ 10 000 |
| Investment outlay | $130 000 |

### Operating cash flows

| End of year | 1 | 2 | 3 | 4 | 5 |
|---|---|---|---|---|---|
| Revenue | $80 000 | $96 000 | $96 000 | $96 000 | $96 000 |
| – Expenses | $44 000 | $52 800 | $52 800 | $52 800 | $52 800 |
| – Depreciation | $26 000 | $20 800 | $16 640 | $13 312 | $10 650 |
| Profit before tax | $10 000 | $22 400 | $26 560 | $29 888 | $32 550 |
| – Taxes (30%) | $ 3 000 | $ 6 720 | $ 7 968 | $ 8 966 | $ 9 765 |
| Profit after tax | $ 7 000 | $15 680 | $18 592 | $20 922 | $22 785 |
| + Depreciation | $26 000 | $20 800 | $16 640 | $13 312 | $10 650 |
| Operating cash flow | $33 000 | $36 480 | $35 232 | $34 234 | $33 435 |

### Terminal value

| | |
|---|---|
| Proceeds on sale of new equipment, year 5 | $42 598 |
| Tax on sale of new equipment | –$ 0 |
| Terminal value | $42 598 |

Net cash flow is calculated as the total of the various cash flows arising for each year. The time-zero net cash flow is usually negative due to the investment outlay, while the other years' net cash flows are usually positive, due to net benefits received. A summary of the net cash flows attributable to the acquisition of the new equipment is presented in Table 11.3.

Table 11.3  Summary of net cash flows for new equipment, Technability Ltd

| End of year | Investment outlay | Operating cash flow | Terminal value | Net cash flow |
|---|---|---|---|---|
| 0 | –$130 000 | | | –$130 000 |
| 1 | | $33 000 | | $ 33 000 |
| 2 | | $36 480 | | $ 36 480 |
| 3 | | $35 232 | | $ 35 232 |
| 4 | | $34 234 | | $ 34 234 |
| 5 | | $33 435 | $42 598 | $ 76 033 |

## Sale of an asset: Tax effects

There may be tax consequences arising from the sale of a depreciable asset. For income tax purposes, any loss on disposal may be written-off as an expense, while a gain on sale is included in income for the year. Note that a loss on disposal and a gain on sale are not cash flows, and therefore for investment evaluation purposes they are not directly relevant to the analysis. However, they do affect a firm's income tax payment, resulting in a tax saving or additional tax to pay, and these represent incremental cash flows that are indeed relevant to an analysis.

The gain or loss upon the sale of an asset is calculated as the proceeds from the sale of the asset minus the adjusted tax value.

$$\begin{aligned} & \text{Proceeds, sale of new asset} \\ - \ & \underline{\text{Adjusted tax value, new asset}} \\ = \ & \text{Gain(loss) on sale of new asset} \end{aligned}$$

The calculation of a gain on sale can be complicated by the existence of capital gains. A capital gain arises when an asset is disposed of for proceeds greater than its cost. For depreciable assets, this circumstance arises infrequently, as their values more commonly decrease over time. However, in a highly inflationary environment (as in New Zealand in the 1970s and 1980s), it is possible for depreciable assets to rise rather than decline in value. In New Zealand, capital gains are not normally taxable, so if a depreciable asset is sold for greater than its cost, the capital gain element is excluded from the calculation of gain on sale. To do this, we simply revise our formula for the calculation of a gain on sale by taking the lower of (1) the proceeds or (2) the cost of the new asset, and deducting the adjusted tax value.

$$\begin{aligned} & \text{Take the lower of:} \\ & \quad \text{(1) Proceeds, sale of new asset, or} \\ & \quad \text{(2) Cost, new asset} \\ \textit{Deduct:} \ & \underline{\text{Adjusted tax value, new asset}} \\ = \ & \text{Gain on sale of new asset} \end{aligned}$$

Next we calculate the tax implications which arise from the gain or loss by multiplying the respective amount by the tax rate (t). A gain on sale implies that excessive depreciation was claimed; consequently it results in extra tax to pay.

$$\text{Tax to pay} = \text{Gain on sale of new asset} \times t$$

A loss on sale indicates that the depreciation claimed on the tax return was insufficient. An additional expense is allowed equal to the loss on sale, resulting in a tax benefit.

$$\text{Tax savings} = \text{Loss on sale of new asset} \times t$$

The example on the following pages works through calculations of terminal value for our fictitious company Technability Ltd.

### Example 4: Terminal value, Technability Ltd

**1 Sale of an asset at the adjusted tax value**

In the previous example of Technability Ltd, we assumed that the new equipment was to be disposed of at the end of year 5 for proceeds equal to the adjusted tax value calculated in Table 11.1 as $42 598. Whenever assets are sold for a price equal to the adjusted tax value, there will be no gain or loss on sale, and consequently there will be no income tax implications.

| | |
|---|---|
| Proceeds, sale of new asset | $42 598 |
| Adjusted tax value, new asset | $42 598 |
| Gain (loss) on sale of new asset | $ 0 |

In this case the terminal value is expected to be equal to the sales proceeds of $42 598.

| | |
|---|---|
| Proceeds, sale of new asset | $42 598 |
| Tax on sale of new asset | –$ 0 |
| Terminal value | $42 598 |

**2 Sale of an asset for greater than the adjusted tax value**

Now let us revise our estimate of the year 5 proceeds on disposal of the new equipment, assuming sales proceeds are $50 000. In this case a gain on sale of $7 402 results. In effect, the company has claimed too much depreciation ($7 402), and the tax department will require the excessive depreciation to be added back into income as a gain on sale. Assuming a tax rate of 30%, extra tax of $2 221 is due to be paid.

| | |
|---|---|
| Proceeds, sale of new asset | $50 000 |
| Adjusted tax value, new asset | $42 598 |
| Gain (loss) on sale of new asset | $ 7 402 |
| Tax at 30% | × 0.30 |
| Tax to pay | $ 2 221 |

Assuming that the equipment is sold for $50 000, we can now recalculate the terminal value for the Technability investment as the proceeds minus the tax to pay, or $47 779.

| | |
|---|---|
| Proceeds, sale of new asset | $50 000 |
| Tax on sale of new asset | – $ 2 221 |
| Terminal value | $47 779 |

## 3 Sale of an asset for greater than its cost

Let us now assume that the equipment is expected to be sold at the end of year 5 for $140 000, which is greater than the time-zero cost of $130 000. In this case there is a non-taxable capital gain of $10 000 ($140 000 − $130 000). To correctly calculate the gain on sale we use the alternative formula.

| | | | |
|---|---|---|---|
| Take the lower of: | | | |
| | (1) Proceeds, sale of new asset, or | $140 000 | |
| | (2) Cost, new asset | $130 000* | $130 000* |
| Deduct: | Adjusted tax value, new asset | | −$ 42 598 |
| Gain on sale of new asset | | | $ 87 402 |
| Tax at 30% | | | × 0.30 |
| Tax to pay | | | $ 26 221 |

In this case the entire amount of depreciation taken to date ($87 402) must be added back into income in the year of sale. However, the difference between the proceeds from the sale of the asset and its initial purchase price ($140 000 − $130 000) is not subject to tax, as it represents a non-taxable capital gain. The result is a tax liability of $26 221.

The terminal value will now be the after-tax proceeds from the sale of the asset, or $113 779.

| | |
|---|---|
| Proceeds, sale of new asset | $140 000 |
| Tax on sale of new asset | −$ 26 221 |
| Terminal value | $113 779 |

## 4 Sale of an asset for less than its adjusted tax value

Now assume that the year 5 proceeds on disposal of the new equipment are expected to be only $20 000. In this case a loss on sale of $22 598 results. This means that the company has claimed insufficient depreciation expense, and the tax department allows the company to deduct the loss from ordinary operating income. This results in tax savings of $6 779.

| | |
|---|---|
| Proceeds, sale of new asset | $20 000 |
| Adjusted tax value, new asset | $42 598 |
| Loss on sale of new asset | $22 598 |
| Tax at 30% | × 0.30 |
| Tax savings | $ 6 779 |

Assuming that the equipment is expected to be sold for $20 000, we can now recalculate the terminal value for the Technability investment as the proceeds plus the tax savings, or $26 779.

| | |
|---|---|
| Proceeds, sale of new asset | $20 000 |
| Tax savings on sale of new asset | + $ 6 779 |
| Terminal value | $26 779 |

## Conclusion

Long-term investment decisions are critical for most organisations. They involve a major commitment of resources and determine a course of action for a considerable time. Consequently, it is essential that managers use the best available means of selecting appropriate investments.

The process of determining, evaluating and implementing long-term investment opportunities is called capital budgeting. The financial evaluation of long-term investments involves measuring the benefits and costs of each proposal, and then applying quantitative techniques to select the acceptable projects that will add the most value to the firm. The benefits and costs are classified into three categories:

- investment outlay
- operating cash flows
- terminal value.

One or more quantitative techniques are then applied to assist in the decision as to whether to accept or reject each project. The techniques used to evaluate investment proposals will be the subject of the next chapter.

Chapter 11: Investments in long-term assets – Concepts **267**

**SELF-TEST QUESTION**

Eco-Tours Ltd is a new eco-tourism business taking mostly overseas visitors on bicycle tours throughout New Zealand. The owner-manager of Eco-Tours Ltd has gathered the following financial information regarding the potential purchase of a fleet of mountain bikes. The initial outlay will be $80 000. Revenues are expected to be $50 000 in year 1, $80 000 in year 2 and $100 000 in year 3. Annual expenses relevant to the decision will be equal to 50% of sales for direct costs and $8 000 per year for selling and administration. The new fleet will be depreciated at 12.5% diminishing value. The bicycles are expected to be sold at the end of three years for $4 000, and the firm pays tax at a rate of 30% of net profits.

a   Calculate the depreciation expense and adjusted tax value for the new fleet for each of the three years.
b   Determine the investment outlay, operating cash flows and terminal value attributable to the proposed project.
c   Prepare a summary of the net cash flows from years 0–3.

**ANSWER TO SELF-TEST QUESTION**

a   Depreciation schedule

| Year | Adjusted tax value, beginning of year | Depreciation expense 12.5% d.v. | Adjusted tax value, end of year |
|---|---|---|---|
| 1 | $80 000 | $10 000 | $70 000 |
| 2 | $70 000 | $ 8 750 | $61 250 |
| 3 | $61 250 | $ 7 656 | $53 594 |

b   Investment outlay, time zero            $80 000

| Operating cash flows | | | |
|---|---|---|---|
| End of year | 1 | 2 | 3 |
| Revenue | $50 000 | $80 000 | $100 000 |
| Direct costs (50% revenue) | –$25 000 | –$40 000 | –$ 50 000 |
| Selling & administration | –$ 8 000 | –$ 8 000 | –$ 8 000 |
| Profit before depreciation & tax | $17 000 | $32 000 | $ 42 000 |
| *Less*: Depreciation | $10 000 | $ 8 750 | $ 7 656 |
| Profit before tax | $ 7 000 | $23 250 | $ 34 344 |
| Taxes 30% | $ 2 100 | $ 6 975 | $ 10 303 |
| Profit after tax | $ 4 900 | $16 275 | $ 24 041 |
| *Add back*: Depreciation | $10 000 | $ 8 750 | $ 7 656 |
| Operating cash flow | $14 900 | $25 025 | $ 31 697 |

**Terminal value**

| | |
|---|---|
| Sales proceeds | $ 4 000 |
| – Adjusted tax value | $53 594 |
| Loss on sale | $49 594 |
| Tax at 30% | × 0.30 |
| Tax savings | $14 878 |
| | |
| Sales proceeds | $ 4 000 |
| Tax savings | $14 878 |
| Terminal value | $18 878 |

**c Summary of net cash flows**

| End of year | Investment outlay | Operating cash flow | Terminal value | Net cash flow |
|---|---|---|---|---|
| 0 | –$80 000 | | | –$80 000 |
| 1 | | $14 900 | | $14 900 |
| 2 | | $25 025 | | $25 025 |
| 3 | | $31 697 | $18 878 | $50 575 |

## QUESTIONS AND PROBLEMS

1. Describe how stakeholders' interests may be considered in long-term investment decision-making.

2. Describe the steps of determining, evaluating and implementing long-term investment opportunities.

3. Is interest expense included in operating expenses for the purpose of calculating operating cash flow? Explain.

4. What is *depreciation expense*? Why is it deducted and then added back to arrive at operating cash flow? Does this not result in a nil effect?

5. Why should the financial evaluation of long-term investments consider only incremental benefits and costs?

6. For the financial evaluation of long-term investments, it is necessary to calculate the gain or loss upon the disposal of assets, and yet it is not correct to include the gain or loss in the net operating cash flows. Explain why this is so.

7. Conrad Entertainment Ltd has purchased new gaming equipment at a cost of $90 000. Installation costs will be $10 000. Calculate the allowable depreciation expense for tax purposes for each of the next four years if the depreciation rate is 33% diminishing value.

8. Exotic Foods Café is considering the purchase of new food-processing equipment. The initial outlay will cost $60 000 and installation costs will total $6 000. Sales are expected to increase by $20 000 per year for four years as a result of the acquisition. The purchase will not affect Exotic's wages expense, which will remain unchanged at $45 000 per year; power costs will increase by $4 000 per year; and rent expense will be unchanged at $50 000 per year. Assume that all annual increases are non-cumulative and that the new equipment will be depreciated at 20% diminishing value. The equipment is expected to be sold at the end of year 4 at a price equal to the year 4 adjusted tax value. The firm pays tax at a rate of 30% of net profits.

    a. Identify those cash flows that are not incremental to the investment proposal under consideration.
    b. Determine the investment outlay for the purchase of new equipment.
    c. Calculate the incremental operating cash flows relevant to the proposed purchase.
    d. Determine the terminal value attributable to the proposed acquisition.

9. Calculate the terminal value for an investment decision when, at the end of the useful life of the asset the expected salvage value is nil, the adjusted tax value is $12 000, and the tax rate is 30%. The original purchase cost of the asset was $30 000.

10. Calculate the terminal value in each of the following circumstances when, at the end of the useful life of the asset, the adjusted tax value is $46 000 and the tax rate is 30%. The original purchase cost of the asset was $58 000.

    a. The asset is sold for $46 000.
    b. The asset is sold for $40 000.
    c. The asset is sold for $55 000.
    d. The asset is sold for $60 000.

11 Miller International Ltd is considering the purchase of new equipment at a cost of $480 000 plus installation of $20 000. There will be no increase in revenue if the equipment is purchased, but operating costs will decrease by $100 000 per year for the five-year life of the equipment. Assume that all annual savings are non-cumulative and that the new equipment will be depreciated at 12.5% diminishing value as per the following schedule:

|  | End of year | | | | |
|---|---|---|---|---|---|
|  | 1 | 2 | 3 | 4 | 5 |
| Depreciation | $62 500 | $54 688 | $47 852 | $41 870 | $36 636 |

At the end of five years, it is expected that the equipment will be sold for $200 000, although the adjusted tax value will be $256 454. The firm's tax rate is 30%.

Calculate the investment outlay, operating cash flows and terminal value attributable to the purchase of the new equipment.

12 Secura-T Systems Ltd is evaluating the possibility of manufacturing a new security alarm system. Company policy dictates that a maximum cut-off point of six years is used for the evaluation of all proposed projects. New manufacturing equipment would be purchased at a cost of $230 000. Equipment modifications would cost another $20 000. As a result of the acquisition, sales are expected to increase by $75 000 in year 1, $150 000 in year 2, and $300 000 in each of years 3 to 6. Assume that all annual increases are non-cumulative. The cost of goods sold is expected to be 60% of the new sales, and selling and administrative expenses for the new system will be 10% of the new sales. Depreciation expense will be at 12.5% diminishing value. The company expects to dispose of the equipment at the end of year 6 for $120 000. The company tax rate is 30%.

   a  Calculate the investment outlay, operating cash flows and terminal value attributable to the proposed project.

   b  Prepare a summary of the net cash flows from years 0–6.

# Investment in long-term assets – Evaluation techniques

**CHAPTER 12**

## Learning objectives

By the end of this chapter, you should be able to:

- explain the four techniques of investment evaluation – accounting return on investment (AROI), payback period, net present value (NPV), and internal rate of return (IRR) – assess their advantages and disadvantages, and use them to determine the acceptability of proposed investment projects
- explain how to apply the NPV technique when capital rationing is present
- discuss the treatment of inflation in the context of capital budgeting
- describe sensitivity analysis and risk-adjusted required returns, and how they apply to capital budgeting problems.

## Introduction

In the last chapter we introduced the concept of capital budgeting, which we defined as the process of determining, evaluating and implementing long-term investment opportunities. We also determined how to measure the relevant cash flows for an investment evaluation decision, being the investment outlay, the operating cash flows, and the terminal value. We will now consider various quantitative techniques of investment evaluation that will help a firm to determine the acceptability of a proposed project.

You should recall that the objective of financial management is to maximise the wealth of the firm's owners. It is therefore preferable to use investment evaluation techniques that will help us achieve this objective.

We will commence our discussion with the assumption that all proposed investment projects are of equal risk. However, we will later relax this assumption and examine two alternative approaches for dealing with risk.

## Techniques of investment evaluation

Once the benefits and costs of a project have been estimated, the proposal must be evaluated to assess its financial acceptability in view of the firm's selection criteria. The four techniques of investment evaluation that are most commonly used in capital budgeting are:

- accounting return on investment
- payback period
- net present value
- internal rate of return.

### Accounting return on investment

**Accounting return on investment (AROI)**
The profit from an investment as a percentage of the investment outlay.

The **accounting return on investment** (AROI) is a measure of the profit from an investment as a percentage of the dollars invested. It is an accounting-based measure that is commonly used to measure the annual performance of an investment or a business unit (such as a department, a division or a firm). However, it is also used to assess the desirability of proposed projects.

AROI can be measured in many different ways. To measure annual performance it may be calculated as follows:

$$\text{Annual AROI} = \frac{\text{Profit after taxes}}{\text{Investment outlay}} \qquad \textit{Equation 12.1}$$

A formula such as Equation 12.1 shown above would give a different AROI for each year of a proposed project, which is not particularly useful for comparing with a required rate of return over the life of the project. Consequently, an alternative formula that averages the annual profits is more useful:

$$\text{Average AROI} = \frac{\text{Average profit after taxes}}{\text{Investment outlay}} \qquad \textit{Equation 12.2}$$

It is necessary for the firm to define a minimum required average AROI. The proposal is then accepted if the forecast average AROI is greater than or equal to the minimum required average AROI.

#### Example 1: Evaluating AROI

Using the information for Technability Ltd presented in Table 11.2 of the last chapter, the annual AROI and average AROI for the proposed equipment purchase can be calculated. In Table 12.1, the annual AROI is calculated for each year by dividing the profit after tax by the investment outlay.

**Table 12.1** The calculation of AROI, Technability Ltd

|  | End of year | | | | |
| --- | --- | --- | --- | --- | --- |
|  | 1 | 2 | 3 | 4 | 5 |
| Revenue | $ 80 000 | $96 000 | $96 000 | $96 000 | $96 000 |
| – Expenses | $ 44 000 | $52 800 | $52 800 | $52 800 | $52 800 |
| – Depreciation | $ 26 000 | $20 800 | $16 640 | $13 312 | $10 650 |
| Profit before tax | $ 10 000 | $22 400 | $26 560 | $29 888 | $32 550 |
| – Tax at 30% | $ 3 000 | $ 6 720 | $ 7 968 | $ 8 966 | $ 9 765 |
| (1) Profit after tax | $ 7 000 | $15 680 | $18 592 | $20 922 | $22 785 |
| (2) Investment outlay | $130 000 | | | | |
| Annual AROI (1)/(2) | 5.4% | 12.1% | 14.3% | 16.1% | 17.5% |

The average AROI is calculated by finding the average of profits after taxes from years 1 to 5, and then dividing by the investment outlay.

$$\text{Average profit} = \frac{\$7\,000 + \$15\,680 + \$18\,592 + \$20\,922 + \$22\,785}{5} = \$16\,996$$

$$\text{Average AROI} = \frac{\$16\,996}{\$130\,000} = 13.1\%$$

If Technability Ltd needs a minimum required average AROI of 12% on proposed investments, then the equipment purchase would be accepted.

### Advantages

The AROI technique has some advantages.
- It is simple to calculate.
- It uses accounting profit concepts that are familiar to most managers.
- It is useful in performance evaluation for evaluating whether actual annual returns live up to previous forecasts.

### Disadvantages

However, AROI has several disadvantages.
- It uses accounting data, not cash flows. Recall from Chapter 8 that cash flows provide a more relevant measure because they reflect owners' returns, they can be measured more objectively, and they determine liquidity and solvency.
- It fails to consider the time value of money. Cash flows arising in different time periods cannot be compared directly, as earlier cash flows are preferred over later cash flows. Neither the annual AROI nor the average AROI consider this preference.
- The **criterion** of a minimum required average AROI is arbitrary and is not consistent with the firm's financial goal of owner wealth maximisation. There are no guidelines on how to set an optimal average AROI that will achieve owner wealth maximisation.

> **Criterion**
> A decision rule used to evaluate the acceptability of a proposed investment.

## Payback period

The **payback period** is the number of years to recover an investment outlay. It represents the length of time it will take for the money spent on the investment outlay to be paid back from the project cash flows. The payback period is calculated by accumulating the annual net cash flows for the investment. The payback period is found when the cumulative cash flow is equal to zero.

The example on the next page calculates the payback period for Technability Ltd.

> **Payback period**
> The number of years to recover, through operating cash flows, the money spent for an investment outlay.

> ### Example 2: Calculating the payback period
>
> Table 11.3 from the last chapter summarised the net cash flows for the proposed equipment purchase by Technability Ltd. This table is reproduced here as Table 12.2. We can see that the investment outlay of $130 000 is recovered through the receipt of operating cash flows. Table 12.3 reveals that it is sometime during year 4, when the cumulative cash flow is equal to zero, that the investment outlay of $130 000 is fully recovered.
>
> Some firms have a policy that in order to be accepted, a project must pay back the investment outlay within a maximum payback period. So, if Technability Ltd has a policy of only accepting projects with a payback period of three years or less, then the proposed equipment purchase would be rejected as the equipment investment is recovered sometime during year 4.
>
> Table 12.2 Summary of net cash flows for new equipment, Technability Ltd
>
> | End of year | Investment outlay | Operating cash flow | Terminal value | Net cash flow |
> |---|---|---|---|---|
> | 0 | −$130 000 | | | −$130 000 |
> | 1 | | $33 000 | | $ 33 000 |
> | 2 | | $36 480 | | $ 36 480 |
> | 3 | | $35 232 | | $ 35 232 |
> | 4 | | $34 234 | | $ 34 234 |
> | 5 | | $33 435 | $42 598 | $ 76 033 |
>
> Table 12.3 Payback period for new equipment, Technability Ltd
>
> | End of year | Net cash flow | Cumulative cash flow |
> |---|---|---|
> | 0 | −$130 000 | −$130 000 |
> | 1 | $ 33 000 | −$ 97 000 |
> | 2 | $ 36 480 | −$ 60 520 |
> | 3 | $ 35 232 | −$ 25 288 |
> | 4 | $ 34 234 | +$ 8 946 |
> | 5 | $ 76 033 | +$ 84 979 |
>
> If we make the assumption that the operating cash flows are earned consistently throughout each year, then we can refine our estimate further to identify the point during the year at which the equipment investment is recovered. We know from Table 12.3 that it is at some point after the end of year 3 but before the end of year 4. The fraction of a year is calculated by dividing the last negative cumulative cash flow by the amount recovered from cash flows in the following year. Based on the data from Table 12.3, the payback period is now estimated as:
>
> $$3 \text{ years} + \frac{\$25\,288}{\$34\,234} = 3.7 \text{ years}$$

## Advantages

The payback period is widely used for the following reasons.

- It uses cash flows rather than accounting profits. Cash flows can be objectively calculated, whereas profits are determined by accounting policies.
- It is simple to calculate.
- It provides a measure of risk exposure. The longer the time to recovery of the investment outlay, the riskier the project. The estimates of distant cash flows are more uncertain due to unforeseen changes in economic or environmental factors, and are therefore subject to more risk. The longer the payback period, the higher the risk.

## Disadvantages

Nevertheless, the payback period has several disadvantages.

- It fails to explicitly consider the time value of money. As we saw earlier, cash flows arising in different time periods cannot be compared directly, as earlier cash flows are preferred over later cash flows. Yet the payback technique aggregates the cash flows, ignoring the fact that the purchasing power is lower for distant cash flows.
- It ignores cash flows that arise after the payback period. Two alternative investment proposals may have identical payback periods, and yet one may return considerably higher cash flows after the payback period than the other.
- The criterion of a maximum payback period is arbitrary and is not consistent with the firm's goal of owner wealth maximisation. There are no guidelines on how to set an optimal payback period that will achieve owner wealth maximisation.

Despite these disadvantages, the payback period is a useful technique when used in conjunction with more sophisticated techniques such as those described below.

## Net present value

The **net present value (NPV)** is the present value of all cash flows pertaining to a project, including the investment outlay which will normally be a negative value. The technique incorporates the time value of money through the present value formula introduced earlier in this book:

$$\text{NPV} = C_0 + \sum_{t=1}^{n} \frac{C_t}{(1+r)^t} \qquad \text{Equation 12.3}$$

> **Net present value (NPV)**
> The present value of all cash flows pertaining to a project minus the investment outlay. Measures the value added to a firm as a result of undertaking a project.

where  $C_0$ = investment outlay, time zero
  $C_t$ = expected cash flow, time t
  r = cost of capital
  t = the period in which a cash flow arises
  n = life of the project.

The NPV equation finds the present value of the forecast net operating cash flows, and deducts from this the investment outlay at time zero. The numerator of the equation includes all operating cash flows. Financing costs, being the required returns of both lenders and owners, are incorporated in the cost of capital as the discount rate in the denominator. Consequently, the NPV equation measures the value added after meeting all relevant operating and financing costs.

The NPV indicates the value in current dollar terms that will be added to the firm as a result of undertaking a project. When value is added to the firm, share prices should increase. Consequently, use of the NPV techniques is consistent with the financial management goal of owner wealth maximisation.

The NPV decision criterion for whether to accept or reject a project can be stated as:

**If NPV ≥ 0, accept the project. Otherwise reject.**

A positive or zero NPV indicates that the project should be accepted, whereas a negative NPV indicates that the project should be rejected.

### Example 3: Determining NPV

Continuing our example of the purchase of new equipment by Technability Ltd, the net cash flows from the last column of Table 12.2 are reproduced below. Assuming that the firm has a cost of capital of 12%, what is the NPV of the proposed purchase?

| End of year | Net cash flow |
|---|---|
| 0 | –$130 000 |
| 1 | $ 33 000 |
| 2 | $ 36 480 |
| 3 | $ 35 232 |
| 4 | $ 34 234 |
| 5 | $ 76 033 |

The NPV of the proposed purchase is calculated as follows:

$$NPV = C_0 + \sum_{t=1}^{n} \frac{C_t}{(1+r)^t}$$

$$NPV = -\$130\,000 + \frac{\$33\,000}{(1+0.12)^1} + \frac{\$36\,480}{(1+0.12)^2} + \frac{\$35\,232}{(1+0.12)^3} + \frac{\$34\,234}{(1+0.12)^4} + \frac{\$76\,033}{(1+0.12)^5}$$

$$= -\$130\,000 + \$29\,464 + \$29\,082 + \$25\,077 + \$21\,756 + \$43\,143$$

$$= \$18\,523$$

The NPV is positive, suggesting the equipment should be purchased, as it will add $18 523 to the value of the firm after covering all operating and financing charges.

### Advantages

Conceptually, the NPV technique is preferred over other techniques for the following reasons.

- It uses cash flows rather than accounting profits. Cash flows can be calculated objectively, whereas profits are determined by accounting policies.
- It takes account of the time value of money. The cash flows are discounted at the cost of capital, which includes a component to compensate investors for the time value of money.

- Risk is considered through the cost of capital. The cost of capital includes a risk premium to reward investors for the amount of risk undertaken.
- It is consistent with the financial objective of owner wealth maximisation. NPV measures the present dollar value added to the firm as a result of undertaking a project. When value is added, investors will benefit by increases in share prices or dividend income.

### Disadvantages

The NPV technique has two disadvantages.

- Some managers are reluctant to use the NPV technique because the results are not expressed in percentage terms, and some managers are more comfortable with techniques that yield rates of return.
- The NPV technique requires an estimate of the organisation's cost of capital. The calculation of cost of capital is not straight-forward for public-sector organisations and is not well understood by small-business managers. Furthermore, if forecasts fail to consider future increases in interest rates, then the cost of capital may be understated and the NPV of projects could be overstated.

Note that in the previous example, the project was discounted at the firm's cost of capital. Recall from Chapter 10 that the weighted average cost of capital represents the average cost of financing the firm's assets. This is the rate that is most frequently used as the discount rate. A simplified example may help to clarify why.

#### Example 4: Using WACC as the discount rate

A company is considering the purchase of new equipment that will cost $100. The only benefit from the purchase will arise in year 1, when the operating cash flow will be $110. The firm is financed 100% with ordinary-share equity, and shareholders require a return of 10% on average-risk investments. Ignoring depreciation and taxes, should the new equipment be purchased? How much value will be added to the firm as a result of undertaking this new investment?

If we first examine this problem intuitively, ignoring NPV, we can conclude that this project will earn sufficient profits to exactly satisfy shareholders' required returns, but will add no further value to the firm.

| | |
|---|---|
| Operating cash flow received | $110 |
| Cost of equipment | − $100 |
| Net profit | $ 10 |
| Financing costs ($100 × 10%) | − $ 10 |
| Value added to the firm | $ 0 |

The operating cash flow of $110 received, less the cost of the equipment of $100, will generate a net profit of $10. Shareholders have funded this project, as the firm is financed 100% with equity. Their required return on investment is 10% or $10 ($100 invested × 10%), so the $10 profit exactly meets their required return. Irrespective of whether the profit is retained or paid out as dividends, the shareholders will benefit. As the purchase of equipment will satisfy shareholders' required returns, the project should be undertaken. Nevertheless, no further value will be added to the firm over and above these financing costs.

**Economic value added (EVA)**
An alternative performance measure that takes into account cash flows and the total cost of debt and equity in order to measure annual value added.

The above method of measuring value added is similar to an annual performance evaluation tool called **economic value added (EVA)**, a registered trademark of Stern Stewart & Co. EVA has become popular among large companies worldwide as it is a performance measure that takes into account the total cost of capital – including the cost of debt and equity. EVA is used as an alternative to the conventional profit figure in the income statement, as it more closely reflects the goal of shareholders' wealth maximisation. A full discussion of EVA is beyond the scope of this book, but its acceptance by many businesses makes it an important topic for more advanced finance study.

The NPV technique gives the same answer as that intuitively concluded above:

$$NPV = C_0 + \sum_{t=1}^{n} \frac{C_t}{(1+r)^t}$$

$$= -\$100 + \frac{\$110}{(1+0.10)^1} = \$0$$

The difference between the two sets of calculations is that it is much easier to handle multi-period calculations and complex financing situations using NPV than using our intuitive technique. The NPV technique allows for a mixture of debt and equity in the capital structure by discounting the project cash flows at the weighted average cost of capital. Recall that the weighted average cost of capital takes into account the after-tax interest return required by debt holders, as well as the required return of equity holders. But the interpretation of results is the same. Accept the project, as it will earn sufficient profits to meet all costs including financing costs. However, the NPV of zero indicates that no additional value will be added to the firm.

## Assumptions of the weighted average cost of capital

The NPV developed above could be restated as follows:

$$NPV = \sum_{t=1}^{n} \frac{\text{Cash flows to debt and equity holders}}{\text{Required returns of debt and equity holders}} - \text{Funds invested by debt and equity holders} \quad \textit{Equation 12.4}$$

By using operating cash flows in the numerator, the weighted average cost of capital (WACC) as the discount rate, and total funds invested at time zero, the conventional NPV technique measures the returns to all long-term sources of financing. By maximising the value of debt and equity, we maximise the value of the firm.

However, it is important to note that the WACC assumes that the capital structure of the firm will remain constant. This means that the proportions of debt and equity used to finance the firm overall will not change as a result of undertaking the proposal. In a large firm where there are several projects routinely under consideration, the particular financing method for the accepted projects is unlikely to materially change the firm's capital structure. Consequently, for a large firm it is generally appropriate to discount all projects at an overall cost of capital that reflects the overall target proportions of debt and equity financing employed by the firm.

In contrast, for a small firm there may be very few projects under consideration, and when the accepted projects are undertaken the act of raising new financing may cause significant deviations in the capital structure of the firm.

> **Example 5: Changing capital structure**
>
> Assume that a small manufacturing firm is financed with 20% debt and 80% equity. The firm plans to purchase some new machinery that is to be financed with new debt. This will cause the capital structure to change to 40% debt and 60% equity. The loan will be paid off over a five-year period. The debt–equity ratio will therefore change every year over the next five years as the debt is paid off. Given that the capital structure will change over time, the WACC is not suitable as the discount rate to assess the proposed project.

## NPV(ER)

When the capital structure of a firm is expected to change materially over time as a result of accepting projects, it is necessary to undertake a slightly different approach to calculate the NPV. This approach, called the **equity residual NPV**, or **NPV(ER)**, requires modifications to the initial investment, the numerator and the denominator of the conventional NPV.

$$\text{NPV(ER)} = \sum_{t=1}^{n} \frac{\text{Cash flows to equity holders}}{\text{Required return of equity holders}} - \text{Funds invested by equity holders} \qquad \textit{Equation 12.5}$$

> **Equity residual net present value, NPV(ER)**
> An alternative calculation of NPV, measuring the present value of equity cash flows pertaining to a project, minus the equity investment outlay.

The NPV(ER) measures the return to equity holders. The numerator represents cash flows to equity holders by taking the net operating cash flows and deducting any principal and interest payments on debt. The cash flows are then discounted solely at the return to equity holders. The relevant investment outlay is that portion of the purchase price that is to be funded by equity. In contrast to the conventional NPV that maximises the value of the firm, the NPV(ER) maximises the value of shareholders' equity. The NPV(ER) is a useful technique for small businesses and real estate investments when the proportion of debt may change considerably over time. We will look at applying the NPV(ER) technique to evaluate property investments in Chapter 13.

## Internal rate of return

The **internal rate of return (IRR)** is the percentage return that discounts all cash flows from a project, including the investment outlay, to zero. In other words, it is the discount rate that makes the NPV of an investment equal to zero. It is calculated as follows:

$$0 = C_0 + \sum_{t=1}^{n} \frac{C_t}{(1 + \text{IRR})^t} \qquad \textit{Equation 12.6}$$

> **Internal rate of return (IRR)**
> The percentage return that discounts all cash flows from a project, including the investment outlay, to zero.

where  $C_0$ = investment outlay, time zero
$C_t$ = expected cash flow, time t
IRR = the discount rate where NPV = 0
t = the period in which a cash flow arises
n = life of the project.

The internal rate of return is the expected percentage return to be earned from a project, taking into account the time value of money. The decision criterion used to assess whether a project should be accepted can be stated as:

**If IRR ≥ r, accept the project. Otherwise reject.**

If the IRR is greater than the cost of capital (r) then the project should be accepted, as it will add value to the firm. If the IRR is equal to r, then the project should be accepted as it will satisfy investors' required rates of return, although no additional value will be added to the firm. If the IRR is less than r, then the project should be rejected as it will not return enough to compensate the suppliers of capital at their respective required rates of return.

### Example 6: Determining the IRR using Excel, Technability Ltd

Manually calculating IRR is a laborious trial-and-error process. As such, in practice a project's IRR is calculated using Excel. Continuing our illustration of the purchase of new equipment by Technability Ltd, the net cash flows from the last column of Table 12.2 are reproduced below. Cell B10 shows the IRR is 16.9%, while cell B11 displays the Excel formula used to calculate the IRR. As the rate of return of 16.9% is greater than the cost of capital at 12%, the project should be accepted.

|    | A | B |
|----|---|---|
| 1  |   |   |
| 2  | End of Year | Net Cash Flow |
| 3  | 0 | -$130 000 |
| 4  | 1 | $33 000 |
| 5  | 2 | $36 480 |
| 6  | 3 | $35 232 |
| 7  | 4 | $34 234 |
| 8  | 5 | $76 033 |
| 9  |   |   |
| 10 | IRR | 16.9% |
| 11 | Formula used | =IRR(B3:B8) |

Note that an error will typically occur when the initial investment in year 0 is shown as a positive rather than a negative cash flow. In this case Excel will return an error code of #NUM!. It is important to remember that cash outflows must be shown as negative numbers in order for the Excel IRR formula to work correctly.

### Advantages

The advantages of the IRR technique are similar to those of the NPV technique.
- It uses cash flows rather than accounting profits. Cash flows can be calculated objectively, whereas profits are determined by accounting policies.
- It takes account of the time value of money. By using the IRR as the discount rate, investors' time preferences are recognised.

- Risk can be considered by adjusting the cost of capital. The cost of capital includes a risk premium to reward investors for the amount of risk taken.
- It is consistent with the financial objective of owner wealth maximisation when the decision is simply to accept or reject a proposed investment. In these circumstances, when the IRR is greater than or equal to the cost of capital, acceptance of the project will increase owners' wealth.

## Disadvantages

Despite having several advantages, the IRR technique also has some weaknesses.

- To use the IRR technique correctly, an estimate of the organisation's cost of capital is required. Recall our earlier point that the calculation of the cost of capital is not straight-forward for public-sector organisations, is not well understood by small-business operators, and can change over time.
- The IRR can result in sub-optimal decisions when alternative projects must be ranked in order to determine their relative acceptability. This will be discussed in the next section.
- In certain circumstances a project can have more than one IRR solution. This can make the IRR difficult to interpret. Multiple IRRs may arise when the sign of the cash flows changes more than once over the project's life. An example of two sign reversals would be when the initial investment is a cash outflow (a negative value) followed by a series of cash inflows (positive values) and then a further cash outflow (a negative value) when the project is terminated.

## Comparing NPV and IRR

NPV and IRR are sophisticated techniques of investment evaluation in that they both take account of the time value of money. The decisions that result from using NPV are particularly justifiable, as the NPV is consistent with the financial management goal of owner wealth maximisation. This is only true for the IRR when the decision is simply about whether to either accept or reject the proposed investment. The IRR may not give the best decision when alternative projects must be ranked to determine the relative acceptability of each. This may occur when projects are mutually exclusive, or when capital is rationed.

### Mutually exclusive projects

When projects are **mutually exclusive** it means that they are alternatives to each other. It is an either/or situation, such as whether to repair existing machinery or to replace it with new machinery. Only one alternative can be chosen, so a ranking of the alternatives in order of acceptability may be needed. An incorrect ranking can occur using the IRR when the magnitude or timing of the project cash flows differs considerably.

The example on the next page compares NPV and IRR for two mutually exclusive projects.

> **Mutually exclusive**
> Alternatives where only one can be accepted; an either/or decision.

> **Example 7: Mutually exclusive projects**
>
> A suburban university is examining two alternatives for upgrading its lawn-mowing equipment. Equipment A will require an investment outlay of $8 000 and will generate savings of operating expenses of $3 000 per year for six years. Equipment B is more expensive, costing $60 000 initially, but will generate higher savings of operating expenses of $18 000 per year for six years. Given a cost of capital of 10%, the financial controller has calculated the NPV and IRR of the alternatives as shown in Table 12.4.
>
> Table 12.4    A comparison of the NPV and IRR of alternative equipment purchases
>
> |                | Equipment A | Equipment B |
> | --- | --- | --- |
> | NPV (r = 10%)  | $5 066      | $18 395     |
> | IRR            | 30%         | 20%         |
>
> When it is necessary to rank alternative projects in order of their acceptability, the NPV and IRR can give conflicting results. In this example, the NPV criterion indicates that Equipment B is better as it has the higher NPV. In contrast, the IRR criterion indicates that Equipment A would be better as it has the higher IRR. Where the NPV and IRR give conflicting results, the proposal with the higher NPV should be chosen.

### Capital rationing

When there is insufficient funding available to undertake all desirable investment projects, capital is said to be rationed. To ensure that only the best projects are undertaken, they must be ranked in order of acceptability. Yet using the IRR technique may mean that the projects are not ranked correctly. In these circumstances it is preferable to use the NPV, as it will always give the correct decision.

To use the NPV in a situation of **capital rationing**, it is necessary to select the group of projects that will maximise the aggregate NPV. To do this, the following steps should be undertaken:

- rank the projects in order of their IRRs, from best to worst
- reject all projects for which NPV < 0
- determine the combination of projects that maximises the aggregate NPV without exceeding the maximum available investment funding.

> **Capital rationing**
> A condition of insufficient funding to undertake all desirable investment projects.

### Example 8: Capital rationing

The financial controller for the New Zealand office of JRP Ltd is reviewing the investment proposals for the coming year. Seven proposals with a total investment outlay of $2 100 000 have been received from several different operating departments. Given budget constraints, only $1 200 000 will be available for undertaking new investments. Given the following data in Table 12.5 and a cost of capital of 10%, which projects should be undertaken?

Table 12.5 Alternative investment proposals, JRP Ltd

| Project | Investment outlay | IRR | NPV r = 10% |
|---|---|---|---|
| F | $100 000 | 20% | $ 9 100 |
| C | $600 000 | 16% | $32 700 |
| A | $200 000 | 14% | $ 7 300 |
| G | $500 000 | 13% | $13 600 |
| D | $200 000 | 12% | $ 3 600 |
| E | $300 000 | 9% | –$ 2 700 |
| B | $200 000 | 8% | –$ 3 600 |

The projects are first ranked in order of their IRRs. Then the unacceptable projects are rejected. Projects E and B each have a negative NPV, and therefore should not be considered further. The remaining projects must then be examined to find the combination that maximises the aggregate NPV.

Table 12.6 summarises the NPVs for the best combinations of acceptable investment proposals. If only those investments with the highest IRRs are accepted, and bearing in mind that JRP Ltd is constrained by a maximum allowable investment of $1 200 000, projects F, C, A, and D will result in an aggregate NPV of $52 700. This investment combination would leave an 'unspent' balance of $100 000 that could be invested in marketable securities or elsewhere. Yet the interest earned on the additional $100 000 would at best be sufficient to only just cover the cost of capital, thus yielding a zero NPV.

Table 12.6 Aggregate NPV of acceptable investment proposals, JRP Ltd

| Combination of projects | Total investment outlay | Aggregate NPV |
|---|---|---|
| F, C, A, D | $1 100 000 | $52 700 |
| F, C, G | $1 200 000 | $55 400 |

Acceptance of projects F, C and G will give the highest aggregate NPV of $55 400, given the capital budget constraint. Other combinations could give a higher NPV only if there was no capital rationing. Acceptance of projects F, C and G will maximise the value of the firm, subject to the capital constraint.

## Other capital budgeting considerations

Underlying the discussion of the financial evaluation of long-term investment projects are two further issues that need to be considered. These are:

- the treatment of inflation
- approaches for dealing with risk.

### Capital budgeting and inflation

The recognition of inflation is particularly important when inflation rates are high, as they were in Australia and New Zealand in the 1970s and 1980s. Inflation erodes the purchasing power of the dollar, so some recognition of this is required when capital budgeting estimates are made.

The recommended treatment for inflation is to express future cash flows in future dollar terms. For example, cash flows arising in 2027 should be expressed in 2027 dollars and cash flows arising in 2032 should be expressed in 2032 dollars. However, as different cash flows may be subject to different changes in price levels, each different type of cash flow should be estimated independently. For example, some revenues and operating expenses may increase annually in accordance with the inflation rate, but the depreciation expense for tax reporting purposes will not. Note that tax is equal to a fixed percentage of profit, so it will grow at the same rate as profits.

> **Example 9: Capital budgeting and inflation**
>
> Assume that revenues from a new investment are forecast to be $100 000 per year for years 1 to 5, with no allowance for inflation. If price level changes are expected to be 2% per annum for the five-year period, then the revised cash flows will be as follows:
>
> |  | Year | | | | |
> |---|---|---|---|---|---|
> |  | 1 | 2 | 3 | 4 | 5 |
> | Revenue | $100 000 | $102 000 | $104 040 | $106 121 | $108 243 |
>
> The first-year revenue is forecast to be $100 000. To calculate the estimated revenue for subsequent years, the next year's revenue is equal to last year's revenue multiplied by (one plus the price level change), which in this case is (1 + 0.02), or 1.02.
>
> Note that no inflation adjustment is required for the discount rate. This is because the cost of capital, reflecting the required return of suppliers of capital, already incorporates an inflation premium (see discussion in Chapter 6).

### Capital budgeting and risk

In the context of capital budgeting, risk is the variability of the cash flows. From a practical point of view, however, risk is the possibility that a project will generate insufficient cash flows to cover all operating and financing cash flows. In such a case, the NPV of the project would be negative.

Some projects, such as the manufacture of new products or the application of new technologies, carry very high risk. In fact, firms involved in research and development activities may spend millions of dollars on a wide variety of different projects, although only one or two may result in a pay-off. However, given the nature of the risk–return trade-off, the research activities would be undertaken only if the aggregate expected return from all successful projects was sufficient to cover the aggregate costs from all successful and unsuccessful projects.

Other projects may be less risky. A geographical expansion may be of average risk, while replacement of equipment is generally considered to be of low risk. The implication for investment decisions is that lower returns will be acceptable for investment in lower-risk projects.

There are many different approaches for considering risk in capital budgeting. Two approaches that are used frequently will be briefly discussed here. They are:

- sensitivity analysis, which focuses on adjusting the cash flows in the NPV equation
- risk-adjusted required returns, which adjust the discount rate.

### Sensitivity analysis

**Sensitivity analysis** is a modelling technique frequently used in financial decisions. When applied in investment evaluation, it involves changing the estimated cash flows to see the effect on the NPV and/or IRR of an investment. It answers the question 'What if?' The following are some examples.

- What if actual revenue is only 80% of forecast revenue?
- What if the cost of goods sold is 120% of the forecast cost of goods sold?
- What if manufacturing overheads are 140% of the forecast manufacturing overheads?

> **Sensitivity analysis**
> A risk assessment technique that changes one or two variables at a time to determine the effect on an outcome.

The purpose of sensitivity analysis is to examine the effect on NPV or IRR of a change in the most uncertain variables. An example of sensitivity analysis is presented below.

#### Example 10: Sensitivity analysis, Technability Ltd

Returning to the example of the purchase of new equipment by Technability Ltd, the finance manager is concerned that competitive conditions may prevent the company's forecast market share from being achieved. This could cause actual sales to be as low as 70% of forecast sales. The NPV and IRR have therefore been calculated assuming that actual sales are 70%, 80%, 90%, 100% or 110% of forecast sales. It is assumed that expenses will be 55% of actual sales. The results of the analysis are presented in Table 12.7.

Table 12.7 Sensitivity analysis of new equipment purchase, Technability Ltd

|     | Percentage of sales | | | | |
| --- | --- | --- | --- | --- | --- |
|     | 70% | 80% | 90% | 100% | 110% |
| NPV | −$12 830 | −$2 379 | $8 072 | $18 523 | $28 974 |
| IRR | 8.5% | 11.4% | 14.2% | 16.9% | 19.7% |

The results show that if actual sales are less than or equal to 80% of forecast sales, then the project will not be successful. However, when actual sales are greater than or equal to 90% of forecast sales, then the project will generate a positive return.[1]

---

[1] Using the Excel Goal Seek feature we can determine the financial breakeven point, being the point at which the NPV will equal zero. This will occur when actual sales are 82% of forecast sales.

Sensitivity analysis has two major benefits. First, the increased accessibility of spreadsheet packages on computers has made sensitivity analysis relatively easy to perform. Once a computerised spreadsheet has been constructed, it is a simple matter to change one or two variables that will cause a recalculation of the entire spreadsheet and a revision of the NPV and IRR. Another benefit of sensitivity analysis is that it gives an indication of those variables that will most significantly affect the success of the project. It may be possible for the firm's managers to follow up with further action, such as market research, refinement of product, cost control measures or some other action to avoid a negative outcome.

### Risk-adjusted required return

Some approaches adjust the discount rate in the denominator of the NPV equation to allow for risk. These techniques attempt to explicitly specify the risk–return trade-off values. For low-risk projects only low returns will be required, while for high-risk projects high returns are required. While there are some very sophisticated techniques to determine the **risk-adjusted required return (RARR)**, the approach discussed here is more subjective but much simpler. This approach involves three steps:

1 categorise each project according to its level of risk
2 define the return required for each level of risk
3 use the RARR as the cost of capital to discount the cash flows in NPV calculations, and as the benchmark for comparison in IRR calculations.

> **Risk-adjusted required return (RARR)**
> A risk-adjustment technique that adjusts the discount rate applied to projects' cash flows in order to compensate for risk.

For projects that are not of average risk, the decision criterion for the NPV remains unchanged while the IRR criterion should be reformulated:

If NPV ≥ 0, accept the project. Otherwise reject.
If IRR ≥ RARR, accept the project. Otherwise reject.

The first two steps may involve subjective judgement. For example, the guidelines in Table 12.8 may be set for a particular firm:

Table 12.8  **Examples of risk-adjusted required returns for different types of investment project**

| Risk | Types of project | RARR |
|---|---|---|
| **Risk-free** | Government securities | 4% |
| **Low** | Cost reduction<br>Replacement of equipment | 8% |
| **Average** | Geographical expansion<br>Upgrading of equipment<br>Expansion of capacity | 12% |
| **High** | Expansion of product lines<br>Introduction of new technology | 18% |

There will be a different RARR for each project risk level. For a low-risk project, the RARR will be less than the firm's WACC but more than the risk-free rate earned on a riskless investment such as government securities. Projects of average risk should return the normal return target for the firm, being the WACC. High-risk projects will need to return considerably more than the WACC before they will be accepted. Within these broad guidelines, managers may need to use a considerable amount of subjective judgement to set the risk-adjusted required return.

## Conclusion

This chapter examined several quantitative investment evaluation techniques that are used to help in the decision to accept or reject investment proposals. Four techniques that are commonly used are the accounting return on investment (AROI), payback period, net present value (NPV) and internal rate of return (IRR). These were explained and illustrated.

Inflation and risk can significantly affect capital budgeting problems. The forecast cash flows should be inflation-adjusted, particularly when the rate of overall inflation is high. Some consideration must also be given to the risk level of the alternative proposals. Techniques such as sensitivity analysis and risk-adjusted required return are methods for dealing with risk in capital budgeting.

### SELF-TEST QUESTION

Eco-Tours Ltd is evaluating the potential purchase of a fleet of mountain bikes at a cost of $80 000. The acquisition is expected to generate net cash flows as follows:

| End of year | Net cash flow after tax |
|---|---|
| 1 | $15 000 |
| 2 | $24 000 |
| 3 | $50 000 |

Assuming a cost of capital of 14%, calculate the payback period, net present value and internal rate of return for the proposed acquisition. Is it a good investment?

### ANSWER TO SELF-TEST QUESTION

**Payback period**

| End of year | Net cash flow after tax | Cumulative cash flow |
|---|---|---|
| 0 | −$80 000 | −$80 000 |
| 1 | $15 000 | −$65 000 |
| 2 | $24 000 | −$41 000 |
| 3 | $50 000 | +$ 9 000 |

The payback period is sometime toward the end of year 3.

## Net present value

$$\text{NPV} = C_0 + \sum_{t=1}^{n} \frac{C_t}{(1+r)^t}$$

$$= -\$80\,000 + \frac{\$15\,000}{(1+0.14)^1} + \frac{\$24\,000}{(1+0.14)^2} + \frac{\$50\,000}{(1+0.14)^3}$$

$$= -\$80\,000 + \$13\,158 + \$18\,467 + \$33\,749$$

$$= -\$14\,626$$

## Internal rate of return

|   | A | B |
|---|---|---|
| 1 | End of Year | Net Cash Flow |
| 2 | 0 | -$80 000 |
| 3 | 1 | $15 000 |
| 4 | 2 | $24 000 |
| 5 | 3 | $50 000 |
| 6 | | |
| 7 | IRR | 4.6% |
| 8 | Formula used | =IRR(B2:B5) |

Overall, the returns are inadequate. It takes almost the three full years to pay back the initial outlay, the NPV is highly negative, and the IRR is well below the cost of capital.

### QUESTIONS AND PROBLEMS

1. What is the *accounting return on investment (AROI)*, and what is its decision criterion?
2. What are the advantages and disadvantages of the AROI technique?
3. What is the *payback period*, and what is its decision criterion?
4. What are the advantages and disadvantages of the payback period?
5. Why are cash flows preferred over accounting profits to measure the benefits and costs of a long-term investment project?
6. What is the *NPV*, and what is its decision criterion?
7. What is the *IRR*, and what is its decision criterion?
8. What are *mutually exclusive projects*?
9. Describe two approaches for considering risk in capital budgeting.
10. Which techniques of investment evaluation are consistent with the goal of owner wealth maximisation? Explain.
11. Compare the advantages and disadvantages of the NPV and IRR techniques. Which is theoretically superior? Explain.

12 Some government departments and state-owned enterprises (SOEs) in New Zealand must pay to the Crown an annual capital or financing charge based on the value of their assets. The purpose is to ensure that the cost of the Crown's investment in assets is recognised by government departments and SOEs, in order to improve asset management.

   a How could a capital charge be incorporated into the NPV analyses of proposed investment projects for a government department or SOE?

   b What are the potential benefits and problems associated with using the capital charge in the financial evaluation of long-term investments?

13 Describe the circumstances in which the use of the IRR technique can result in sub-optimal decisions being taken.

14 Why is it that in a circumstance of capital rationing, projects with a short payback period may be preferred?

15 Why would an investment in marketable securities be likely to return less than the firm's weighted average cost of capital?

16 How would the cash flows and discount rate for a proposed investment opportunity be affected by a forecast of high inflation?

17 What would be the effect on the NPV of a project if inflation is higher than expected?

18 Three divisions of a diversified international company have estimated their weighted average cost of capital as follows:

| Division | Weighted average cost of capital |
|---|---|
| Foodstuffs processing | 12% |
| Retail department stores | 15% |
| Oil and gas exploration and refining | 20% |

What would be a reasonable estimate of the required return for each of a low-, average- and high-risk project, for each division? Explain your rationale.

19 In practice, sensitivity analysis is more commonly used than risk-adjusted required returns to deal with risk in capital budgeting. Give a possible reason for this preference.

20 Action Rollerblades is considering a geographical expansion that is expected to affect profits as shown below:

| End of year | Profit after tax |
|---|---|
| 1 | −$2 800 |
| 2 | $1 900 |
| 3 | $4 700 |
| 4 | $7 200 |
| 5 | $7 200 |

To undertake the expansion, an investment outlay of $40 000 is required.

a  Calculate Action's annual accounting return on investment (AROI).

b  Calculate Action's average AROI.

c  If Action's minimum required average AROI is 16% for all new investments, should the expansion be undertaken?

21  Calculate the payback period for each of the following investments, and rank the investments in order of acceptability:

| End of year | Net cash flow after tax | | |
|---|---|---|---|
| | Investment | | |
| | A | B | C |
| 0 | −$50 000 | −$185 000 | −$210 000 |
| 1 | $40 000 | $ 50 000 | $ 0 |
| 2 | $15 000 | $ 50 000 | $ 0 |
| 3 | | $ 50 000 | $100 000 |
| 4 | | $ 50 000 | $100 000 |
| 5 | | | $100 000 |
| 6 | | | $100 000 |

22  Successful Chocolates Ltd is evaluating the purchase of new processing equipment at a cost of $90 000. The acquisition is expected to generate net cash flows as follows:

| End of year | Net cash flow after tax |
|---|---|
| 1 | $15 000 |
| 2 | $40 000 |
| 3 | $38 000 |
| 4 | $36 000 |

Calculate the net present value of the proposed purchase, and indicate whether to accept or reject the investment assuming a cost of capital of:

a  12%

b  14%

c  16%.

23  Green Forestry Products Ltd is considering two alternative investments. One involves upgrading major equipment at a cost of $50 000, while the alternative is to replace the equipment with a newer model costing $125 000.

The net profit attributable to each investment after taxes and incremental cash flows are:

| End of year | Upgrade equipment | | Replace equipment | |
|---|---|---|---|---|
| | Net profit after tax | Net cash flow after tax | Net profit after tax | Net cash flow after tax |
| 1 | $15 000 | $21 250 | $18 000 | $33 625 |
| 2 | $15 000 | $20 469 | $18 000 | $31 672 |
| 3 | $ 5 000 | $ 9 785 | $18 000 | $29 963 |
| 4 | $ 5 000 | $ 9 187 | $24 000 | $34 468 |
| 5 | $ 5 000 | $34 309 | $24 000 | $97 272 |

Green Forestry has a cost of capital of 14%.

a   Calculate the average accounting return on investment for each alternative. Which alternative is preferred?

b   Calculate the payback period for each alternative. Which alternative is preferred using this technique?

c   Calculate the net present value of each alternative. Which alternative is preferred using this technique?

d   Given the results in **a** to **c**, what can you conclude about the different techniques of investment evaluation? Which investment alternative would you recommend? Explain your decision.

24  Investco Ltd is considering three alternative investment opportunities. The incremental cash flows attributable to each investment are:

| End of year | Net cash flow after tax | | |
|---|---|---|---|
| | Investment | | |
| | A | B | C |
| 0 | −$80 000 | −$100 000 | −$120 000 |
| 1 | $15 000 | $ 31 000 | $ 30 000 |
| 2 | $15 000 | $ 31 000 | $ 30 000 |
| 3 | $15 000 | $ 31 000 | $ 30 000 |
| 4 | $15 000 | $ 31 000 | $ 30 000 |
| 5 | $60 000 | $ 85 000 | $ 90 000 |

Investco has a 15% cost of capital.

a   Calculate the payback period for each alternative. Which alternative is preferred?

b   Calculate the net present value of each alternative. Which alternative is preferred using this technique?

c   If you have access to Excel, calculate the internal rate of return of each alternative. Which alternative is preferred using this technique?

d   Comment on your findings in **a** to **c** and recommend the best alternative.

25 Fishing Supplies Ltd is evaluating two mutually exclusive investment opportunities. The incremental cash flows for each investment are as follows:

| End of year | Net cash flow after tax | |
|---|---|---|
| | Investment | |
| | Q | R |
| 0 | −$70 000 | −$140 000 |
| 1 | $17 000 | $ 32 000 |
| 2 | $17 000 | $ 32 000 |
| 3 | $17 000 | $ 32 000 |
| 4 | $17 000 | $ 32 000 |
| 5 | $17 000 | $ 32 000 |
| 6 | $50 000 | $100 000 |

a  Calculate the net present value for each project, given a cost of capital of:

   i    14%

   ii   15%

   iii  16%.

   Which project is preferred at each cost of capital?

b  The IRR for investment Q is 18.8%, compared with R's IRR of 17.3%. Which project is preferred?

c  Comment on your findings in **a** and **b**, and explain the reasons for the different decisions resulting from the net present value and internal rate of return techniques.

26 Wirth International Hotels Ltd is reviewing several investment proposals for the next year. To undertake all eight projects would cost $1 550 000, but due to funding restrictions the firm only has $600 000 available for new investments. Given the data below, and a cost of capital of 13%, which projects should be accepted? Explain your decision.

| Project | Investment outlay | IRR | NPV r = 13% |
|---|---|---|---|
| C | $ 100 000 | 22% | $ 7 965 |
| A | $ 250 000 | 19% | $13 274 |
| F | $ 100 000 | 17% | $ 3 540 |
| B | $ 400 000 | 16% | $13 626 |
| G | $ 300 000 | 15% | $ 5 310 |
| D | $ 150 000 | 14% | $ 1 327 |
| E | $ 175 000 | 12% | −$ 1 549 |
| H | $  75 000 | 10% | −$ 1 991 |
| | $1 550 000 | | |

27 Refer to the Technability Ltd example in this chapter. The firm's financial controller is concerned that future inflation may be higher than expected and that the NPV of the proposed equipment purchase may consequently be lower.

   a  Rework the operating cash flows in the Technability Ltd problem (Table 12.1), assuming that revenues increase by 2% per year beginning in year 3 and expenses increase by 6% per year beginning in year 3. Depreciation is expected to remain unchanged.

   b  Recalculate the net cash flow after tax for the proposed purchase of equipment, using the revised operating cash flows determined in **a**, above. Assume an investment outlay of $130 000 and a terminal value of $42 598.

   c  Calculate the revised net present value of the net cash flow after tax as determined in **b**, above, assuming that the cost of capital is unchanged at 12%. Should the proposed purchase go ahead under the new circumstances?

28 Tillers Ltd is evaluating two mutually exclusive projects, X and Y. A table has been prepared to forecast net cash flow under different economic conditions:

| End of year | Net cash flow after tax | | | | | |
|---|---|---|---|---|---|---|
| | Project X | | | Project Y | | |
| | Recession | Normal | Expansion | Recession | Normal | Expansion |
| 0 | −$50 000 | −$50 000 | −$50 000 | −$50 000 | −$50 000 | −$50 000 |
| 1 | $11 000 | $12 000 | $13 000 | $ 9 000 | $12 000 | $16 000 |
| 2 | $11 000 | $12 000 | $13 000 | $ 9 000 | $12 000 | $16 000 |
| 3 | $11 000 | $12 000 | $13 000 | $ 9 000 | $12 000 | $16 000 |
| 4 | $40 000 | $41 000 | $42 000 | $38 000 | $41 000 | $46 000 |

   a  Calculate the net present value of each project, under each of the three economic scenarios, assuming a cost of capital of 12%.

   b  Assess the relative risk of each project by examining the range of net present values for each. Which project is riskier?

   c  Which project would you recommend? Explain why.

29 Air-o-bics Ltd is considering three proposed investment projects, L, A and H. Project L is of lower-than-average risk and will be evaluated using a risk-adjusted required return of 10%. Project A is of average risk and will be evaluated using the weighted average cost of capital of 13%. Project H is high risk and will be evaluated using a risk-adjusted required return of 18%. The forecast net cash flows for each project are presented below:

| End of year | Net cash flow after tax | | |
|---|---|---|---|
| | Project L | Project A | Project H |
| 0 | −$50 000 | −$60 000 | −$75 000 |
| 1 | $10 000 | $16 000 | $18 000 |
| 2 | $10 000 | $16 000 | $18 000 |
| 3 | $10 000 | $16 000 | $18 000 |
| 4 | $40 000 | $50 000 | $65 000 |

a  Find the risk-adjusted net present value for each project.
b  Assuming that all desirable projects can be undertaken, which project(s) should be accepted? Explain why.

# Investment in long-term assets – Property

**CHAPTER 13**

## Learning objectives

By the end of this chapter, you should be able to:

- discuss the motivations, advantages and disadvantages of investing in property
- explain single-period return measures and apply them to determine the acceptability of proposed property investments
- describe how investor-specific characteristics such as risk preferences, taxation and debt financing requirements affect required returns and the evaluation of property investment decisions
- explain why the NPV(ER) method, rather than the traditional NPV method, is typically used to evaluate property investment decisions
- evaluate property investment decisions using multi-period techniques including discounted cash flow analysis.

## Introduction

Property commonly comprises a large proportion of the total investments people own and is also associated with significant debt financing requirements. The importance of property both as a place to live (personal consumption) and a place to potentially own cannot be overstated. This capstone chapter integrates the prior learning from this textbook by applying it to property investment decisions. For example, Chapter 2 explored property markets and characteristics of property that are important considerations when buying and selling property. This current chapter applies the time value of money formulae from Chapters 4 and 5, including the capitalisation rate valuation method, to help evaluate property decisions for commercial properties. It also considers the risk and return features of property discussed in Chapter 6. Property rights, obligations, forms of property ownership and legal terminology critical to the sale and purchase of property were explored in Chapter 7, while Chapters 11 and 12 focused on investment decision tools and techniques. We now integrate these concepts, tools and techniques in analysing property investment decisions.

The characteristics, concepts and legal framework that underpin investment in property differentiate it from other asset classes (including personal consumption of housing). However, the principles of cash flow estimation and the discounting of these for timing and risk is consistent across the asset classes. Further, while property investments have some unique characteristics and terminology (such as rentals and valuation methodologies), the concepts of determining cash flows and discounting these to allow for required rates of return, and the use of leverage, are consistent.

The chapter begins with a discussion of the advantages and disadvantages of investing in property, which informs property investment risk. It then explores single-period return measures, feasibility analysis and the application of multi-period cash-flow analysis, using NPV principles and techniques covered in prior chapters, to residential and commercial property settings.

## Why invest in property?

Many of the world's wealthiest people have large real estate holdings, and building a property portfolio is one step towards the goal of wealth accumulation. Investors will purchase property for a variety of reasons. For some, the investment income and/or potential capital growth are of primary importance, while others may be looking to complete a diversified portfolio of a range of different investments. Many investors are attracted by the tangible nature of property investment and the ability to have direct control. Some of the motivations that relate specifically to property investment are outlined in Table 13.1. Disadvantages of investing in property are outlined in Table 13.2.

Table 13.1   **Motivations for investing in property**

| | |
|---|---|
| **Tangible** | As real estate can be readily identified, it is often associated with social status. People like to live in certain neighbourhoods because their peers live there; companies may compete to build (and have their name on) the largest and most prestigious office buildings. Real estate can be seen and admired; it creates a physical presence of wealth. |
| **Leverage** | This is the use of borrowed funds to finance a portion of a real estate investment. Because real estate is income-producing and tends to appreciate in value over time, loans may be secured against the real estate asset. In addition, there is a well-established legal framework for the recovery of unpaid debt via mortgage mechanisms. |
| **Personal control** | Many people enjoy the day-to-day decision-making associated with managing ongoing investments. This gives them a direct input into making the investment successful. Unlike equities, where ownership provides no control over the operation of the business, direct property ownership presents the opportunity to add value to the investment rather than being a price-taker. In some cases, however, where the necessary skills are lacking, it also leads to failure. |
| **Owner/ occupier** | Real estate is often purchased for self-occupation and use. The majority of residential purchases would fit this category. Many commercial and industrial properties are owner-occupied or are owned by closely related entities. Purchasers who buy for self-use also take the investment potential of the property into account. |
| **Security** | The physical and long-lasting nature of real estate ranks highly as a secure investment, and as mentioned in leverage above, this allows significant use of debt financing. |
| **Inflation hedge** | The conventional wisdom is that real estate is a relatively good hedge against inflation. During inflationary periods, real estate prices have historically risen after adjusting for inflation, which may be why real estate is considered an inflation hedge. Two potential reasons for this include rents, which tend to rise; and capitalisation rates (as detailed in Chapter 5), which often become compressed when there is high inflation. |

| Capital growth | Some countries, including New Zealand, have no explicit capital gains tax, so any increase in value would typically be tax-free. This can act as a strong incentive to invest in real estate, particularly in residential property, which has experienced consistent capital growth over many decades. However, it should be noted that in New Zealand there is a de facto capital gains tax, called the bright-line test. This was introduced in 2015 and stipulates that any residential investment property (i.e. not the home in which the owner lives) purchased and then on-sold within a certain period is subject to tax on the capital gain at the investor's marginal tax rate. The period was originally set at two years in 2015 and subsequently adjusted by various governments to five years from 2018, and 10 years from 2021. It should be noted that the bright-line test is not conclusive, and tax on capital gains may or may not be payable on residential property transactions outside of the test where the intention in relation to investing for capital gain is shown. |
|---|---|

Table 13.2     **Disadvantages of investing in property**

| Liquidity risk | The loss of liquidity is an economic characteristic of real estate. It may take a long time to sell a property, depending on the type of property and the prevailing market conditions. In times of economic downturn, high-priced investment real estate becomes very difficult to sell. In such circumstances, urgent or distressed sales typically result in sellers accepting lower offers. |
|---|---|
| Complexity and cost of transaction | The purchase and sale of property requires specialist technical and legal advice, which may be costly; and if an agent is involved then this will add further to the transaction costs. |
| Management | Real estate requires specialist management in order to maximise return on investment and to mitigate compliance risks. A property manager needs to be aware that buildings and improvements constantly require repairs and maintenance, tenants may leave leading to vacancy periods without rental income, and laws and planning controls change. Specialist management skills are therefore required to maximise the investment benefits. The cost of either obtaining the skills or paying for them is a disincentive to invest. |
| Statutory control | Governments see real estate (particularly housing) as a social and economic commodity that is subject to policy interventions to suit desired social and political goals. Examples of this are residential rent control (Residential Tenancies Act 1986), which limits the power of landlords, and regular changes to the Building Act 1991 to increase the durability and safety of properties, often at additional cost. |
| Political risk | Political risk is the risk that an investment's returns could suffer as a result of political changes which may, for example, stem from changes to government or legislative bodies. Successive governments have changed property-related legislation around quality, rental reviews and taxation, in particular to do with residential property. These often-unexpected policy changes have an impact on the future realised returns of property. |

As discussed in Chapter 2, property can be held both directly and indirectly. The advantages and disadvantages shown in Tables 13.1 and 13.2 refer to direct investment in property and will continue to apply to the entity holding the property. For an indirect investor, however, these factors may operate quite differently, especially in terms of liquidity and the level of direct control an investor has, but the need for specialist property skills in order to invest is reduced. For example, owning indirectly through listed property investment funds or shares results in much greater liquidity, and therefore lower liquidity risk, but shareholders do not have direct control of the underlying property assets.

## Analysis of a property investment

A critical aspect of investing in property is being able to analyse the return on investment. This section covers investment concepts that can be applied to both residential and commercial property.

### Investment purpose

In Chapter 6 we considered investment in financial assets like shares and bonds, as well as their risk and return. Then in Chapters 11 and 12 we considered investment in real assets or projects where we estimated annual cash flows and changes in asset values. This is similar for investors in property, who will typically be looking for both an annual cash flow, such as rents, and an increase in property value. However, there may be situations where a property investor only receives a return from an increase in value following a development project.

Property investors are concerned with the return a property will provide in relation to their required rate of return. Each investor has their own required return criteria, which relate to alternative investment options and their attitude to risk. To make an informed investment choice, a property investor needs to analyse return and consider the risk of all investment options.

### Property investment risk

We discussed the relationship between risk and return in Chapter 6, and saw that unsystematic risk can be minimised by investing in a well-diversified portfolio of investments. Investors who have a well-diversified portfolio of assets should therefore be more concerned about systematic risk. However, many property investors hold a single property or only a small number of properties, and therefore tend to be over-weighted in property relative to total wealth. This means their personal portfolio of investments is not well-diversified. If this is the case, such investors should be concerned with the unsystematic risk of their investments.

In real estate investment, most risk analysis is still undertaken on an intuitive basis, having regard to those factors that reflect property-specific risk. Factors affecting unsystematic property-specific risk include the quality of tenants (their ability to meet the lease obligations), the quality of the lease agreement, how the property is used, its location, age and condition of buildings, and its price bracket. Decisions relating to these risk factors are essential in ensuring that the highest-quality return from a property is achieved.

## Property investment return

The investment return from real estate is derived from annual cash flow (usually in the form of net rental income after relevant expenses) and changes in property value. Not all measures of performance for property investment consider both these components. Investment return can be measured over single periods (e.g. gross and net income returns with or without capital return) or multiple periods (e.g. discounted cash flow analysis to determine NPV and IRR).

The incomes from properties are based on contracts (usually a lease). These contracts are usually fixed in duration, and as such there may be times when the property is vacant. Once one tenant leaves, there may be time taken to undertake repairs, market the property and re-let, resulting in a period of vacancy. A commercial building may have a long lease (five years or more), but a residential property may have several tenants per year. In this respect, the analysis of property income should include an appropriate allowance for any vacancy period when no rental is received, depending on the nature of the lease.

## Single-period methods

A **single-period return** shows the return achieved over a defined period. The period chosen is normally one year. The one-year period also aligns with the period that rents are fixed for, and enables comparison with other forms of investment where interest rates are usually quoted on an annual basis. However, shorter or longer period lengths could also be informative for investors. For example, an investor may be interested in comparing the returns of various options over their investment horizon, along similar lines to the holding period returns discussed in Chapter 6.

**Single-period return**
Investment return over a specific time period.

These types of return measure are usually based on past and current financial performance at a particular point in time and make no attempt to look into the future to predict future financial performance. Conclusions are usually simple. For example:

- This property is providing a 6% return, and this is considered adequate, or
- Property A provides a 6% return, which is better than alternative property B; therefore, we should purchase property A.

Single-period returns can be income-based measures, such as gross return (based on the total period rents or lease) or net return (rents less expenses), or composite returns which include both the income and changes in the asset's value components. We will now examine the commonly used measures more closely.

### Gross and net returns

Gross and net returns measure the return from cash flow, usually in the form of rental income. The **gross return** and **net return** equations are:

$$\text{Gross return} = \frac{\text{Gross income}}{P_0} \qquad \text{Equation 13.1}$$

$$\text{Net return} = \frac{\text{Net operating income}}{P_0} \qquad \text{Equation 13.2}$$

where  gross income = rental or lease income for the period
       net income = rental or lease income less relevant expenses for the period
       $P_0$ = property value at the beginning of the period.

**Gross return**
Total income generated before expenses divided by value of investment at the beginning of the period.

**Net return**
Investment income after deducting relevant expenses divided by value of investment at the beginning of the period.

Example 1 shows the calculation of gross and net returns for a block of residential flats.

> **Example 1: New residential flats – gross and net return on investment**
>
> A block of three new flats is expected to be leased on a periodic tenancy with a total gross rental income of $600 per week for each flat. The property has a purchase price of $975 000.
>
> The property is management-intensive. This involves regular expenditure to ensure that the rental income continues to be received. The flats are expected to have annual operating expenses of $16 250, comprising $6 000 for insurance, $4 500 for rates, and repairs and maintenance of $5 750.
>
> What is the gross and net return on investment?
>
> $$\text{Gross return} = \frac{\text{Gross income}}{P_0} = \frac{\$93\,600}{\$975\,000} = 0.096 \text{ or } 9.6\%$$
>
> The net income for the flats can be calculated by deducting the expenses from the gross income as follows:
>
> | | |
> |---|---|
> | Gross income | $93 600 |
> | Less operating expenses | $16 250 |
> | Net operating income | $77 350 |
>
> $$\text{Net return} = \frac{\text{Net operating income}}{P_0} = \frac{\$77\,350}{\$975\,000} = 0.079 \text{ or } 7.9\%$$
>
> As properties are not always fully tenanted, the residential flats may be vacant for a short time each year. Later, in Example 5, we will consider the impact of vacancy on investor returns.

Gross and net return measures are simple to calculate and widely used in the marketplace by buyers, sellers, investors and financiers. However, these measures have been criticised for being overly simplistic and not conveying the full picture relating to the investment. The discounted cash flow analysis detailed later in this chapter seeks to overcome these criticisms by considering the relevant future cash flows, risks and required returns for investor(s) related to a property investment.

## Composite returns

The gross and net return methods of evaluation measure the return of income only. Property, like most assets, experiences changes in value over time. As such, the total returns for a property will commonly include both an income return component and a return from the change in value of the property. The measurement of both the net income return and the growth or decline in property value over a single period is called a **composite return**.

$$\text{Composite return} = \frac{(P_1 - P_0) + \text{Net operating income}}{P_0}$$

*Equation 13.3*

where
$P_0$ = property value at the beginning of the period
$P_1$ = property value at the end of the period.

> **Composite return measure**
> Net income plus change in value of the investment over the value of investment at the beginning of the period.

### Example 2: New residential flats – composite return

Continuing with the block of new flats in Example 1, calculate the composite return (before interest and taxes) assuming that the value of the flats in 12 months' time is $1 000 000 (Scenario 1), then again assuming the value has fallen to $925 000 (Scenario 2).

**Scenario 1:**

$$\begin{aligned}
\text{Composite return} &= \frac{(P_1 - P_0) + \text{Net operating income}}{P_0} \\
&= \frac{(\$1\,000\,000 - \$975\,000) + \$77\,350}{\$975\,000} \\
&= \frac{\$102\,350}{\$975\,000} \\
&= 0.105 \text{ or } 10.5\%
\end{aligned}$$

**Scenario 2:**

$$\begin{aligned}
\text{Composite return} &= \frac{(P_1 - P_0) + \text{Net operating income}}{P_0} \\
&= \frac{(\$925\,000 - \$975\,000) + \$77\,350}{\$975\,000} \\
&= \frac{\$27\,350}{\$975\,000} \\
&= 0.028 \text{ or } 2.8\%
\end{aligned}$$

### Profit margins

Composite returns are a suitable evaluation tool for lower-priced direct real estate investments. However, they are not suitable for development, conversion and refurbishment type property investments. For these investment options, there is often no income – only a change in value brought about by the capital expended to improve the property. This is shown in Example 3.

> **Example 3: Property development**
>
> A residential section (bare land) is purchased for $300 000 and the developer builds two townhouses on the section for an additional $800 000. The developed site is sold one year later for $1 300 000. What is the profit margin?
>
> $$\begin{aligned} \text{Profit margin} &= \text{Sale value} - \text{Total investment cost} \\ &= \$1\,300\,000 - (\$300\,000 + \$800\,000) \\ &= \$200\,000 \end{aligned}$$
>
> This equates to a return of 18.2% on total investment cost ($200 000 / $1 100 000).

### Investor-specific considerations

> **Investor-specific considerations**
> Unique factors influencing investment decisions, including choice of debt financing and the investor's marginal tax rates.

The calculations and measures discussed so far relate to property investments at the asset level – that is, the returns to the asset itself. In this regard, these calculations are similar to market-based property valuations (such as the capitalisation of income approach outlined in Chapter 5 for commercial properties) that are commonly considered for sale and purchase purposes and property valuations. Therefore, when we are undertaking a market-based approach (sometimes referred to as an objective approach) such as the capitalisation of income approach, we would use the 'market' rate of return. As tax rates typically apply to investors (e.g. sole traders, companies, trusts, etc.) rather than individual assets, market-based property asset returns are generally before-tax returns. Ignoring individual investor debt financing requirements and using before-tax returns allows an objective comparison of returns across multiple properties, irrespective of who the investor may be.

However, individual investors are also interested in the returns they may generate on a particular property given their own set of specific needs and requirements. For example, each investor is likely to have different financing arrangements, cost of debt, marginal tax rates and risk preferences, and therefore every potential investor in a specific property could have different financing cash flows and required rates of return. Further, potential investors may structure the management of a particular property differently. For example, some may manage the property themselves, while others may engage a property manager to manage it on their behalf. Some investors may undertake repairs and maintenance themselves, while others will contract repairs and maintenance out. Therefore, the financing and operating cash flows (after tax) from the property and the required returns of all potential investors in the property will differ.

Analysis of property returns undertaken from the perspective of a particular investor is sometimes referred to as a subjective approach, as the analysis and returns are subject to that investor's specific circumstances or considerations. The examples discussed so far in this chapter are at the asset level, and would apply similarly to an investor using 100% equity investment. In practice this rarely happens, as property investors generally use both debt and equity financing. Individual investors are primarily interested in their returns after all expenses, including debt servicing and taxes. Investor-specific return calculations consider the investor's subjective required rate of return but also include that investor's particular capital structure for the investment (i.e. the use of debt) and cash flows, and can also include the investor's tax rate, enabling before-tax and after-tax returns to be calculated.

### Property debt financing

Two common types of debt financing include the table loan (or amortised loan) and the flat loan (interest-only loan).

- Table loans are longer-term loans with maturities commonly of around 20–30 years, though the interest rates will normally not be fixed for the duration and will be either variable ('floating') or fixed for periods of up to 10 years. In Chapters 5 and 7 we explored both loan types, including the calculation of table loan payments and repayment schedules showing each payment split between principal and interest expense. In Example 8 later in this chapter we demonstrate how the relevant debt financing for the discounted cash flow analysis is estimated.

- A flat loan is generally a shorter-term loan, typically up to five years (it can be longer or renewed later), during which only interest is paid. The total principal (amount borrowed) is repaid in full at the end of the loan term. For example, if $1 000 000 is borrowed at 6% interest for three years, the annual interest expense would be $1 000 000 x 6% = $60 000 per annum. The $1 000 000 would still be owed at the end of the three years.

As noted above, one of the advantages of property investment is the relative ease of leverage, partly due to the ability of the lender to recover unpaid debt via the mortgage instrument process. It is therefore common to hear property loans referred to as 'mortgages', though technically they are 'mortgage-secured loans'.

### Property taxation

As discussed earlier, when returns or valuations are calculated on the asset itself, these exclude taxes. This is because the tax rate that applies to an investor will depend on a number of factors, in particular the 'intention' of the investment and the business form of ownership (e.g. sole trader, partnership, company, trust, not-for-profit, Māori trust, etc.).

Income from properties is generally taxed in the same manner as any other investment or business, with reasonable expenses and interest being deductible expenses. As noted in Table 13.1, tax related to property, particularly residential property, is subject to regular government intervention. This makes property investment planning and the forecasting of returns difficult as these are subject to political risk. For example, the New Zealand government at the time announced limitations on interest expense tax deductibility for existing (not new) residential properties purchased after 27 March 2021. This was reversed by another government in 2024.

Also, one of the key complexities with property arises from the tax status of capital returns. In general, where investment properties in New Zealand are

> **Equity return measures**
> Equity income (before or after tax) over the investor's equity in the investment at the beginning of the period.

held for the intention of income return and not regularly traded or significantly redeveloped (and are held beyond the relevant bright-line threshold for residential properties), any changes in value are not taxable. Therefore, it is practical for the 'income return on equity' calculation to be undertaken on both a pre-tax and a post-tax basis for a particular investor, based on their marginal tax rate. In these **equity return measures**, equity income before tax refers to net operating income less interest expense, while equity income after tax is net operating income less interest and tax expenses.

$$\text{Equity return before tax} = \frac{\text{Equity income before tax}}{P_e} \quad \text{Equation 13.4}$$

$$\text{Equity return after tax} = \frac{\text{Equity income after tax}}{P_e} \quad \text{Equation 13.5}$$

where $P_e$ = equity in property at the beginning of the period.

### Example 4: New residential flats – equity return measures

**Equity return before tax**

Building on the information in Examples 1 and 2, now assume that the new block of flats costs $975 000 and the investor secures a $625 000 flat loan with an annual interest rate of 7% to finance the project. What is the investor's equity return before tax on this property?

| | |
|---|---|
| Net operating income | $77 350 |
| Less interest expense ($625 000 @ 7% per annum) | $43 750 |
| Equity income before tax | $33 600 |

$$\text{Equity return before tax} = \frac{\text{Equity income before tax}}{P_e} = \frac{\$33\,600}{\$350\,000} = 0.096 \text{ or } 9.6\%$$

Note: $P_e$ = Purchase price – Debt
= $975 000 – $625 000
= $350 000

**Equity return after tax**

For the same residential block of flats, what is the after-tax return on equity if the investor's marginal tax rate is 33%?

| | |
|---|---|
| Net operating income | $77 350 |
| Less debt service ($625 000 @ 7% per annum) | $43 750 |
| Equity income before tax | $33 600 |
| Tax at 33% | $11 088 |
| Equity income after tax | $22 512 |

$$\text{Equity return after tax} = \frac{\text{Equity income after tax}}{P_e} = \frac{\$22\,512}{\$350\,000} = 0.064 \text{ or } 6.4\%$$

Net income returns, profit margins and composite returns could all be calculated on both a before- and an after-tax basis. However, as noted earlier, in practice asset-based property returns are typically done on a before-tax basis. In contrast, individual investors want to know what after-tax returns they will receive on their equity funds invested. This can cause some confusion, and therefore for the sake of simplicity the remainder of this chapter assumes that:

- composite and other *asset-based* return measures are calculated on a before-tax basis (unless specifically mentioned otherwise)
- NPV and other *equity-based* return measures use net cash flows after tax (unless specifically mentioned otherwise).

## Multi-period methods

Measuring property performance for single time periods is not always convenient or appropriate. The cost of obtaining annual valuations to measure changes in value (or price) may be high and, of course, it is past performance that is being measured. The investor needs to be able to look into the future and ask: *What will my return be if I make this outlay, obtain this rent, and these changes (such as rent increases or operating costs escalations) occur?* In other words, evaluating investment performance is not about measuring past events but about assessing the likely impact on returns (both income and capital) of future events.

Chapter 12 discussed two alternative methods of estimating a proposed investment's NPV. The first method, which is traditionally applied in a large firm setting, assumes that the firm's capital structure (i.e. how the firm's assets are financed) does not change significantly as a result of the new investment. This assumption is fine for large firms or where the new project is small. However, property is typically a relatively large investment and/or many property investors (particularly residential investors) have relatively low wealth. As such, acquiring a new property is likely to result in a substantially different capital structure after the acquisition. Therefore, when evaluating property investments, the second method presented in Chapter 12, called the equity residual NPV or NPV(ER) method (Equation 12.5, reproduced below), is typically applied.

$$\text{NPV (ER)} = \sum_{t=1}^{n} \frac{\text{Cash flow to equity holders}}{\text{Required return of equity holders}} - \text{Funds invested by equity holders}$$

In applying this method, we first estimate the cash flows to the investor (equity holder). These are then discounted at the investor's required return.

The equity residual NPV analysis involves several important steps, including:

1. Determining the investment period over which the cash flows are to be estimated
2. Estimating future income such as rent (cash inflows) and property expenses (cash outflows)
3. Estimating financing cash flows (i.e. initial equity outlay, interest and principal repayments)
4. Estimating the value of the property at the end of the investment period
5. Applying appropriate investment decision techniques such as NPV(ER) and IRR.

> **Discounted cash flow analysis**
> Valuation method in which the present value of future cash flows (i.e. NPV) is calculated.

The NPV analysis is also commonly referred to as **discounted cash flow analysis**, as first the relevant cash flows are estimated and then these cash flows are discounted at the investor's required rate of return to determine the present value for each year's cash flows. Further detail on some of the key inputs required to construct discounted cash flow analysis to determine the investment's NPV and IRR include:

### The investment period

The investor needs to make a decision about how far into the future cash flows are to be forecast and at what time intervals. In practice, a five- to ten-year time frame is commonly used in conjunction with annual cash flow forecasts. This coincides with the likely ownership period and the period of rent determination.

### Initial equity outlay

This is the equity outlay that the investor is intending to invest (equity financing component), and is required because we want to analyse the individual investor's return on a specific property investment. The equity outlay will affect the level of debt required to finance the transaction.

### Relevant annual cash inflows

This is the gross income flowing into an investment and could include, for example, property rent, licence payments and parking fees. Note that if a building is vacant there will be no rental income and, as expenses such as local authority rates and insurance are likely to continue, the net cash flow may be negative.

### Relevant annual cash outflows

This is the expenditure that must be met each period in order to produce the cash inflows. It comprises unrecovered property expenses, i.e. that portion of rates, insurance, repairs and maintenance, etc. that is paid by the property owner rather than recovered from the tenant as per the lease. When we apply the equity residual NPV method, annual cash outflows will also include the interest component of debt servicing. (Recall that this differs from the standard NPV method discussed in Chapter 12, which does not include interest expense in the cash flows as the cost of debt financing is included in the WACC used to discount the cash flows.)

As noted earlier, depreciation on residential property assets for tax purposes is in general no longer allowable in New Zealand. This is because most component parts of property are enduring and have historically been seen to appreciate over time, notwithstanding that they experience physical deterioration and potentially functional obsolescence. The property cash flows allow for the deterioration of the assets by way of maintenance, repair and replacement over the period of the cash flow projection. Residential property cash flows therefore exclude an allowance for depreciation but do allow for maintenance and replenishment of the assets over time.

## End-of-investment cash flows

The last cash flow period will include the estimated resale value of the property less expected costs of sale and the balance outstanding on the debt.

## Expected value at end of investment period

The expected value or sales price of the property at the end of the investment period must be estimated. In practice, the capitalisation rate valuation method from Chapter 5 is used to estimate this for commercial property. Example 7 later in this chapter demonstrates how the capitalisation rate valuation method can be applied to determine an end-of-investment-period valuation. It should be noted that the capitalisation rate approach should only be used for residential properties that are specialised rental properties and unlikely to be owner-occupied because the latter likely requires a different valuation methodology.

## The discount rate

The discount rate is the investor's required return on equity and is used to determine the present value of each year's relevant net cash flow.

Developing an NPV(ER) decision model for a property investment requires experience and expertise. The analyst needs to be able to make predictions about the growth or decline in rents, expenses and values, and consideration needs to be given to the state of property markets and economic indicators. Cash flow forecasts are often coupled with a sensitivity analysis that utilises several different predictive scenarios (as discussed in Chapter 12).

### Example 5: New residential flats – NPV(ER)

Estimate the NPV(ER) for acquiring the new residential flats for $975 000 over a five-year investment period. Additional information includes:

| | |
|---|---|
| Debt funding | $625 000 (7% interest-only loan for 5 years) |
| Gross rental income in year 1 | $1 800 per week (3 flats at $600 each) |
| Vacancy allowance | 2 weeks (therefore, use 50 weeks income per year) |
| Operating expenses in year 1 | $16 250 (comprising insurance $6 000, rates $4 500, repairs and maintenance $5 750) |
| Sale proceeds year 5 | $1 150 000 |

Gross rental income is expected to increase at a rate of 1.5% per annum, while operating expenses are expected to increase at a rate of 2% per annum. The investor's after-tax required rate of return on equity invested is 8% and their tax rate is 33%.

Gross rental income in the first year after allowance for vacancies is expected to be $1 800 per week, multiplied by 52 weeks less the 2 weeks vacancy allowance per year, or $1 800 × (52 − 2) = $90 000.

|  | Year | | | | | |
|---|---|---|---|---|---|---|
|  | 0 | 1 | 2 | 3 | 4 | 5 |
| Equity outlay | ($350 000) | | | | | |
| Gross rental income | | $90 000 | $91 350 | $92 720 | $94 111 | $95 523 |
| Operating expenses (OPEX) | | ($16 250) | ($16 575) | ($16 907) | ($17 245) | ($17 590) |
| Net operating income | | $73 750 | $74 775 | $75 814 | $76 866 | $77 933 |
| Loan interest payments | | ($43 750) | ($43 750) | ($43 750) | ($43 750) | ($43 750) |
| Taxable income | | $30 000 | $31 025 | $32 064 | $33 116 | $34 183 |
| Taxation at 33% | | ($9 900) | ($10 238) | ($10 581) | ($10 928) | ($11 280) |
| Sale proceeds | | | | | | $1 150 000 |
| Outstanding loan principal repayment | | | | | | ($625 000) |
| Net cash flow | | $20 100 | $20 787 | $21 483 | $22 188 | $547 903 |
| Cash flows discounted @ 8% | | $18 611 | $17 821 | $17 054 | $16 309 | $372 893 |
| Sum of PV of cash flows | $442 688 | | | | | |
| NPV | $92 688 | | | | | |

### Decision

This investment meets the investor's required return because NPV(ER) > 0. If the block of flats is purchased by the investor, their wealth is expected to increase by over $92 000. Further, using Excel, the IRR for the investment is 13.7%, which meets the investor's minimum required return of 8.0%. Therefore, the investment in the block of new flats is financially viable for this investor.

## Feasibility analysis

Feasibility analysis is a common tool in property investment. It seeks to assess the most favourable of competing options. This could be a number of options, or it could be a single option that is being compared with the 'do nothing' option.

Feasibility analysis is undertaken when an investor is seeking to evaluate a proposed course of action, such as:

- undertake improvements to a property (and potentially improve rentals)
- change the use of a property (say, a conversion from office to apartments)
- undertake a major development of a vacant site
- subdivide a site (say, residential sections) or a building (say, apartments).

In a simple form, the steps of feasibility analysis are as follows:

1. Decide on investment objectives (for example, a % rate of return or profit)
2. Identify options
3. Evaluate options (compare costs, benefits and risks)
4. Select the best alternative based on comparison with the investment objectives.

Feasibility analysis could either compare alternatives or be used to test the feasibility of one option compared to 'do nothing'. For larger scale investments (say, a redevelopment of an office block), this could involve a complex NPV calculation over a number of years including the use of different discount rates that take account of the risk of each option. A simple feasibility analysis for a residential property is shown in Example 6.

---

**Example 6: Feasibility of residential refurbishment**

An investor owns a one-bedroom flat and is deciding whether it is feasible to invest in upgrading the kitchen and bathroom. The investor can achieve a 10% return on other investments of similar risk and therefore considers the achievement of this rate of return to be the investment objective. Is it feasible to undertake the upgrade?

| | |
|---|---|
| Expected property valuation after upgrade | $535 000 |
| Less current property valuation | $500 000 |
| Expected valuation increase | $35 000 |
| Less cost of cosmetic upgrade | $28 000 |
| Profit from cosmetic upgrade ($35 000 – $28 000) | $7 000 |

Return on capital invested: $7 000 / $28 000 = 25%

The investment objective is to achieve a 10% return on funds invested. Based on that investment objective, the analysis shows that the decision would be to proceed with the upgrade.

---

## Capitalisation of property income

In addition to the core concepts of single-period returns and multi-period NPV and IRR calculations, in Chapter 5 we also explored the capitalisation of property income using the perpetuity valuation approach (capitalisation rate valuation). The capitalisation rate valuation method is commonly used to estimate expected sale price, or the market value of the property at the end of the investment period. Recall from Chapter 5 that the capitalisation rate valuation method is based on the perpetuity formula, and therefore estimates the value of the property at a particular point in time, based on all future net operating cash flows.

> **Example 7: Estimating property value at end of investment period**
>
> You need to estimate the market value of a commercial property at the end of the ten-year investment period before you can complete the discounted cash flow analysis. To do so, you first estimate the net operating income in year 11 as $210 000. Next, determine that similar commercial properties have been selling at an 8% capitalisation rate.
>
> $$\text{Value} = \frac{\text{Net operating income}}{r} = \frac{\$210\,000}{0.08} = \$2\,625\,000$$
>
> Therefore, the estimated value of the commercial property at the end of year 10 is $2 625 000. Note that net operating income used is before interest expense and tax because we want to estimate the property's market value in year 10. As discussed in the section *Investor-specific considerations* earlier in the chapter, market-based estimates are before financing and tax cash flows.

### Financing property investments

As noted above and in Chapters 5 and 7, table (or amortised) loans are common in a property context, and it is common for loan contracts to be broken ahead of maturity. This requires the property professional to be able, during the term of an amortised loan, to calculate the outstanding principal remaining on the loan using the loan repayment schedule described in Chapter 5.

Example 8 shows a table loan repayment schedule which contains important financing cash flow information required in the NPV(ER) discounted cash flow analysis. This information is also used by property investors to separate the principal and interest components of loan payments for the purposes of tax calculations.

Also related to the financing of property is the use of sinking funds, which are created to regularly set aside money for the repayment of debt used to finance the property and/or to cover the costs associated with major capital items in large buildings. Examples include funding of upgrades to the building such as future seismic strengthening or conversion into a green building, or the expected replenishing of major plant such as lifts and air-conditioning. A sinking fund is used to create an annualised allowance for these large but infrequent costs. This is particularly important to ensure that these costs are appropriately allowed for on an annual basis, and therefore allocated to lease durations (or to the tenure of apartment ownership) when these are for a shorter term than the life of the asset being replaced. This is particularly relevant to unit-titled apartments to ensure that properties can be sold at any point without an unanticipated major cost being incurred that may have an impact on the fairness of the price.

> **Example 8: Loan repayment schedule**
>
> An investor has secured a $2 500 000 table loan to buy a commercial property. The loan will be repaid in five equal annual payments and the interest rate is 5.5%.
>
> | Year | Beginning balance | Loan payments | Interest payments | Principal payments | Ending balance |
> |---|---|---|---|---|---|
> | 1 | $2 500 500 | $585 441 | $137 500 | $447 941 | $2 052 059 |
> | 2 | $2 052 059 | $585 441 | $112 863 | $472 578 | $1 579 481 |
> | 3 | $1 579 481 | $585 441 | $86 871 | $498 570 | $1 080 911 |
> | 4 | $1 080 911 | $585 441 | $59 450 | $525 991 | $554 920 |
> | 5 | $554 920 | $585 441 | $30 521 | $554 920 | $0 |
>
> The shaded cells in the loan repayment schedule above indicate information that is required in the discounted cash flow analysis using the NPV(ER) method.

## Conclusion

This capstone chapter focuses on property and allowed us to integrate material from throughout the textbook. We initially discussed some of the key motivations for investing in property while also considering the potential drawbacks. We then looked at single-period return calculations that are commonly used in the industry to evaluate property investments.

We then considered investor-specific characteristics such as their personal risk preferences, taxation and debt-financing requirements which affect an individual investor's required returns. These investor-specific characteristics can be directly incorporated into the discounted cash flow analysis commonly used to evaluate property investments over multiple periods. For example, the NPV(ER) method includes the investor's specific financing requirements, including their own equity outlay in the initial investment, annual interest and principal payments, tax liabilities and their risk preferences as reflected in the required rate of return used to discount the cash flows.

## SELF-TEST QUESTION

The following discounted cash flow analysis relating to commercial property is provided as an extension example. It also demonstrates how important information about table loans, loan repayment schedules, and capitalisation of income measures, previously explored in Chapters 5 and 7, are integrated into discounted cash flow analysis of property.

*Background information*

Construct discounted cash flows to analyse an investment in a commercial building with a lettable area of 2 100 square metres which is to be purchased for $7 000 000 (assume $3 000 000 in land and $4 000 000 in improvements). All leases are net leases wherein the tenant is responsible for the building's operating expenses, and as such the unrecoverable operating expenses are nil. Rents are reviewed annually, and there are no leases expiring during the investment period so there is no vacancy allowance.

The investor will invest 40% of the purchase price using their own money. The remaining 60% of the purchase price will be financed with a 15-year table loan at an interest rate fixed at 8%. Other relevant information includes:

| Investment period | 5 years |
|---|---|
| Net lettable area per floor | 2 100 m2 |
| Commencement rent | $300 per m2 net of operating expenses |
| Rental increase | 2% per annum |
| Management fees | 5% of gross income (not recoverable from tenant) |
| Property value at end of investment period | Capitalise the net operating income in year 6 at a capitalisation rate of 7.5% to estimate the expected sale price of the building |
| Balance of loan principal owing to be repaid on sale of the property at end of year 5 | |
| Investor's after-tax required return | 7% |
| Tax rate | 33% |

Finally, it is assumed that no depreciation can be claimed over the investment period (this would be dependent on the current tax rules at the time of the analysis).

a Calculate the annual payment required on the table loan.
b Construct the loan repayment schedule, using the following template to assist

| Year | Beginning balance | Loan payments | Interest payments | Principal payments | Ending balance |
|------|-------------------|---------------|-------------------|--------------------|----------------|
| 1    |                   |               |                   |                    |                |
| 2    |                   |               |                   |                    |                |
| 3    |                   |               |                   |                    |                |
| 4    |                   |               |                   |                    |                |
| 5    |                   |               |                   |                    |                |
| 6    |                   |               |                   |                    |                |
| 7    |                   |               |                   |                    |                |
| 8    |                   |               |                   |                    |                |
| 9    |                   |               |                   |                    |                |
| 10   |                   |               |                   |                    |                |
| 11   |                   |               |                   |                    |                |
| 12   |                   |               |                   |                    |                |
| 13   |                   |               |                   |                    |                |
| 14   |                   |               |                   |                    |                |
| 15   |                   |               |                   |                    |                |

c  Construct the discounted cash flow analysis to analyse the commercial property investment, using the following template to assist.

|  | Year | | | | | | |
|---|---|---|---|---|---|---|---|
|  | 0 | 1 | 2 | 3 | 4 | 5 | 6 |
| Equity outlay |  |  |  |  |  |  |  |
| Gross income |  |  |  |  |  |  |  |
| Less Vacancies |  |  |  |  |  |  |  |
| Effective gross income |  |  |  |  |  |  |  |
| Operating expenses |  |  |  |  |  |  |  |
| Management fee |  |  |  |  |  |  |  |
| Total expenses |  |  |  |  |  |  |  |
| Net operating income |  |  |  |  |  |  |  |
| Interest payments |  |  |  |  |  |  |  |
| Taxable income |  |  |  |  |  |  |  |
| Taxation at 33% |  |  |  |  |  |  |  |
| Loan principal payments |  |  |  |  |  |  |  |
| Ending property value |  |  |  |  |  |  |  |
| Outstanding loan principal repayment |  |  |  |  |  |  |  |
| Net cash flow |  |  |  |  |  |  |  |
| Present value of cash flow at 7% |  |  |  |  |  |  |  |
| Sum of PV of cash flows |  |  |  |  |  |  |  |
| Net present value |  |  |  |  |  |  |  |

**d** Using the capitalisation of income valuation approach in Chapter 5, estimate the value of the commercial property at the end of year 5. *Hint*: You will need to first estimate net operating income in year 6 from the analysis above in part **c**.

**e** What is the investment recommendation?

## ANSWER TO SELF-TEST QUESTION

**a** The initial amount borrowed for the table loan is $4 200 000, which represents 60% of the $7 000 000 purchase price. The initial amount borrowed is the PVA of the loan.

$$\text{PMT} = \frac{\text{PVA} \times r}{1 - (1 + r)^{-n}}$$

$$= \frac{\$4\,200\,000 \times 0.08}{1 - (1 + 0.08)^{-15}}$$

$$= \frac{336\,000}{1 - 0.31524}$$

$$= \$490\,684$$

**b** The highlighted areas below represent information required to complete the discounted cash flow analysis in the next question.

| Year | Beginning balance | Loan payments | Interest payments | Principal payments | Ending balance |
|---|---|---|---|---|---|
| 1 | $4 200 000 | $490 684 | $336 000 | $154 684 | $4 045 316 |
| 2 | $4 045 316 | $490 684 | $323 625 | $167 059 | $3 878 257 |
| 3 | $3 878 257 | $490 684 | $310 261 | $180 424 | $3 697 834 |
| 4 | $3 697 834 | $490 684 | $295 827 | $194 857 | $3 502 976 |
| 5 | $3 502 976 | $490 684 | $280 238 | $210 446 | $3 292 530 |
| 6 | $3 292 530 | $490 684 | $263 402 | $227 282 | $3 065 249 |
| 7 | $3 065 249 | $490 684 | $245 220 | $245 464 | $2 819 784 |
| 8 | $2 819 784 | $490 684 | $225 583 | $265 101 | $2 554 683 |
| 9 | $2 554 683 | $490 684 | $204 375 | $286 309 | $2 268 373 |
| 10 | $2 268 373 | $490 684 | $181 470 | $309 214 | $1 959 159 |
| 11 | $1 959 159 | $490 684 | $156 733 | $333 951 | $1 625 208 |
| 12 | $1 625 208 | $490 684 | $130 017 | $360 667 | $1 264 540 |
| 13 | $1 264 540 | $490 684 | $101 163 | $389 521 | $875 020 |
| 14 | $875 020 | $490 684 | $70 002 | $420 683 | $454 337 |
| 15 | $454 337 | $490 684 | $36 347 | $454 337 | $0 |

**c** Please note that the ending property value in year 5 of $8 810 565 is based on the calculation in part **d** below.

|  | Year | | | | | | |
|---|---|---|---|---|---|---|---|
|  | 0 | 1 | 2 | 3 | 4 | 5 | 6 |
| Equity outlay | ($2 800 000) | | | | | | |
| Gross income | | $630 000 | $642 600 | $655 452 | $668 561 | $681 932 | $695 571 |
| Less vacancies | | Nil | Nil | Nil | Nil | Nil | Nil |
| Effective gross income | | $630 000 | $642 600 | $655 452 | $668 561 | $681 932 | $695 571 |
| Operating expenses | | Nil | Nil | Nil | Nil | Nil | Nil |
| Management fee | | $31 500 | $32 130 | $32 773 | $33 428 | $34 097 | $34 779 |
| Total expenses | | $31 500 | $32 130 | $32 773 | $33 428 | $34 097 | $34 779 |
| Net operating income | | $598 500 | $610 470 | $622 679 | $635 133 | $647 836 | $660 792 |
| Interest payments | | $336 000 | $323 625 | $310 261 | $295 827 | $280 238 | |
| Taxable income | | $262 500 | $286 845 | $312 419 | $339 306 | $367 598 | |
| Taxation at 33% | | $86 625 | $94 659 | $103 098 | $111 971 | $121 307 | |
| Loan principal payments | | $154 684 | $167 059 | $180 424 | $194 857 | $210 446 | |
| Ending property value | | | | | | $8 810 565 | |
| Outstanding loan principal repayment | | | | | | $3 292 530 | |
| Net cash flow | | $21 191 | $25 127 | $28 897 | $32 478 | $5 553 879 | |
| Present value of cash flow at 7% | | $19 805 | $21 947 | $23 589 | $24 777 | $3 959 839 | |
| Sum of PV of cash flows | $4 049 956 | | | | | | |
| Net present value | $1 249 956 | | | | | | |

d First estimate the net income in year six (reason: the time value of money formulas assume cash flows are end-of-period cash flows). The net operating income in year six, from part c above, is the numerator in the capitalisation rate valuation formula (from Chapter 5) as follows.

$$\text{Capitalisation rate valuation} = \frac{\text{Net operating income}}{r}$$

$$= \frac{\$660\,792}{0.075}$$

$$= \$8\,810\,565$$

The $8,810,565 becomes the estimated ending property value shown in the discounted cash flow analysis above.

e The NPV of the project is greater than $0 and therefore meets the investor's financial requirements. By accepting the project, the investor will be adding approximately $1 250 000 to their wealth.

## QUESTIONS AND PROBLEMS

1 List and briefly explain the advantages of owning property.
2 List and briefly explain the disadvantages of owning property.
3 How can indirect investment affect the advantages and disadvantages of owning property?
4 What are some of the factors affecting unsystematic risk of a real estate investment?
5 If a property produces a gross income of $50 000, unrecovered building operating expenses of $10 000 and the property is worth $500 000:
   a Calculate the gross return of the property.
   b Calculate the net return of the property.
6 What are the main differences between a flat and a table (i.e. amortised) loan?
7 Why is the equity residual NPV method typically applied to the evaluation of property investments?

8. *Residential rental investment.* Using the investment template below, construct a discounted cash flow analysis to analyse a five-year investment in a new residential townhouse which can be purchased for $650 000.
   - Debt financing is by way of a $300 000 flat loan at 8% interest. The loan is to be repaid on sale of the property in year 5.
   - Current rental will be $850 per week (per annum, assume 50 weeks of rental income and 2 weeks of vacancy).
   - Annual rental increase: 2% per annum.
   - Annual increase in expenses: 4% per annum.
   - Sale price in year 5 is expected to be $750 000.
   - Local authority rates, repairs and maintenance, and insurance in year 1 are expected to be $12 000 in total.
   - A property manager will be hired to manage the property at a cost of 7% of gross rental income.
   - The investor requires an after-tax return of 7% on the investment and their tax rate is 33%.

|  | Year | | | | | |
| --- | --- | --- | --- | --- | --- | --- |
|  | 0 | 1 | 2 | 3 | 4 | 5 |
| Equity outlay | | | | | | |
| Gross rental income | | | | | | |
| Operating expenses | | | | | | |
| Rates, R&M, insurance | | | | | | |
| Management | | | | | | |
| Total operating expenses | | | | | | |
| Net operating income | | | | | | |
| Mortgage interest payment | | | | | | |
| Taxable income | | | | | | |
| Taxation at 33% | | | | | | |
| Sale of flats | | | | | | |
| Loan principal repayment | | | | | | |
| Net cash flow | | | | | | |
| Present value of cash flow at 7% | | | | | | |
| Sum of PV of cash flows | | | | | | |
| Net present value | | | | | | |

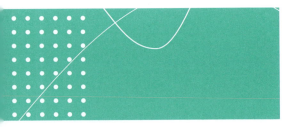

# Glossary

**accounting return on investment (AROI)** The profit from an investment as a percentage of the investment outlay. (Ch. 12)

**accounting system** A method of recording financial transactions. (Ch. 9)

**accounts** Items accounted for on a balance sheet, income statement, or cash flow statement. (Ch. 9)

**accounts payable** Current debts arising from the purchases of goods and services. (Ch. 9)

**accounts receivable** Short-term debt due from a customer, on account of goods sold in the normal course of business. Also known as *debtors*. (Ch. 8)

**accrual** Accrual accounting records cash and credit transactions as they are incurred and not when the cash flows arise. (Ch. 1)

**Act** A codified decision provided by a legislative body. (Ch. 1)

**adjusted tax value** For income tax purposes, the undepreciated balance of the depreciable value of an asset (also known as an asset's book value for tax purposes). (Ch. 11)

**agency costs** Costs incurred to monitor management and costs associated with offering financial incentives to act consistently with shareholder wealth maximisation. (Ch. 8)

**agency problems** Issues that arise when managers who are hired as agents of a company, work in their own interests rather than in those of the shareholders. (Ch. 1)

**amortisation** Process of discharging a debt by a set of regular and equal or unequal payments that include the amount borrowed and interest owing. (Ch. 5)

**annual holding period yield** The annual percentage return received on an investment. (Ch. 6)

**annual percentage rate (APR)** The annualised interest rate that uses simple interest ratios to annualise an interest rate quoted on a fraction of a year. (Ch. 4)

**annual retirement income** The various sources of income that can be used to fund retirement. (Ch. 7)

**annuity** A regular stream of payments over a fixed time. (Ch. 5)

**annuity due** An annuity with a payment made immediately; that is, the first payment is at time zero. (Ch. 5)

**arbitrage** The simultaneous buying and selling of a product to take advantage of price differences. In this process, the price differences are reduced. (Ch. 2)

**arbitrageur** A market player who carries out arbitrage. (Ch. 2)

**arm's length transaction** Fair, uncoerced property exchange between unrelated parties at market value. (Ch. 2)

**asset** A commodity or quality that is useful or valuable. (Ch. 1)

**auction** A market where the orders of traders are matched directly with the brokers. (Ch. 2)

**average age of inventory (AAI)** Average length of time between the purchase and sale of inventory. (Ch. 9)

**average collection period (ACP)** Average length of time between the sale of inventory and the receipt of cash for payment from the customer. (Ch. 9)

**average payment period (APP)** Average length of time to pay for materials and labour consumed. (Ch. 9)

**balance sheet** Statement of an individual's or organisation's assets, liabilities and equity at a given date. (Ch. 2)

**bank bills** Unsecured short-term marketable securities issued by companies with payment arranged through a bank. (Ch. 2)

**bank overdraft** A short-term loan whereby a bank gives permission to a borrower to have a negative bank balance up to a pre-arranged limit. (Ch. 8)

**beta, β** Measures the volatility of an individual security or portfolio in relation to the market (Ch. 6)

**bill** A short-term debt instrument that is issued at a discount to its face value. (Ch. 2)

**blockchain** Decentralised, immutable (i.e. permanent, irreversible) ledger technology ensuring secure and transparent record-keeping for cryptocurrency transactions. (Ch. 2)

**bonds** Fixed-interest investments whereby the individual receives a number of payments at fixed intervals until the bond is repaid. They represent the long-term debt obligations of a company or government. (Ch. 1)

**borrower** An individual, or organisation, who obtains or receives something, such as money, temporarily from another individual or organisation, with the intention of repaying it. (Ch. 1)

**broker** An agent who, for a fee or commission, carries out transactions such as the buying and selling of shares for a client. (Ch. 2)

**budgeting** Process of allocating income and expenditure over a future period. (Ch. 7)

**bundle of rights** Ownership rights encompassing possession, use, exclusion, and transfer of property. (Ch. 2)

**business plan** Plan developed for a proposed business venture based on a preliminary evaluation and information gathered from research. (Ch. 7)

**business risk** Fluctuations in cash flows, such as sales. (Ch. 6)

**call deposit** A deposit that can be redeemed immediately. (Ch. 3)

**call option** An option where the buyer has the right, but not the obligation, to buy the underlying asset at a predetermined price before a specified date. (Ch. 2)

**callable deposits** Deposits that are available on demand from a bank without penalty for early payment. (Ch. 3)

**capital** Wealth that is available to be used to produce more wealth. (Ch. 7)

**capital asset pricing model (CAPM)** The CAPM calculates the required rate of return for any risky asset. (Ch. 6)

**capital budgeting** The process of determining, evaluating and implementing long-term investment opportunities. (Ch. 11)

**capital gain** Amount by which the selling price of an asset exceeds its purchase price. (Ch. 6)

**capital loss** Amount by which the selling price of an asset is below its purchase price. (Ch. 6)

**capital markets** The financial markets where the longer-term, relatively riskier debt and equity securities trade. (Ch. 2)

**capital notes** Bond issues that are not supported by any underlying security and that pay higher interest than corporate bonds supported by underlying assets. (Ch. 2)

**capital rationing** A condition of insufficient funding to undertake all desirable investment projects. (Ch. 12)

**capital structure** The proportionate mix of debt and equity used to finance a firm. (Ch. 10)

**capitalisation approach** Valuation method for determining property value by dividing income by the capitalisation rate. (Ch. 5)

**capitalisation rate** Yield-based rate used to estimate property value in the capitalisation approach. (Ch. 5)

**capitalise** To treat an outlay as a long-term asset on the balance sheet, and not as an expense on the income statement. (Ch. 11)

**cash conversion cycle (CCC)** Average length of time that cash is tied up in net working capital. Calculated as AAI + ACP − APP. (Ch. 9)

**cash disbursements** Cash payments. (Ch. 9)

**cash flow statement** Statement showing the inflows and outflows of cash over a defined period of time. (Ch. 7)

**cash flows** The inflow (receipts) and outflow (disbursements) of funds. (Ch. 1)

**cash management** The management of cash-on-hand, bank balances and marketable securities. (Ch. 9)

**cash receipts** Cash inflows received. (Ch. 9)

**certificates of deposits (CDs)** Short-term debt instruments mainly issued by banks on behalf of corporates requiring short-term funding. Investors providing the funds do have the flexibility to sell them in the liquid secondary market before the deposit held by the bank matures. (Ch. 2)

**clearing house** A financial institution that guarantees the contract exchange between buyers and sellers of financial contracts; for example, futures contracts. (Ch. 2)

**collateral** Assets, such as inventory, that are pledged as security for a loan. (Ch. 10)

**collection policy** Procedures adopted to collect accounts receivable. (Ch. 9)

**commercial** Relating to commerce, profit-oriented. (Ch. 8)

**commercial bills** Unsecured short-term marketable securities issued either by companies or by banks. (Ch. 10)

**commercial paper** Short-term debt instrument issued directly into the market by companies with good credit ratings, with the aid of a financial institution, and known in New Zealand as *promissory notes*. (Ch. 2)

**commodity money** Money that has value in itself or is redeemable as something of value; for example, gold coins. (Ch. 3)

**company** A legal entity that operates and functions independently from its owners, and as such is responsible for all debts incurred in the course of business. (Ch. 1)

**compliance costs** Costs incurred to comply with laws, regulations or standards. (Ch. 11)

**composite return** Net income plus change in value of the investment over the value of investment at the beginning of the period. (Ch. 13)

**compound interest** Interest is calculated each period on the principal plus any interest. It is then added to the principal. (Ch. 4)

**compounding** The process of finding future amounts where interest is paid on interest already earned. (Ch. 4)

**conflicts of interest** Issues that arise when a manager, or director, uses company information to benefit themselves or another organisation. (Ch. 1)

**consolidated** The combined financial accounts of a group of companies, composed of a parent and its subsidiaries. (Ch. 10)

**Consumer Price Index (CPI)** Annual index updated quarterly that reflects changes in the general level of prices. (Ch. 6)

**contagion** An effect in which the uncertainty about one bank's finances can spill over to other banks and lead to heavy withdrawals by depositors. (Ch. 3)

**contributed capital** Funds contributed to a business by the owner(s). Represents a portion of owners' or shareholders' equity. (Ch. 8)

**convertible notes** Debt instruments that can be converted into shares. (Ch. 2)

**convertible securities** Securities that begin their life in one form (usually debt) and that may be converted to another form (usually equity) at a later date. Includes convertible notes, capital notes and convertible preference shares. (Ch. 10)

**corporate governance** The set of policies and procedures that direct and control how a company conducts its business. (Ch. 8)

**corporate social responsibility (CSR)** Business practice integrating ethical, social and environmental concerns into goals and operations, contributing to sustainable development and stakeholder well-being. (Ch. 8)

**correlation** A measure of the relationship between two sets of variables (Ch. 6)

**cost of capital** The cost of raising and using funds. (Ch. 10)

**cost of debt** The cost of financing with debt. Composed of interest and issue costs, less any interest tax shield. (Ch. 10)

**cost of equity** The cost of financing with equity. Composed of dividends and issue costs. (Ch. 10)

**country risk** Refers to the uncertainty of returns from investments in another country. (Ch. 6)

**coupon** The interest paid to the holder of a bond, based on a percentage of a bond's face value. (Ch. 4)

**creating shared value** Business strategy aligning corporate success with societal progress, aiming to address social issues while achieving economic goals. (Ch. 8)

**credit creation** The process by which banks create money from their lending of investors' deposits. (Ch. 3)

**credit period** The period ending with the final date for payment of an invoice. (Ch. 9)

**credit policy** Setting standards and guidelines that govern the management of accounts receivable. Consists of credit standards, credit terms and collection policy. (Ch. 9)

**credit standards** Criteria used to evaluate the creditworthiness of customers who are seeking to purchase goods or services on credit. (Ch. 9)

**credit terms** The time-frame requirements for customer repayments of trade credit. (Ch. 9)

**criterion** A decision rule used to evaluate the acceptability of a proposed investment. (Ch. 12)

**crowdfunding** A means of raising relatively small amounts of funds from the public to finance a business venture or project. (Ch. 10)

**cryptocurrency** Digital or virtual currency commonly built on blockchain technology. (Ch. 2)

**currency** An exchange medium within a country; that is, money. (Ch. 1)

**current assets** Cash, or assets which are expected to be converted to cash within one year. (Ch. 8)

**current liabilities** Debts that are due to be paid within the year. (Ch. 7)

**dealer** In the case of financial markets, an agent that takes ownership of the financial assets, and then makes a market by buying and selling those assets to investors. (Ch. 2)

**debenture** A medium-term to long-term loan agreement secured by assets of the borrower. (Ch. 6)

**debt** An obligation of one party (the borrower) to repay a specified amount of money to another party (the lender). (Ch. 1)

**debt–equity ratio** A measure of the proportion of long-term debt relative to shareholders' equity. (Ch. 10)

**debt ratio** A measure of the proportion of debt relative to total financing; or alternatively, the proportion of assets financed by debt. (Ch. 10)

**deep markets** Markets where there are numerous buyers and sellers. (Ch. 2)

**delivery date** Date at which the contract expires and the specified transaction is carried out. (Ch. 2)

**deposit** Amount given in part-payment of an asset. (Ch. 7)

**depreciable asset** A long-term asset that has a limited life, such as buildings and equipment. (Ch. 11)

**depreciable value** The value of an asset that is to be depreciated. Includes the purchase price plus installation costs. (Ch. 11)

**depreciation** The allocation of the cost of a long-term asset to the periods benefiting from its use. Represents a non-cash expense. Relates only to assets that decline in value over time. (Ch. 8)

**derivative instrument** Any instrument whose value is derived from the underlying asset on which it is based. (Ch. 2)

**digital wallets** Tools for storing and managing cryptocurrencies, providing secure access to private keys for transactions and balances. (Ch. 2)

**diminishing value (d.v.)** A method of depreciation that allows for higher depreciation expense in the early years of an asset's life. (Ch. 11)

**direct property investment** Ownership of physical real estate for income or capital appreciation. (Ch. 2)

**discount** The difference between the face value and the price of a financial asset, such as a bond or bill, where the face value exceeds the price. (Ch. 2)

**discount instrument** Financial asset that, when first issued, is below its face or par value, and when repaid at maturity includes principal and interest. (Ch. 2)

**discounted cash flow analysis** Valuation method in which the present value of future cash flows (i.e. NPV) is calculated. (Ch. 13)

**discounting** The process of finding current amounts by the process of present value. (Ch. 4)

**discounts** This means to find the present values of future amounts. This is the inverse of compounding interest. (Ch. 4)

**diversification** Practice of spreading risk by investing in a number of different assets. (Ch. 6)

**diversify** Place funds in a range of assets in order to spread risk. (Ch. 6)

**dividend policy** A strategic policy that considers the need for profits to be retained within the firm for reinvestment and the preferences of shareholders for the amount and consistency of dividends. (Ch. 10)

**dividends** The portion of a company's net profit paid to its shareholders (owners). (Ch. 1)

**earnings per share** Net profit after taxes divided by the number of ordinary shares on issue. (Ch. 8)

**economic life** The useful life of a business asset. (Ch. 8)

**economic order quantity (EOQ)** The optimal order quantity that minimises total holding and ordering costs. (Ch. 9)

**economic value added (EVA)** An alternative performance measure that takes into account cash flows and the total cost of debt and equity in order to measure annual value added. (Ch. 12)

**economies of scale** Economies of scale occur when the average cost of producing a product or service decreases as the amount produced increases. (Ch. 2)

**effective rate ($r_e$)** The actual rate of interest that includes an adjustment to the nominal rate for the frequency of compounding. (Ch. 4)

**efficient market** This market exists when the price of any good (asset) fully reflects all information associated with it. (Ch. 1)

**equity** Money, in the form of shares, supplied to a company or organisation by its owners. (Ch. 1)

**equity residual net present value, NPV(ER)** An alternative calculation of NPV, measuring the present value of equity cash flows pertaining to a project, minus the equity investment outlay. Uses the cost of equity capital or RARR as the discount rate. (Ch. 12)

**equity return measures** Equity income (before or after tax) over the investor's equity in the investment at the beginning of the period. (Ch. 13)

**ethics** The ability to know the difference between right and wrong. (Ch.1)

**eurobonds** Bonds issued outside the country of the currency in which they are denominated. (Ch. 10)

**eurocurrency loans** Loans issued by an international bank, denominated in a major currency other than the legal currency of the country in which it is issued. (Ch. 10)

**euroequities** Equity funds issued in offshore centres to achieve a wider distribution of ownership and greater capital than would otherwise be possible. (Ch. 10)

**Euromarket** An international financial market that facilitates the trading of debt and equity securities outside the country of origin. (Ch. 10)

**ex ante** Before the event. (Ch. 6)

**ex post** After the event. (Ch. 6)

**exchange rate** The price at which one foreign currency can be exchanged for another. (Ch. 2)

**exchange rate risk** The risk associated with fluctuations in exchange rates. (Ch. 6)

**exercise an option** When the holder of an option uses or takes up the option on or before the expiration date. (Ch. 2)

**exercise price** The price at which an option is to be settled; also known as the *strike* price. (Ch. 2)

**expectations** Beliefs or views about possible outcomes, such as the future direction of interest rates. (Ch. 2)

**expiry date** The date when an option terminates, also known as the *expiration date*. (Ch. 2)

**explicit interest cost** A stated interest charge. (Ch. 9)

**externality** An influence on the activities of an individual or business that is not controlled by the individual or business. (Ch. 1)

**face value** The maturity value of a bond, usually the principal, that is repaid to the lender. (Ch. 5)

**factoring** The discounted sale of accounts receivable to a factoring company or financial institution in return for immediate receipt of funds. Credit and collection activities are undertaken by the factor. (Ch. 10)

**finance** The allocation of scarce resources, such as money, over time. (Ch. 1)

**finance company** Finance companies raise funds in the markets and then lend to people for purchasing durables such as cars or home improvements. They normally charge higher interest rates to compensate for their riskier lending. (Ch. 1)

**financial assets** Securities issued by a corporation or economic unit for purchase by another individual or corporate investor. (Ch. 1)

**financial crises** Major disturbances in financial markets typified by steep declines in asset prices and widespread company failures. (Ch. 1)

**financial forecasting and planning** An ongoing process that involves forecasting financial performance, planning the sources and uses of funds, and monitoring cash flows. (Ch. 8)

**financial instruments** Instruments, such as convertible debt or preference shares, that allow funds to be transferred between investors (or lenders) and borrowers. (Ch. 1)

**financial intermediaries** Banks, insurance companies and other organisations that facilitate the flow of funds between investors and borrowers. (Ch. 1)

**financial lease** A lease contract whereby the lessee acquires the use of an asset over a period approximately equal to the useful life of the asset. (Ch. 10)

**financial management** Activities and decisions undertaken with regard to the financing and investment requirements of an organisation. (Ch. 8)

**financial market** A market used to transfer financial assets between borrowers and investors. (Ch. 1)

**financial planning activities** Those activities relating to managing money. (Ch. 1)

**financial risk** Relates to the amount of debt used to fund a firm's operations. (Ch. 6)

**financial system** A network which operates via a set of financial markets, bringing together investors and borrowers who buy and sell both real and financial assets; includes financial intermediaries, individuals, corporations, regulatory bodies and financial service organisations. (Ch. 1)

**financing cash flows** Cash inflows received and cash outflows incurred as part of the firm's financing activities. (Ch. 9)

**finished goods inventory** Fully completed goods available for sale. (Ch. 9)

**fixed assets** Assets that are real (for example, buildings, equipment, vehicles). (Ch. 7)

**fixed-rate mortgage** Mortgage where the interest rate is set at the beginning of the period and does not change. (Ch. 7)

**floating debenture** Medium-term or long-term debt funds secured by a charge over all otherwise unsecured assets. (Ch. 10)

**floating-rate mortgage** Mortgage where the interest rates rise and fall. (Ch. 7)

**foreign bonds** Bonds issued in a foreign country, denominated in the currency of that foreign country. (Ch. 10)

**foreign exchange** The process of converting New Zealand dollars into the currency of another country. (Ch. 1)

**forward contract** An agreement by two parties to carry out a financial transaction at a future (forward) point in time. (Ch. 2)

**forward market** A market for forward contracts that involve delayed settlement. (Ch. 2)

**freehold interest** Absolute ownership of real property with no time constraints; considered the highest form of ownership. (Ch. 7)

**future value** The value of a sum after receiving interest on it over one or more periods. Also called *compound value* when interest is compounded. (Ch. 4)

**futures contract** An exchange-traded, legal contract between a buyer, who agrees to take delivery of a specified asset at a predetermined time, and a seller who agrees to deliver the asset. (Ch. 2)

**global financial crisis** A worldwide financial crisis arising when financial-market participants recognise the risk and over-inflated values of financial contracts, leading to a severe contraction in the flow of funds and rapidly declining asset values. (Ch. 1)

**goal** The object (or aim) of a person's ambitions or efforts. (Ch. 7)

**goods and services tax (GST)** A type of value-added tax collected by suppliers of goods and services on behalf of the government. (Ch. 9)

**greenwashing** Misleading or deceptive marketing to create a false impression of a company's environmental responsibility. (Ch. 8)

**gross return** Total income generated before expenses divided by value of investment at the beginning of the period. (Ch. 13)

**ground lease** Lease of land for a specified period, with the lessee permitted to improve or build on the land. (Ch. 7)

**hedger** A market player who wishes to protect their position by reducing risk. (Ch. 2)

**hedging** The practice of managing risk exposure, often by using contracts (such as derivatives) that have an offsetting exposure. (Ch. 2)

**holding period yield** Percentage return recieved on an investment over the period it was owned. (Ch. 6)

**homogeneous** Something that is of a similar kind or nature. (Ch. 1)

**immobility of land** The inability of land to move to another location, which affects its value. (Ch. 2)

**implicit interest cost** An implied, but unstated, interest charge. (Ch. 9)

**income statement** Statement showing the income/deficit resulting from income and expenditure over a period. (Ch. 7)

**incremental** Directly relevant; additional; over and above the status quo. (Ch. 11)

**indefeasible title** Undisputed ownership rights providing legal certainty. (Ch. 7)

**indirect property investment** Investing in real estate through securities like listed property companies or real estate funds. (Ch. 2)

**inflation** Increase in the level of prices as a result of changes in demand or money supply. (Ch. 6)

**initial margin** The preliminary amount that needs to be deposited with a broker by the market player so that a futures contract may be bought or sold. (Ch. 2)

**insolvent** The status of an individual or a company with insufficient assets to meet their financial commitments. (Ch. 6)

**interest** The rate paid for borrowing or lending money. (Ch. 4)

**interest-free period** The period over which a supplier will extend credit to a customer with no explicit or implicit interest charge. (Ch. 9)

**interest tax shield** The savings a business makes due to the tax-deductibility of interest payments. (Ch. 10)

**intermediary** A financial institution that facilitates the transfer of funds between borrowers and lenders. (Ch. 2)

**intermediated** Parties are brought together by the help of a mediator. (Ch. 2)

**internal rate of return (IRR)** The percentage return that discounts all cash flows from a project, including the investment outlay, to zero. (Ch. 12)

**intertemporal** An adjective meaning *across time*. (Ch. 2)

**inventory** Goods for resale, or to be used in production of goods for sale. Also known as *stock in trade*. (Ch. 8)

**invest** To apply or put money to some use in order to defer consumption and receive a return in the future. (Ch. 1)

**investment** The activity of investing real and/or financial resources. (Ch. 1)

**investment banks** Institutions or divisions of firms that originate and distribute securities to open market investors. (Ch. 3)

**investment outlay** The net cash outflow normally paid out at time zero in order to undertake a project. (Ch. 11)

**investors** Individuals who acquire the financial assets of corporations or other organisations in order to receive compensation for the loan of their funds. (Ch. 1)

**investor-specific considerations** Unique factors influencing investment decisions, including choice of debt financing and the investor's marginal tax rates. (Ch. 13)

**invoice discounting** The discounted sale of accounts receivable to a factoring company or financial institution in return for immediate receipt of funds. Unlike factoring, credit and collection activities are retained by the seller of the accounts. (Ch. 10)

**issue costs** Administration, selling and underwriting costs associated with the issue of a new security. (Ch. 10)

**just-in-time system** An arrangement with suppliers for inventory to be delivered at the time when it is needed for production. (Ch. 9)

**KiwiSaver** A voluntary, mainly workplace, incentive savings scheme open to all New Zealanders to save for their retirement via a variety of investment options, from conservative to growth, offered by various financial intermediaries. (Ch. 3)

**landlord** Person who owns or leases property. (Ch. 7)

**lease interest** A contractual relationship between a tenant (lessee) and a property owner (lessor) where the tenant has the right to use the land for the period specified in the lease agreement in return for rental payments and other obligations. (Ch. 10)

**lender** Person who grants the use of money or any other asset to another for a set period of time and receives income in return. (Ch. 1)

**lender of last resort (LLR)** Banks which provide liquid funds to financial institutions in need. (Ch. 3)

**liability** Debts of an individual or company that represent obligations for repayment. (Ch. 4)

**limited liability** The state of being liable for all debts and monies owed up to a pre-defined amount. (Ch. 1)

**line of credit** An informal arrangement with a bank to allow a firm to borrow up to a maximum specified amount over a set period of time. (Ch. 10)

**liquidation** The process of winding up the assets of an organisation and distributing the funds to creditors and owners. (Ch. 1)

**liquidity** The quickness and ease of converting assets into cash. Sometimes called *marketability*. (Ch. 2)

**liquidity risk** The risk that an investor holding equity or fixed-income investments in a company may be unable to sell them to another investor. (Ch. 6)

**long hedge** This is when a market player buys a futures contract to protect an underlying physical position. (Ch. 2)

**long position** To agree to buy at a future date. (Ch. 2)

**long-term assets** Assets which are expected to provide benefits over more than one accounting year. (Ch. 8)

**loss** A negative 'profit' arising when expenses exceed income. (Ch. 10)

**macroeconomic** The relationships and forces that affect variables such as national income, prices and employment. (Ch. 3)

**margin call** The call for extra funds when adverse movements in the price of a contract erode the initial deposit to below a specified level. (Ch. 2)

**marginal analysis** Technique used in managerial finance whereby a proposal is accepted only when the added benefits exceed the added costs. (Ch. 1)

**market** A network whereby buyers and sellers are able to come together, either physically or through communication channels, to trade goods and/or services. (Ch. 1)

**market index** A measure of price levels in a market. (Ch. 2)

**market portfolio** The portfolio containing all risky assets. (Ch. 6)

**market risk premium (MRP)** The MRP is the additional return investors must earn to compensate them for investing in the market portfolio. (Ch.6)

**marketable securities** Short-term interest-earning financial claims that can be quickly converted to cash without any significant loss of value. (Ch. 9)

**marking to market** The process of adjusting an initial deposit of a good to its current market value. Usually occurs daily in the futures markets. (Ch. 2)

**maturity** The date when a security, for example, a bond, will be redeemed. (Ch. 4)

**maturity date** The date at which the last bond payment is due. (Ch. 5)

**maturity risk** The risk that changes in interest rates will adversely affect the prices or yields of long-term assets compared with short-term assets. (Ch. 3)

**merchant banks** Intermediaries who specialise in servicing the funding needs of medium and large companies. Also called *investment banks*. (Ch. 10)

**mining** Process of validating transactions and securing a cryptocurrency network by the solving of complex mathematical problems which is rewarded with new coins. (Ch. 2)

**monetary policy** The management of a nation's money supply and its links to interest rates, prices and other economic variables. (Ch. 2)

**money markets** A market in which short-term debt instruments with maturities up to a year are traded. (Ch. 2)

**moral hazard** A theory that the existence of insurance may induce undesirable behaviour. In relation to banks, it is the idea that banks may take excessive risks with depositors' funds. (Ch. 3)

**mortgage** A form of financial asset where the lender (mortgagee) has the right to recover their money by selling the property if the borrower (mortgagor) defaults on payment. (Ch. 4)

**mutually exclusive** Alternatives where only one can be accepted; an either/or decision. (Ch. 12)

**needs** Items of necessity. (Ch. 7)

**net present value (NPV)** The present value of all cash flows pertaining to a project minus the investment outlay. Measures the value added to a firm as a result of undertaking a project. Uses the WACC or RARR as the discount rate. (Ch. 12)

**net return** Investment income after deducting relevant expenses divided by value of investment at the beginning of the period. (Ch. 13)

**net working capital** Current assets minus current liabilities. (Ch. 9)

**net worth** Net worth represents the amount of money a person would have left over if all their assets were sold to pay off their debts. (Ch. 7)

**nominal interest rate** Interest rate that includes inflation. (Ch. 4)

**nominal rate** The quoted rate that includes inflation. (Ch. 4)

**non-recourse basis** With respect to the sale of accounts receivable, when the factor takes on the risk of bad debts. (Ch. 10)

**objective valuation** Unbiased assessment of a property's value based on market conditions and comparable sales. (Ch. 2)

**offshore currencies** The monetary medium of exchange relating to other countries. (Ch. 6)

**offshore finance** Capital raised overseas. (Ch. 10)

**operating cash flows** Cash inflows received and outflows incurred as a result of the firm's day-to-day operating activities. (Ch. 9)

**operating lease** A short-term, cancellable lease where the lessee gains the use of an asset without ever buying the asset. (Ch. 10)

**opportunity cost** The next best rate of return that would be achieved through an alternative course of action: the rate of return (market yields) in the financial markets is often used as a benchmark for opportunity costs. (Ch. 4)

**optimal capital structure** The best mix of debt and equity that minimises the cost of capital and maximises the value of the firm. (Ch. 10)

**ordinary annuity** An annuity with a first payment that occurs one period hence. Sometimes referred to as a *simple annuity* or an *annuity in arrears*. (Ch. 5)

**over-the-counter (OTC) market** A market that is not organised by an exchange organisation. (Ch. 2)

**owners' equity, partnership capital** A residual claim by the owner(s) on the assets of the business, after payment of all liabilities. (Ch. 8)

**par value** The face value on a bond, usually $1 000 in the United States and $100 in New Zealand. The face value is normally equal to the maturity value. (Ch. 5)

**parent company** A company that owns and controls another company. (Ch. 10)

**payback period** The number of years to recover, through operating cash flows, the money spent for an investment outlay. (Ch. 12)

**perpetuity** A security that promises regular cash flows forever. (Ch. 5)

**personal financial planning** Process of setting financial goals in order to satisfy a need. (Ch. 7)

**personal financial statement** Statement listing the items an individual owns (assets) and the amount of debt they owe to someone else (liabilities). (Similar to a balance sheet.) (Ch. 7)

**physical characteristics of property** The tangible attributes like size, location, and structure that affect a property's value and use. (Ch. 2)

**pledge** To put up assets as security for a loan. (Ch. 10)

**post-audit** An investigation, after the implementation of a project, to compare the actual and expected financial results. (Ch. 11)

**preference shares** Shares that give their holders priority over ordinary shareholders and have some characteristics common to debt instruments. (Ch. 2)

**premium** The payment from the buyer to the seller of an option. (Ch. 2)

**present value** The value of a future amount discounted at the appropriate market interest rate; that is, the current dollar value of a future amount. (Ch. 4)

**price discovery** The revealing of information about future cash market prices. (Ch. 2)

**primary market** Financial market in which new securities are sold and most of the funds raised go to the issuer. (Ch. 2)

**principal** The outstanding balance owing on a loan. (Ch. 4)

**private placement** A placement of shares or debt offered only to selected investors. (Ch. 10)

**private sector** The business sector of the economy. Excludes government departments and state-owned enterprises. (Ch. 8)

**profit** Excess of income over expenses. Alternatively referred to as *net profit, net income* or *net earnings*. (Ch. 1)

**promissory note** A written promise by the borrower to pay the lender a specified amount of money at some future specified date. Usually a short-term instrument issued by a corporate of good credit standing. (Ch. 2)

**prospectus** A document required by law to inform prospective investors in a firm of the details of the security and the firm's financial position. (Ch. 1)

**public goods** Goods or services, such as education, provided by the government for use by members of its society. (Ch. 1)

**public offering** Issue of securities by a company to the public. (Ch. 10)

**public sector** Government departments and state-owned enterprises. (Ch. 8)

**pure market system** A system in which all scarce resources are freely allocated so that the maximum benefit is received by everyone as a result of the allocation. (Ch. 1)

**put option** An option where the buyer has the right, but not the obligation, to sell an underlying asset at a predetermined price before a specified date. (Ch. 2)

**rate of return** The rate of increase or decrease between the present and future values of an amount over time, normally on an annual basis. (Ch. 4)

**raw materials inventory** Unprocessed materials inventory held while awaiting production. (Ch. 9)

**real assets** Assets that are tangible, such as land, buildings and machinery. (Ch. 1)

**real interest rate** The underlying interest rate with no inflation or uncertainty about future cash flows. (Ch. 6)

**recession** An economic decline or a contraction in business activity. (Ch. 7)

**record of title** Official document detailing property ownership and rights. (Ch. 7)

**repos** Repurchase agreements where financial institutions sell some of their government securities in exchange for cash, simultaneously agreeing to buy them back at some fixed later date. (Ch. 2)

**residential property** Property in which people live. (Ch. 7)

**resource consent** Formal permission by a government authority to allow an individual or an organisation to undertake a specified activity that may otherwise contravene environmental laws. (Ch. 11)

**retained earnings** Profits retained and reinvested in assets of the firm. Represents an internal source of equity finance. (Ch. 10)

**retirement income gap** The surplus or deficit in income required to fund one's retirement. (Ch. 7)

**return** Gains or losses received from the investment of funds for a given period of time. (Ch. 1)

**revolving credit facility** A legal commitment by a bank to provide credit to a borrower up to a maximum specified amount when requested. Similar to a line of credit. (Ch. 10)

**rights issue** If a company is seeking extra funds, it may offer the existing shareholders the right to subscribe for the extra shares. The right is renounceable if it can be sold to another party. The right is non-renounceable if it can be exercised only by the shareholder and not be sold. (Ch. 2)

**risk** The variability of returns resulting from an investment. (Ch. 1)

**risk-adjusted required return (RARR)** A risk adjustment technique that adjusts the discount rate applied to projects' cash flows in order to compensate for risk. (Ch. 12)

**risk aversion** The avoidance of risk. (Ch. 6)

**risk-free** Free from default risk. A government Treasury bill is regarded as risk-free. (Ch. 6)

**risk premium** Additional return investors require for investing in risky assets. (Ch. 6)

**safety motive** Maintaining additional cash balances for unforeseen day-to-day cash needs. (Ch. 9)

**salvage value** The price received from the sale of a fixed asset at the end of its useful life. (Ch. 9)

**secondary market** Financial market in which existing securities are bought and sold between investors. (Ch. 2)

**securities** The type of financial instruments used to finance an organisation's operations. (Ch. 1)

**securitisation** The process of repackaging and grouping loans so they have the characteristics of more liquid securities. For example, many of the mortgage loans in the United States have been repackaged into securities called *collateralised mortgage obligations* (CMOs). (Ch. 3)

**security market line (SML)** The SML displays the expected return of an individual security or portfolio in relation to its systematic, non-diversifiable risk (Ch. 6)

**sensitivity analysis** A risk assessment technique that changes one or two variables at a time to determine the effect on an outcome. (Ch. 12)

**settlement date** Also known as *expiry date*. It refers to the date when a contract expires. (Ch. 2)

**share options** A financial asset that gives the holder the right to purchase shares at a given price. (Ch. 8)

**shareholder** Any individual or entity owning shares in a company (Ch. 1)

**shareholders' equity (net worth)** The total of funds contributed by the shareholders plus earnings retained and reinvested in the firm. (Ch. 7)

**share** An entitlement to a proportion of the ownership of a company or firm. (Ch. 1)

**short hedge** This is when a market player sells a futures contract. (Ch. 2)

**short position** A selling position — the sale of a financial asset. (Ch. 2)

**simple interest** Interest calculated on the original amount. (Ch. 4)

**single-period return** Investment return over a specific time period. (Ch. 13)

**solvency** The ability of a person or an organisation to meet their financial commitments as they come due. (Ch. 8)

**speculative motive** Maintaining additional cash balances in interest-earning marketable securities in order to take advantage of unexpected investment opportunities. (Ch. 9)

**speculator** A market player who takes on risk in order to make a potential profit. (Ch. 2)

**spot market** A market that involves transactions that are settled without delay. (Ch. 2)

**spread** The difference between buying and selling quotations. (Ch. 2)

**stakeholders** Groups such as investors, suppliers, regulators, employees, customers and the public with interests in a firm. (Ch. 1)

**standard deviation** Measures the variability of a set of values. (Ch. 6)

**straight-line** A method of depreciation that expenses an asset by equal annual deductions. (Ch. 11)

**strategy** A plan of action designed to achieve a goal. (Ch. 7)

**strike price** The price at which an option is to be settled or exercised. (Ch. 2)

**subscribe** To agree to purchase a security, often shares. (Ch. 10)

**subsidiary** A company owned and controlled by another company. (Ch. 10)

**sunk costs** Cash outflows that have occurred and cannot be reversed irrespective of whether the project is accepted or rejected. (Ch. 11)

**superannuation** A scheme that allows individuals to invest funds over their working life to create income for when they retire. (Ch. 3)

**swaps** Financial instruments that involve the exchange of cash flows between two parties. (Ch. 2)

**SWOT** Analysis of a venture in order to determine its Strengths, Weaknesses, Opportunities and Threats. (Ch. 7)

**syndicate** A group of lending institutions which pool funds on a one-off basis to lend to a very large borrower. Limits risk exposure for any one given lender. (Ch. 10)

**systematic risk** Risk that cannot be diversified away because it pertains to the market. (Ch. 6)

**target annual retirement income** Amount of income required to cover estimated retirement expenses. (Ch. 7)

**tax credit** A deduction from taxes payable. (Ch. 10)

**term** The time between the beginning of an annuity's first payment and the end of its last payment. (Ch. 5)

**term loan** A loan from a bank with a specific maturity. (Ch. 4)

**term structure of interest rates** Relationship between time to maturity and percentage yield. (Ch. 6)

**terminal value** An estimate of the value to the firm of a long-term asset at either the end of the life of the project or at a predetermined cut-off point. (Ch. 11)

**thin markets** Markets in which there are not many buyers or sellers. (Ch. 2)

**time value of money** The concept that a dollar owned today is worth more than the same dollar would be worth in the future. (Ch. 1)

**trade credit** The purchase of goods or services on account, for payment at a later date. (Ch. 9)

**transaction costs** The costs involved in making financial deals, such as the costs of issuing new securities. (Ch. 2)

**transactions motive** Maintaining additional cash balances to pay for predictable day-to-day cash needs. (Ch. 9)

**Treasury bill** Short-term debt instruments issued by the government for short-term financing. (Ch. 2)

**underwriting** The agreement by an investment bank to purchase any securities that are not subscribed by the public in a new issue. (Ch. 10)

**unethical behaviour** A breach of a written or unwritten moral code. (Ch. 3)

**unlimited liability** The state of being personally liable for all debts and monies owed by a business or organisation. (Ch. 1)

**unpledged assets** Assets that have not been used as security for a loan. (Ch. 10)

**unsecured** When no collateral is offered as security against a loan. (Ch. 10)

**unsystematic risk** Risk that can be diversified away. (Ch. 6)

**variance** Measures how far each return is from the mean, or average, of all returns. (Ch. 6)

**venture capital** Funds (usually equity) provided to relatively new businesses by public companies or government-sponsored enterprises. (Ch. 10)

**wants** Items of desire. (Ch. 7)

**wealth maximisation** Represents the goal of financial management. Refers to maximising the wealth of the firm's owners. For a company, this is achieved by maximising the market price of the company's shares. (Ch. 8)

**weighted average cost of capital (WACC)** The overall cost to a firm of all long-term sources of finance. (Ch. 10)

**withholding tax** Tax deducted from a payment and remitted to the IRD on behalf of a recipient who receives the after-tax payment. (Ch. 10)

**work-in-process inventory** Partly completed goods that are still in production. (Ch. 9)

**writer of an option** The seller of an option. (Ch. 2)

**yield** The return on an investment, normally expressed as a percentage of its current value. By convention, it is quoted as an annual rate. (Ch. 2)

**zero-coupon bond** A bond that makes no interest payments during its lifetime. The interest is included with the repayment of principal at maturity. (Ch. 4)

# Appendix 1 – Some useful formulae

## Chapter 4

*Simple interest*

$$I = Prn \qquad (4.1)$$

*Future value, simple interest*

$$FV = P(1 + rn) \qquad (4.3)$$

*Present value, simple interest*

$$PV = \frac{FV}{(1 + rn)} \qquad (4.4)$$

*Future value of a single payment*

$$FV = PV(1 + r)^n \qquad (4.5)$$

*Present value of a single payment*

$$PV = \frac{FV}{(1 + r)^n} \qquad (4.6)$$

*Future value – multiple compounding periods*

$$FV = PV \times \left(1 + \frac{r}{m}\right)^{m \times n} \qquad (4.7)$$

*Present value – multiple compounding periods*

$$PV = \frac{FV}{\left(1 + \frac{r}{m}\right)^{m \times n}} \qquad (4.8)$$

*Continuous compounding/discounting*

$$FV = PVe^{rn} \qquad (4.9)$$

*Effective interest rate*

$$r_e = \left(1 + \frac{r}{m}\right)^m - 1 \qquad (4.10)$$

*Unknown interest rate*

$$r = \left(\frac{FV}{PV}\right)^{\frac{1}{n}} - 1 \qquad (4.11)$$

*Unknown time period*

$$n = \frac{\ln(FV/PV)}{\ln(1 + r)} \qquad (4.12)$$

## Chapter 5

*Future value – multiple cash flows*

$$FV = C_1 \times (1 + r)^{n-1} + C_2 \times (1 + r)^{n-2} + \ldots C_{n-1} \times (1 + r)^1 + C_n \times (1 + r)^0 \qquad (5.1)$$

*Annuity – present value*

$$PV = \frac{C_1}{(1 + r)^1} + \frac{C_2}{(1 + r)^2} + \ldots + \frac{C_n}{(1 + r)^n} \qquad (5.2)$$

*Annuity – future value*

$$FVA = PMT\left[\frac{(1 + r)^n - 1}{r}\right] \qquad (5.3)$$

*Annuity – present value*

$$PVA = PMT\left[\frac{1 - (1 + r)^{-n}}{r}\right] \qquad (5.4)$$

*Annuity (FV) – regular payments*

$$\text{PMT} = \frac{\text{FVA} \times r}{(1+r)^n - 1} \quad (5.5)$$

*Annuity (PV) – regular payments*

$$\text{PMT} = \frac{\text{PVA} \times r}{1 - (1+r)^{-n}} \quad (5.6)$$

*Annuity due (FV) – regular payments*

$$\text{FV Annuity due} = \text{PMT}\left[\frac{(1+r)^n - 1}{r}\right](1+r) \quad (5.7)$$

*Annuity due (PV) – regular payments*

$$\text{PV Annuity due} = \text{PMT}\left[\frac{1-(1+r)^{-n}}{r}\right](1+r) \quad (5.8)$$

*Constant perpetuity (PV)*

$$\text{PV} = \frac{C_1}{r} \quad (5.9)$$

*Growing perpetuity (PV)*

$$\text{PV} = \frac{C_1}{r - g} \quad (5.10)$$

*Capitalisation valuation approach*

$$V = \frac{\text{Net operating income}}{r} \quad (5.11)$$

*Capitalisation rate*

$$r = \frac{\text{Net operating income}}{V} \quad (5.12)$$

*Bond price*

$$P = \text{PMT}\left[\frac{1-(1+r)^{-n}}{r}\right] + \frac{F}{(1+r)^n} \quad (5.13)$$

## Chapter 6

*Risk-free interest rate*

$$\text{Risk-free interest rate} = \text{Real interest rate} + \text{Expected inflation rate} \quad (6.1)$$

*Nominal interest rate*

$$\text{Nominal interest rate} = [(1 + \text{Real interest rate}) \times (1 + \text{Expected inflation rate})] - 1 \quad (6.2)$$

*Real interest rate*

$$\text{Real interest rate} = \left(\frac{1 + \text{Nominal interest rate}}{1 + \text{Rate of expected inflation}}\right) - 1 \quad (6.3)$$

*Nominal interest rate*

$$\text{Nominal interest rate} \approx \text{Real interest rate} + \text{Expected inflation rate} \quad (6.4)$$

*Real interest rate*

$$\text{Real interest rate} \approx \text{Nominal interest rate} - \text{Expected inflation rate} \quad (6.5)$$

*Nominal return*

$$\text{Nominal return} = \text{Risk-free return} + \text{Risk premium} \quad (6.6)$$

*Risk premium*

$$\text{Risk premium} = \text{Nominal return} - \text{Risk-free return} \quad (6.7)$$

*Holding period yield*

$$\text{HPY} = \frac{(\text{EV} - \text{BV}) + C}{\text{BV}} \quad (6.8)$$

*Annual holding period yield*

$$\text{Annual HPY} = \left(\frac{EV+C}{BV}\right)^{1/n} - 1 \qquad (6.9)$$

*Mean*

$$\bar{r} = \frac{\sum r}{n} \qquad (6.10)$$

*Variance*

$$\sigma^2 = \frac{\sum_{i=1}^{n}(r_i - \bar{r})^2}{n-1} \qquad (6.11)$$

*Standard deviation*

$$\sigma = \sqrt{\text{variance}} = \sqrt{\sigma^2} \qquad (6.12)$$

*Expected return*

$$\bar{r} = \sum_{i=1}^{n} r_i \times \text{probability}_i \qquad (6.13)$$

*Variance*

$$\sigma^2 = \sum_{i=1}^{n} (r_i - \bar{r})^2 \times \text{probability}_i \qquad (6.14)$$

*Capital asset pricing model (CAPM)*

$$r_i = r_f + \beta_i(\text{MRP}) \qquad (6.15)$$

## Chapter 7

*Surplus (Deficit)*

Income − Expenses = Surplus (Deficit)     (7.1)

*Net worth*

Assets − Liabilities = Net worth     (7.2)

## Chapter 8

*Net profit after taxes*

Net profit after taxes = Income − expenses     (8.1)

*Earnings per share*

$$\text{EPS} = \frac{\text{Net profit after taxes}}{\text{Number of ordinary shares on issue}} \qquad (8.2)$$

## Chapter 9

*Cash discount*

$$CD = \frac{D}{100\% - D} \times \frac{365}{N} \qquad (9.1)$$

*Cash conversion cycle*

$$CCC = AAI + ACP - APP \qquad (9.2)$$

## Chapter 10

*Debt ratio*

$$\text{Debt ratio} = \frac{\text{Total liabilities}}{\text{Total assets}} \quad (10.1)$$

*Debt–equity ratio*

$$\text{Debt–equity ratio} = \frac{\text{Long-term debt}}{\text{Shareholders' equity}} \quad (10.2)$$

*Cost of debt*

$$r_d = r_i \times (1 - t) \quad (10.3)$$

*Cost of preference shares*

$$r_p = \frac{C_1}{PV} \quad (10.4)$$

*Weighted average cost of capital*

$$r_{cc} = (r_d \times w_d) + (r_p \times w_p) + (r_e \times w_e) \quad (10.5)$$

## Chapter 12

*Annual AROI*

$$\text{Annual AROI} = \frac{\text{Profit after taxes}}{\text{Investment outlay}} \quad (12.1)$$

*Average AROI*

$$\text{Average AROI} = \frac{\text{Average profit after taxes}}{\text{Investment outlay}} \quad (12.2)$$

*Net present value*

$$NPV = C_0 + \sum_{t=1}^{n} \frac{C_t}{(1+r)^t} \quad (12.3)$$

*Internal rate of return*

$$0 = C_0 + \sum_{t=1}^{n} \frac{C_t}{(1+IRR)^t} \quad (12.6)$$

## Chapter 13

*Gross return*

$$\text{Gross return} = \frac{\text{Gross income}}{P_0} \quad (13.1)$$

*Net return*

$$\text{Net return} = \frac{\text{Net operating income}}{P_0} \quad (13.2)$$

*Composite return*

$$\text{Composite return} = \frac{(P_1 - P_0) + \text{Net operating income}}{P_0} \quad (13.3)$$

*Equity return before tax*

$$\text{Equity return before tax} = \frac{\text{Equity income before tax}}{P_e} \quad (13.4)$$

*Equity return after tax*

$$\text{Equity return after tax} = \frac{\text{Equity income after tax}}{P_e} \quad (13.5)$$

# Appendix 2 – Suggested solutions for selected end-of-chapter questions and problems

### Chapter 4
- 4   $5 795.61
- 10   $78 943.83
- 12   $89 215.44
- 13   a   $6 077.53
-      c   $1 214.72
-      d   $2 188.32
-      g   $12 996.34
- 14   $11 972.17
- 17   $6 989.25
- 20   $8 010.21
- 23   10.38%
- 27   23.33%

### Chapter 5
- 1   $11 182.25
- 2   $937.96
- 5   $10 636.63
- 7   $4 667.58
- 9   $46.12
- 13   $4 304.12
- 16   $150 000
- 17   $1 094.18

### Chapter 6
- 2   Annual HPY = 0.237 or 23.7%
- 8   a   $E(r)$ = 0.1225 or 12.25%
-      b   $\sigma^2$ = 0.03012
-        $\sigma$ = 0.1736 or 17.36%
-      c   $E(r_{TTT})$ = 0.0599 or 5.99%

### Chapter 7
- 12   $67 634.75
- 13   $15 843.70

### Chapter 8
- 20   b   PVAQ = $3.43, PVR = $2.94
- 21   Select investment C
- 22   Accept projects G, J, L, M and N

### Chapter 9
- 24   $580 000 March, $720 000 April, $800 000 May
- 26   a   Closing cash balance 30 June $11 000
-      b   Closing cash balance 31 July ($2 000)
- 28   a   December net cash inflow $29 900
-      b   Cumulative financing needed – September $1 300, October $22 500, November $7 500

  Surplus cash to invest – July $9 500, August $9 700, December $22 400
- 36   18.3%. Interest at 15% take discount, 20% forego discount and pay in full
- 39   a   100 days
-      b   70 days

## Chapter 10

39  a   $5 480
    b i $5 880
    b ii $5 080

40  a
|   |                  | NWC      | TAFC    |
|---|------------------|----------|---------|
|   | Current:         | $10 000  | $8 700  |
| b | Incr. ST funds:  | $16 000  | $9 240  |
|   | Incr. LT funds:  | $ 4 000  | $8 160  |

43  a   EPS $0.0728
    b   EPS $0.0719
    c   EPS $0.0742

44  WACC = 14.3%

46  a   WACC = 15.3%
    b   Accept projects A and B

48  b   10%
    c   12.5%

49  a   10%

## Chapter 11

7   $9 925

9   $3 600

11  Investment outlay $500 000

    Operating cash flows: Yr 1 $88 750; Yr 2 $86 406; Yr 3 $84 356; Yr 4 $82 561; Yr 5 $80 991

    Terminal value $216 936

## Chapter 12

20  a   Yr 1, −7%; Yr 2, 4.75%; Yr 3, 11.75%; Yr 4, 18%; Yr 5, 18%
    b   9.1%
    c   No, average AROI < required 16% AROI

24  a   A 4–5 years; B 3–4 years; C 4 years
    b   A −$7 345; B $30 764; C $10 395
    d   Investment B is the best alternative

26  Accept projects C, A, F, D

29  a   L $2 189; A $8 444; H −$2 337
    b   Accept projects L and A, NPV > 0

# Acknowledgements

In 1999, Professor Lawrence Rose (former pro vice-chancellor and finance professor at Massey University and later dean and finance professor at California State University, San Bernardino, USA) asked the original authors of this textbook (Andrea Bennett, Jenny Parry and Carolyn Wirth) to write a finance textbook from a New Zealand perspective. His vision was to enhance students' appreciation of local as well as international markets by creating a finance book that would be particularly relevant to first-year business students. We acknowledge his foresight, as well as the contributions and assistance of the original authors.

In late 2023, the original authors kindly assigned their authorship rights including any royalties due for this fifth edition to the Massey Business School. All royalties are collected by the Massey Foundation and set aside to provide ongoing support for students in the School of Economics & Finance including, prizes, and scholarships. The Massey Business School is grateful for their very kind gesture.

We thank Hamish Anderson, David Smith, David White and Liping Zou, who generously gave of their time to update materials for this edition. We also thank Jenny Parry and Andrea Bennett for their thorough proofreads.

We also acknowledge the assistance of staff at Massey University Press. We particularly owe a debt of gratitude to Nicola Legat and Anna Bowbyes, who have been enthusiastic supporters of the book and provided timely advice and assistance.

# About the original authors

**Andrea Bennett** (BSc Hons, MBS, DipBusStud, DipTeaching) is a former lecturer in finance at Massey University. Andrea taught investments, financial markets and institutions, and researched in the areas of investments, especially managed funds and performance, and financial market analysis.

**Jenny Parry** (PhD), formerly a senior lecturer in finance at Massey University, is a self-employed consultant in investments and personal financial planning. Jenny has taught introductory finance and investments. Her PhD research topic was the financing of biotechnology companies.

**Carolyn Wirth** (BCom, MBA, PhD, CPA, CGA) is a former senior lecturer in finance at Massey University. She taught managerial finance and researched the capital-market impacts of disclosure and environmental information.

# Index

## A

accounting  6–7, 17, 183, 211
   and cash flows  183
accounting information system  179, 206
accounting return on investment (AROI)  271–73, 287, 318; *see also* profit
   criterion  273, 320
accounting system  211, 318
accounts  199, 318
   consolidated  235–36, 320
accounts payable  200, 202, 207–11, 213, 318
   cost of financing  207, 210–11, 213
accounts receivable  180, 200, 204–05, 213, 245, 318
   collection policy  205, 319
   factoring  230
   invoice discounting  230
   management of  17, 204–05, 228, 230
   pledging  42, 230
   *see also* credit
accrual accounting  6, 257, 318
Acts of Parliament  8–10
adjusted tax value  259–60, 261, 263–65, 318
agency problems and costs  13, 185, 189, 318
amortisation  104, 318
annual holding period yield  121–23, 209, 318
annual percentage rate (APR)  75, 318
annual retirement income  151, 318
annuities  87–95, 107, 318
   annuity due payments  88, 95–96, 318
   future value  88–90, 92
   ordinary  87–91, 93, 95, 325
   payment calculations  93–4
   present value and annuities  90–91
   value calculations  88–92
arbitrage  22, 33, 318
arbitrageurs  32, 33, 318
arm's length transaction  39, 318
assets  2, 5, 318
   current  146–47, 179, 199–201, 211, 237, 320; *see also* net working capital
   depreciable  259–66, 321
   financial  2–5, 19–23, 43, 51, 53, 57, 120, 146–47, 322
   fixed  147, 203, 322
   liquid and illiquid  22–23
   long-term  146–47, 179, 324; *see also* investment in long-term assets
   non-financial  121
   pledged  230, 325
   prices  21
   real (tangible)  3–5, 14, 20, 326
   risk-free  113–17
   risky  112, 117–19
   roles of  21
   sales  263–66
   terminal value  257, 261–66, 327
   transformation of assets  54–56
   unpledged  229, 328
auctions  24, 27, 318
auditors  13
Australian Prudential Regulatory Authority  46
Australian Stock Exchange  30–31
average age of inventory (AAI)  211–13, 318
average collection period (ACP)  211–13, 318
average payment period (APP)  211–13, 318

## B

balance sheets  21, 26, 47, 48, 145, 169, 231, 259, 318
   forecast  169
   personal  145–47, 325
bank bills  24, 232–3, 235, 318
banks  5, 14, 28, 45–52
   business financing  170, 223, 224–26, 228, 229–33
   central banks  2, 45–52
   credit creation  48–49
   foreign exchange  28
   forward contracts  33
   lines of credit  229–30, 324
   loans  54, 104–06, 164, 225–26, 229, 230–31, 232–38; *see also* mortgages
   overdrafts  178, 210, 212, 225–26, 229, 318
   property financing  164, 303, 310–11
   regulation of  47–48
   in transfer of funds  14, 52
   *see also* global financial crisis (GFC); investment banks (merchant banks)
Basel Accords  46–47
behavioural sciences  6, 7
beta (β) measurements  132–34, 318
bills  20–21, 24–25, 31, 233, 319
   bank bills  24–25, 31, 232, 233, 235, 318
   Treasury bills  20–21, 24–25, 114, 119, 201, 328
Bitcoin  35
blockchain  35, 319
bonds  4–5, 129, 319
   convertible  26
   Eurobonds  234, 321
   foreign  234, 322
   government  20, 21, 25–26, 50, 61, 134, 241
   markets  25
   par and face (maturity) values  100
   price calculations  21, 74, 100–04
   zero-coupon  73–74, 77, 328
      book value  *see* adjusted tax value
borrowers  3–5, 20, 12, 19, 20, 22, 25, 48, 53–57, 59–60, 104–05, 113, 178, 225–26, 230, 232, 233, 319
brokers  24, 27, 31, 54, 56, 57, 70, 319
brokerage  27, 54, 55
budgets/budgeting  145, 146, 319
   capital budgeting  255–66, 271–87
   personal budgeting  145–47, 155
Building Act (1991)  164, 297
building consents  164
bundle of rights  38, 157, 319
business environment  7–10
business starting or buying  166–70, 225
   business plans  169–70, 225, 319
   personality traits  167–68
   primary evaluation  168–69
business plans  17, 169–71, 225, 319

## C

calculators  62, 65, 69, 78, 79, 89, 91, 95
call options  34, 319
callable deposits  44, 319
capital  156, 319
   contributed  179, 320
   cost of  192, 240–45, 257, 275–78, 280–86, 320
   optimal capital structure  240, 325
   partnership  180, 225, 325
   structure  240
   venture capital  224, 225, 227–28, 328
   *see also* debt finance; equity finance; financing businesses; net working capital; working capital
capital asset pricing models (CAPM)  112, 133–35, 319
capital budgeting  255–66, 271–87, 319
   capital budgeting and inflation  284
   capital budgeting and risk  284–87
capital gains and losses  21, 102, 104, 123–24, 156, 263, 265, 297, 303–04, 319
capital markets  23, 25–8, 53, 56, 77, 319
   borrowing on  56, 77
capital notes  26, 56, 234, 236, 319
capital rationing  282–83, 319
capital structure  240–41, 244–45, 278–79, 305, 319, 325
capitalisation approach  98–99, 259, 298, 302, 307, 310–11, 319
capitalisation rate  98–99, 295, 307, 310, 319
cash and near-cash  200, 201
cash conversion cycle (CCC)  211–13, 319
cash disbursements  182, 202–04, 319
cash flows  6, 7–8, 21, 59, 97, 118, 178, 182–83, 201, 258–59, 273–81, 284–85, 302, 305–07, 319
   company  8
   discounted  306, 310–11, 321
   financing cash flows  202, 322
   future value of multiple cash flows  84–85
   holding cash  201
   incremental  258
   level cash flows  87–92
   liquidity and solvency  183
   measuring owners' returns  182
   multiple cash flows  84–87
   operating cash flows  202, 223–24, 257–62, 273, 310
   perpetuity  97–98
   present value of multiple cash flows  85–87
   single cash flows  78
   visibility/objectivity of  183
cash flow statements  170, 201–04, 319
   forecast statements  201–04
cash management (in business)  201–04, 319
cash management trusts  53
cash markets  21, 24, 32
cash receipts  182, 202–04, 319
caveats  162
central banks  2, 45–52
certificates of deposits (CDs)  24–25, 201, 319
chattels  157, 162
clearing houses  31–32, 319
Climate Change Response Act (2002)  10
collateral  230, 319
collection periods  211–13, 318
collection policies  204, 205, 213, 319
commercial bills  201, 232, 233–36, 320
commercial paper  24, 25, 56, 320
commodity money  43, 320
Companies Act (1993 and amendments)  9, 47, 202
company  5, 12–13, 19, 20–21, 26, 117–18, 169–70, 184–85, 190, 320
   parent  180, 235, 325
   private-sector  180, 326
   structure  184–85
company directors *see* directors
compliance costs  16, 257–58, 320
composite returns  299, 301–02, 320
compound interest  61, 63–8, 320
   and future value  63–67
compounding  64, 70–75, 106–07, 320
   compounding frequency  71–75, 106–07
   continuous compounding/ discounting  74–75
Computer Freehold Register (CFR)  160
conflicts of interest  13, 189, 320
consolidated accounts  235–36, 320
Consuls  97
Consumer Guarantees Act (1993)  9
Consumer Price Index (CPI)  113–14, 320
consumer protection laws  8–9, 45, 47
contagion  45, 320
contracts  12, 15, 22, 23
   forward  23–24, 29, 33
   futures  29–33
   options  34–5
contributed capital  179, 320
convertible notes  26, 320
convertible securities  234, 235, 320
corporate governance  8, 184–85, 187–89, 320
corporate social responsibility (CSR)  186–89, 320
correlation  132, 320
cost of capital  192, 240–45, 257, 275–78, 280–86, 320
cost of debt  222, 241–42, 320
cost of equity  242–44, 320
country risk  118–19, 320
coupon interest  21, 74, 100–04, 320
covenants
   loan  55
   property  159, 161, 162
   restrictive  162
creating shared value (CSV)  187, 188, 320
credit  6, 40, 211–12
   lines of credit  229–30, 324
   personal buying  145, 150
   policy/terms  190, 204–05, 319, 320
   ratings  25, 56, 119
   revolving credit  229–30, 326
   standards  204, 205, 320
   terms  204, 205, 320
   trade credit  205, 207–10, 227, 232, 238, 328
credit creation  48–49, 50, 320
   credit multiplier  49
credit period  205, 207, 208–10, 320
credit unions  52
creditors  7–8, 9, 11, 12, 185, 186, 229, 239
crowdfunding  224, 225, 227–28, 320
Crown and non-Crown instruments  25
Crown Minerals Act (1991 and amendments)  159
cryptocurrency markets  35, 320
   mining  35
currencies  5, 7, 21, 23, 28–29, 118, 168, 234, 320
   offshore  118, 325
   *see also* cryptocurrency; foreign exchange
current assets  146–47, 179, 199–201, 211, 237, 320
   *see also* net working capital
current liabilities  199–201, 206–07, 211, 237, 320
   *see also* net working capital

## D

dealers  24, 28, 32, 321
debentures  56, 119, 179, 229, 231, 232, 234, 241, 321
   floating  225, 322
debt  12, 147–48, 180, 321
   amortisation  104, 318
   cost of  241–43, 302, 320
   debt ratio  240, 321
   debt–equity ratio  179, 240, 321
   personal  165
debt finance  36, 39, 53, 118, 156, 178–79, 222–23, 225–26, 228–29, 232, 234–35, 239–40, 278–79, 295, 302–03
debt instruments  19, 21, 74, 100, 235
debt markets  232–4, 25–27, 62, 321
debt ratio  240, 321
debt servicing  98–9, 150, 165, 306
debt vs equity claims  20–21
decision sciences  6, 7

decision-making
  corporate 10–12
  financial 5, 6, 7, 178, 191, 193, 256, 296
  levels of 10–12
  partnerships 10–12
  personal 10–11, 142
  sole-proprietorship 10–11
deep markets 22, 24, 321
delivery date 33, 321
deposit insurance 46
depository institutions 46, 52, 56; see also non-depository institutions
deposits (as initial payments) 147, 153, 155, 164–65, 321
deposits (in banks and other financial institutions) 31, 46, 49, 52, 61–4, 86, 89
depreciable assets/depreciation 259–66, 321
  adjusted tax value 259–60, 261, 263–65, 318
  diminishing-value (d.v.) method 259–61, 321
  straight-line 259, 327
derivative (futures) markets 23, 24, 29–35
  clearing house role 31
  contract closing 31
  forward contracts 33
  margin requirements 31
  operation 30–32
  options contracts 34
  participants 32–33
  types of derivative instruments 29–30, 321
digital wallets 35, 321
directors 9, 12, 13, 184–85, 202, 222
disclosure of information 9, 15, 45, 47, 190, 227
discount instruments 20, 25, 321
discount windows 46
discounted cash flow (DCF) 67, 299, 300, 303, 306, 321
  analysis 306, 310–11, 321
discounts 20, 321
discounts on invoices 207–10, 230
discounting 20, 25, 63, 67–68, 71, 74–75, 88, 90, 295, 321
  annuities 88, 90
  continuous 74–75
  discount rate 50, 67–68, 85, 97–98, 277–80, 284–86, 307
  invoice 207–10, 230, 324
district plans 156, 163
diversification (of investment) 39, 53, 111, 112, 129–33, 298, 321
dividends 8, 10, 12, 121–22, 145, 180, 182, 186, 190, 220, 321
  payment of 21, 26, 118, 178, 182, 202, 222–23, 239, 242–44

policy 239, 321
taxation of 10, 223

## E

earnings per share (EPS) 181–82, 239, 321
easements 157, 162
economics 6, 7
  economic theories 6–7
economic life 180, 321
economic order quantity (EOQ) 206, 321
economic value added (EVA) 278, 321
economies of scale 22, 53, 54, 321
effective interest rates 75–6, 321
efficient markets 14–16, 23, 28, 321
encumbrances 162
environmental protection 10, 16, 163–64, 180, 186–88, 258
equities markets 23, 26–8; see also sharemarket
  operations and participants 27–28
  types of equity traded 267
equity 12, 26–27, 46, 129, 278, 321
equity claims 20–21
equity crowdfunding 227
equity finance 47, 118, 178–79, 206–07, 222–23, 225, 227, 231, 239–40, 306, 307–08
  cost of 240–03, 278–79, 320
equity residual net present value (NPV(ER)) 279, 305, 307–08, 310–11, 321
  cf. internal rate of return 281–82
equity return measures 304–05, 321
ethics 9, 13, 16, 56, 186–89, 192, 321
  agency problems 13, 189, 318
  conflicts of interest 13, 189, 320
  ethics and financial institutions 56
  ethics in property 189
  unethical behaviour 56, 191–92, 328
eurobanks 234
eurobonds 234, 321
eurocurrency loans 234, 235, 322
euroequities 234, 322
Euromarket 234, 322
exchange rates 21, 24, 28–29, 33, 322
  risks 21, 29, 118, 322
exercise price 34, 322
expiry/expiration date 29, 31, 34, 322
explicit interest costs 207, 322
external factors/externalities 16, 178, 189–90, 192, 322
external funding 239

## F

face value/par value (on bonds) 20, 74, 100–03, 322
factor markets 19
factoring 229, 230, 322

non-recourse basis 230
Fair Trading Act (1986) 9
finance companies 5, 8, 53, 56, 119, 322
  as lenders 8, 224–26, 233
finance
  and business 7–12
  definitions 4, 322
  interdisciplinary nature 6–7
  studying 5–6
finance companies 8, 9, 53, 119, 241, 322
financial assets 2–5, 19–23, 43, 51, 53, 57, 120, 146–47, 322
  markets and 2–4, 26, 29, 39, 53, 57, 60, 62, 120, 177
financial crises 8, 322
  financial decision-making 178, 191, 193, 256, 296
  financial intermediaries 3–5, 19–20, 35, 43–44, 45, 46, 52–57, 177, 232, 322
  see also global financial crisis (GFC)
financial decision-making see decision-making
financial forecasting 170, 178, 322
financial institutions 43–57
  credit creation 48–49
  development of financial system 43–48
  ethics 56
  financial intermediaries 52–56
  monetary policy 49–52
  types of financial transfer 56–57
financial instruments 4, 5, 19, 21–22, 25, 30, 189, 322
financial intermediaries 3–5, 19–20, 35, 43–46, 52–57, 177, 232, 322
  benefits of intermediation 53
  brokerage 54
  depository institutions 52
  non-depository institutions 52–53
  transformation 54–56
financial leases 226, 322
financial management 5–6, 176–98, 193, 322
  business ethics 187–89, 192
  cash flows 182–83
  decision-making process 193
  corporate governance 184, 187–89
  creating shared value (CSV) 187–88
  external environment 189–90
  financing 178–79
  investment in assets 179
  managers as agents 185
  objectives 180–87
  organisational context 179–80
  profit maximisation 181, 185–87
  risk–return trade-off 190–93
  risks and risk assessment 183–84
  role of 178–80

social responsibility  186–87
time value of money  181–82
wealth maximisation and economic implications  185–87
financial markets  3–6, 13–16, 21–41, 178–79, 189–90, 322
    capital markets  25–28
    cost reduction  22
    cryptocurrency markets  35
    deep  22
    derivate markets  29–35
    efficient  15, 16, 321
    establishing prices  22
    foreign exchange market  28–29
    forward  23, 29
    freedom of choice  14
    government role  15–16
    incentives  14–15
    instruments  24–25
    international  22
    intertemporal function  23, 323
    maintaining liquidity  22–23
    money markets  24–25
    participants  23
    primary  23–24
    private wealth  14
    property markets  36–41
    regulation of  9–10, 15–16
    risk transfer  23
    retail  23
    roles of  22–23
    secondary  24
    spot  29
    thin  22
    types of  23–24
    wholesale  23
    *see also* capital markets; debt markets; derivative (futures) markets; equity markets; foreign exchange (FX) market; money markets; property markets
Financial Markets Authority (FMA) 9–10, 13, 28, 47, 227
Financial Markets Conduct Act (2013) 9, 47
financial planning activities  3, 166, 178–79, 193, 201, 322
    cash inflows and outflows  201–02, 204, 213; *see also* liquidity
    for life  147–49
    personal  111, 142–44
    property investment planning  303
    retirement plan  150
financial risk *see* risk
financial statements  6, 13, 145–47, 170
financial system  4–5, 14–16, 36, 41, 56, 322
    development  43–45
financial transfers  56–57
    direct  56
    indirect  56–57

financing businesses  169–70, 178–79, 222–45
    cost of capital  240–45
    cost of debt capital  241–42
    cost of equity capital  242–44
    debt or equity finance  222–23, 239–40
    financing mix  237–40
    growth stage  228–32
    internal or external sources  239–40
    maturity stage  228–36
    short or long-term sources  237–9
    start-up stage  224–28
    weighted average cost of capital  244–45, 328
financing property  39, 104–05, 155–56, 164–65
finished goods inventory  205–06, 211–12, 230, 322
Fisher equations  115
floating debentures  225, 322
flotation (of shares)  26, 333
forecast cash flow statement  201–04
forecast financial statements  170
    cash flow  200–04, 261
forecasting and planning  178–79, 322
foreign bonds  234, 322
foreign exchange  5, 322
    forward contracts  23, 29, 30, 33, 323
    risk  21
foreign exchange (FX) market  24, 28–29, 33
    operation and participants  28–29
    types of instruments traded  29
formulae  329–32
forward contracts  23, 29, 30, 33, 323
    forward rate agreement  33
forward markets  29, 33, 323
freedom of choice  14
freehold homes  156, 159
freehold interest  156, 159, 161, 323
future value  60, 61–9, 71, 75, 78–79, 84–86, 323
    annuities  88–90, 92, 95–96
futures contracts  29, 30–33, 323

## G

global financial crisis (GFC)  8, 22–23, 40, 45, 46, 115, 323
    related recession  41, 47, 115–16, 237
goal attainment  111, 142–44, 146, 147, 149–50, 166, 167, 180–81, 187–88, 198, 255, 275, 281, 296, 323
gold and goldsmiths  43–45
goods and services tax (GST)  113, 202, 323
government bonds *see under* bonds
governments
    role of  15–16, 40, 45, 56, 178, 189, 303
    as stakeholders  10
    *see also* regulatory bodies

greenwashing  187–88, 323
gross return measure  299–300, 323

## H

hedge  32
    long  32, 324
    short  32, 327
hedger  32, 323
hedging  23, 30, 32–33, 323
hire-purchase loans  87, 190, 226
holding period yields (HPY)  121–24, 209, 323
    annual holding period yields  123–24
homogeneous goods  15, 121, 323
housing  36, 40–41, 104, 189
    owner-occupied  36, 41, 296
    role of housing in economic cycle  297
    statutory control  297
    *see also* land, landlords, loans, leases, mortgages, property, rent

## I

implicit interest cost  207, 323
imputation  10, 223, 242, 243
incentives  14–15
income statements, personal  145, 146–47, 323
income tax  10, 193, 226, 258, 259, 263
Income Tax Act: (1994) 259; (2007) 10
indefeasible (undisputed) title  160, 323
inflation  29, 48, 50, 51–52, 323
    capital budgeting and  284
    expected  113–14
    inflation hedge  296
    interest rates and  75, 113–17
inflation-indexed bonds  25
information disclosure  47
Inland Revenue Department (IRD)  73, 202, 210, 223, 259
insolvency  9, 26, 40, 45, 117, 200, 227, 228, 237, 323
institutional investors  27, 35, 228, 229
insurance companies  5, 27, 46, 52, 56, 91, 226, 229
insurance premiums  87, 145, 147, 152, 164, 227, 306
intangibles  157
interdisciplinary nature of finance  6–7, 17
interest  20, 60–61, 241, 323
    compound  61, 63–70, 320
    compounding frequency  70–75
    explicit cost  207, 322
    implicit cost  207–08
    simple  61–63, 327
interest-free period  207–09, 323
interest rates  5, 6, 7, 8, 21, 22, 26, 29, 40, 46, 49, 53, 60–61, 77–79
    annual percentage rate (APR)  75
    economic effects  40, 49–50

effective 75–76, 325
forward contracts 33
forward rate agreements (FRAs) 33
nominal 75–76, 114–15, 325
official cash rate 5 0
rate of return 75
real 112, 113–15, 326
risk-free 114
risk premium 115
solving for unknown interest rate 77–78
solving for unknown time period 78–79
spot 29
term structure 115–17, 327
volatility 23, 33
interest tax shields 241–42, 323
intermediaries *see* financial intermediaries
intermediated markets 24, 323
internal funding 239
internal rates of return (IRR) 270, 279–83, 323
inventories 180, 190–91, 200, 205–06, 224, 228, 229, 230, 323
average age of (AAI) 211–13, 318
as collateral 230, 319
computerised control system 206
economic order quantity (EOQ) 206, 321
finished goods 205–06, 211–12, 230, 322
just-in-time system 206, 324
management 205–06
raw materials 205, 206, 211, 326
work-in-process 205, 328
investment 4–7, 121, 323
investment banks (merchant banks) 53, 56, 232–33, 323, 324
investment companies 53, 153, 229
investment in long-term assets 255–311
capital budgeting 255–56
cost and benefit measurement 256–66
evaluation techniques 271–87
investment outlay 257, 323
operating cash flows 257–61
property investment 295–311
terminal value 261–66, 327
investment period 306
investors 4–10, 12, 20, 21, 24, 25, 26, 27, 35, 43, 47, 53, 117, 324
attitudes to risk 112–13, 119–21, 132, 183–84
institutional 27, 35, 228, 229
property investors 36, 163, 164, 296, 298–99, 302–03, 305
protection of 9, 47
requirements 54–55, 113, 115
invoice discounting 207–10, 230, 324
issue costs 26, 233, 241, 242–43, 324

## J
just-in-time inventory system 206, 324

## K
Kiwi bonds 25–26, 119
KiwiSaver 52–53, 147, 152, 153–55, 324
choosing a fund 153–55
Kyoto Protocol 10

## L
land 36–39, 157–59
bundle of rights 38, 157–58, 319
concepts of land 157
Crown ownership 36, 38
economic characteristics 38–39
fixed asset 147
immobility of land 38, 323
legal characteristics 38
Māori land 36, 38
ownership forms 159
ownership of land defined 157–59
permanence of land 39
physical characteristics 38
planning regulations 164
protection 163–64
real asset 3, 4, 19, 326
record of title 160–62, 326
registration of land 160–01
*see also* property; Resource Management Act
Land Act (1948) 36
Land Information Memorandum (LIM) 163
Land Information New Zealand (LINZ) 160
Land Transfer Act (1952, 2017) 160
landlords 156, 227, 297, 324
lease interest 159, 226, 324
leasehold 159, 161
leases 38, 88, 226–27
financial 53, 226–27
ground lease 159, 323
lease interest 159, 226, 324
operating 226
property 157, 159, 162, 226, 227
lenders 3, 4, 12, 19, 20, 23, 24, 29, 43, 53–54, 56, 57, 60, 61, 75, 100, 105, 113, 190, 222–23, 225, 226, 233, 237, 238–39, 241, 324
lenders of last resort (LLRs) 45, 46, 50, 324
lessee 157, 159, 226
lessor 157, 159, 162, 226
leverage 295, 296, 303
liabilities 12, 13, 60–61, 324
current 147, 199–201, 206–11, 320; *see also* net working capital
limited 12, 324
long-term 147
personal 147
unlimited 11–12, 328

life insurance companies 226
limited liability 12, 324
lines of credit 229, 230, 324
liquidation 12, 222–3, 230, 239, 324
liquidity (in businesses) 35, 44, 45, 46, 48, 55, 179, 180, 183, 199, 228, 238, 273, 324
liquidity (in markets) 24, 33, 39, 54
liquidity risk
in investment 24, 118, 297, 324
in property 297, 298
loans 38, 48, 54, 55, 61, 75, 88, 104–05, 113, 145, 146, 150, 190, 202, 223, 225–26, 241, 303, 310
amortised loan 104, 303, 310
calculating repayment schedule 105–07, 310–11
collateral 230, 319
fixed loan 164–65, 303
interest costs 241
interest-only loan 104, 303
interest tax shield 242–43
issue costs 241
flat loan 303
floating loan *see* variable loan
pledges 230, 325
secured loans 230
security for 225, 226, 230, 233
table loan 104, 303, 310–11
term loan 61
types 104–05
unsecured loans 233, 328
variable loan 164–65, 303
*see also* debenture; hire-purchase loans; lines of credit; mortgages; overdrafts
long position 30, 324

## M
macroeconomic performance 35, 45, 324
managed funds 53
management team 170
managers 5–7, 12–13, 56, 170, 176, 177, 178, 181, 182, 190, 222, 237, 240, 255, 256, 277, 287
as agents 184–85
roles 184–86, 190, 240
Māori Fisheries Act (2004) 180–81
margin 31, 202
call 31, 324
initial 31, 323
marking to market 31, 324
margin requirements (in futures contracts) 31
marginal analysis 7, 324
marginal tax rate 242, 297, 302, 304
market indices 28, 324
market portfolios 132, 133–34, 324
market risk premium (MRP) 133–34, 324

marketable securities 24, 201–02, 204, 208, 210, 233, 238, 242, 324
marketing plan 170
markets 5, 14–16, 20, 324
　see also financial markets and individual types of market
marking to market 31, 324
maturity 8, 20, 21, 23, 31, 61, 74, 77, 100, 116, 229, 233, 310, 324
　date 26, 100, 243, 324
　risk 44, 324
　transformation 54
merchant banks see investment banks
mining 35, 325
monetary policies 6–7, 29, 46, 49–52, 325
　inflation control 51–52
　official cash rate 49, 50–51
money management (personal) 144–47
　balance sheet development 146–47
　budget preparation 146
　gathering financial information 145
　income statement preparation 146
money markets 23, 24–25, 53, 62, 325
　instruments traded 24–25
　operation and participants 24
　over-the-counter (OTC) 24
moral hazards 46–47, 325
mortgages 38, 46–47, 52, 53, 61, 104–05, 147, 148, 155, 156, 162, 164–65, 226, 303, 325
　fixed rate 164, 322
　floating rate 164, 322
　market for 46–47, 56
　residential property 155–56, 303
multi-period methods 305–08
multiple payments per annum and compounding frequency 106–07
mutual funds 53
mutually exclusive projects 281, 325

## N

net present value (NPV) 271, 275–78, 281–83, 305–08, 325
　equity residual net present value (NPV(ER)) 279, 305, 307–08, 321
net working capital 199–221, 237, 325
　accounts receivable management 204–05
　cash conversion cycle 211–13
　cash management 201–04
　current liabilities management 206–11
　inventory management 205–06
　net working capital management 200–01
　risk–profitability trade-off 200
net worth 146–49, 325; see also shareholders' equity
　life cycle 147–49

New Zealand Exchange Ltd (NZX) 9–10, 13, 25, 28, 56
　debt market (NZDX) 25, 241
　derivatives market 30
　listing rules 47
New Zealand Stock Exchange (NZSX) 25, 27–28
nominal interest rates 75–76, 325
nominal returns 113–15, 117
non-depository institutions 52–53
not-for-profit organisations 181

## O

official cash rate (OCR) 40, 49, 50–51, 116
offshore currencies 118, 325
offshore finance 232, 234–35, 325
offshore investments 118
offshore securities 234–35
open market operations (OMOs) 50–51
operating cash flows 202, 223–24, 257–61, 262, 273–74, 275, 277–78, 310, 325
　calculating 26–21
operating leases 226, 325
opportunity costs 67, 85, 142, 144, 145, 209, 243, 325
option exchanges 34
options contracts 34
　call options 34, 39
　put options 34–35, 326
options market 34–35
　exercising an option 34
　options writers 34, 35, 328
　participants 34–35
ordinary shares 20–21, 26, 180, 181, 189, 192, 225, 229, 232, 234, 235, 241, 242–44
overdrafts 178, 210, 212, 225–26, 229, 318
over-the-counter (OTC) market 24, 25, 28, 30, 33, 325
owners' equity 180, 225, 325

## P

par value (on bonds) 20, 74, 100–03, 325
parent companies 235, 325
Paris Agreement 10
partnerships 180, 225, 325
　partnership capital 180, 225, 325
payback periods (on investment outlays) 272, 273–75, 325
payment periods 211–13
　average payment period (APP) 211–13, 318
　maximising 213
perpetuities 97–98, 310, 325
personal decision-making 142
personal financial goals 111, 142–44, 146, 147, 149–50

personal financial management 142–75
　balance sheet development 146–47
　budget preparation 146
　financial goal attainment 149–50
　financial information collection 145
　income statement preparation 146
　money management 144–47
　residential property and mortgages 155–65
　retirement plan funding 150–55
　risk and return 112–41
　starting or buying a business 166–70
personal financial planning 5, 6, 10–11, 142–44, 325
　financial planning for life 147–49
　planning process 142–44
personal financial statements 145–47, 325
personal investment 225
plant and equipment 180, 226
pledges (of assets) 230, 325
political risk 297, 303
pollution 16, 192
post-audits 256, 325
preference shares 4, 26, 225, 229, 232, 234, 241, 242, 243–44, 325
premiums (on options) 34–35, 325
present value 63, 65, 67–73, 77, 78–79, 85–87, 100, 105, 190, 306, 307, 326
　annuities 88, 90–91
　discounts 63
　perpetuities 97–98
　present value of a single payment 67–70
　see also net present value
price discovery 22, 24, 35, 326
pricing of financial assets 5, 21, 23, 39, 170
pricing of goods 15
primary financial markets 2, 23–24, 26, 326
principal 8, 20, 53, 60–61, 63–64, 67, 70, 74, 98, 100, 104–06, 117, 162, 222, 226, 239, 279, 303, 305, 310–11, 326
private placements 228, 229, 230, 232, 234, 326
private sector 180, 326
private wealth 14
profit 6, 326
　profit margins 302
　profit maximisation 181–84
promissory notes 24–25, 326
property concepts 156–57
property investment 8, 12, 16, 23, 156–60, 295–317
　analysis of a property investment 298–311
　bright line test 297, 304
　capital gains tax 297
　capitalisation of income 309
　direct investment 321

direct property investment 39, 321
disadvantages 297–98
economic characteristics 38–41
equity outlay 307
ethical considerations 189
financing 155–56, 164–65, 303, 310–11
government intervention in market 40, 41
home ownership 156
housing and economic cycles 40–41
indirect property investment 39, 323
investor-specific considerations 302–08
land and land ownership 157–59
land registration 160–62
landowners 38
leases 157, 159, 162, 226–27, 324
legal characteristics of property 38
loans for 104–05
motivations for 296–97
physical characteristics of property 36, 37–38, 325
property concepts 156–57
property management 297, 302
property markets 36–41
purpose/reasons for investment 296–98
real property 157, 159
record of title 160–62, 326
rent 298, 299
residential property financing and mortgages 155–56, 164–65, 326
returns 298, 302, 304–08
rights and ownership 156–59
risks 237, 298
security 296
taxation 297, 303–05
tenants 298, 299
valuation of property 39, 98–99, 319
*see also* housing; land; leases; mortgages
prospectuses 9, 233, 326
protection for consumers and investors 9, 45, 47, 163–64, 190
public goods 16, 326
public offerings 232–34, 326
public-sector organisations 181, 277, 281, 326
pure market system 14, 326
put options 34–35, 326

**R**

rate of return 67, 75, 78, 98–99, 106, 112, 115, 133–34, 154–55, 200, 223, 239, 240, 271–72, 298, 302, 303, 306, 309, 326; *see also* internal rate of return
Rating Powers Act (1988) 162
raw materials inventory 205, 206, 211, 326

recessions 47, 115–16, 117, 168, 237, 293, 326
record of title 160–62, 326
regulatory bodies 5, 8–10, 13, 35, 46, 178, 190
rent 36, 38, 87, 88, 147, 155, 159, 162, 226, 297, 305, 306
repurchase agreements (repos) 24, 50, 326
Reserve Bank of Australia 46
Reserve Bank of New Zealand (RBNZ) 2, 25, 40, 46, 49, 56
bond issues 119
residential property 23, 36, 40, 41, 99, 155–56, 164–65, 189, 297, 298–308, 326
financing 164–65
*see also* property
Residential Tenancies Act (1986) 189, 297
residual claims 20, 180, 223
resource consents 257, 326
Resource Management Act (1991) 10, 159, 163–64
compliance 163–64
planning environment 164
retained earnings 46, 228–29, 230, 232, 239, 241, 242–43, 244, 326
retirement income 52–53, 142, 147–55, 165, 318
funding a retirement plan 150–55
income gap 151–55, 326
KiwiSaver 52–53, 147, 152, 153–55, 324
target annual retirement income 151, 327
*see also* superannuation funds and schemes
returns 3, 6, 10, 24, 36, 39, 53, 75, 111–13, 115, 117–32, 134, 147, 148, 153, 181–82, 190–92, 239–40, 273, 275, 277–78, 285–86, 297, 299–305, 326
accounting return on investment (AROI) 271–73, 287, 318
composite returns 301–02
gross returns 299–300, 323
holding period yields (HPY) 121–23, 209
internal rates of return (IRR) 270, 279–83, 323
net returns 299–300, 325
real rate of return 115
risk-adjusted required return (RARR) 286–87, 326
single-period returns 299–302, 327
*see also* risk–return trade-off
revolving credit 229–30, 326
reward-based crowdfunding 227
rights issues 26–7, 233–34, 326
risk 3, 20, 21, 23, 25–26, 29, 35, 36, 39, 111–41, 167, 183, 189–90, 199, 238–39, 295–97, 280–81, 309, 326
agency risk 189

assessing/measuring 183–84, 205
business risk 118, 179, 319
capital asset pricing model 133–35
capital budgeting 284–87
capital investment 271, 275–77, 280–81, 284–87
country risk 118, 320
crowdfunding 224
default risk 44, 50, 227, 233, 241
diversification benefit 129–33
exchange rate risk 21, 29, 118, 322
financial risk (in firms) 118, 322
foreign exchange risk 21
future risk and return 127–29
historical risk and return 121–27
interest rate risk 54
liquidity risk 24, 118, 324
maturity risk 44, 324
non-diversifiable risk 112
perceptions and preferences 7, 149, 302; *see also* risk aversion
political risk 297, 303
reduction 29–33, 53, 54, 55, 60, 100, 129–33, 184; *see also* diversification
standard deviation measure 124–27
systematic risk 132–33, 298, 327
transfer of 21, 23
unsystematic risk 132–33, 298, 328
risk aversion 121, 143, 191, 326
risk premiums 26, 115, 117, 119, 133–34, 183, 243, 277, 326
risk-adjusted required return (RARR) 286–87, 326
risk-free assets 117–19, 326
risk–profitability trade-off 200, 207, 213, 237
risk–return trade-off 119–21, 149, 190–93, 222, 239–40
in business 190–03, 222, 239–40
in personal finance 112–41, 148–49, 153, 167
in property 298–99, 302
risky assets 113–15

**S**

safety and soundness of financial system 45–48
banking regulation 47–48
consumer and investor protection 9, 45, 47, 163–64, 190
fairness and information disclosure 47
safety motive 201, 326
Sale of Goods Act (1908) 9
salvage value 203, 259, 326
secondary financial markets 2, 24, 25, 26, 326
securities 4–5, 7, 8, 9, 19, 22–24, 25, 26, 39, 43, 46–47, 52–56, 97, 117–20, 147, 148, 189, 190, 229, 232–35, 327

## Index

convertible 234, 235, 320
hybrid 26
offshore 234–35
public offerings 233–34, 326
subscribed 26, 233, 327
toxic 47
*see also* marketable securities
Securities Commission of New Zealand 9
securitisation 53, 327
security market line (SML) 134–35, 327
self-employment 165–67
sensitivity analysis 285–86, 307, 327
settlement date 29–30, 327
share markets *see* equity markets
share options 34–35, 185, 327
shareholders 7–10, 12, 13, 21, 26, 177, 178, 179, 180, 182, 184–86, 190, 192, 202, 222–23, 225, 233, 235, 239, 242–43, 255, 277–78, 298, 327
roles of 12, 222–23
*see also* investors
shareholders' equity 179, 207, 231, 236, 240, 279, 327
shares 27–28, 118, 123, 132–3, 145, 178, 180–82, 184, 185, 189–90, 192, 227–28, 232–36, 256, 298, 327
ordinary 20–21, 26, 180, 181, 189, 192, 225, 229, 232, 234, 235, 241, 242–44
preference 4, 26, 225, 229, 232, 234, 241, 242, 243–44, 325
rights issues 26–27, 233–34, 326
trading apps 54
trading in 27–28
share statement 27
short position 30
simple interest 61–63, 327
and calculating present value 63
and future value 61–62
social responsibility *see* corporate social responsibility
sole-proprietorship decision-making 11
solvency 183, 202, 273, 327
speculative motive 201, 327
speculators 32, 33, 35, 327
spot markets 29, 327
spread (in FX transactions) 28, 327
spreadsheet program use 6, 106, 286
calculation examples 65–66, 69, 79, 90, 91, 93–94, 96
staff 170
stakeholders 7–10, 13, 56, 181, 187, 256, 258, 327
protection of 9, 190
rights 187
wealth maximisation and 185–68
standard deviation technique 124–27, 128, 129, 130, 132, 183, 327

stock exchanges 9, 27–28
regulation of 9–10
*see also* equity markets
stratum title 161
strike price 34, 327
subscribe 26, 233, 327
subsidiaries 235, 327
sunk costs 259, 327
superannuation funds and schemes 27, 52–53, 148, 152, 229, 327
suppliers 227
swaps 30, 327
SWOT analysis 169, 327
syndicates (of banks) 233, 327

## T

taxation 8, 10, 12, 98, 178, 181, 186, 189, 201, 210, 257, 258
deductibility of depreciation 261
deductibility of interest payments 241–42, 303
of dividends 10, 223
income tax 10, 190, 258, 259, 260–61
land tax 38
property 303–5
tax credit 223, 327
withholding tax 223, 328
term loans 61, 178, 225, 230, 303, 327
term structure of interest rates 115–17, 327
terminal value 257, 261–66, 275, 276, 280, 281, 295, 327
Territorial Local Authority (TLA) 163
thin markets 22, 327
time value of money 3, 21, 144, 181–82, 241, 273, 327
asset valuation 98
multiple payments 84–110
regular payments 93–94
single payments 60–83
trade credit 205, 207–10, 227, 232, 238, 328
transaction costs 15, 22, 23, 44, 53, 297, 328
transactions motive 201, 328
transformation of assets 54–56
Treasury bills 20–21, 24–25, 114, 119, 201, 328

## U

uncertainties 6, 166
underwriting 233, 239, 241, 328
unethical behaviour 56, 191–92, 328
Unit Titles Act (2010) 158
unit trusts 27, 53
unlimited liability 11–12, 328
unpledged assets 229, 328

## V

valuation
asset valuation 98–104, 147
calculating price of a bond 100–04
capitalisation method of property valuation 98–99, 309, 319
capitalisation rate 98–99, 295, 307, 309, 319
current value 21, 26, 73–74, 98, 100
fees 164
government valuation 147
objective valuation 39, 325
and pricing 39
*see also* discounted cash flow analysis
variance technique 125–27, 128, 129, 328
venture capital 224, 225, 227–28, 328
volatility 23, 50, 132, 164

## W

wealth maximisation 178, 180, 185–87, 255, 256, 273, 275–78, 281, 328
economic implications 185–87
weighted average cost of capital (WACC) 244–45, 277–79, 328
withholding tax 223, 328
working capital 232, 242
*see also* net working capital
work-in-process inventory 205, 328

## Y

yields 25–26, 63, 78, 98, 100, 241, 328
annual holding period yields 123–24
holding period yields (HPY) 121–24, 209, 323
yield curves 115–17

## Z

zero-coupon bonds 73–74, 77, 328

First published in 2000 by Pearson Education New Zealand; revised in 2017
This updated and revised edition published in 2024 by Massey University Press

Massey University Press, Private Bag 102904
North Shore Mail Centre, Auckland 0745, New Zealand
www.masseypress.ac.nz

Text © Massey University Business School, 2024

Typesetting by Sarah Elworthy
Text design updated from original design by Marie Low and BookNZ

All rights reserved. Except as provided by the Copyright Act 1994, no part of this book may be reproduced, stored in or introduced into a retrieval system or transmitted in any form or by any means (electronic, mechanical, photocopying, recording or otherwise) without the prior written permission of both the copyright owners and the publisher.

A catalogue record for this book is available from the National Library of New Zealand

Printed and bound in China by 1010 Printing Asia Ltd

ISBN: 978-1-99-101688-1
eISBN: 978-1-99-101696-6